DATE DUE

DEC 7			
MAR 29			
DEC 1 8 1973			
NOV 2 1 1995			
FEB 1 9 1997			
FEB 2 5 1998			
APR 0 8 1998			
GAYLORD			PRINTED IN U.S.A.

The Combat Series

Editor: Don Congdon

The War with Germany

The War with Japan

European Theater—World War II

Pacific Theater—World War II

COMBAT:
World War I

Edited by DON CONGDON

Foreword and Afterword by William Manchester

Introduction by Herbert Mitgang

A Delacorte Press Book · Distributed by The Dial Press, New York

ACKNOWLEDGMENTS

"Foreword" and "Afterword" are from "The First World War" from Holiday Magazine. Copyright 1962 by The Curtis Publishing Company. Reprinted by permission of Harold Matson Company.

"The First Month" is from DARE CALL IT TREASON, published by Simon & Schuster. Copyright 1963 by Richard M. Watt. Reprinted by permission of the publisher and Chatto & Windus, London.

"The Marne" is from THE WORLD CRISIS, published by Charles Scribner's Sons. Copyright 1923, 1927, 1929, 1931 by Charles Scribner's Sons. Reprinted by permission of the publisher and Odham's Press Limited, London.

"The Anzac Beachhead" is from GALLIPOLI, published by Harper & Borthers. Copyright 1956 by Alan Moorehead. Reprinted by permission of the publisher and Laurence Pollinger, Limited, London.

"In the Cambrin and Cuinchy Trenches" is from GOODBYE TO ALL THAT. Copyright 1929, 1957 by International Authors, N.V. Reprinted by permission of the author's agent, A. P. Watt, London, and Doubleday.

"Loos: First and Second Days" is from THE DONKEYS, published by William Morrow & Company. Copyright 1961 by Alan Clark. Reprinted by permission of the publisher and The Hutchinson Publishing Group, London.

"Verdun: The Fall of Fort Douamont" is from THE PRICE OF GLORY Copyright 1962 by Alistair Horne. Reprinted by permission of the publisher, St. Martin's Press.

"The Battle of Jutland" is from SEA FIGHTS AND SHIPWRECKS published by Garden City Publishing Company. Copyright 1955 by Hanson Baldwin. Reprinted by permission of Doubleday & Company, Inc., and the author's agent, Willis Kingsley Wing.

"Up to Mametz" is from UP TO MAMETZ published by Faber & Faber, London, and reprinted by permission of the publisher.

"A Bombing Party" is from MEMOIRS OF AN INFANTRY OFFICER, published by Coward McCann, Inc. and Faber & Faber, London. Copyright 1930, 1958 by Siegfried Sassoon. Reprinted by permission of Faber & Faber.

"The Tunnels at Messines" is from FLANDERS FIELD, published by The Viking Press. Copyright 1958 by Leon Wolff. Reprinted by permission of the publisher and Longmans Green & Co. Limited, London.

"The Third Battle of Ypres" is from OLD SOLDIERS NEVER DIE. Reprinted by permission of the publisher, Faber & Faber, London.

"The Charge at Soissons" is from FIX BAYONETS, published by Charles Scribner's Sons. Reprinted by permission of the publishers. Copyright 1925, 1953 by Charles Scribner's Sons.

"Blowing Up Trains" is from THE SEVEN PILLARS OF WISDOM, published by Doubleday, Doran Co., Inc. Copyright 1926, 1935, 1963. Reprinted by permission of Doubleday, the executors of the T. E. Lawrence Estate and Jonathan Cape, London.

"Alamo of the Argonne" is from True Magazine. Copyright 1960 by Fawcett Publications, Inc. Reprinted by permission of the author.

"Mick Mannock" is from THE ACES, published by G. P. Putnam's. Copyright 1960 by Frederick Oughton. Reprinted by permission of the publishers and the Author.

"Zeebrugge" is from ZEEBRUGGE, published by Ballantine Books. Copyright 1958, 1959 by Barrie W. Pitt. Reprinted by permission of the publishers and Cassell, London.

"Remember Always to Dare" is from SEA FIGHTS AND SHIPWRECKS, published by Garden City Publishing Co. Copyright 1955 by Hanson Baldwin. Reprinted by permission of Doubleday & Co., Inc. and the author's agent, Willis Kingsley Wing.

Selections were also taken from the following books:

THE FIRST BATTLE OF THE MARNE, published by J. B. Lippincott Company. Reprinted by permission of the publisher. Copyright 1962 by Robert B. Asprey.

THE BIG PUSH, published by William Morrow & Co. Copyright 1961 by Brian Gardner. Reprinted by permission of the publisher and Cassell, London.

THE GREAT WAR, published by G. P. Putnam's. Copyright 1959 by Cyril Falls. Reprinted by permission of the publisher and Longmans Green & Co., Limited, London.

WORLD WAR I, published by Harper & Row. Copyright 1962 by Hanson W. Baldwin. Reprinted by permission of the publisher.

THE REAL WAR, published by Little Brown & Co. Copyright 1930, by B. H. Liddell Hart. Reprinted by permission of the publisher and Curtis Brown, London.

Editor's Note

This anthology is fifth in a series. In each the editor has selected narratives, wherever possible, to show the experience of an individual or a small group in combat. Most selections deal with important battles as well.

The editor believes this method, while arbitrary, supplies a more intimate picture of the men fighting in the front lines.

This is by no means an overall history of World War I or even of the Western Front, but the reader will find each selection is supplemented with introductory material to help clarify the larger outlines of battle.

CONTENTS

INTRODUCTION

by Herbert Mitgang

Funny Little Figures Called Mankind

From time immemorial, always there have been two wars: the war, and the war remembered. When Virgil wrote "Arma virumque cano" as the opening line of the epic *Aeneid,* he began a terrible tale of warring Greeks and Trojans, full of glory without purpose and death by primitive sword. And yet he began, "Arms and the man I sing." Thus have come many singers of war afterward, up to our own time of overkill.

Does the roseate recollection of war do a disservice to actual war? The aim of the battle well fought is to enhance the reputations of the living and to kill unknown and often unseen enemies; to gain or regain a trench, a hedgerow, a hill, a town; eventually, to triumph for some cause once eloquently expressed but excised by casualty lists and dimmed by time. Deaths alone lead to victory, not generalship; the beast's nature is to win by bleeding. So those who write cleverly about strategy and intelligence insult war. Government leaders of stature long have realized that war is too important to be left to the generals and marshals. But is not war too painful to be left to the singers, too? For their voices and words survive; the warriors die.

The Great War of 1914–18 began as a charade, full of pomp, cousins on thrones of rivalry, insults, dying duchies and alliances signifying nothing. The opening gun meant little more in the long history of warfare than a glove slap across the face, yet the death rattle of chivalry shook the Balkans and all Europe. Foolishness and revenge put the torch to peace. The politicians and standing armies strutted, the bloated men of commerce and munitions nodded patriotically, the nations became nationalistic. And the singers sang.

The funny little figures called mankind—civilized mankind—moved as dolls into training camps, lunged in bayonet quickstep at each other's throats, boarded steamers to the tune of "Over There" that sank in a cacophony of hissing U-boat torpedoes, and settled down to a lullaby of Mausers and Gatlings and Enfields and Springfields, under a barbed-wire tent and a sky filled with yellow mustard gas. Half a century later, the old men who were once young and breathed that gas are still in hospitals, and they are called Incompetent Veterans. The young women they did not marry then are called old maids, their bodies barren of life. Oh, what a lovely war, the jerky figures in costumes of Pierrot khaki moving across our film of memory.

This was the beautifully measured war: as soon as the Hohenzollerns and Hapsburgs and Huns capitulated, the world would be made safe for democracy. The times were idealistic, sentimental and unhurried. The old order had not yet changed; the world still lived with one foot in the nineteenth century. For the military, that foot was in a cavalry stirrup. For government and business, that foot was still on the neck of the lower classes. The death of the horse and the rise of man in states concerned with his welfare coincided. The mustached field marshals and corps commanders, veterans of the Boer War, campaigns to put down insurrectionists and Indians from the North American to the Asian continents, were names to remember—though not with affection. Dismounted from their beasts, they and their war became quite ordinary.

The war began in exaltation and ended in the mud. The victors were the graves registration units. Where the parts of the bodies did not match, there was always the out of "missing in action" or "unknown soldier." Total losses were estimated at 10 million soldiers and another 10 million civilians dead; 20 million wounded; another 20 million dead from war epidemics and famines.

Though the League of Nations failed to limit war or even provide a forum to discuss war's consequences intelligently, the hidden and open revolutions for mankind continued. Social orders in the Tsar's Russia, in Germany and Italy, realigned radically, leading to dictatorships. But other nations recognized—though for some it took a second world war—that the terrible disparities between rich and poor that existed in the nineteenth century had to die in the twentieth century; that lasting evils and economic oppressions were deeply imbedded in the permanent causes of war. These could be uprooted by quiet revolutions, such as the New Deal in the United States and the Welfare State in England and many other nations in Europe.

That the inherent causes could be ameliorated by man himself and his statecraft was realized long before President Wilson dreamed of a great world forum. "Wars, battles, and revolutions come from the body and the lusts of the body. For wars are occasioned by the love of money, and money has to be acquired for the sake and in the service of the body." So spoke Plato, adding: "War, whether external or civil, is not the best, and the need of either is to be deprecated." World War II became a continuation of World War I, which was a continuation of the wars that had engaged mankind for all his recorded years. There are more spears than olive branches in the windswept monuments of antiquity. And yet, today, in the age of the intercontinental ballistic missile, the folly of worlds at war seems greater and clearer than ever in the past. Thermonuclear warfare, which would eliminate the victor along with the vanquished, may at last turn man's mind inward toward the ultimate weapon: himself.

In his Nobel Peace Prize lecture, Linus Pauling plucked a neutron of hope from the core of the killers: "I believe that there will never again be a great world war—a war in which the terrible weapons involving nuclear fission and nuclear fusion would be used. And I believe that it is the discoveries of scientists upon which the development of these terrible weapons was based that are now forcing us to move into a new period in the history of the world, a period of peace and reason, when world problems are not solved by war or by force, but are solved in accordance with world law, in a way that does justice to all nations and that benefits all people."

America has fought Germany in two world wars. Although a quarter of a century has passed since the Nazis first began their paranoic drive to enslave the world by arms and terror, the stench of the Auschwitz and Buchenwald concentration camps still fills the nostrils of this generation. We are hopeless; we cannot condone and forget. Nor should we if World War II is to have meaning and bear a message to history.

But the World War I *is* now history. Its follies can speak to us across the divide of half a century. The message is this: We must think the unthinkable—of civilized world law to insure peace. And we must sing of men without arms.

FOREWORD*

by William Manchester

In my childhood the statue of the lean bronze doughboy was already darkening on its marble Lest-We-Forget plinth in the square downtown, but people still sang *There's a Long, Long Trail* as they drove the family flivver in from the country Sunday evenings, and at least once a week there would be an argument down at the white clapboard Legion Hall over whether the Hindenburg Line had been broken by the Yankee Division, the Rainbow, or the Marines. I used to hang around the hall cadging doughnuts, and the figure I remember best was a town card who had been too old to fight and couldn't have found France, let alone the Argonne, on a map of Europe. Every Memorial Day he would clown around in a mishmash of military livery—an overseas cap, a Navy blouse, sky blue trousers, and rolled puttees. He wasn't a verteran of anything—even I knew that—so he wasn't allowed in the A. E. F. parade. I regretted that then, and I still do. Then I wanted him to march because he looked so dashing, but now I think he was truer to his time than he knew. The war he never fought, like the uniform he always wore, was first to last a hopeless muddle, and like his costume it was carried off with a flair that almost made you forget how senseless it all was.

Never was a war more fouled up. It was so confusing that when the guns stopped historians couldn't even decide what to call it. Most of them were divided between The Great War and The World War. After Hitler showed his fist it was filed away as World War I, a forgotten curtain raiser, but they were really right the first time. It

* Adapted from "The Great War" published in *Holiday*.

was a great war, in its own right. It was a kind of cultural hinge—Lieutenant Colonel Winston S. Churchill wrote that afterward "We seemed separated from the old life by a measureless gulf," and to the most idealistic youth the world had ever known it came as a crisis of the spirit. They had marched off to the lilt of *Tipperary* or *Die Wacht am Rhein* or *Over There,* dreaming of braid and heroism. When they found that their generation was bleeding to death, with each month's casualty lists redder than the last, the thoughtful among them recoiled, stunned, and fled into cynicism and despair. The composer of *Keep the Home Fires Burning* acquired an exemption and lolled around in a silk dressing gown, burning incense; thrice-wounded young Harold Macmillan of Britain retreated into a study of Horace; Siegfried Sassoon flung his military cross in the sea and wrote bitterly:

> *Pray God that you may never know*
> *The hell where youth and laughter go.*

They were the sensitive. Most men fought stolidly. They had been bred to valor, taught fealty to the tribal deities of God or *Gott* or *Dieu,* and with numb certitude they sacrificed themselves to a civilization that was vanishing with them. Perceived now down the corridor of time they seem to have been marked by a quiet sense of dedication that could only have been instinctive. In that war, said Dick Diver, touring old trenches in F. Scott Fitzgerald's *Tender Is the Night,* "You had to have a whole-souled sentimental equipment going back further than you could remember. You had to remember Christmas, and postcards of the Crown Prince and his fiancée, and little cafés in Valence and beer gardens in Unter den Linden and weddings at the *mairie,* and going to the Derby, and your grandfather's whiskers." "This," he said, "was the last love battle." That was in 1917, the penultimate year, when the lovelight was glimmering. The Central Powers—Germany, Austria-Hungary, Bulgaria, Turkey—and the Allies—England, France, Russia, Italy—seemed lost in a dark maw of madness. On the Western Front the lines moved a few inches a day, "Leaving the dead," said Dick Diver, "like a million bloody rugs."

In that remote day of derbies, ostrich-plume bonnets and hansom cabs, civilization was in the middle of a profound transition. Culturally it remained gyved to the horsy Victorian past, while signs multiplied that the machine age was coming, and coming fast. Europe lay half in one period, half in the other. Until the assassination of the Austrian Archduke on June 28, 1914 set off the chain reaction of alliances, it had not been a bad time. Churchill remembered how "The world on the verge of its catastrophe was very brilliant. Nations and Empires crowned with princes and potentates rose majestically on every side, lapped in the accumulated treasures of the long peace." The flaw was that of all customs, war was the most rooted in the folklore of the past, and its traditional leaders—the princes and potentates and field marshals—were the most conservative men in society, the least capable of understanding the new mechanized war they were to lead.

French yearning for *la gloire* was almost as great as their talent for self-hypnosis. They never stopped dreaming of Murat and Ney and the ghostly glint of Austerlitz moonlight on the lance heads of the Emperor's cavalry. Their speech was studded with Napoleonic phrases. They plotted the *offensive à outrance*, carried out with *toujours l'audace* by gallant men singing *La Marseillaise* and crying *En avant! À la baïonette!* Of course this was for the younger man, *les jeunes Turcs*. The generals themselves stayed out of the chilling rain, in the ballrooms of splendid old commandeered *châteaux*. At their age they had to take care of themselves. When the Germans sprang at Verdun in 1916 the courier who brought the news was told that "Papa" Joffre, the constable of France, was asleep behind a double-locked door and couldn't be disturbed.

England's military Boeotians were equally convinced that a chap could smash through that barbed wire if he had enough sand, and they were even more devoted to peacetime military routine and Quetta manners. They strode around in gleaming field boots and jingling spurs and toured the lines in Rolls Royces, cursing bad march discipline. It was a pretty thin time for the regular service, they agreed; so many of the officer replacements weren't really gentlemen. Something had to be done about it. The new fellows were sharply reminded that they should keep servants in their dugouts, that slack privates were to be struck on sight, and that before going over the top everyone must check to be sure the senior regiment was on the right. In rest camp subalterns were actually required to attend riding school and learn polo, and during the worst fighting on the Somme fussy divisional horse shows were ceremoniously held just behind the front. The British failed in the Somme, though not for that reason; the German generals were just as bad. Junkers cherished their monacles, spotless white gloves, black and silver saberknots, and cement *Kommandanturs* with the Prussian eagles molded in cement above the entrances. Everywhere the military cliques abused the almost ecclesiastical status they had acquired when pre-war diplomacy broke down. Interlopers like Churchill, who spoke bitterly of their "pomp and power" were looked upon as cads. When the British Prime Minister questioned England's strategy, Haig said tightly, "I could not have believed that a British minister could have been so ungentlemanly." The general staffs insisted no one should have a voice in the war unless he had spent forty years in uniform, which, as Liddell Hart acidly observed, would have blackballed Alexander, Hannibal, Caesar, Cromwell, Marlborough, and Napoleon.

American officers were of the same stodgy breed. Theodore Roosevelt noted that some of them were too fat to mount a saddle, and others seemed to belong back at Little Big Horn. They sent white horses to France in anticipation of triumphal entries when they had slimmed down a bit; they showed their sympathy with the stale defensive tactics on the Western Front by ordering, at the outset, a hundred million sandbags from India, and they insisted enlisted men wear parade-ground tunics so binding that they were crippling in combat. Doughboys complained, but they had been spared a lot. By then the more fantastic anachronisms had disappeared from field uniforms. The Germans had shed the impractical spikes on their steel helmets; the French and British, who hadn't any helmets at all in 1014, were protected now. French infantrymen no longer wore scarlet trousers and blue coats, nor French artillerymen black and gold, and the British army had abandoned the practice of having new subalterns visit an armorer to have their swords sharpened, like Henry V, before sailing for France.

The decision wasn't made lightly. Sword sharpening had been a sentimental ceremony, like Flirtation Walk. The idea of attacking a machine gun with a saber is inconceivable today, but the generals hadn't been thinking about the machine gun much. They had considered it before the war, decided it was an over-rated weapon, and turned back to what they considered real soldiering. Each year the mechanical revolution clanked out more new engines of death, but the alumni of Sandhurst and *Saint-Cyr-l'École* accepted them grudgingly or not at all. They belonged to that older generation which still called electric light "the electric" and distrusted it as newfangled. Joffre wouldn't use a telephone. Kitchener of England dismissed the tank as a "toy." Planes and submarines were deplored; poison gas, adopted reluctantly after the Germans had used it, was delicately called "the accessory." The trench mortar was rejected twice at the British War Office and finally introduced by a cabinet minister who begged the money for it from an Indian maharajah. In the gleaming chateaux this was regarded as both bad form and foolishness. The epauletted marshals there placed their main reliance in great masses of cavalry (as late as 1918 Pershing was cluttering up his supply lines with mountains of fodder for useless horses) and their staffs rarely visited the front, where a very different kind of war was being fought.

There, by the junk heap of no-man's-land, the great armies squatted on the Western Front year after year, living troglodytic lives in candlelit dugouts and trenches hewn from Fricourt chalk or *La Bassée* clay, or scooped from the porridge of swampy Flanders. They had been there since the gray tide of the German right wing (undiscovered by a hundred thousand galloping French cavalry) had made its sinister sweep through Belgium, lapped at the breakwater of Verdun, recoiled on the Marne at the very gates of Paris, and receded to the Aîsne. The efficient Prussians had tacked up propaganda signs there (*Gott Strafe England; Frankreich, du bist betragen*) and settled down to teach the children German while the Allies furiously counterattacked. The titantic struggles that followed were called battles, but although they were fought on a fantastic scale, with nearly two million men lost at Verdun and on the Somme, strategically they were only seige assaults. Every attack found the Kaiser's defenses stronger. The poilus and tommies who crawled over their parapets, lay down in front of jump-off tapes, and waited for their officers' zero-hour whistles; they faced as many as ten aprons of barbed wire thick as a man's finger, backed by the pullulating Boche. A few trenches would be taken at shocking cost, one gain of seven hundred mutilated yards cost twenty-six thousand men, and then the siege would start again. At home newspapers spoke of "hammer blows" and "the big push," but the men knew better; a soldier's *mot* had it that the war would last a hundred years, five years of fighting and ninety-five of winding up the barbed wire.

COMBAT: World War I

SOME DAMNED FOOLISH THING
IN THE BALKANS

The political background of World War I has been set forth in many recently published histories.* It will be enough to say here that the onslaught of the German armies in August, 1914, was a result of the power diplomacy among the European nations begun in the days of Bismarck, the father of the German Empire. As the Germans expanded their overseas trade, they commenced to build a navy that would soon offer a challenge to the British Royal Navy, which had ruled the seas for many decades. Germany's rise to power caused anxieties in the governments of England, France and Russia. By 1914 various political treaties had produced an alignment of the British, French, and Russians against Germany and Austria-Hungary; any spark of conflict between nations might provoke a collision between the major powers, precipitating a general conflict between the Alliances. Long before 1914 Bismarck had forecast the spark would be "some damned foolish thing in the Balkans." **

"One incident was as good as another. On the sunny morning of June 28, 1914, a young Serbian student named Gavrilo Prinzip pushed through a crowded Sarajevo street, leaped onto a royal motorcar, fired two shots into a uniformed, bulky body and became the assassin of Archduke Francis Ferdinand, Austria's future Emperor.

"Shocked by the murder, European diplomats hoped that Austria would not convert it into a *casus belli*. Count Berchtold, Austria's Foreign Minister, whose own position was as shaky as his country's prestige did exactly this. Backed by Conrad von Hötzendorf, Chief of the Imperial General Staff, who had wanted war against Serbia for years, Berchtold persuaded the old Emperor Francis Joseph to

* see *The Guns of August,* by Barbara Tuchman; *The Great War,* by Cyril Falls; *World War I,* by Hanson Baldwin.
** *The Guns of August,* p. 91.

ask Germany to support an aggressive Austrian action. On July 5 Emperor Wilhelm's reply—the famous 'blank check'—announced that Austria 'could depend on the complete support of Germany.'

"While the European powers, particularly Germany and Austria, began quiet military preparations, Berchtold on July 23 delivered an ultimatum to Serbia and demanded her reply in forty-eight hours. The extreme insult of the terms, which Serbia could not have accepted without forfeiting her sovereignty, shocked all of Europe, even Kaiser Wilhelm who recovered to reaffirm his military support of Austria the next day. Simultaneously Russia reiterated her support of Serbia, France pledged her aid to Russia, and Sir Edward Grey, England's Foreign Minister, urged Germany to arrange an extension of time for Serbia to answer the Austrian note. This request was ignored as were Grey's frantic attempts in the following days to settle the affair by a conference of European powers. Serbia, however, met the deadline and agreed to all except two of Austria's terms—a conciliatory effort rejected by Austria. On July 28 she declared war on Serbia and began a partial mobilization on the Serbian frontier.

"The next three days witnessed a frenzied exchange of formal ultimatums and informal propositions among Berlin, Vienna, St. Petersburg, Rome, Paris and London that at times seemed to hold hope of peace but in the end came to naught. On July 31 Russia ordered general mobilization. Austria followed a few hours later. Germany immediately declared a preliminary mobilization that, despite actual mobilization measures and armed raids into France, kept from her the stigma of general mobilization while she carried out pathetic and futile last-minute attempts to gain England's neutrality, the more important since Italy on July 31 declared herself neutral.

"With general mobilization under way in Russia and Austria nothing in the world could have saved the peace of Europe after July 31. On August 1 Germany declared war against Russia and ordered general mobilization; on August 2 she delivered an ultimatum to Belgium demanding the right to cross Belgian territory; on August 3 she declared war on France; on August 4 German troops crossed the Belgian border.

"Europe was at war." *

THE ARMIES

The conflagration was soon worldwide; before the end of the war thirty nations and sixty-five million men were involved.

Germany had the strongest military establishment at the beginning of the war, although Russia numbered more divisions of men. The German army put eighty-seven divisions in the field to begin the fighting. Hanson Baldwin says, "Her army was the best equipped of the time; one German division was reckoned about equal to one and a half or even two Russian and Austro-Hungarian divisions. The Mauser rifle and the Maxim heavy machine gun were standard and highly effective weapons for the infantry. The Germans had a great advantage in medium and heavy artillery. Their horsed cavalrymen—also taught to fight dismounted—still carried saber and lance . . . the German staff and logistical organization was unexcelled. The use of the railroad to transport and supply armies had been more highly developed in Germany than in any other country. The German tactics and training, though by no means prophetic of what was to come, nevertheless had absorbed the lessons of the Russo-Japanese War (trench systems, importance of artillery, etc.) to a greater degree than other armies." **

The French had a standing army of sixty-two divisions, most of

* *The First Battle of the Marne,* by Robert Asprey, pp. 4, 5, 6.
** Baldwin, *World War I,* p. 10.

4   THE ARMIES

whom were first-class troops. Their famous 75-millimeter gun was the most efficient piece of artillery in the war.* They were weak in heavy artillery; the Germans had ten times more big guns. Unfortunately, the French commanders had been contemptuous of the weapon that was largely responsible for trench warfare—the machine gun, and while their regiments were each equipped with six, they were of poorer quality than Germany's Maxim. Their doctrine of "attack, attack, always attack" which permeated their whole strategy for battle would prove to be disastrous when they were forced to the defense against the slashing German colums. The French commanders were incapable of adopting another more flexible strategy during the first months of the war.

The British, in contrast to the Germans and French, maintained a small, but highly trained army which was used mostly as a constabulary force in their colonies. Only seven British divisions were on hand at the beginning of the war, but their armies would increase to almost six million men before the war ended. Britian's most potent fighting force was the Royal Navy, the strongest on the seas.

If the British land force was small, it was highly trained and effective. "The British Tommy carried the excellent if heavy Lee-Enfield clip-fed, bolt-action rifle, wore a light khaki uniform ideal except for winter wear, and was trained for offense and defense—equipment and training both having resulted from experience gained in the Boer War. Much more individualistic in outlook than the German or Frenchman, he had been taught and partially understood the importance of fast, accurate rifle fire, of advance by fire and movement, and of cover and concealment." **

The armies in the East—Russia's and Austria-Hungary's—were comparable in size, but this volume will not deal with their campaigns. (For discussion of their size and effectiveness as well as their major battles, see Baldwin's *World War I* and Cyril Falls' *The Great War.*

The armies were largely horse-drawn. Men were moved by railway if the track systems were available in the areas of battle. Other-

* Because of its accuracy and speed of firing.
** Asprey, pp. 27, 28.

wise movement of army units was still by foot. Men would soon learn to fly and fight in the air, but at the war's beginning there were only "about five to seven hundred military aircraft and some four hundred pilots in all of Europe." *

THE FIRST MONTH **

by Richard M. Watt

Fortunate is the general staff which sees a war fought the way it intends. Indeed, if there is one thing which can be counted upon in war it is that you can count on nothing. This the French Army was soon to rediscover.

To begin with, the French Army was commanded by General Joseph Joffre. Sixty-two years old at the time war broke out, Joffre was almost the antithesis of the soldier in appearance as well as in manner. Fat, unbelievably phlegmatic, routine-loving, he had never been accused of being a military genius, but for three peacetime years he had commanded the French Army.

Prior to 1911 Joffre had been primarily an engineer officer. Only once in his life had he held a real field command—in 1894, when he had led a little expeditionary force to Timbuktu to put down a colonial insurrection. Joffre had no reputation as a strategist or tactician, and although in 1910 he became a junior member of the War Council, the job that had been assigned to him in the event of mobilization was the direction of the lines of communication.

But in 1911 General Michel, the designated commander of the

* Baldwin, *World War I*, p. 12.
** From *Dare Call It Treason*, published by Simon & Schuster.

French Army in time of war, fell from favor. He had advanced the disagreeable theory that the German plan for invading France involved a huge attack through Belgium and had recommended that the French Army prepare itself to stand on the defensive. This last was, of course, anathema to the influential "Young Turks" of the School of the Attack, whose influence by this time was such that they could pull down even the Commander in Chief designate of the French Army. So Adolphe Messimy, the Minister of War in the government of the hour, looked about for a new Army commander. Several senior generals, notably Joseph Gallieni and Paul Marie Pau, were considered but were rejected for one reason or another. Pau, for example, demanded the right to make his own senior military appointments, a privilege which the distrustful government would not allow. Finally, the most obvious choices having been exhausted, Joffre was selected.

What did he have to recommend him? First, he was politically acceptable—neither an aristocrat (his father was a cooper) nor an ardent Catholic. Second, he was acceptable to the General Staff, which probably regarded him as "a solid shield behind which subtler brains could direct French military policy." * At any rate, Joffre well knew to whom he owed his appointment and also the ousting of his predecessor—to the influential young officers of the School of the Attack. Accordingly, Joffre gave his blessing to the development of their Plan XVII, the violent offensive into Alsace and Lorraine.

But although Joffre was, to an extent, beholden to the Young Turks of the General Staff, this is not to say that he was in any way subservient. In his exalted position as ruler of the French Army, he developed a species of Olympian detachment. Solemn, somber, never ruffled, he seemed like a brooding presence hanging over the General Staff and, indeed, the entire Army. His age, girth and imperturbability gave an impression of paternal grandeur which accentuated and reinforced the confidence the French Army had always had in itself. With "Papa" Joffre in command, what could possibly go wrong? With his blessing upon them, how could the plans go awry, how could the tactics be in error?

* *Reputations,* by Liddell Hart, B. H., p. 7.

Immediately upon mobilization the French Army began to put Plan XVII into force. Since it was thought that the Germans would have to divide their forces to meet an attack in the east by the huge Russian Army, the French saw no insurmountable difficulty in carrying out their own attacks. So Joffre began a series of tentative assaults which were designed to clear the way for the audacious drive into Alsace and Lorraine. But before these offensives had the opportunity to gather headway, there was ominous news from the north. The Germans had burst across the Belgian frontier and, using immense howitzers of a size unknown to other armies, were reducing the vaunted Belgian fortress system into so much crushed concrete.

Now, prewar French doctrine had been to completely ignore the enemy's activities in favor of pursuing Plan XVII. This procedure, it was held, would rapidly place the Germans in such a position that they would have to abandon any offensive of their own in favor of countering the French thrust, and thus the French would retain the initiative with the privilege of directing their attack where and when they wanted. In practice, this theory was found to be valid—but it worked the other way. The Germans outnumbered the French by three to two, and it was only a matter of days before their drive began to exert tremendous pressure.

For the first two weeks of the war, Joffre attempted to follow the doctrine of the offensive. The German incursion into Belgium was officially ignored; it was regarded as a feint or a cavalry raid. How could it be anything else? It was obvious that the Germans could not possibly have enough troops to provide the necessary manpower for a serious attack through Belgium. Moreover, the Second Bureau had advised that the German railheads opposite Belgium were too small to support anything more than twenty-two divisions.

But gradually and sickeningly it became clear that the German thrust into Belgium was no mere smash-and-grab raid. It was nothing less than the most powerful military offensive the world had ever seen, mounted by five German armies which totaled nearly two million fighting men. And its aim was to debouch on the French left, outflank the entire French Army (together with the handful of divisions which the British had brought across to support their allies) roll it up, smash it, and then transfer the German troops east to deal with the ponderous Russian forces. The Germans had found enough manpower by training and arming their reserve divisions to a far greater degree than the French thought possible. The proficiency of the German reserves was such that they were being used in almost the same manner as the active divisions.

But, despite this evidence of the immensity of the German offensive on his undefended left, Joffre continued with the attacks envisioned in Plan XVII. A French drive into Alsace and Lorraine was thrown back; in its stead, Joffre launched two other armies into the Ardennes Forest where he foresaw no serious German opposition. He could not have been more wrong. The German Fourth and Fifth Armies were just beginning their own scheduled advance and the two forces met head-on. On one day, August 22, four bloody engagements were fought—Virton, Ethe, Rossignol, and Neufchâteau. The French lost them all.

Under the circumstances, it would seem apparent that the logical, the prudent, the accepted tactics for the French Army would have been to conduct a series of rear-guard actions: to beat a slow retreat, pausing along a river, a height, or some other naturally defensible terrain feature and to dig trenches (they had proved their value in the Balkan War of two years before) site artillery and machine guns, string barbed wire and shred the advancing German columns in a blast of firepower. But so steeped was the French Army in the School of the Attack, in the idea of the irresistible bayonet attack that, as Winston Churchill pointed out, "Though the Germans invaded, it was more often the French who attacked."

This, then, was the way the French Army fought. In nineteenth century massed formations, the troops were assembled in fields or on roads in full view of the efficient German artillery observers. There was no attempt at surprise or concealment—indeed, the French infantrymen, with their bright red trousers and dark blue coats, were superbly visible.

When all was ready, bayonets were fixed and the attack began. Flags snapping in the air, regimental bands playing "The Marseillaise," the officers in white gloves and twenty paces forward, they

swept forward to the sound of bugles—full tilt into the massed
firepower of the twentieth century.

And now a ghastly truth became evident. No amount of *élan,* no
Napoleonic traditions, no exhortations by officers crying *"En avant!"*
and *"à la baïonnette!"* could save from slaughter the troops charging
over open fields at the hands of an entrenched, numerically superior
enemy which possessed machine guns, modern magazine rifles and
long-range artillery.

A British Army officer was horrified. "Whenever the French
infantry advance," he wrote, "their whole front is at once regularly
covered with shrapnel and the unfortunate men are knocked over
like rabbits. They are very brave and advance time after time to the
charge through appalling fire, but so far it has been of no avail. No
one could live through the fire that is concentrated on them. The
officers are splendid; they advance about twenty yards ahead of
their men as calmly as though on parade, but so far I have not seen
one of them get more than fifty yards without being knocked over." *

But somehow the German onrush had to be checked and a spirited
charge was the only method the School of the Attack knew. Every
man was thrown into the battle. Even cavalrymen, dismounted and
with their horses either dead or exhausted, made suicidal charges on
foot across the fields, their only weapons their long lances. The
French artillery was helpless against the entrenched Germans—
"What were they to fire at, anyhow, when all that could be seen of
the enemy was a few faint gleams of well-aligned cannon?" ** To a
French corporal the German machine guns seemed "like a coffee mill
—*tac-tac-tac.* The bullets stream past; it is an infernal uproar. For
each bullet that I hear I think, That one is for me."

By August 25, the tremendous force of the Schlieffen Plan had
become evident to Joffre in its fullest scope. Plan XVII was dead. An
irresistible mass of Germans was pouring across the Franco-Belgian
frontier, well north of the French armies. Now it had become a
matter of the starkest necessity for the French to avoid being
outflanked and encircled.

* From *The Times History of the War,* Vol. II, p. 146.
** De Gaulle, *France and Her Army,* p. 92.

So, for day after day during the hottest summer in years, the French Army retreated southward and westward. Always in danger of being outflanked and caught in reverse, the French streamed back in long, dusty columns. Every road was filled with men, guns and horses—and hanging over the exhausted troops like an invisible pall was the knowledge that in a few hours, a few days at most, these same French roads would be filled with the gray-clad, spike-helmeted Germans.

It is a difficult undertaking to rewrite tactical doctrine in the midst of a war. It is almost impossible to rewrite it when an army is in full retreat, when it is deathly tired, confused and decimated and utter ruin is looming. Nevertheless, the useless sacrifice of the French Army to the gods of the Attack could not continue and Joffre sent the following modifying instruction to his army commanders:

> The engagements which have taken place so far have served to display the admirable qualities of our infantry. Without in any way wishing to impair this dash, in which lies the principal factor of success, it is of the greatest importance, especially when it is a question to carrying fortified positions, to learn to await artillery fire and to prevent the troops from exposing themselves hastily to the enemy's fire. . . .
>
> As many guns as possible should be engaged from the beginning of an engagement. The attacks will be all the more successful, all the less costly, in proportion to the care with which they have been prepared.

Thus, as Plan XVII had proved a failure, so did the theories of the School of the Attack. And still the German offensive rolled onward while, tottering with exhaustion, the French armies fled before its enveloping thrust. The world stood aghast. Could Paris possibly be defended? Could the French Army possibly come back from this great retreat which by now had left northeastern France naked to the invader?

By August 30 the rumble of German guns in the northeast was audible in Paris and the city experienced its first air raid. A German plane let loose five bombs on the Rue Albouy and the Quay Valmy, and with the bombs a message was dropped. Signed by a Lieutenant von Heidessen, it said: "The German Army is at the gates of Paris; there is nothing left to you but to surrender."

On September 2 the situation had become desperate and the French government fled Paris for Bordeaux, announcing: "If this formidable struggle is to be given all its dash and efficiency, the government must remain free to act. . . . The government, therefore, transfers its residence to a spot where it can remain in constant communication with the whole country." The announcement closed with admiring references to the Paris population and recommendations of "calm and resolution." Nevertheless, more than a third of the citizens of Paris saw fit to flee the oncoming Germans. The railroad stations were mobbed with refugees and the roads filled with carts and automobiles heading south.

To explain the stunning defeats of August 1914, it is customary for apologists for the French Army command to complain that the Germans possessed great superiority in artillery and automatic weapons; anyway, they say, the French Army gave as good as it got. To proffer this explanation is to deny the facts. Agreed, the Germans possessed the heavier artillery. This was the reason why the French armies came under long-range artillery fire to which they could not even reply. Yet in their 75-mm. artillery piece the French had a quick-firing weapon which in most respects was superior to its German 77-mm. counterpart and which, if they had grasped the secret of its proper use, should have helped to even out the German edge. With regard to automatic weapons, the French and German armies were alike in possessing two machine guns per battalion. But the Germans invariably used theirs better, probably simply because they had faith in their effectiveness and the French School of the Attack did not. Finally, while it is true that the Germans suffered severe losses, it is probable that at no time did their casualty totals exceed two thirds of the combined French and British—this despite the fact that the Germans were the invaders.

No, the inescapable conclusion is that the French Army theorists, while convinced that they had grasped the secret of success in modern warfare, had in reality seized upon its antithesis. They had actually done their unwitting best to destroy their Army. And, almost symbolically, one of the dead was the high priest of offensive action, Colonel Loiseau de Grandmaison, killed leading an infantry brigade charge. Now the French Army could be saved only by the one quality the Army theorists did not believe their troops possessed —tenacity on the defensive.

To the neutral observer in August 1914, it seemed as if nothing could save France. But, actually, there was still a glimmer of hope. Even though the French Army had been disastrously defeated in almost every battle, it had not been routed. Though the troops had been marched to the point where they were in a stupor, though the Army had lost more than a third of its effectiveness, it still existed as an organized force. Each corps had always taken the right road in its retreat, fewer than ten thousand unwounded prisoners had been taken by the Germans, and the cry of "Every man for himself" had never been raised. The Army had been pushed to the brink, but it still was capable of marching and fighting another day. And as long as this was the case, the French had not yet lost the war. Moltke, the Chief of the German General Staff, realized this, and when gleeful subordinates came to tell him that the Schlieffen Plan was victorious and that the French Army was routed, he said, "Don't let's deceive ourselves. . . . When armies of millions stand facing one another, the victor has prisoners. Where are our prisoners?"

By September 3 the German armies were nearly at the gates of Paris. A few more days of uncontested marching would have finished the war. But Joffre had taken a number of steps to prevent this from happening. First, on the insistence of the Minister of War, he had appointed General Gallieni as the military governor of Paris. Gallieni was an old and respected French soldier, passed over in favor of Joffre as Commander in Chief but possessed of imagination and energy all out of keeping with his sixty-five years. In the absence of the government, Gallieni became undisputed master of Paris. There had been some official discussion of evacuating Paris and declaring it an open city. Gallieni would have none of it. He posted the following announcement:

To the Army of Paris and the Population of Paris

The members of the Government of the Republic have left Paris in order to give a new impulse to the national defense. I have received the order to defend Paris against the invader. This order I shall fulfill to the end.

Gallieni

He then busied himself with readying Paris for a siege. Out of the half-deserted city he dragooned up masses of manpower and marched them out to the ring of fortifications which surrounded Paris. There they began to dig rifle pits, repair crumbling masonry and clear fields of fire. Gallieni remembered the siege of Paris in 1870, when the animals in the zoo and the rats in the gutters had been eaten, so the Bois de Boulogne, the infields of the race tracks and every park he could find were filled with cattle ready for slaughter.

But more had been done to defend France than simply placing Paris in an attitude of defense. At the French Army's Grand Quartier Général—G.Q.G.—Joffre was slowly evolving his answer to the Schlieffen Plan. Somewhere, sometime, he theorized, the Germans would make a mistake. For the moment he must continue his retreat, get his troops out of the German grip, reorganize them and then give battle. In addition, to strengthen his left flank, which by now was almost bent back to Paris, Joffre had been shuffling reserves over from his fortress-defended right. Finally, he had formed two new armies to supplement the two he already had in the field. One of these, the Sixth Army, was based in Paris and originally consisted of a handful of reserve divisions, but shortly it was stiffened by the arrival from Algeria of two first-class regular divisions.

In all of this, the imperturbability of Joffre was astounding. Granted, the man was no strategic genius, but his nerve was phenomenal. This Commander in Chief who had not won a battle and whose enemy had already conquered an area containing a sixth of the population of France gave not the slightest evidence of the awful strain which any normal man would have felt. Every night Joffre retired punctually at ten, leaving strict instructions that his slumber should not be disturbed. His meals were eaten with a gourmet's zest and with a calm which his anguished subordinates found shattering.

In a way, Joffre's *sang-froid* had some justfication. Much had begun to go wrong with the Schlieffen Plan, especially with German communications. Radio messages were a haphazard thing, and in the line of the German advance the French cavalry patrols had cut telegraph wires in countless places.* The result was that neither the German Supreme Headquarters nor any of the five German armies slicing into France had a very clear idea where the others were or what they were doing.

Even more important was the fact that the German commander, General von Moltke, had tampered with the purity of the dead Schlieffen's scheme. One of the keys to its success had been the intentional weakening of the German left flank so as to draw the French right wing out of its fortifications. But Moltke had been unable to resist the urgings of the commanders on the German left to strengthen their forces. The result was that these armies had actually driven the French back into their fortresses, thus unintentionally giving Joffre the reserves of manpower which he was now railing to his own left. Moreover, two of the five German invading armies had been weakened by detachments to defend East Prussia against the advancing Russians and were now becoming too small to carry out their task.

And finally, it must be recalled that the German thrust was a wheeling movement, which meant that the outer sections had to move a much greater distance than the inner. This imposed a tremendous strain upon the flankers—the armies on the outside.

It was the two outside German armies, the First Army, commanded by General Alexander von Kluck, and the Second Army, under General Karl von Bülow, who were to prove weak links in the German chain.

These two armies had marched so far and so fast that they were

---

* According to Asprey (p. 171), "German front-to-rear communications were hopeless. Radio was in its infancy, telephones were scarcely reliable, cable-wireless was slow and uncertain. OHL operated only one radio receiver—as incredible as this may seem."

now fully as exhausted as their French and British adversaries. Moreover the Allies, in their retreat, had pretty much broken contact with the Germans, who did not have a clear idea where they had gone. Kluck in particular was in a quandary. He seems not to have realized that Joffre's new Sixth Army was forming on his flank. Thus Kluck thought that he was outside the Allied forces and that his flank was secure. In addition Bülow was urging him to wheel inward to help crush the French Fifth Army. Thus, lacking information and direction from Moltke, Kluck edged out of his assigned path and began to march south and east. This was tremendously significant. The German "wheel" had now been pushed in. The hitherto sacred Schlieffen Plan had been drastically altered and instead of passing *behind,* or to the west of Paris, the German armies were altering their direction to pass *in front,* to the east of Paris. Thus the arc of the German wheel was made smaller by some eighty miles, and this was to prove its undoing.

BATTLE FOR SURVIVAL

The Battle of the Marne was, in the estimation of many, the turning point of the war. Military authorities agree that while the German armies were not really defeated in the field, their own miscalculations coupled with the stiffening of the French forced a change in the German strategy. The German high command ordered a retreat because their lines were overextended and their First Army's flank was dangerously exposed. At this point, the German armies were not driven back, but the momentum of attack disappeared.

Until September 6, the first day of the Marne battle, "The German soldier looked ahead to this day being like the day before and the day after—forward always forward, until finally he crushed the enemy as his grandfather had crushed the enemy nearly half a century before . . . nowhere did the soldier or the officer or the general expect the enemy to attack, no one doubted final victory." [*]

Even so, many changes had occurred within the German war machine since August 4. "The three right-wing armies originally marched with 17 infantry corps; on September 6 they counted 12 corps, a transfer loss of 225,000 troops, plus further severe losses in the numerous encounter battles and from attrition much greater than planned. The boots of men had worn thin . . . and their bodies were tired. As long ago as Mons the First Army had started to outrun its supply trains. Above and below the Marne some units now were living off the country and sometimes the country did not feed them too well." [**]

The French armies, meanwhile, had been severely dealt with by the invading Germans. By the end of the Battle of the Marne they

[*] Asprey, p. 102.
[**] Asprey, p. 103.

would have lost almost half the personnel of their field armies including two-thirds of their field officers. Out of 1,300,000 men, more than 600,000 had been killed, wounded and captured.

"The men on the line were mostly veterans now. They knew what it was to march to the sound of cannon, to hear the shells whistling overhead, making that same revolting noise of some giant dog vomiting. They knew what the cannon did to you inside, that ghastly feeling of impotence against a far-sprung evil, suddenly the *karoomp, karoomp, karoomp* to tear the heart from your company, to foul an honest landscape with entrails of men and horses and twisted broken wagons, and finally if time permitted rude crosses in a field, man's attempt to dignify indignant death.

"The Germans outgunned the Allies by far, the big sooty shells from their heavy artillery being called *marmites* or caldrons by the French, 'Jack Johnsons' by the English. The men respected the shells because they were lethal but they no longer feared them, because if you were there you would be killed but if you were forty yards away you would live, and besides many were duds, so you never knew, especially at night. Not so with the 75s, and these the Germans both respected and feared, because they were fast and accurate and lent themselves to a method of firing the French called *rafale*—a squall of shrapnel shells, metal casings that exploded to release iron balls that smothered an area in agony and death. But if the French held the upper hand here, the Germans claimed it back when it came to the machine gun, for this the *poilu* failed to understand; he loathed and feared the dreadful *mitrailleuse* that spit death: you could see it and it mocked you because it was far away and your rifle and bayonet could not reach and when you tried running for it you met death or sometimes wounds." *

Joffre's armies in front of the German thrust southeast of Paris were "disorganized, and stood anywhere from five to fifteen miles behind their scheduled departure lines." ** Joffre had ordered his troops to turn and fight but if the Germans broke through again, it might mean the end of France.

* Asprey, pp. 99, 100.
** Asprey, p. 104.

The Battle of the Marne would be a battle for survival. Its success would gain time for Joffre to rebuild the French armies.

THE MARNE*

by Winston Churchill

As the German armies rolled southwards Paris loomed before them like an enormous breakwater. The enemy capital was not only the heart of France, it was also the largest fortress in the world. It was the center of an intricate spider's web of railways. Masses of troops could debouch in almost unlimited numbers in any direction upon passers-by. No one could count on entering it without a formal seige, the German cannon for which were at this moment deploying before Antwerp. To advance upon both sides of Paris, the Germans had not the troops; to enter Paris, they had not at this moment the guns. What then remained? They must march between Paris and Verdun—which exerted a similar influence—and guarding their flanks from both these fortresses push on to the destruction of the French field armies. Surely also this was the classical tradition? Had not Moltke—not this one but the great Moltke, now dead a quarter of a century—proclaimed "Direction: Paris! Objective: the enemy's field armies!"

At noon on August 31 a Captain Lepic sent to reconnoitre with his squadron reported from Gournay-sur-Aronde that the interminable columns of Kluck's First Army were turning southeast towards Compiègne instead of continuing their march on Paris. This news was confirmed the next day both by British and French aviators. By

* From *The World Crisis*, published by Charles Scribner's Sons.

nightfall on the 2nd General Maunoury's Sixth Army, which had now arrived in the northern environs of Paris, reported that there were no German troops west of the line Senlis-Paris. It was upon these indications, confirmed again by British aviators on the 3rd, that Galliéni acted.

Assuredly no human brain had conceived the design, nor had human hand set the pieces on the board. Several separate and discrepant series of events had flowed together. First, the man Galliéni is on the spot. Fixed in his fortress, he could not move towards the battle; so the mighty battle has been made to come to him. Second—the weapon has been placed in his hands—the army of Maunoury. It was given him for one purpose, the defence of Paris; he will use it for another—a decisive manœuvre in the field. It was given him against the wish of Joffre. It will prove the means of Joffre's salvation. Third, the Opportunity: Kluck, swinging forward in hot pursuit of, as he believed, the routed British and demoralized French, will present his whole right flank and rear as he passes Paris to Galliéni with Maunoury in his hand. Observe, not one of these factors would have counted without the other two. All are interdependent; all are here, and all are here now.

Galliéni realised the position in a flash. 'I dare not believe it,' he exclaimed; 'it is too good to be true.' But it is true. Confirmation arrives hour by hour. He vibrates with enthusiasm. Instantly on the 3rd, he orders the army of Maunoury to positions on the north-east of Paris, which in 48 hours will enable them on the 5th to strike Kluck and with him the whole advancing line of German armies behind their right shoulder blade. But this is not enough. What can one army—hastily improvised—do by itself amid events on such a scale? He must secure the British; he must animate Joffre. At half-past eight on the evening of the 3rd he wrote requesting Joffre's authority for the movement, which he has already ordered Maunoury's army to make, and urging a general offensive by all the French armies between Paris and Verdun simultaneously with his attack.

Joffre and Great Headquarters had arrived that day at Bar-sur-Aube. The numerous bureaux composing the elaborate staff machine

had been on the move for two days and were now installing
themselves at a new centre. We must not suppose that Joffre and his
assistants have not been thinking about things. It was evident to any
trained observer that if the fortresses of Verdun and Paris were
strongly defended by mobile armies, the German invasion would
bulge forward into a wide crescent between these two points; and
that this would give an opportunity for a general French attack.
Somehow, somewhere, sometime, Joffre and his Staff intended this.
In principle they and Galliéni were agreed. From the beginning of
the retreat he had said, 'I will attack when my two wings have an
enveloping position.' But the How, the Where, and the When. These
were the rubs; and on these vital matters it is certain that not only no
resolve or design had been formed, but that important orders had
been issued inconsistent with such a plan.

Galliéni's messenger reached Bar-sur-Aube on the night of the 3rd,
and all the next morning while Maunoury's army was marching into
its preparatory stations Galliéni waited in acute anxiety. In the afternoon of the 4th he set off by motor-car to Melun to ask Sir John
French for British co-operation. Remember that this man had had
Joffre under his command in Madagascar and that he is his formally
designated successor. He is not thinking only of the local situation
around Paris. He thinks for France and he behaves with the
spontaneous confidence of genius in action. But French is out with
his troops. Murray, Chief of his Staff, receives the Governor of Paris.
The interview is lengthy and somewhat bleak.

It was an unpropitious moment for a subordinate French General
to propose a new and desperate battle to the British command. On
September 2 Sir John French had written to Joffre offering, if the
French would turn and fight a general battle on the Marne, to throw
in the British Army and put all things to the proof; and Joffre had
written back, 'I do not think it possible to contemplate at this moment (*actuellement*) a general operation on the Marne with the
whole of our forces.' And the British leader who had braced himself
for a supreme ordeal with his small, weary and shot-torn army had
been chilled. By a swift reaction, remembering all that had passed
since the battle of Mons began, he had reached precipitately but not

inexcusably the conclusion that the French had lost heart and did not feel themselves capable of regaining the offensive—at any rate for some time to come. So far, his allies had produced nothing but repulse, defeat and retreat. All their plans, in so far as he was informed of them, seemed to have failed. He knew that the Government was quitting Paris for Bordeaux. He saw that the rearmost lines of places mentioned in Joffre's Instruction No. 2 as the limits of the retreat were far behind the positions he occupied at the moment. He could not exclude from his mind, on the morrow of his offer being declined, the possiblity of a general collapse of French resistance. Indeed it was evident that the Germans, by the very fact of disdaining Paris, sought nothing less than the destruction of the French armies. Had he been in the German Headquarters, he would have learned that at this moment Moltke looked confidently forward to driving the French masses either into Switzerland or, if Rupprecht could break through between Nancy and Toul, on to the back of their own eastern fortress line, thus swiftly compelling a universal surrender. If he had been admitted to the secrets of the French Headquarters, he would have learned that Joffre had proposed to declare Paris an open town and to surrender it to the first German troops who arrived; that he had simultaneously sent orders to General Sarrail to abandon Verdun; and that only Messimy's intrusion and Sarrail's stubbornness had prevented both these catastrophes from being already accomplished facts. One really cannot blame Sir Archibald Murray on the knowledge that he had, and in the absence of his Chief, from viewing with scepticism the ardent and admittedly unauthorised projects of the Governor of Paris. However he promised provisionally to stop the southward movement of the British Army and to face about on a certain rather rearward line.

Meanwhile, early on the 4th, Joffre at Bar-sur-Aube had received Galliéni's letter of the night before. All the morning he pondered upon it. Then at noon he authorised Galliéni by telegram to use the army of Maunoury as he had proposed, but with the express condition that it should not attack north, but south of the Marne. A little later he telegraphed to Franchet d' Espérey, now commanding the

Fifth French Army, asking him when he could be ready to take part in a general offensive. Franchet replied at 4 p. m. on the 4th that he could attack on the morning of the 6th. This answer reached Joffre between 5 and 6 o'clock. But for the next three hours he did nothing. He took no decision; he sent no orders.

Galliéni arrived back in Paris from Melun shortly before 8 o'clock. He had been absent from his Headquarters for five hours, and meanwhile Joffre's reply to his letter had arrived. He was disturbed by the Commander-in-Chief's express condition that the army of Maunoury should not attack north but only south of the Marne. Other disconcerting news reached him. He heard by telegram from Sir Henry Wilson (Murray's assistant) that the British Army was continuing its retreat; and soon after he received from Colonel Huguet, the French *liaison* officer at the British Headquarters, Sir John French's reply to his proposals: 'Prefer on account of continual changes of the situation to re-study it before deciding on further operations."

It was now 9 o'clock. Apparently nothing was happening. All the armies would before dawn resume their retreat. So far as he knew, he had received nothing but the permission to make an isolated flank attack with Maunoury's army. Galliéni went to the telephone. He called up Joffre. The Commander-in-Chief came. The two men talked. As the Commander-in-Chief of the French armies circulating his orders through the official channels, Joffre towered above Galliéni; but now, almost in personal contact, Galliéni and his old subordinate spoke at least as equals; and Joffre, to his honour, rising above jealousies and formalities, felt the strong, clear guidance of his valiant comrade. He agreed that Galliéni should attack *north* of the Marne on the 5th, and returning to his circle of officers, ordered the general battle for the 6th. Unfortunately his hesitation and previous delays bred others. We can see from the times quoted how long these vital orders take to prepare and encipher for telegraph, and decipher on arrival. It was nearly midnight before they were dispatched. They were in fact outstripped by duplicates carried by officers in motor cars. Foch, being nearest, received his orders at 1.30 a.m. But neither Franchet nor Sir John French learned of the great decision until after 3 a.m., when their armies had already begun a further day's march to the south.

Nevertheless the die is now cast. The famous order of the day is sent out; and from Verdun to Paris the electrifying right-about-turn points a million bayonets and 1,000 cannon upon the invading hosts. The Battle of the Marne has begun.

Since the war laborious studies have been set in train, and an enormous mass of publications, official, non-official and counter-official, has been produced. These have together assembled a multitudinous array of facts. But there are so many facts adduced and some few vitally important facts withheld, and such disputations over the one or the other, that half a dozen explanatory theories may well be championed; and the world, harassed with paying the bill, has been content to rest on the solid assurance that the French beat the Germans at the Battle of the Marne.

The French official history carries its discreet narration down to midnight on September 5. According to this account, with little generosity to Galliéni, the battle of the Marne does not begin till the 6th, and in the presence of this event the French military historians are mute. From the evening of September 5 till January 1915 their pages are blank. Obviously the controversies of rival schools of professional opinion, fierce disputes about facts and their valuations, respect for the feelings of illustrious men, have induced the chroniclers to leave this climax of their tale till time has wrought its smoothing work.

So far as we may judge from the French account of the preliminaries, they consider the battle as having reached from Paris to Verdun. The German account, on the other hand, in harmony with their own schemes, comprehends it as extending from Paris right round the corner of Verdun to the Vosges Mountains. The Germans consider that all their seven armies were engaged at the Marne; the French that only five of theirs and the British Army were comprised in the battle. We have to contemplate on either view the collision of thirteen or fourteen armies, each containing the adult male population of a very large city, and all consuming food, material, ammunition, treasure and life at a prodigious rate per hour.

We have to remember also that the French and British are armies whose springs are compressed back on their reserves and supplies; and that the German armies have hurried on far beyond their rearward organisation and their rail-heads. The French have perfect communications sideways and otherwise; the Germans have not yet restored the broken roads and bridges over which their rapid advance had been made. The French are upon interior lines; the Germans are stretched round the fortified Verdun corner. It was upon this basis that the battle began.

It was less like a battle than any other ever fought. Comparatively few were killed or wounded. No great recognisable feat of arms, no shock proportionate to the event can be discerned. Along a front of more than 200 miles weary, war-ravaged troops were in a loose, desperate contact; then all of a sudden one side sustained the impression that it was the weaker, and that it had had the worst of it. But what was the mechanical causation which induced this over-powering psychological reaction? I can only try to furnish a few links of a chain that is still partly buried.

The popular conception of the Battle of the Marne as a wild counter-rush of France upon Germany, as a leopard spring at the throat of the invaders, as an onslaught carried forward on the wings of passion and ecstasy, is in singular contrast to the truth. It took some time to turn round the French armies retreating between Verdun and Paris. These ponderous bodies could only effectually reverse their motion after a substantial number of hours and even days. No sooner had the French turned about and begun to advance, than they met the pursuing Germans advancing towards them. Most prudently they stopped at once and fired upon the Germans, and the Germans withered before their fire. It is the Battle of the Frontiers fought the other way round. No longer the French advance madly to the strains of the Marseillaise while the German invaders stop and shoot them down with machine guns and artillery; the conditions are reversed. It is the Germans who try to advance and feel for the first time the frightful power of the French artillery. If only the French had done this at the frontiers; if only they had used modern firearms upon hostile flesh and blood at the outset, how different the picture of the world might look to-day!

The Battle of the Marne was won when Joffre had finished his conversation with Galliéni on the night of September 4. Although the French armies had been defeated, had suffered grievous losses, and had retreated day after day, they were still an enormous, unbeaten, fighting force of a very high order. Although the British had retreated with great rapidity and had lost 15,000 men, the soldiers knew they had fought double their numbers and had inflicted far heavier casualties upon the German masses. Drafts and reinforcements had reached them, and they were at the moment of the turn certainly stronger than they had ever been. Although the Germans had 78 divisions on their western front compared to 55 French and British, this superiority was not enough for the supreme objective which they had in view. The Schlieffen plan, the 'receipt for victory,' had prescribed 97 divisions against France alone, and of these 71 were to execute the great offensive wheel through Belgium. Moltke had 19 fewer divisions in the west and 16 fewer in the great offensive wheel. From these again he had withdrawn 2 army corps (4 divisions) to send to the eastern front. He had not thought it worth while to attempt to stop or delay the transport of the British Expeditionary Force across the Channel. According to the German naval history 'the chief of the General Staff personally replied that the Navy should not allow the operations that it would have otherwise carried out to be interfered with on this account. It would even be of advantage if the armies in the west could settle with the 160,000 English at the same time as with the French and Belgians.' Thus when Joffre's decision was taken the balance had already turned strongly in favour of the Allies.

Contrary to the French official narrative, the battle began on the 5th when Maunoury's army came into action on the Ourcq. Let us hasten thither.

General von Kluck's army is marching south and passes Paris in sight of the Eiffel Tower. One of his five corps is acting as flank guard. Bright and cloudless skies! Suddenly about one o'clock the flank corps begins to brush against French troops advancing upon it from Paris. In order to test the strength of their assailants, the Germans attack. At once a violent action flares out and spreads. The French appear in ever-growing strength; the flank guard is beaten. The corps retreats seven miles with heavy losses. The attack from Paris grows and lengthens with more and more weight behind it. Night comes on. The defeated General, hoping to retrieve his fortunes with the morning, sends no word to Kluck. But a German aviator has noticed the conflict far below and the unexpected position of the fighting lines and his report goes to the Army Headquarters. It is not till nearly midnight that Kluck is informed that the shield on which he had counted has been shivered. Then, and not till then did he remember Moltke's orders, namely that in the main advance to drive the French into Switzerland, the armies of Kluck and Bülow should form a defensive flank against attacks from Paris. So far from giving protection to the line of German armies, he has had his own flank torn open; and in four hours another day will break!

So Kluck without more ado pulls back the two corps of his centre, and bids them recross the Marne and form to the north of his defeated flank guard; and as the pressure of Maunoury's attack continues during the 6th, he next takes the last of his army, the two corps of his left, marches them 60 miles in 48 hours, resolved whatever befall not to be out-flanked in the north, and have his communications cut. So here is Kluck who was pressing southward so fast to find the remains of the defeated English, now suddenly turned completely round and drawing up his whole army facing west to ward off Maunoury's continuing attack from Paris. But all this takes time and it is not till the morning of the 9th that Kluck has got himself into his new position and is ready to fall upon Maunoury in superior strength and drive him back upon the Paris fortifications. Meanwhile the war has been going on.

Next in the line to Kluck is Bülow. He too remembers his orders to form a flank guard against Paris. Moreover the withdrawal of Kluck's army corps has left his right in the air. So Bülow pivots on his centre. His right arm goes back, his left arm comes forward, and in the course of the 6th, 7th, 8th and 9th he draws himself up in position facing Paris, and almost at right angles to his previous front. But both Kluck and Bülow have now exposed their left hands to the attack of any allied forces who may be advancing upon them from the south. We know that the British Army and the Fifth French Army (Franchet d'Espérey) have turned about on the morning of the 5th and are advancing. This was only the beginning. Not only had Kluck and Bülow exposed their left flanks to the attack of powerful forces, but a hideous gap had opened between them. A gap of over 30 miles, and practically nothing to fill it with except cavalry! A great mass of cavalry indeed, two cavalry corps, the corps of Marwitz provided by Kluck and of Richthofen provided by Bülow —still only cavalry and without a common commander! An awful gap merely skinned over! We may imagine the feelings of the German Main Headquarters in Luxemburg as this apparition gradually but inexorably resolved itself upon the map. 'If we only had a couple of corps marching forward behind the main front, here is their place and this is their hour.' 'What did we do with the two corps that were to have besieged Namur?' 'Ah! yes, we sent them to the Vistula! So we did! How far have they got?' 'They are now disembarking from 80 trains 700 miles away.' Well might the Kaiser have exclaimed, 'Moltke, Moltke, give me back my legions!'

If the immense organisms of modern armies standing in a row together find there is a wide gap in their ranks, and have no reserves to come up and fill it, they cannot edge towards one another sideways like companies or battalions. They can only close the gap by an advance or by a retreat. Which is it to be? To answer this question we must see what has been happening on the rest of the long battle line.

Beginning round the corner at the extreme left of the German invasion, Prince Rupprecht has found he cannot pierce the front between Toul and Épinal. The heavy guns of the French fortresses, the prepared positions and the obstinate armies of Dubail and Castelnau have, with much slaughter, stopped him and his Bavarians. He has been dragging the heavy cannon out of Metz; but it takes a long time to move them. Now they are called for elsewhere. Rupprecht therefore reports on September 8 that he cannot break through the Trouée des Charmes and that he is in fact at a standstill. North-east of Verdun Sarrail faces the army of the German Crown Prince. Here again the guns of the fortress strike heavy blows. The Crown Prince's columns skirting Verdun at a respectful distance are mauled and hampered. Next come the armies of the Duke of Wurtemberg and General von Hausen. These are confronted respectively by the army of de L'Angle le Carré and around the marshes of St. Gond by the army of General Foch.

Throughout the centre the fighting was confused, obscure, and to say the least, indecisive. On the left of Bülow's army (with which was now associated nearly half of Hausen's) an attempt was made to advance against Foch with a desperate, gigantic bayonet attack at dawn. The Germans claim that this assault was successful. The outposts and advance troops of one of Foch's army corps were certainly driven back; but the main line of the French field artillery intact continued its devasting fire. Every one remembers Foch's staccato phrases: 'My flanks are turned; my centre gives way; I attack!'

Three German armies had tried to advance directly against the French and had failed. The French wisely and though hardly with a conscious decision abstaining from their own onslaught, had been content to shoot them down. Broadly speaking, the armies of the German Crown Prince, the Duke of Wurtemburg and General von Hausen were by September 8 at a complete standstill in front of those of Sarrail, de L'Angle and Foch. The centres of the French and German fronts were leaning up against each other in complete equipoise. We are witnessing the birth throes of trench warfare.

But what meanwhile has been happening to the gap? We must not forget the gap. It is still open, thirty miles of it between the two armies of the German right. Into this gap are now marching steadily the British Army together with the left of the Fifth French Army (Franchet's). On they march, these 5 British divisions preceded by 5 brigades of their own cavalry and a French cavalry division. They go on marching. The German aeroplanes see five dark 15-mile long caterpillars eating up the white roads. They report 'heavy British masses advancing.' And what was there to stop them? Only one corps of cavalry now, the other has been called away by Bülow; 6 battalions of Jäger, and—a long way back—one rather battered infantry division. There is no possibility of such forces stopping or indeed delaying the march of a professional army of 120,000 men. There are three rivers or streams to cross; four wooded ridges of ground to be cleared. But nothing can prevent this wedge from being driven into the gap. With every hour and every mile of its advance the strategic embarrassments of Bülow and Kluck increased. Nothing had happened so far. The German cavalry and Jäger were being driven back before aggressive British rifle-using cavalry, backed by swiftly gathering bayonets and cannons. But in the whole four days the British lost under 2,000 men. The effects were not tactical; they were strategic.

No human genius planned that the British Army should advance into this gap. A series of tumultuous events had cast them into this position in the line. When they advanced, there was the gap in front of them. On the whole front it was the line of least resistance. Along it they bored and punched, and it led into the strategic vitals of the German right wing. High destiny, blind fate regulated the none too vigorous, but nevertheless decisive, movements of this British Army. It marches on, wondering what has happened to the monster which had pursued it with whip and yell since Mons. Bülow finds his right flank being rolled back by the Fifth French Army, and himself cut off continually from his right-hand comrade, Kluck, by the British advance. Kluck, just as he has got himself into a fine position to fight Maunoury, finds his left and all the rear of his left, hopelessly compromised and exposed.

All these developments present themselves in the first instance upon the maps at Bülow's and Kluck's headquarters, loaded with a hundred details concerning the supplies, the safety and even the escape of at least one-third of the whole of both their armies. And the sum of these disquietudes, unwillingly disclosed item by item, reveals its terrors to the highest centre of authority.

We must now transport ourselves, as is our privilege, to the Emperor's headquarters at Luxemburg. Time: the morning of September 8. The magnates there assembled were already alarmed

at the lack of reports of the hourly victories to which they had
become accustomed. Instead comes Rupprecht's tale that he is at a
standstill. Next there is brought a captured copy of Joffre's battle
orders of the 5th. The whole French army is attacking! The Crown
Prince says he is pinned down. 'We can make only contemptible
advances' he reports. 'We are plagued with artillery fire. The
infantry simply get under cover. There are no means of advancing.
What are we to do?' The Duke of Wurtemburg and Hausen tell the
same tale in similar terms, varied only by the bayonet attack episode.
As for Bülow and Kluck, one has only got to look at the map. One
does not need to read the tactical reports from these armies, when
their strategic torture is disclosed, by aeroplane and other reports.
Here at the summit in spacious rooms, in an atmosphere of order,
salutes and heel-clicking, far from the cannonade and desperate,
squalid, glorious confusion of the fighting lines, the resultants of the
pressures upon the immense body of the German invasion of France
are totalled and recorded, as if by a Wall Street ticker during a crash
of the market. Values are changing from minute to minute. The
highest authorities are reconciling themselves to new positions. The
booming hopes of the 3rd are replaced by the paper collapse of the
8th. It is the same story in terms of blood instead of scrip.

Colonel Bauer, an accomplished Staff Officer of middle rank, has
furnished us with a picture of the scene.

'Desperate panics seized severely the entire army, or to be more
correct the greater part of the leaders. It looked at its worst at the
supreme command. Moltke completely collapsed. He sat with a
pallid face gazing at the map, dead to all feeling, a broken man.
General von Stein [Moltke's deputy] certainly said "We must not
lose our heads," but he did not take charge. He was himself without
confidence and gave expression to his feelings by saying "We cannot tell how things will go." Tappen [head of the Operations Section
of whom we have heard before] was as calm as ever and did not
consider that the failure was altogether his fault; nor was it, for he
did not lose his nerve. But he did nothing. We younger people could
not get a hearing.'

Thus Bauer!

Everything now converged upon Moltke. Who was Moltke? He was the shadow of a great name; he was the nephew of the old Field Marshal and had been his aide-de-camp. He was an ordinary man, rather a courtier; a man about the Palace agreeable to the Emperor in the palmy days of peace. The sort of man who does not make too much trouble with a Sovereign, who knows how to suppress his own personality—what there is of it; a good, harmless, respectable, ordinary man. And on to this ill-fated being crashes the brutal, remorseless, centripetal impingement of tides and impulsions under which the greatest captains of history might have blenched!

There is hardly any doubt what he should have done. A simple message to all the German armies to be imparted to every division, 'If you cannot advance, hold on, dig in, yield not a scrap of conquered territory; *vestigia nulla retrorsum*,' might well have stablished the situation. At this time, however, only the British Army knew (from the Boer War) the power of modern weapons on the defensive. The French were just enjoying their first exultant experience of it. None of the military men on the other side yet knew that as a matter of fact a 30-mile gap in a front of 200 is only a trap for the attackers who enter into it. Almost instantly it becomes not a victory but a dangerous salient, a bulge subject to cross-fire and counter-attack from both flanks, the worst place in the world for a further offensive.

The officers of the German General Staff formed a close corporation and confraternity, and bore the same relation to the German army and its leaders, as the Jesuits of the seventeenth and eighteenth centuries bore to the priests and cardinals of the Roman Catholic Church. They spoke their own language, they had their own special affiliations, they moved men and things with the higher intelligence which comes from knowledge and organisation. To one of these officers, Colonel Hentsch, the head of the Intelligence, about midday September 8, Moltke imparted his views or mood. Both men are now dead. Neither has left a record of the conversation. We only know what followed from it. Colonel Hentsch got in his long grey car and went along the whole line of the armies, stopping at each of their headquarters and finally reached Bülow's headquarters about dark. He saw his brother Staff Officer of that army. He wrestled with him long. It was agreed between them that if the British Army was actually found to be across the Marne in force and advancing into the gap between Bülow and Kluck, Bülow should retreat to the Aisne in conformity with all the other German armies of the right and centre. Hentsch spared a few moments for a civil chat with old Bülow. The conversation, we are told, was pessimistic. He slept the night at Bülow's headquarters. He started at 7 o'clock the next morning, and the old man not being called till 9, he talked again with the General Staff Officer. It is clear that by this time—the reports of the previous day having been considered—there was no doubt about the heads of the British columns being across the Marne. Therefore the conditions established the night before had been fulfilled. Bülow 'on his own initiative,' as directed by his Staff Officer, ordered the retreat of the Second Army when in due course he entered his Headquarters' office.

Hentsch, knowing what the Second Army was doing, proceeded on his way. He had some difficulty in reaching Kluck. He had to cross the grisly gap and his car was blocked by masses of retreating German cavalry. He was involved in a 'panic,' as he describes it, following a British aeroplane raid. It was not till after noon that he reached Kluck's headquarters. Here again he dealt only with the Staff Officer. He never saw Kluck at all. He told von Kühl, Kluck's Chief of Staff, that as the English were now known to be advancing into the gap, Bülow's army would be retreating. But according to Hentsch, Kühl, some two hours before, had issued an order for retreat. Kühl, who is still alive and has written a massive book, admits that such an order had been telephoned by his subordinate (now dead), but that his subordinate had misconceived what he had intended. He declares that Hentsch gave him a positive order to withdraw Kluck's army to the Aisne, and seeks to lay the whole burden upon him.

At the inquiry into this celebrated episode ordered by Ludendorff in 1917 Colonel Hentsch was exonerated. It was found that his mission from Moltke was in short to see if a retreat was necessary, and if so to co-ordinate the retrograde movements of the five German armies. For this he had been given plenary authority in the name of the Supreme Command. And he had been given it only by word of mouth! But the duel between Kühl and Hentsch has been continued by Kühl over his adversary's grave. He declares the order to retreat was positive. It is however to be noted that he did not ask for this vital order in writing and that he did not tell Kluck about it till several hours had passed.

However it may be, Hentsch, a peripatetic focus of defeat, traversed and retraversed the entire line of the German armies. On the outward journey he gathered evil tidings, and as he returned he issued fateful orders. He used the powers confided to him to order successively the First, Second, Third, Fourth and Fifth German armies to retreat upon the line of the Aisne or in general conformity with that line. Only at one point was any objection raised. The German Crown Prince, who has been so mocked at, received Moltke's emissary in person. Confronted with an order to retreat, he demanded it in writing, and refused otherwise to obey. All Hentsch's directions had been verbal as from one General Staff Officer to another. Here was the first Commander with whom he had come in contact. So he said 'he would have a formal order sent from Luxemburg.' And sent it was by telegraph the next day.

So ended the Battle of the Marne. Until a retreat began, the only Ally army which had crossed the Marne was the British. In fact we may say that along the whole front from Verdun to Paris the French did not advance at all in the battle of the Marne. Some of them indeed on the left of Foch and the right of Franchet actually retreated. The only Ally army which advanced continually was the British. They advanced northwards in the four days September 5-8 more than 4 miles. But lest the reader should think this an assertion of national vainglory, let me hasten to repeat *first* that at the moment when the British Army was turned round, it had further to go than the others before it came into contact; and *secondly* that when it met the enemy it found in the main only a cavalry screen covering the fatal gap. Nevertheless the fact remains that it probed its way into the German liver.*

Thus, by a succession of unforeseeable and uncontrolled events was decided almost at its beginning the fate of the war on land, and little else was left but four years of senseless slaughter. Whether General von Moltke actually said to the Emperor, 'Majesty, we have lost the war,' we do not know. We know anyhow that with a prescience greater in political than in military affairs, he wrote to his wife on the night of the 9th, 'Things have not gone well. The fighting east of Paris has not gone in our favour, *and we shall have to pay for the damage we have done.*'

* Cyril Falls, *The Great War*, pp. 67, 68 says, "Most British historians have done their utmost to make as good a story as possible of the B.E.F.'s advance. In fact it was a crawl. The chief blame must undoubtedly fall upon the head of Sir John French, who never seems to have sensed that he was moving into what was virtually a void, and never drove his troops forward. Undoubtedly too there was among French and British troops alike a certain caution, degenerating at times into timidity. Commanders could not believe that the tide had turned and kept wondering whether or not they were walking into a gigantic ambush. Anyhow, the British infantry's advance measured only about eight miles a day from September 7 to 9, when half as much again, a mere 12 miles, would have been enough to sever Kluck's three corps from the rest of the German array and enable the British to attack them in rear while Maunoury was attacking them frontally."

GALLIPOLI

After the Battle of the Marne, the armies, to use Churchill's phrase, were "leaning up against each other." Neither side could budge the other all along the 400 mile front. The troops dug their rifle pits, then dug deeper until whole trench systems came into being.

As the stalemate continued through the fall and into the winter of 1915, the British turned their attention away from the Western Front, seeking a vulnerable spot on the flanks of the Central Powers. Largely through the influence of the First Lord of the Admiralty, Winston Churchill, it was decided to launch an attack through the Dardanelles, the narrow sea passage reaching from Constantinople to the Mediterranean. These waters were dominated by Turkish coastal gun installations located on the western end of the Gallipoli peninsula. The terrain of the peninsula was hilly, rocky and unsettled. The breadth of the strait measured from less than a mile to four and a half miles. All sea traffic came directly under the guns along the shore.

The British hoped their navy could force the passage and open a supply line to the Russians through the Black Sea, as well as accomplish the isolation of the Turks from their allies in Europe. Twice, in February and in March, the navy attacked the coastal installations, and almost got through; in fact, they succeeded in quelling the fire from the coastal guns, but they withdrew when three old Allied battleships went down in the mine fields.

An expeditionary force was then considered; its mission was to land on the peninsula, march overland to the Narrows, and destroy the guns.

"It is a matter of some surprise that the expedition ever got to sea at all. On March 26 Hamilton's* administrative staff had still not arrived from England (it did not get to Alexandria until April 11), many of the soldiers were still at sea, no accurate maps existed, there was no reliable information about the enemy, no plan had been made, and no one had yet decided where the Army was to be put ashore.

"The simplest of questions were unanswered. Was there water on the shore or not? What roads existed? What casualties were to be expected and how were the wounded men to be got off to the hospital ships? Were they to fight in trenches or in the open, and what sort of weapons were required? What was the depth of water off the beaches and what sort of boats were needed to get the men, the guns and the stores ashore? Would the Turks resist or would they break as they had done at Sarikamish; and if so how were the Allies to pursue them without transport or supplies?

"It was perhaps the very confusion of this situation which made it possible for the staff to get things done. Since no one could really calculate what the difficulties were going to be it was simply a matter of taking the material that came to hand, and of hoping for the best. A period of hectic improvisation began. Men were sent into the bazaars of Alexandria and Cairo to buy skins, oildrums, kerosene tins—anything that would hold water. Others bought tugs and lighters on the docks; others rounded up donkeys and their native drivers and put them into the Army. There were no periscopes (for trench fighting), no hand grenades and trench-mortars; ordnance workshops set to work to design and make them. In the absence of maps staff officers scoured the shop for guide-books." **

But by late April, two main landings were successfully made; one at Cape Helles at the tip of the peninsula, and the second, thirteen miles up the coast which quickly became known as the Anzac*** Landing. Both landings gained initial surprise but the troops failed to press inland before the Turks could organize their counterattacks.

* General Sir Ian Hamilton, Commander-in-Chief of the Gallipoli expedition.
** From Gallipoli, by Alan Moorehead.
*** Anzac: Australian and New Zealand Army Corps.

According to Cyril Falls, the ". . . two . . . landing forces unopposed or nearly so, lay on their objectives and enjoyed the scenery. They did not go to help their comrades because they knew nothing about them. The plan had for reasons of security been kept too secret." * On the other hand, the Turks, with help from a German staff, were more successful at concentrating their troops at critical points. After the initial surprise, the Turks at the Anzac Landing, under the command of Mustafa Kemal, put up a fierce resistance.

"At 4 p.m. the Dominion troops began to fall back towards the coast from the outlying positions they had taken in their first rush. By nightfall they were in a state of siege. But this alone had not caused the crisis . . . the fatal error of the original misplaced landing was beginning to take its effect.** Birdwood *** had expected to seize a strip of coast at least a mile in length, instead of which he found himself in possession of one small beach barely 1000 yards long and 30 yards wide. Everything coming ashore had to be fed through this bottleneck. Earlier in the day a small jetty had been built. But in the afternoon the congestion on the shore became intense. Animals, guns, ammunition and stores of every kind were dumped together in confusion on the sand, and there was no question of dispersing them until more territory had been gained. The whole Anzac position was less than two miles long and about three-quarters of a mile deep. No one could get inland. Bridges and Godley, the two divisional commanders and their staffs were crammed together in a gully a few yards from the beach, and the headquarters of the brigades were almost on top of them. Hospitals, signalling units, artillery batteries and even prisoners' cages perched where they could among the rocks.

"The wounded meanwhile were coming down from the hills in an endless stream, and were dumped in their stretchers in rows along the shore. Soon the whole of one end of the beach was covered with

* Falls, p. 130.
** In the dark, the landing parties had been swept by strong currents a mile north of the intended beach.
*** General Sir William Birdwood, Commander of Anzac Landing.

them, and there they lay, many of them in great pain, waiting to be taken off to the ships. While they waited a constant storm of bullets and shrapnel broke over their heads; and indeed, everyone on that crowded beach from generals to donkey drivers was under fire, for the Turks overlooked them from three sides. In desperation one of the officers in charge on the beach ordered every boat that came ashore to help in taking the casualties away, and this not only disorganized and delayed the disembarkation programme, it exposed the wounded to further suffering as well. Some were taken from transport to transport only to be sent away since there were no medical facilities on board; all the doctors and their staffs had gone to the shore.

"On the front line—or rather at the changing points of contact with the enemy—the soldiers had had little opportunity of digging in. Their light trenching tools were not very effective among the rocks and the tough roots of the scrub, and at some places the slopes were too steep for them to dig in at all. They were in desperate need of artillery support, but because of the ragged nature of the country and the uncertainty of the front line there was very little the naval guns could do. By nightfall the situation was not yet critical but it was becoming so. It had been a long exhausting day, and the men were beginning to feel the intense psychological strain of always being looked down upon from above, their every move watched, their smallest gestures attracting the snipers' bullets." *

It began to look as though the Turks were not strong enough to drive the Allied troops into the sea, and the British and Anzacs needed reinforcements if they were to reach the Narrows. While General Hamilton waited for help the Turks launched an attack at Cape Helles on May 1, which got nowhere; the British counter-attacked, having shifted some of their troops to Cape Helles, and got nowhere. Now "there was desultory fighting from time to time, but hardly more than a few yards of ground changed hands, and it seemed that nothing could break the deadlock. Yet the situation could not remain as it was, some sort of decision would have to be taken. And, in fact, at this ultimate moment of hesitation, a

* Moorehead, pp. 151-52.

glimpse of reality was on its way. A few moments before dawn, on this same day, May 19, General Birdwood was woken in his dugout at Anzac with the news that, in a packed mass of many thousands, the Turks were streaming across to his trenches in the darkness." *

THE ANZAC BEACHHEAD**

by Alan Moorehead

There is some dispute as to who ordered the attack on the Anzac bridgehead on the night of May 18. Liman von Sanders*** says that he himself made the plan and he takes the responsibility for it; others believe that it was conceived by Enver when he first visited the peninsula on May 10, and the circumstances of the enterprise do, in fact, bear the impress of Enver's headlong cast of mind. There was no subtlety or caution about the matter: some 42,000 men under the command of Essad Pasha were assembled, and their orders were nothing less than to demolish the whole Anzac bridgehead at a single blow. By nightfall it was hoped that the last Dominion soldier would have been killed, captured or driven into the sea, and that the entire Turkish army would have then been free to turn south to deal with the remainder of Hamilton's forces at Cape Helles.

At this time the Australian and New Zealand Corps had dwindled to some 10,000 effective men, and it was only by luck that a brigade which had been sent round to Cape Helles earlier in the month was returned to Birdwood on the eve of the battle. This brought his

* Moorehead, pp. 173-74.
** From *Gallipoli*, published by Harper and Bros.
*** The German general, under whose command the Turks fought.

numbers to a total of about 17,000, of which 12,500 were available for fighting in the front line. They were thus outnumbered by more than three to one.

The Anzac position had by now become very clearly defined: it was a shallow triangle, covering about 400 acres, its base, a mile and a half long, resting on the sea, its apex reaching to the slopes of Sari Bair about a thousand yards from the shore. In order to avoid the fire of the British Fleet the Turks had dug their trenches almost on top of the Anzac lines, and at some places the two sides were divided by not more than ten yards. The situation at Quinn's and Courtnay's Posts in the centre of the line was fantastic; directly behind the Australian trench (which was kept packed with men by day and night), a steep cliff fell away to the gully below, and the Turks had only to make an advance of five yards in order to drive a wedge through the bridgehead to the sea. But this they never could succeed in doing, though they attacked repeatedly during the first half of May. No-man's-land at these and other points was no larger than a small room, and it was the easiest thing in the world for the Turks to toss a hand grenade into the Anzac trenches. The only real defence against this was to throw the grenade smartly back again before it exploded; except for a few jam tins which were filled with explosive at a makeshift workshop on the beach, the Australians had no such weapons of their own. No man could expose the smallest fraction of his body for an instant without being shot, and even a periscope hoisted for a moment above the parapet was immediately shattered. An extreme tension prevailed in the bridgehead; there was no hour when some new raid was not expected or delivered, no minute when shells were not crashing among them or bullets screaming overhead. The soldiers managed to sleep through this racket at odd hours of the day and night, but it was never a sufficient rest. No one was ever safe. On May 14 General Bridges, the commander of the Australian Division, was mortally wounded, and the following day Birdwood had his hair parted by a bullet while he was looking through a periscope. The wound turned septic and was very painful but he continued in command.

There was an intense hatred of the Turks among the Dominion

soldiers. Most of them had grown up in a world of clear and obvious values; a fight was a fight, you knew who your enemy was and you stood up to him and had it out, fairly and squarely, in the open. It was in this spirit that they had volunteered for service in the Army. The charge was the thing, the quick and palpable blow in the face that knocked the man down. War, in fact, was an extension of the pub brawl, and it had in it the elements of rioting, of street fighting, of instant physical revenge.

But nothing of the kind had happened at Gallipoli. From the day they had landed the soldiers had scarcely ever seen the enemy; he lurked unseen in the heights above, he sniped down on them and caught them unawares, he stood back at a safe distance with his guns and burst his shrapnel above their heads, and there seemed to be no effective way of retaliating. After more than three weeks of this the soldiers were beginning to feel an increasing sense of frustration and of impotent anger in their narrow bridgehead. A claustrophobia had developed; they felt that they had been caught in a trap, and there seemed to be something unfair in this kind of fighting in which they were never given a chance of showing their real courage and their strength.

Beyond this there was at this early stage another and perhaps deeper feeling that there was a monstrosity and inhumanity about the Turks: they were cruel and sinister fanatics, capable of any sort of vice and bestiality—in brief, it was the popular picture that had been drawn of them by Byron and the emotions of Gladstonian liberal England. The Turks were 'natives'—but natives of a peculiarly dangerous and subtle kind. And so the Australian and New Zealand soldiers fought, not an ordinary man, but a monster prefigured by imagination and by propaganda; and they hated him.

Despite these things, perhaps even because of them, an extraordinary cheerfulness and exaltation possessed the men in the front line. Living with the instant prospect of death, all pettiness, all the normal anxieties and jealousies of life, deserted them, and they developed an almost mystical feeling towards the extreme danger that surrounded them. The fighting became an elaborate and exciting game in which they were all immensely engrossed, and it was only when they were retired to rest for a while in some half-haven under the cliffs that they became aware again of the miseries of their situation, the monotonous food, the endless physical discomfort, the impossible limits of a life in which even a canteen of fresh water or a bathe in the sea were the utmost luxuries.

By now death had become familiar, and they often talked about it in a half-derisive deprecating slang. In the same way as the Chinese will laugh at other people's pain it became a huge joke when the men bathing off the beach were caught in a burst of shrapnel, or when some poor devil had his head blown off while he was in the latrine. There had to be some sort of expression which would help to rationalize the unbearable circumstances of their lives, some way of obtaining relief from the shock of it all, and since tears were impossible this callous hard-boiled laughter became the thing. They were not fatalists. They believed that a mistake had been made in the landing at Gaba Tepe and that they might easily have to pay for it with their lives; but they very much wanted to go on living, they were all for the battle and they hoped and believed obscurely that in the end they would win.

These high spirits, this fineness and integrity created by the powerful drug of risk, might not perhaps have continued indefinitely under such a strain, but there had certainly been no weakening in morale when, on May 18, the soldiers became aware that something unusual was happening in the enemy lines.

An unaccountable silence spread through the hills before them. For the first time since they had landed the fearful racket of the Turkish howitzers died away, and for several minutes at a stretch no rifle or machine gun was fired. In this strange quiet most of the day went by. Then at five o'clock in the evening a tremendous artillery barrage broke out, and it continued for about half an hour. It chanced that on this day a naval aircraft had been sent out to fix the position of an enemy warship in the straits, and on his return the pilot reported that he had seen large numbers of men massing behind the Turkish lines. Later in the day this information was confirmed by a second pilot who had also seen enemy soldiers coming across the straits in boats from the Asiatic side; and from the battleship *Triumph* there was a further report that Turkish reinforcements were marching north from Cape Helles to the Anzac front. On hearing this, Birdwood sent a message to his two divisional commanders warning them to expect an attack that night; the men were to stand to arms at 3 a.m., which was half an hour before the usual time.

The night turned cold and misty, and when the moon went down at 11.35 p.m. there was hardly a sound along the front except for the breaking of the waves on the shore. Suddenly at fifteen minutes to midnight, a fusillade of rifle fire which was heavier than anything that had been heard before burst out from the Turkish trenches, and as it spread along the line the Anzac commanders kept telephoning to their outposts to ask if they were being attacked. But nothing followed, and presently the uproar dwindled into silence again. At 3 a.m. the men were roused, and they took their places on the firing steps with their bayonets fixed to their rifles. It was still cold and most of them were wearing their overcoats.

Hardly five minutes had gone by when a shout of warning went up from one of the outposts, and a company of Turks was seen advancing down a ravine known as Wire Gully in the centre of the line. There had been no preliminary bugle call, none of the usual shouts of Allah, Allah: merely these shadowy forms in the half-darkness and the long line of bayonets. The Australians opened fire from either side of the gully, and immediately the enemy bugles sounded and the charge began. Everywhere along the line the Turks jumped up from their hiding places and in a dark cloud swept forward over the broken ground.

At most places the oncoming enemy had to cross two or three hundred yards before they reached the Anzac entrenchments, and so there was half a minute or more when they were exposed in the open and quite defenceless. Very few of them survived even that amount of time. There was a kind of cascading movement in the battle; directly one line of soldiers had come over the parapet and been destroyed another line formed up, emerged into view and was cut down. For the first hour it was simply a matter of indiscriminate killing, but presently the Australians and New Zealanders began to adopt more systematic methods: when a Turkish officer appeared they deliberately withheld their fire until he had assembled the full company of his men in the open. Then all were destroyed together. At some points it became a kind of game to pick off the survivors as they ran back and forth across the battlefield like terrified rabbits in search of cover. Here and there some few of the Turks did manage to get into the Anzac trenches, but they survived only for a few minutes; there was a quick and awful bayoneting and then the tide receded again.

As daylight broke the battle assumed the character of a hunt, with the Turkish officers serving in the role of beaters driving the game on to the guns. A wild, almost berserk excitement filled the Australian and New Zealand ranks. In order to get a better view many of the soldiers jumped up and sat astride the parapets and from there they blazed away at the screaming mass of Turks before them. The Anzac soldiers who had been held in reserve could not bear to be left out of the fight; they came pressing forward offering to pay for a place on the firing line. In one trench two soldiers actually fought one another with their fists for a vacant position on the parapet, and there was a kind of mad surrealism in the shouts and cries along the line as each new Turkish rush came on. 'Backsheesh', 'Imshi Yallah', 'Eggs is cooked'.* Once an Australian was heard shouting to the Turks as they fell back from his trench, 'Saida (good-bye). Play you again next Saturday.'

By 5 a.m., when a hot sun was beginning to stream down on to the battlefield, the attack was broken. But the orders to the Turks were that they should continue the fight until they got through to the sea, and so they went on with the struggle for another six hours, each new charge getting a little feebler than the last. Mustafa Kemal had been reduced to the command of a single division, the 19th, for the period of the offensive, and he alone, of the four divisional commanders engaged, had succeeded in making any headway. When at midday Essad Pasha decided to break off the action 10,000 of his

---

* Or 'Eggs-a-cook,' an expression used by the Egyptian vendors when they sold eggs to the Anzac troops during their stay in Egypt.

men had fallen, and of these some 5,000, dead, dying and wounded, were lying out in the open between the trenches.

Other heavier battles than this were fought at Gallipoli, but none with such a terrible concentration of killing, none so one-sided, and none with so strange an aftermath. Through the long afternoon the wounded lay with the dead on the battlefield, and although the trenches on either side were only a yard or two away no one could go out and bring them in without taking the risk of being instantly shot.

'No sound came from that dreadful space,' the Australian history of the campaign relates, 'but here and there some wounded or dying man, silently lying without help or any hope of it under the sun which glared from a cloudless sky, turned painfully from one side to the other, or slowly raised an arm towards heaven.'

Birdwood was warned by his medical staff that, quite apart from any feelings of humanity, the dead should be buried as quickly as possible to prevent infection spreading through the Army. When the afternoon had passed without any sign of the Turks renewing the attack, he sent off Aubrey Herbert to ask Hamilton aboard the *Arcadian* if he might arrange an armistice.

Herbert was an odd figure on the Anzac bridgehead—indeed, he would have been odd in any army on any battlefield: a Member of Parliament turned soldier, an eccentric, a poet and a scholar who, far from hating the Turks, was captivated by them. This did not mean he was disloyal—he was determined that they should be defeated— but he knew Turkey and Turkish very well, and he believed that with better handling by the politicians they might have been converted into allies. Of all the band who had been with Rupert Brooke at Alexandria he was the one most possessed of ideas, and despite his short-sightedness, his impulsive and agitated manner, he was very brave and saw very clearly under the façade of things. Hamilton was glad enough to have him on his staff as an intelligence officer with the rank of lieutenant-colonel, but he noted in his diary that he was 'excessively unorthodox'.

Herbert chose to do his intelligence work in the front line at

Anzac, and he proceeded to war in the manner of a nineteenth-century gentleman-adventurer. Servants were engaged at Lemnos, suitable horses and mules acquired, an adequate kit assembled, and off he went with an extraordinary assemblage of Greek and Levantine interpreters to the peninsula. There were staff troubles almost at once. A spy mania was raging through the Anzac bridgehead—the fear of spies seems to be endemic in every crisis in every military campaign—and his interpreters were arrested as many as four and five times a day. A terrible hail of shrapnel once fell on Herbert's dugout, and the cook, a Greek named Christopher of the Black Lamp, with the tears pouring down his face gave two hours' notice, though why it should be two hours and not two minutes he was unable to explain. Among these and other domestic anxieties Herbert continued with his work of questioning the Turkish prisoners and of acting as a kind of general confidant of the commanders in all questions relating to the habits and character of the enemy.

His methods of propaganda were very direct. He crawled into the foremost trenches and from there he addressed the enemy soldiers in their own language, urging them to desert, promising them good treatment and pointing out that the real quarrel of the Allies was not with Turkey but with the Germans. At times he actually got into trenches which communicated directly into the enemy emplacements, and lying on the dead bodies there, he called to the Turks through a single barrier of sandbags. Occasionally they would listen and enter into argument with him. More often they replied with hand-grenades—a thing which did not make Herbert very welcome with the Anzac troops—and in Constantinople one of the newspapers announced that there was someone in the Anzac bridgehead who was making a low attempt to lure the Turks from their duty by imitating the prayers of the *muezzin*.

It now fell to Herbert to put the case to Hamilton for an armistice. He argued that unless something was done quickly the situation would become intolerable: our own wounded as well as Turkish were still lying in the open, and in the hot sun the dead bodies were decomposing rapidly. Hamilton answered that he would not initiate any proposal himself, because the enemy would make propaganda of it, but if the Turks liked to come forward he was willing to grant them a cessation of hostilities for a limited period. It was agreed finally that notes could be thrown into the Turkish trenches telling them of this.

Meanwhile all May 20 had gone by and unknown to Hamilton and Herbert the soldiers at the front had already taken matters into their own hands. Towards evening an Australian colonel caused a Red Cross flag to be hoisted on a plateau at the lower end of the line. He intended to send out his stretcher-bearers to bring in a number of wounded Turks who were crying out pitiably in front of his trenches. Before they could move, however, the Turks put two bullets through the staff of the flag and brought it down. A moment later a man jumped up from the Turkish trenches and came running across no-man's-land. He stopped on the parapet above the Australians' heads, spoke a few words of apology, and then ran back to his own lines again. Immediately afterwards Red Crescent flags appeared above the enemy trenches, and Turkish stretcher-bearers came out. All firing ceased along the line, and in this eerie stillness General Walker, the commander of the 1st Australian Division, got up and walked towards the enemy. A group of Turkish officers came out to meet him, and for a while they stood there in the open, smoking, and talking in French. It was agreed that they should exchange letters on the subject of an armistice at 8 p.m. that night.

While this was going on another impromptu parley with the enemy had opened on another section of the line. It was now growing late and Birdwood, as soon as he heard what was happening, issued an order that no further burials were to be made that night. A note signed by the General's A.D.C. was handed to a Turkish officer: 'If you want a truce to bury your dead,' it said, 'send a staff officer, under a flag of truce, to our headquarters via the Gaba Tepe road, between 10 a.m. and 12 noon tomorrow.'

At this stage neither side seems to have been absolutely sure of themselves; there was a tense feeling that some act of treachery might occur at any moment, that an attack might be launched under the cover of the white flags—and indeed, an Australian soldier who

had been out in no-man's-land came back with the report that the
enemy trenches were filled with men who were apparently ready to
attack. Upon this the Australians opened fire on a party of stretcher-
bearers who were still wandering about in the failing light. At once
the Turkish artillery started up again and the bombardment continued intermittently all night.

Hamilton says he was very much annoyed when he heard of these
irregular dealings with the enemy, and he dispatched Braithwaite to
Anzac to handle the negotiations. The following letter, addressed to
'*Commandant en chef des Forces Britanniques*, Sir John Hamilton,'
arrived from Liman von Sanders.

> 'Grand Quartier Général de la 5 me. Armée Ottomane.
> le 22 mai 1915.
> Excellence,
> J'ai l'honneur d'informer Votre Excellence que les propositions
> concernant la conclusion d'un armistice pour enterrer les morts et
> secourir les blessés des deux parties adverses, ont trouvé mon plein
> consentement—et que seuls nos sentiments d'humanité nous y ont
> déterminés.
> J'ai investi le lieutenant-colonel Fahreddin du pouvoir de signer
> en mon nom.
> J'ai l'honneur d'être avec assurance de ma plus haute considéra-
> tion.
>   LIMAN VON SANDERS,
>   Commandant en chef de la 5 me. Armée Ottomane.'

There is an air of fantasy about the conference that took place at
Birdwood's headquarters on May 22. Herbert walked through heavy
showers of rain along the Gaba Tepe beach, and a 'fierce Arab officer
and a wandery-looking Turkish lieutenant' came out to meet him.
They sat down and smoked in a field of scarlet poppies. Presently
Kemal himself arrived on horseback with other Turkish officers, and
they were blindfolded and led on foot into the Anzac bridgehead.
The British intelligence officers were anxious to give the impression
that a great deal of barbed-wire entanglement had been erected on
the beach, and they forced Kemal to keep goose-stepping over
imaginary obstacles as he went along. Presently the Turks were
remounted and taken to Birdwood's dugout by the beach.

The conference in the narrow cave was a stiff and strained affair, the Turkish Beys in their gold lace, the British generals in their red tabs, each side trying to make it clear that it was not they who were eager for the armistice. But the atmosphere was relieved by one moment of pure farce: an Australian soldier, not knowing or caring about what was going on inside the dugout, put his head round the canvas flap and demanded, 'Have any of you bastards got my kettle?'

Herbert meanwhile had been taken into the Turkish lines as a hostage. He was mounted on a horse and blindfolded, and then led round and round in circles to confuse his sense of direction. At one stage the fierce Arab officer cried out to the man who was supposed to be leading the horse, 'You old fool. Can't you see he's riding straight over the cliff?' Herbert protested strongly and they went on again. When finally the bandage was taken from his eyes he found himself in a tent in a grove of olives, and the Arab officer said, 'This is the beginning of a lifelong friendship'. He ordered cheese, tea and coffee to be brought, and offered to eat first to prove that the food was not poisoned. They had an amiable conversation, and in the evening when Kemal and the other Turks came back from Birdwood's headquarters Herbert was blindfolded again and returned to the British lines.

The terms of the truce had been settled as precisely as possible; it was to take place on May 24 and was to continue for nine hours. Three zones were to be marked out with white flags for the burial of the dead—one Turkish, one British and the third common to both sides. Priests, doctors and soldiers taking part in the burials were to wear white armbands and were not to use field-glasses or enter enemy trenches. All firing was of course to cease along the line, and the soldiers in the opposing trenches were not to put their heads above their parapets during the period of the truce. It was also agreed that all rifles minus their bolts were to be handed back to whichever side they belonged to—but this move was circumvented to some extent by the Australians, who on the previous evening crept out into no man's-land and gathered up as many weapons as they could find.

The morning of May 24 broke wet and cold, and the soldiers were in their greatcoats. Soon after dawn the firing died away, and at six-thirty Herbert set out again with a group of officers for Gaba Tepe beach. Heavy rain was falling. After an hour the Turks arrived— Herbert's acquaintance of two days before and several others, including a certain Arif, the son of Achmet Pasha, who handed Herbert a visiting card inscribed with the words, *Sculpteur et Pein-tre. Etudiant de Poésie.*

Together the two parties left the beach, and passing through cornfields flecked with poppies walked up to the hills where the battle had taken place. 'Then,' Herbert says, 'the fearful smell of death began as we came upon scattered bodies. We mounted over a plateau and down through gullies filled with thyme, where there lay about 4,000 Turkish dead. It was indescribable. One was grateful for the rain and the grey sky. A Turkish Red Crescent man came and gave me some antiseptic wool with scent on it, and this they renewed frequently. There were two wounded crying in that multitude of silence.'

Many of the dead had sunk to the ground in the precise attitude they had adopted at the moment when the bullets stopped their rush, their hands clasping their bayonets, their heads thrust forward or doubled up beneath them. Nothing was missing except the spark of life. They lay in mounds on the wet earth, whole companies of soldiers, like some ghastly tableau made of wax.

Among the living men there was at first some little friction. Everyone was nervous, everyone expected that even in these awful nightmarish surroundings some kind of treachery had been planned by the other side. There were complaints: the Australians were stealing arms: the Turks were coming too close to the Anzac trenches. At Quinn's Post, where the lines were only ten or fifteen yards apart, the tension was almost a palpable thing in the air, an inflammable essence that might explode at any moment. Hands on their triggers the men watched one another across the narrow space, expecting at every minute that someone would make some foolish gesture that would start the fighting again. On the wider stretches of the battlefield, however, Turks and Anzac troops worked together in digging great communal graves, and as the hours went by they began to fraternize, offering cigarettes to one another, talking in broken scraps of English and Arabic, exchanging badges and gadgets from their pockets as souvenirs.

Herbert was kept busy settling points of difference. He allowed the Turks to extract for burial some bodies which had been built into their emplacements, and once he was even permitted to go into the enemy trenches to satisfy himself that the Turks were not using this lull to fortify and advance their positions. He found there a group of soldiers whom he had known previously in Albania. They gathered round him cheering and clapping, and he had to stop them because they were interrupting the burial services which were being conducted round about by the Moslem Imams and the Christian priests. From this time onwards the Turks were constantly coming up to him for orders, and even getting him to sign receipts for money taken from the dead. Intervals of bright sunshine had now followed the rain.

Compton Mackenzie and Major Jack Churchill (the brother of Winston Churchill) had come over from the *Arcadian* for the day, and they stood on a parapet constructed chiefly of dead bodies to watch the scene. 'In the foreground,' Mackenzie writes, 'was a narrow stretch of level scrub along which white flags were stuck at intervals, and a line of sentries, Australians and Turks, faced one another. Staff officers of both sides were standing around in little groups, and there was an atmosphere about the scene of local magnates at the annual sports making suggestions about the start of the obstacle race. Aubrey Herbert looked so like the indispensable bachelor that every country neighbourhood retains to take complete control of the proceedings on such occasions. Here he was shuffling about, loose-gaited, his neck out-thrust and swinging from side to side as he went peering up into people's faces to see whether they were the enemy or not, so that, if they were, he could offer them cigarettes and exchange a few courtesies with them in their own language. . . .

'The impression which that scene from the ridge by Quinn's Post made on my mind has obliterated all the rest of the time at Anzac. I cannot recall a single incident on the way back down the valley. I know only that nothing could cleanse the smell of death from the nostrils for a fortnight afterwards. There was no herb so aromatic but it reeked of carrion, not thyme nor lavender, nor even rosemary.'

By three in the afternoon the work was practically done. There were two crises: it was discovered at the last minute that the Turks' watches were eight minutes ahead of the British, and a hurried adjustment had to be made. Then, as the hour for the ending of the truce was approaching, a shot rang out. Standing there in the open with tens of thousands of rifles pointed towards them the burial parties stood in a sudden hush, but nothing followed and they returned to their work again.

At four o'clock the Turks near Quinn's Post came to Herbert for their final orders, since none of their own officers were about. He first sent back the grave-diggers to their own trenches, and at seven minutes past four retired the men who were carrying the white flags. He then walked over to the Turkish trenches to say good-bye. When he remarked to the enemy soldiers there that they would probably shoot him on the following day, they answered in a horrified chorus, 'God forbid.' Seeing Herbert standing there, groups of Australians came up to the Turks to shake hands and say good-bye. 'Good-bye, old chap; good luck.' The Turks answered with one of their proverbs: 'Smiling may you go and smiling may you come again.'

All the remaining men in the open were now sent back to their lines, and Herbert made a last minute inspection along the front, reminding the Turks that firing was not to begin again for a further twenty-five minutes. He was answered with salaams, and he too finally dropped out of sight. At 4.45 p.m. a Turkish sniper fired from somewhere in the hills. Immediately the Australians answered and the roar of high explosive closed over the battlefield again.

There had been some irregularities. On both sides a good deal of surreptitious digging had been done, and both Turkish and British staff officers had strolled about no-man's-land, covertly studying the lie of each other's trenches. It was even said—and the story has never been denied in Turkey—that Kemal had disguised himself as a sergeant and had spent the whole nine hours with various burial parties close to the Anzac trenches.

Much the most important results of the battle and the truce, however, was that from this time onwards all real rancour against the Turks died out in the Anzac ranks. They now knew the enemy from their own experience, and he had ceased to be a propaganda figure. He was no longer a coward, a fanatic or a monster. He was a normal man and they thought him very brave.

This camaraderie with the enemy—the mutual respect of men who are committed to killing one another—was not peculiar to Gallipoli for it existed also in France; but on this isolated battlefield it had a special intensity. The Australian and New Zealand troops refused to use the gas-masks that were now issued to them. When they were questioned about this they made some such reply as, 'The Turks won't use gas. They're clean fighters.' *

Had the soldiers known Enver a little better they might not have been so certain of this; yet perhaps they did know Enver, for politicians generally were held in contempt at Gallipoli and by both sides, and in a way that seldom occurred in the second world war. Soon many of the British began to feel as Herbert felt: that the campaign need never have been fought at all had only the politicians acted more responsibly in the beginning.

The extreme ferocity with which the battles were fought at Gallipoli gives no inkling of the compassion that the opposing soldiers in the front line felt for one another. In the periods of comparative calm which followed May 19 at Anzac, the most bizarre incidents occurred. Once a staff officer visiting the front saw with astonishment that a number of Turks were walking about behind their lines in full view of the Australians. He asked, 'Why don't you shoot?' and was answered, 'Well, they're not doing any harm are they? Might as well leave the poor beggars alone.' Later in the campaign there was an old Turk who apparently had been given the job of doing the washing for his platoon. Regularly each day he emerged from his trench and hung out the wet shirts and socks in a line along the parapet, and no Allied soldier would have dreamed of

* Gas was never used at Gallipoli.

shooting him. The Turks on their side usually withheld their fire from the survivors of wrecked ships, and in the front line at least their prisoners were treated with kindness.

There was a constant traffic of gifts in the trenches, the Turks throwing over grapes and sweets, the Allied soldiers responding with tinned food and cigarettes. The Turks had no great love for British beef. A note came over one day: '*Bully beef—non. Envoyez milk.*' It became an accepted practice to wave a 'wash-out' to a sniper who missed: there would be the sudden crack of a rifle, the bullet scream-ing past the Turk's head, then the laugh from the enemy trench, the waving of a spade or a bayonet and the words in English softly shouted, 'Better luck next time, Tommy.'

Once or twice private duels were fought. While the rest of the soldiers on both sides held their fire an Australian and a Turk would stand up on the parapets and blaze away at one another until one or the other was wounded or killed, and something seemed to be proved—their skill, their wish 'to dare', perhaps most of all their pride. Then in a moment all would dissolve into the horror and frenzy of a raid or a setpiece battle, the inhuman berserk killing.

Between the two extremes, between the battles and the truce, between fighting and death, the men had to come to terms with their precarious existence. They soon developed habits that fitted their mad surroundings, and they did this very rapidly and very well. The rabbit warren of trenches and dugouts at Anzac became more famil-iar to them than their own villages and homes. By night ten thou-sand shaded fires were lit in niches in the cliffs, ten thousand crude meals were cooked; they slept, they waited for their precious mail, their one reminder of the lost sane world, they put the individual extra touch to their dug-outs—another shelf in the rock, a blanket across the opening, a biscuit tin to hold a tattered book. They knew every twist in the paths where a sniper's bullet would come thudding in, they accepted wounding as they might have accepted an accident on the football field, they argued about the war and the confined beehive politics of their battalions, they took the risk of bathing in the sea under the bursting shrapnel and nothing would stop them

doing it. They cursed and complained and dreamed and this in fact
was home.

No stranger visiting the Anzac bridgehead ever failed to be moved
and stimulated by it. It was a thing so wildly out of life, so
dangerous, so high-spirited, such a grotesque and theatrical setting
and yet reduced to such a calm and almost matter-of-fact routine.
The heart missed a beat when one approached the ramshackle jetty
on the beach, for the Turkish shells were constantly falling there,
and it hardly seemed that anyone could survive. Yet once ashore a
curious sense of heightened living supervened. No matter how
hideous the noise, the men moved about apparently oblivious of it
all, and with a trained and steady air as though they had lived there
all their lives; and this in itself was a reassurance to everyone who
came ashore. The general aspect was of a vast mining camp in some
savage desert valley. Close to the shore were the dug-outs of the
generals, the wireless station, the telephone exchange, the searchlights, a factory for making bombs, a corral for Turkish prisoners, a
smithy. Scores of placid mules sheltered in the gully until at nightfall
they began their work of taking ammunition and supplies to the men
in the trenches in the hills above—the water ration was a pannikin a
day. There was a smoking incinerator near the jetty, and it erupted
loudly whenever an unexploded bullet fell into the flames. An empty
shellcase served as a gong for the headquarters officers' mess. They
ate bully beef, biscuits, plum and apple jam, and just occasionally
frozen meat; never vegetables, eggs, milk or fruit.

Above the beach a maze of goat tracks spread upward through
furze and the last surviving patches of prickly oak, and at every step
of the way some soldier had made his shelter in the side of the
ravine: a hole dug into the ground, the branches of trees or perhaps
a piece of canvas for a roof, a blanket, a few tins and boxes, and that
was all. As one progressed upward there were many crude notices of
warning against the enemy snipers: Keep Well to Your Left. Keep
Your Head Down. Double Across One at a Time. Then finally the
trenches themselves, where all day long the men stood to their arms,
watching and watching through their periscopes for the slightest

movement in the enemy lines. Cigarettes dangled from their mouths. They talked quietly.

Hamilton came over to the bridgehead on May 30 and saw, 'Men staggering under huge sides of frozen beef: men struggling up cliffs with kerosene tins full of water; men digging; men cooking; men cardplaying in small dens scooped out from the banks of yellow clay —everyone wore a Bank Holiday air; evidently the ranklings and worries of mankind—miseries and concerns of the spirit—had fled the precincts of this valley. The Boss—the bill—the girl—envy, malice, hunger, hatred—had scooted away to the Antipodes. All the time, overhead, the shell and rifle bullets groaned and whined, touching just the same note of violent energy as was in evidence everywhere else. To understand that awful din, raise the eyes twenty-five degrees to the top of the cliff which closes in the tail end of the valley and you can see the Turkish hand-grenades bursting along the crest, just where an occasional bayonet flashes and figures hardly distinguishable from Mother Earth crouch in an irregular line. Or else they rise to fire and are silhouetted against the sky and then you recognize the naked athletes from the Antipodes and your heart goes into your mouth as a whole bunch of them dart forward suddenly, and as suddenly disappear. And the bomb shower stops dead—for the moment; but, all the time, from that fiery crest line which is Quinn's, there comes a slow constant trickle of wounded— some dragging themselves painfully along; others being carried along on stretchers. Bomb wounds all; a ceaseless silent stream of bandages and blood. Yet three out of four of "the boys" have grit left for a gay smile or a cheery little nod to their comrades, waiting for their turn as they pass, pass, pass, down on their way to the sea.

'There are poets and writers who see naught in war but carrion, filth, savagery and horror. The heroism of the rank and file makes no appeal. They refuse war the credit of being the only exercise in devotion on the large scale existing in this world. The superb moral victory over death leaves them cold. Each one to his taste. To me this is no valley of death—it is a valley brim full of life at its highest power. Men live through more in five minutes on that crest than they do in five years of Bendigo or Ballarat. Ask the brothers of these very

fighters—Calgoorlie or Coolgardie miners—to do one quarter of the
work and to run one hundredth the risk on a wages basis—instanter
there would be a riot. But here—not a murmur, not a question; only
a radiant force of camaraderie in action.'

From May onwards many of the men discarded their uniforms,
and except for a pair of shorts, boots and perhaps a cap, went naked
in the sun. Even in the frontlines they fought stripped to the waist, a
girl, a ship or a dragon tattooed on their arms.

There was a toughness mixed with touchiness in this ant-heap life.
Compton Mackenzie relates that on his visit to Anzac he overtook
Lieutenant-Colonel Pollen, Hamilton's military secretary, who was
talking to three Australians all well over six feet tall. 'Pollen, who
had a soft, somewhat ecclesiastical voice, was saying, "Have you
chaps heard that they've given General Bridges a posthumous
K.C.M.G.?"

' "Have they?" one of the giants replied. "Well, that won't do him
much good where he is now, will it, mate?"

'Poor Pollen, who was longing to be sympathetic and not to mind
the way these Australians would stare at his red tabs without saluting, walked on a little depressed by his reception at making
conversation, perhaps at the very spot where General Bridges had
been mortally wounded. He looked carefully at the ground when he
met the next lot, whereupon they all gave him an elaborate salute,
and then because he had looked up too late to acknowledge it one of
them turned to the others and said: "I suppose that's what they call
breeding." They really were rather difficult.'

But it was the physical appearance of the Dominion soldiers—
Colonials as they were then called—that captivated everybody who
came to Anzac, and there is hardly an account of the campaign
which does not refer to it with admiration and even a kind of awe.
'As a child,' Mackenzie wrote, 'I used to pore for hours over those
illustrations of Flaxman for Homer and Virgil which simulated the
effect of ancient pottery. There was not one of those glorious young
men I saw that day who might not himself have been Ajax or
Diomed, Hector or Achilles. Their almost complete nudity, their
tallness and majestic simplicity of line, their rose-brown flesh burnt

by the sun and purged of all grossness by the ordeal through which they were passing, all these united to create something as near to absolute beauty as I shall hope ever to see in this world.'

The soldiers themselves might not have thought of it in this way, but here perhaps, in this unlikely place, was the expression of Rupert Brooke's dream of war, the Grecian frieze, the man entirely heroic and entirely beautiful, the best in the presence of death. Just for this moment at the end of May and in the months that followed they were the living embodiment of the legend they were creating. This was the highest moment of their countries' short history; they had fought and won their first great battle, they were still in the glow of it, they knew suffering and they were not afraid. They had made a fortress of this wretched strip of foreign soil on which they had so haphazardly drifted, and they were quite determined to hold on. Never again in the whole course of the campaign did the Turks attempt an assault in force upon the Anzac bridgehead.

EARLY DAYS IN THE TRENCHES

The Western Front now stretched from Switzerland to the English Channel at Nieuport. After the Battle of the Marne, the Germans had shifted their attention to the northern provinces of France, seeking to outflank the Allied armies, but the French and British sidestepped right along with them.

The possibilities of a real breakthrough occupied the minds of the commanding officers on both sides. Once the breakthrough was achieved, the cavalry would pour through and mobility in warfare would once again be possible. The cavalry had been the Sunday punch for too many wars to be put aside so early in the day. But it was clear to many, if not to the commanders, that cavalry was ineffective; in face of the fire power that could be generated by the fast-firing British riflemen, the machine gun and the deadly French .75's, mounted horsemen were a sacrifice to the Gods of War.

Battle positions continued to harden. Neither side could move the other out of their defense positions and so the trench systems grew more comprehensive. Between the trenches, nests of barbed wire were planted as a barrier to surprise attacks. Massed artillery probed and blasted at each other's lines and the land in the battle area was pockmarked with shell holes. At times the shell holes themselves were integrated into the trench systems; they were frequently used for listening posts, sniper positions and defense positions to harass the enemy on his way to his own first line trenches.

The area between the trenches was patrolled at night, if the front was active. Attacks and counterattacks flowed back and forth unceasingly; this area would be known as "no-man's-land," an irony in face of the bloodletting of hundreds of thousands of men killed there.

A revealing glimpse of life in the trenches in 1915 can be found in Robert Graves' *Goodbye to All That*. The following observations were made as he moved into the trenches for the first time.

"At Cambrin village, which was about a mile from the front trenches, we were taken into a ruined house. . . . Here we were issued with gas-respirators and field dressings. This was the first respirator issued in France. It was a gauze pad filled with chemically treated cotton waste, to be tied across the mouth and nose. It seems it was useless against German gas. I never put it to the test. A week or two later came the "smoke-helmet," a greasy grey felt bag with a talc window to look through, but no mouthpiece. This also was probably ineffective against gas. The talc was always cracking and there were leaks where it was stitched into the helmet.

"These were early days of trench-warfare, the days of the jam-tin bomb and the gas-pipe trench-mortar. It was before Lewis or Stokes guns, steel helmets, telescopic rifle-sights, gas-shells, pill-boxes, tanks, trench-raids, or any of the later improvements of trench-warfare.

"After a meal of bread, bacon, rum and bitter stewed tea sickly with sugar, we went up through the broken trees to the east of the village and up a long trench to battalion headquarters. The trench was cut through red clay. I had a torch with me which I kept flashed on the ground. Hundreds of field mice and frogs were in the trench. They had fallen in and had no way out. The light dazzled them and we could not help treading on them. So I put the torch back in my pocket. . . .

"The trench was wet and slippery. The guide was giving hoarse directions all the time. "Hole right." "Wire high." "Wire low." "Deep place here, sir." "Wire low." I had never been told about the field telephone wires. They were fastened by staples to the side of the trench, and when it rained the staples were always falling out and the wire falling down and tripping people up. If it sagged too much one stretched it across the top of the trench to the other side to correct the sag, and then it would catch one's head. The holes were the sump-pits used for draining the trenches. We were now under rifle-fire. I always found rifle-fire more trying than shell-fire. The gunner was usually, I knew, firing not at people but at map-references—cross-roads, likely artillery positions, houses that suggested billets for troops, and so on. Even when an observation officer in an aeroplane or captive balloon or on a church spire was directing the gun-fire it seemed unaimed, somehow. But a rifle bullet even when fired blindly always had the effect of seeming aimed. And we could hear a shell coming and take some sort of cover, but the rifle bullet gave no warning. So though we learned not to duck to a rifle bullet, because once it was heard it must have missed, it gave us a worse feeling of danger. Rifle bullets in the open went hissing into the grass without much noise, but when we were in a trench the bullets, going over the hollow, made a tremendous crack. Bullets often struck the barbed wire in front of the trenches, which turned them and sent them spinning in a head-over-heels motion—ping! rockety-ockety-ockety-ockety into the woods behind.

"Battalion headquarters was a dug-out in the reserve line about a quarter of a mile from the front companies. . . . It was a cosy dug-out for so early a stage of trench-warfare. . . . There was an ornamental lamp, a clean cloth, and polished silver on the table. The colonel, adjutant, doctor, second-in-command, and signalling officer were at dinner. It was civilized cooking, with fresh meat and vegetables. Pictures were pasted on the walls, which were wallpapered; there were beds with spring mattresses, a gramophone, easy chairs. It was hard to reconcile this with accounts I had read of troops standing waist-deep in mud and gnawing a biscuit while shells burst all around.

"Our guide took us up to the front line. We passed a group of men huddled over a brazier. They were wearing waterproof capes, for it had now started to rain, and cap-comforters, because the weather was cold. They were little men, daubed with mud, and they were talking quietly together in Welsh. Although they could see we were officers, they did not jump to their feet and salute. I thought that this was a convention of the trenches, and indeed I knew that it was laid down somewhere in the military textbooks that the courtesy of the salute was to be dispensed with in battle. But I was wrong; it was just slackness.

"I reported to the company commander. I had expected him to be a middle-aged man with a breastful of medals, with whom I would have to be formal; but Dunn was actually two months younger than myself. . . . Dunn had not let the war affect his morale at all. He greeted me very easily with: 'Well, what's the news from England? Oh, sorry, first I must introduce you. This is Walker—clever chap, comes from Cambridge and fancies himself as an athlete. This is Jenkins, one of those patriotic chaps who chucked up his job to come here. This is Price, who only joined us yesterday, but we like him; he brought some damn good whisky with him. Well, how long is the war going to last and who's winning? We don't know a thing out here. And what's all this talk about war-babies? Price pretends he knows nothing about them.' I told them about the war and asked them about the trenches.

" 'About trenches,' said Dunn. 'Well, we don't know as much about trenches as the French do and not near as much as Fritz does. We can't expect Fritz to help, but the French might do something. They are greedy; they won't let us have the benefit of their inventions. What wouldn't we give for parachute-lights and their aerial torpedoes! But there's no connection between the two armies except when there's a battle on, and then we generally let each other down.

" 'When I was out here first, all that we did in the trenches was to paddle about in water and use our rifles. We didn't think of them as places to live in, they were just temporary inconveniences. Now we work all the time we are here, not only for safety but for health. Night and day. First, the fire-steps, then building traverses, improving the communication trenches, and so on; lastly, on our personal comfort—shelters and dug-outs. Our time-table is like this. Breakfast at eight o'clock in the morning, clean trenches and inspect rifles, work all morning; lunch at twelve, work again from one till about six, when the men feed again. "Stand-to" at dusk for about an hour, work all night, "stand-to" for an hour before dawn. That's the general program. Then there's sentry duty. The men do two-hour sentry spells, then work two hours, then sleep two hours. At night sentries are doubled, so our working parties are smaller. We officers are on duty all day and divide up the night in three-hourly watches.' "

◆ ◆ ◆

Later—"He showed me round the line. The battalion frontage was about eight hundred yards. Each company held two hundred of these with two platoons in the front line and two platoons in the support line about a hundred yards back. Dunn introduced me to the platoon sergeants, more particularly to Sergeant Eastmond of the platoon to which I was posted. He asked Sergeant Eastmond to give me any information that I wanted, then went back to sleep, telling me to wake him up at once if anything was wrong. I was left in charge of the line. Sergeant Eastmond was busy with a working-party, so I went round by myself. The men of the working-party, who were building up the traverses with sandbags (a traverse, I learned, was a safety-buttress in the trench), looked curiously at me. They were filling sandbags with earth, piling them up bricklayer fashion, with headers and stretchers alternating, then patting them flat with spades. The sentries stood on the fire-step at the corners of the traverses, stamping their feet and blowing on their fingers. Every now and then they peered over the top for a few seconds. Two parties, each of an N.C.O. and two men, were out in the company listening-posts, connected with the front trench by a sap about fifty yards long. The German front line was about three hundred yards beyond them. From berths hollowed in the sides of the trench and curtained with sandbags came the grunt of sleeping men.

"I jumped up on the fire-step beside the sentry and cautiously raising my head stared over the parapet. I could see nothing except the wooden pickets supporting our protecting barbed-wire entanglement and a dark patch or two of bushes beyond. The darkness seemed to move and shake about as I looked at it; the bushes started travelling, singly at first, then both together. The pickets were doing the same. I was glad of the sentry beside me; his name, he told me, was Beaumont. 'They're quiet tonight, sir,' he said, 'a relief going on; I think so, surely.' I said: 'It's funny how those bushes seem to move.' 'Aye, they do play queer tricks. Is this your first spell in trenches, sir?' A German flare shot up, broke into bright flame, dropped slowly and went hissing into the grass just behind our trench, showing up the bushes and pickets. Instinctively I moved. 'It's bad to do that, sir,' he said, as a rifle bullet cracked and seemed to pass right between us. 'Keep still, sir, and they can't spot you. Not but what a flare is a bad thing to have fall on you. I've seen them burn a hole in a man.'

"At stand-to rum and tea were served out. I had a look at the German trenches through a periscope—a streak of sandbags four hundred yards away. Some of these were made of coloured stuff, whether for camouflage or from a shortage of plain canvas I do not know. There was no sign of the enemy, except for a wisp or two of wood-smoke where they, too, were boiling up a hot drink. Between us and them was a flat meadow with cornflowers, marguerites and poppies growing in the long grass, a few shell holes, the bushes I had seen the night before, the wreck of an aeroplane, our barbed wire and theirs. A thousand yards away was a big ruined house, behind that a red-brick village (Auchy), poplars and haystacks, a tall chimney, another village (Haisnes). Half-right was a pithead and smaller slag-heaps. La Bassée lay half-left; the sun caught the weathervane of the church and made it twinkle." *

IN THE CAMBRIN
AND CUINCHY TRENCHES**

by Robert Graves

Now as the summer advanced there came new types of bombs and trench-mortars, heavier shelling, improved gas-masks and a general tightening up of discipline. We saw the first battalions of the new army and felt like scarecrows by comparison. We went in and out of the Cambrin and Cuinchy trenches, with billets in Béthune

* From *Goodbye to all That*, by Robert Graves, excerpted from pp. 121-32.

** From *Goodbye to All That*.

and the neighbouring villages. By this time I had caught the pessimism of the division. Its spirit in the trenches was largely defensive; the policy was not to stir the Germans into more than their usual hostility. But casualities were still very heavy for trench warfare. Pessimism made everyone superstitious. I became superstitious too: I found myself believing in signs of the most trivial nature. Sergeant Smith, my second sergeant, told me of my predecessor in command of the platoon. "He was a nice gentleman, sir, but very wild. Just before the Rue du Bois show he says to me: 'By the way, sergeant, I'm going to get killed tomorrow. I know that. And I know that you're going to be all right. So see that my kit goes back to my people. You'll find their address in my pocket-book. You'll find five hundred francs there too. Now remember this, Sergeant Smith, you keep a hundred francs yourself and divide up the rest among the chaps left.' He says: 'Send my pocket-book back with my other stuff, Sergeant Smith, but for God's sake burn my diary. They mustn't see that. I'm going to get it *here!*' He points to his forehead. And that's how it was. He got it through the forehead all right. I sent the stuff back to his parents. I divided up the money and I burnt the diary."

One day I was walking along a trench at Cambrin when I suddenly dropped flat on my face; two seconds later a whizz-bang struck the back of the trench exactly where I had been. The sergeant who was with me, walking a few steps ahead, rushed back: "Are you killed, sir?" The shell was fired from a battery near Auchy only a thousand yards away, so that it must have arrived before the sound of the gun. How did I know that I should throw myself on my face?

I saw a ghost at Béthune. He was a man called Private Challoner who had been at Lancaster with me again in F Company at Wrexham. When he went out with a draft to join the First Battalion he shook my hand and said: "I'll meet you again in France, sir." He had been killed at Festubert in May and in June he passed by our C Company billet where we were just having a special dinner to celebrate our safe return from Cuinchy. There was fish, new potatoes, green peas, asparagus, mutton chops, strawberries and cream, and three bottles of Pommard. Challoner looked in at the window, saluted and passed on. There was no mistaking him or the cap-badge he was wearing. There was no Royal Welch battalion billeted within miles of Béthune at the time. I jumped up and looked out of the window, but saw nothing except a fag-end smoking on the pavement. Ghosts were numerous in France at the time.

There was constant mining going on in this Cambrin-Cuinchy sector. We had the prospect of being blown up at any moment. An officer of the R. E. tunnelling company was awarded the Victoria Cross while we were here. A duel of mining and counter-mining was going on. The Germans began to undermine his original boring, so he rapidly tunnelled underneath them. It was touch and go who would get the mine ready first. He won. But when he detonated it from the trench by an electric lead, nothing happened. He ran down again into the mine, retamped the charge, and was just back in time to set it off before the Germans. I had been into the upper boring on the previous day. It was about twenty feet under the German lines. At the end of the gallery I found a Welsh miner, one of our own men who had transferred to the Royal Engineers, on listening duty. He cautioned me to silence. I could distinctly hear the Germans working somewhere underneath. He whispered: "So long as they work, I don't mind; it's when they stop." He did his two-hour spell by can-dle-light. It was very stuffy. He was reading a book. The mining officer had told me that they were allowed to read; it didn't interfere with their listening. It was a paper-backed novelette called *From Mill Girl to Duchess*. The men of the tunnelling companies were notorious thieves, by the way. They would snatch things up from the trench and scurry off with them into their borings; just like mice.

After one particularly bad spell of trenches I got bad news in a letter from Charterhouse. Bad news in the trenches might affect a man in either of two ways. It might drive him to suicide (or reckless-ness amounting to suicide), or it might seem trivial in comparison with present experiences and be disregarded. But unless his leave was due he was helpless. A year later, when I was in trenches in the same sector, an officer of the North Staffordshire Regiment had news from home that his wife was living with another man. He went out on a raid the same night and was either killed or captured; so the men with him said. There had been a fight and they had come back without him. Two days later he was arrested at Béthune trying to board a leave-train to go home; he had intended to shoot up the wife and her lover. He was court-martialled for deserting in the face of the enemy, but the court was content to cashier him. He went as a private soldier to another regiment. I do not know what happened afterwards.

The bad news was about Dick, saying that he was not at all the innocent sort of fellow I took him for. He was as bad as anyone could be. The letter was written by a cousin of mine who was still at Charterhouse. I tried not to believe it. I remembered that he owed me a grudge and decided that this was a very cruel act of spite. Dick's letters had been my greatest stand-by all these months when I was feeling low; he wrote every week, mostly about poetry. They were something solid and clean to set off against the impermanence of trench life and the uncleanness of sex-life in billets. I was now back in Béthune. Two officers of another company had just been telling me how they had slept, in the same room, one with the mother and one with the daughter. They had tossed for the mother because the daughter was a "yellow-looking little thing like a lizard." And the Red Lamp, the army brothel, was around the corner in the main street. I had seen a queue of a hundred and fifty men waiting outside the door, each to have his short turn with one or the other of the three women in the house. My servant, who had been in the queue, told me that the charge was ten francs a man—about eight shillings at that time. Each woman served nearly a battalion of men every week for as long as she lasted. The assistant provost-marshal had told me that three weeks was the usual limit, "after which the woman retires on her earnings, pale but proud." I was always being teased because I would not sleep even with the nicer girls. And I' excused myself, not on moral grounds or on grounds of fastidiousness, but in the only way they could understand: I said that I didn't want a dose. A good deal of talk in billets was about the peculiar bed-manners of the French women. "She was very nice and full of games. I said to her: 'S'il vous plaît, ôtes-toi la chemise, ma chérie.' But she wouldn't. She said, 'Oh no'-non, mon lieutenant. Ce n'est pas convenable.'" I was glad when we were back in trenches. And there

I had a more or less reassuring letter from Dick. He told me that I was right, that my cousin had a spite against him and me, that he had been ragging about in a silly way, but that there was not much harm to it; he was very sorry and would stop it for the sake of our friendship.

At the end of July, I and Robertson, one of the other five Royal Welch officers who had been attached to the Welsh, got orders to proceed to the Laventie sector, some miles to the north. We were to report to the Second Battalion of the Royal Welch Fusiliers. Frank Jones-Bateman and Hanmer Jones, two more of us, went to the First Battalion. The remaining two of the six had already gone back, Mc-Lellan sick and Watkin with bomb wounds that have kept him limping ever since. We were sorry to say good-bye to the men; they all crowded round to shake hands and wish us luck. And we felt a little sorry too that we had to start all over again getting to know a new company and new regimental customs. But it would be worth it, to be with our own regiment. Robertson and I agreed to take our journey as leisurely as possible. Laventie was only seventeen miles away, but our orders were to go there by train; so a mess-cart took us down to Béthune. We asked the railway transport officer what trains he had to Laventie. He told us one was going in a few minutes; we decided to miss it. There was no train after that until the next day, so we stopped the night at the Hôtel de la France. (The Prince of Wales, who was a lieutenant in the Fortieth Siege Battery, was billeted there sometimes. He was a familiar figure in Béthune. I only spoke to him once; it was in the public bath, where he and I were the only bathers one morning. He was graciously pleased to remark how emphatically cold the water was and I loyally assented that he was emphatically right. We were very pink and white and did exercises on the horizontal bar afterwards. I joked to Frank about it: "I have just met our future King in a bath." Frank said: "I can trump that. Two days ago I had a friendly talk with him in the A. S. C. latrines." The Prince's favourite rendezvous was the *Globe,* a café in the Béthune market square reserved for British officers and French civilians; principally spies by the look of them. I once heard him complaining indignantly that General French had refused to let him go up into the line.)

The next day we caught our train. It took us to a junction, the name of which I forget. Here we spent a day walking about in the fields. There was no train until next day, when one took us on to Berguette, a railhead still a number of miles from Laventie, where a mess-cart was waiting for us in answer to a telegram we had sent. We finally rattled up to battalion headquarters in Laventie High Street. We had taken fifty-two hours to come seventeen miles. We saluted the adjutant smartly, gave our names, and said that we were Third Battalion officers posted to the regiment. He did not shake hands with us, offer us a drink, or give us a word of welcome. He said coldly: "I see. Well, which of you is senior? Oh, never mind. Give your particulars to the regimental sergeant-major. Tell him to post whoever is senior to A Company and the other to B Company." The sergeant-major took our particulars. He introduced me to a young second-lieutenant of A Company, to which I was to go. He was a special reservist of the East Surrey Regiment and was known as the Surrey-man. He took me along to the company billet. As soon as we were out of earshot of battalion headquarters I asked him: "What's wrong with the adjutant? Why didn't he shake hands or give me any sort of decent welcome?"

The Surrey-man said: "Well, it's your regiment, not mine. They're all like that. You must realize that this is a regular battalion, one of the only four infantry battalions in France that is still more or less its old self. This is the Nineteenth Brigade, the luckiest in France. It has not been permanently part of any division, but used as army reserve to put in wherever a division has been badly knocked. So, except for the retreat, where it lost about a company, and Fromelles, where it lost half of what was left, it has been practically undamaged. A lot of the wounded have rejoined since. All our company commanders are regulars, and so are all our N. C. O.'s. The peace-time custom of taking no notice of newly-joined officers is still more or less kept up for the first six months. It's bad enough for the Sandhurst chaps, it's worse for special reservists like you and Rugg and Robertson, it's

worse still for outsiders like me from another regiment." We were
going down the village street. The men sitting about on the door-
steps jumped up smartly to attention as we passed and saluted with
a fixed stony glare. They were magnificent looking men. Their
uniforms were spotless, their equipment khaki-blancoed and their
buttons and cap-badges twinkling. We reached company headquarters, where I reported to my company commander, Captain G. O.
Thomas. He was a regular of seventeen years' service, a well-known
polo-player, and a fine soldier. This is the order that he would
himself have preferred. He shook hands without a word, waved me
to a chair, offered a cigarette and continued writing his letter. I
found later that A was the best company I could have struck.

The Surrey-man asked me to help him censor some company
letters before going over to the battalion mess for lunch; they were
more literate than the ones in the Welsh regiment, but duller. On the
way to the mess he told me more about the battalion. He asked me
whether it was my first time out. "I was attached to the Second
Welsh Regiment for three months; I commanded a company there
for a bit." "Oh, were you? Well, I'd advise you to say nothing at all
about it, then they'll not expect too much of you. They treat us like
dirt; in a way it will be worse for you than for me because you're a
full lieutenant. They'll resent that with your short service. There's
one lieutenant here of six years' service and second-lieutenants who
have been out here since the autumn. They have already had two
Special Reserve captains foisted on them; they're planning to get rid
of them somehow. In the mess, if you open your mouth or make the
slightest noise the senior officers jump down your throat. Only
officers of the rank of captain are allowed to drink whisky or turn on
the gramophone. We've got to jolly well keep still and look like
furniture. It's just like peace time. Mess bills are very high; the mess
was in debt at Quetta last year and we are economizing now to pay
that back. We get practically nothing for our money but ordinary
rations and the whisky we aren't allowed to drink.

"We've even got a polo-ground here. There was a polo-match
between the First and Second Battalions the other day. The First
Battalion had had all their decent ponies pinched that time when

they were sent up at Ypres and the cooks and transport men had to come up into the line to prevent a breakthrough. So this battalion won easily. Can you ride? No? Well, subalterns who can't ride have to attend riding-school every afternoon while we're in billets. They give us hell, too. Two of us have been at it for four months and haven't passed off yet. They keep us trotting round the field, with crossed stirrups most of the time, and they give us pack-saddles instead of riding-saddles. Yesterday they called us up suddenly without giving us time to change into breeches. That reminds me, you notice everybody's wearing shorts? It's a regimental order. The battalion thinks it's still in India. They treat the French civilians just like 'niggers,' kick them about, talk army Hindustani at them. It makes me laugh sometimes. Well, what with a greasy pack-saddle, bare knees, crossed stirrups, and a wild new transport pony that the transport men had pinched from the French, I had a pretty thin time. The colonel, the adjutant, the senior major and the transport officer stood at the four corners of the ring and slogged at the ponies as they came round. I came off twice and got wild with anger, and nearly decided to ride the senior major down. The funny thing is that they don't realize that they are treating us badly—it's such an honour to be serving with the regiment. So the best thing is to pretend you don't care what they do or say."

I protested: "But all this is childish. Is there a war on here or isn't there?"

"The battalion doesn't recognize it socially," he answered. "Still, in trenches I'd rather be with this battalion than in any other that I have met. The senior officers do know their job, whatever else one says about them, and the N. C. O's are absolutely trustworthy."

The Second Battalion was peculiar in having a battalion mess instead of company messes. The Surrey-man said grimly: "It's supposed to be more sociable." This was another peace-time survival. We went together into the big château near the church. About fifteen officers of various ranks were sitting in chairs reading the week's illustrated papers or (the seniors at least) talking quietly. At the door I said: "Good morning, gentlemen," the new officer's customary greeting to the mess. There was no answer. Everybody

looked at me curiously. The silence that my entry had caused was
soon broken by the gramophone, which began singing happily:

> We've been married just one year,
> And Oh, we've got the sweetest,
> And Oh, we've got the neatest,
> And Oh, we've got the cutest
> Little oil stove.

I found a chair in the background and picked up *The Field*. The
door burst open suddenly and a senior officer with a red face and
angry eye burst in. "Who the blazes put that record on?" he shouted
to the room. "One of the bloody warts I expect. Take it off somebody. It makes me sick. Let's have some real music. Put on the
Angelus." Two subalterns (in the Royal Welch a subaltern had to
answer to the name of "wart") sprang up, stopped the gramophone,
and put on *When the Angelus Is Ringing*. The young captain who
had put on *We've Been Married* shrugged his shoulders and went on
reading, the other faces in the room were blank.

"Who was that?" I whispered to the Surrey-man.

He frowned. "That's Buzz Off," he said.

Before the record was finished the door opened and in came the
colonel; Buzz Off reappeared with him. Everybody jumped up and
said in unison: "Good morning, sir." It was his first appearance that
day. Before giving the customary greeting and asking us to sit down
he turned spitefully to the gramophone: "Who on earth puts this
wretched *Angelus* on every time I come into the mess? For heaven's
sake play something cheery for a change." And with his own hands
he took off the *Angelus*, wound up the gramophone and put on *We've
Been Married Just One Year*. At that moment a gong rang for lunch
and he abandoned it. We filed into the next room, a ball-room with
mirrors and a decorated ceiling. We sat down at a long, polished
table. The seniors sat at the top, the juniors competed for seats as far
away from them as possible. I was unlucky enough to get a seat at
the foot of the table facing the commanding officer, the adjutant and
Buzz Off. There was not a word spoken down that end except for an
occasional whisper for the salt or for the beer—very thin French

stuff. Robertson, who had not been warned, asked the mess waiter for whisky. "Sorry, sir," said the mess waiter, "it's against orders for the young officers." Robertson was a man of forty-two, a solicitor with a large practice, and had stood for Parliament in the Yarmouth division at the previous election.

I saw Buzz Off glaring at us and busied myself with my meat and potatoes.

He nudged the adjutant. "Who are those two funny ones down there, Charley," he asked.

"New this morning from the militia. Answer to the names of Robertson and Graves."

"Which is which?" asked the colonel.

"I'm Robertson, sir."

"I wasn't asking you."

Robertson winced, but said nothing. Then Buzz Off noticed something.

"T'other wart's wearing a wind-up tunic." Then he bent forward and asked me loudly. "You there, wart. Why the hell are you wearing your stars on your shoulder instead of your sleeve?"

My mouth was full and I was embarrassed. Everybody was looking at me. I swallowed the lump of meat whole and said: "It was a regimental order in the Welsh Regiment. I understood that it was the same everywhere in France."

The colonel turned puzzled to the adjutant: "What on earth's the man talking about the Welsh Regiment for?" And then to me: "As soon as you have finished your lunch you will visit the master-tailor. Report at the orderly room when you're properly dressed."

There was a severe struggle in me between resentment and regimental loyalty. Resentment for the moment had the better of it. I said under my breath: "You damned snobs. I'll survive you all. There'll come a time when there won't be one of you left serving in the battalion to remember battalion mess at Laventie." This time came, exactly a year later.*

We went up to the trenches that night. They were high-command trenches; because water was struck when one dug down three feet,

* The quartermaster excepted.

the parapet and parados were built up man-high. I found my platoon curt and reserved. Even when on sentry-duty at night they would never talk confidentially about themselves and their families like my platoon in the Welsh Regiment. Townsend, the platoon-sergeant, was an ex-policeman who had been on the reserve when war broke out. He used to drive his men rather than lead them. A Company was at Red Lamp Corner; the front trench broke off short here and started again further back on the right. A red lamp was hung at the corner, invisible to the enemy, but a warning after dark to the company on our right not to fire to the left of it. Work and duties were done with a silent soldier-like efficiency quite foreign to the Welsh.

The first night I was in trenches my company commander asked me to go out on patrol; it was the regimental custom to test new officers in this way. All the time that I had been with the Welsh I had never once been out in No Man's Land, even to inspect the barbed wire. In the Welsh Regiment the condition of the wire was, I believe, the responsibility of the battalion intelligence officer. I never remember any work done on it by C Company. I think we left it to the Royal Engineers. When Hewitt, the machine-gun officer, used to go out on patrol sometimes it was regarded as a mad escapade. But with both battalions of the Royal Welch Fusiliers it was a point of honour to be masters of No Man's Land from dusk to dawn. There was not a night at Laventie that a message did not come down the line from sentry to sentry: "Pass the word; officer's patrol going out." My orders for this patrol were to see whether a German sap-head was occupied by night or not.

I went out from Red Lamp Corner with Sergeant Townsend at about ten o'clock. We both had revolvers. We pulled socks, with the toes cut off, over our bare knees, to prevent them showing up in the dark and to make crawling easier. We went ten yards at a time, slowly, not on all fours, but wriggling flat along the ground. After each movement we lay and watched for about ten minutes. We crawled through our own wire entanglements and along a dry ditch; ripping our clothes on more barbed wire, glaring into the darkness till it began turning round and round (once I snatched my fingers in horror from where I had planted them on the slimy body of an old corpse), nudging each other with rapidly beating hearts at the slightest noise or suspicion, crawling, watching, crawling, shamming dead under the blinding light of enemy flares and again crawling, watching, crawling. (A Second Battalion officer who revisited these Laventie trenches after the war was over told me of the ridiculously small area of No Man's Land compared with the size it seemed on the long, painful journeys that he made over it. "It was like the real size of the hollow in a tooth compared with the size it feels to the tongue.")

We found a gap in the German wire and came at last to within five yards of the sap-head that was our objective. We waited quite twenty minutes listening for any signs of its occupation. Then I nudged Sergeant Townsend and, revolvers in hand, we wriggled quickly forward and slid into it. It was about three feet deep and unoccupied. On the floor were a few empty cartridges and a wicker basket containing something large and smooth and round, twice as large as a football. Very, very carefully I groped and felt all around it in the dark. I couldn't guess what it was. I was afraid that it was some sort of infernal machine. Eventually I dared to lift it out and carry it back. I had a suspicion that it might be one of the German gas-cylinders that we had heard so much about. We got back after making the journey of perhaps two hundred yards in rather more than two hours. The sentries passed along the word that we were in again. Our prize turned out to be a large glass container quarter-filled with some pale yellow liquid. This was sent down to battalion headquarters and from there sent along to the divisional intelligence officer. Everybody was very interested in it. The theory was that the vessel contained a chemical for re-damping gas masks. I now believe it was the dregs of country wine mixed with rainwater. I never heard the official report. The colonel, however, told my company commander in the hearing of the Surrey-man: "Your new wart seems to have more guts than the others." After this I went out fairly often. I found that the only thing that the regiment respected in young officers was personal courage.

Besides, I had worked it out like this. The best way of lasting the war out was to get wounded. The best time to get wounded was at night and in the open, because a wound in a vital spot was less likely. Fire was more or less unaimed at night and the whole body was exposed. It was also convenient to be wounded when there was no rush on the dressing-station services, and when the back areas were not being heavily shelled. It was most convenient to be wounded, therefore, on a night patrol in a quiet sector. You could usually manage to crawl into a shell-hole until somebody came to the rescue. Still, patrolling had its peculiar risks. If you were wounded and a German patrol got you, they were as likely as not to cut your throat. The bowie-knife was a favourite German patrol weapon; it was silent. (At this time the British inclined more to the "cosh," a loaded stick.) The most important information that a patrol could bring back was to what regiment and division the troops opposite belonged. So if a wounded man was found and it was impossible to get him back without danger to oneself, the thing to be done was to strip him of his badges. To do that quickly and silently it might be necessary first to cut his throat or beat in his skull.

Sir P. Mostyn, a lieutenant who was often out patrolling at Laventie, had a feud on with a German patrol on the left of the battalion frontage. (Our patrols usually consisted of an officer and one or, at the most, two men. German patrols were usually six or seven men under an N. C. O. German officers left as much as they decently could to their N. C. O.'s. They did not, as one of our sergeant-majors put it, believe in "keeping a dog and barking themselves.") One night Mostyn caught sight of his opponents; he had raised himself on one knee to throw a percussion bomb at them when they fired and wounded him in the arm, which immediately went numb. He caught the bomb before it hit the ground and threw it with his left hand, and in the confusion that followed managed to return to the trench.

Like everyone else I had a carefully worked out formula for taking risks. We would all take any risk, even the certainty of death, to save life or to maintain an important position. To take life we would run, say, a one-in-five risk, particularly if there was some wider object than merely reducing the enemy's man-power; for instance, picking off a well-known sniper, or getting fire ascendancy in trenches where the lines were dangerously close. I only once refrained from shooting a German I saw, and that was at Cuinchy about three weeks after this. When sniping from a knoll in the support line where we had a concealed loop-hole I saw a German, about seven hundred yards away, through my telescopic sights. He was having a bath in the German third line. I somehow did not like the idea of shooting a naked man, so I handed the rifle to the sergeant who was with me and said: "Here, take this. You're a better shot than me." He got him, he said; but I had not stayed to watch.

About saving the lives of enemy wounded there was disagreement; the convention varied with the division. Some divisions, like the Canadians and a division of Lowland territorials, who had, they claimed, atrocities to avenge, would not only take no risks to rescue enemy wounded, but would go out of their way to finish them off. The Royal Welch Fusiliers were gentlemanly: perhaps a one-in-twenty risk to get a wounded German to safety would be considered justifiable. An important factor in taking risks was our own physical condition. When exhausted and wanting to get quickly from one point in the trenches to another without collapse, and if the enemy were not nearer than four or five hundred yards, we would sometimes take a short cut over the top. In a hurry we would take a one-in-two-hundred risk, when dead tired a one-in-fifty risk. In some battalions where the *morale* was not high, one-in-fifty risks were often taken in mere laziness or despair. The Munsters in the First Division were said by the Welsh to "waste men wicked" by not keeping properly under cover when in the reserve lines. In the Royal Welch there was no wastage of this sort. At no time in the war did any of us allow ourselves to believe that hostilities could possibly continue more than nine months or a year more, so it seemed almost worthwhile taking care; there even seemed a chance of lasting until the end absolutely unhurt.

The Second Royal Welch, unlike the Second Welsh, believed themselves better trench fighters than the Germans. With the Second Welsh it was not cowardice but modesty. With the Second Royal Welch it was not vainglory but courage: as soon as they arrived in a new sector they insisted on getting fire ascendancy. Having found out from the troops they relieved all possible information as to enemy snipers, machine-guns, and patrols, they set themselves to deal with them one by one. They began with machine-guns firing at night. As soon as one started traversing down a trench the whole platoon farthest removed from its fire would open five rounds rapid at it. The machine-gun would usually stop suddenly but start again after a minute or two. Again five rounds rapid. Then it usually gave up.

The Welsh seldom answered a machine-gun. If they did, it was not with local organized fire, beginning and ending in unison, but in ragged confused protest all along the line. There was almost no firing at night in the Royal Welch, except organized fire at a machine-gun or a persistent enemy sentry, or fire at a patrol close enough to be distinguished as a German one. With all other battalions I met in France there was random popping off all the time; the sentries wanted to show their spite against the war. Flares were rarely used in the Royal Welch; most often as signals to our patrols that it was time to come back.

As soon as enemy machine-guns had been discouraged, our patrols would go out with bombs to claim possession of No Man's Land. At dawn next morning came the struggle for sniping ascendancy. The Germans, we were told, had special regimental snipers, trained in camouflaging themselves. I saw one killed once at Cuinchy who had been firing all day from a shell-hole between the lines. He had a sort of cape over his shoulders of imitation grass, his face was painted green and brown, and his rifle was also green fringed. A number of empty cartridges were found by him, and his cap with his special oak-leaf badge. Few battalions attempted to get control of the sniping situation. The Germans had the advantage of having many times more telescopic sights than we did, and steel loopholes that our bullets could not pierce. Also a system by which the snipers were kept for months in the same sector until they knew all the loopholes and shallow places in our trenches, and the tracks that our ration-parties used above-ground by night, and where our traverses came in the trench, and so on, better than we did ourselves. British snipers changed their trenches, with their battalions, every week or two, and never had time to learn the German line thoroughly. But at least we counted on getting rid of the unprofessional German sniper. Later we had an elephant-gun in the battalion that would pierce the German loopholes, and if we could not locate the loophole of a persistent sniper we did what we could to dislodge him by a volley of rifle-grenades, or even by ringing up the artillery.

It puzzled us that if a sniper were spotted and killed, another sniper would begin again next day from the same position. The Germans probably underrated us and regarded it as an accident. The willingness of other battalions to let the Germans have sniping ascendancy helped us; enemy snipers often exposed themselves unnecessarily, even the professionals. There was, of course, one advantage of which no advance or retreat of the enemy could rob us, and that was that we were always facing more or less east; dawn broke behind the German lines, and they seldom realized that for several minutes every morning we could see them though still invisible ourselves. German night wiring-parties often stayed out too long, and we could get a man or two as they went back; sunsets were against us, but sunset was a less critical time. Sentries at night were made to stand with their head and shoulders above the trenches and their rifles in position on the parapet. This surprised me at first. But it meant greater vigilance and self-confidence in the sentry, and it put the top of his head above the level of the parapet. Enemy machine-guns were trained on this level, and it was safer to be hit in the chest or shoulders than in the top of the head. The risk of unaimed fire at night was negligible, so this was really the safest plan. It often happened in battalions like the Second Welsh, where the head-and-shoulder rule was not in force and the sentry just took a peep now and then, that an enemy patrol would sneak up unseen to the British wire, throw a few bombs and get safely back. In the Royal Welch the barbed-wire entanglement was the responsibility of the company behind it. One of our first acts on taking over trenches was to inspect and repair it. We did a lot of work on the wire.

Thomas was an extremely silent man; it was not sullenness but shyness. "Yes" and "no" was the limit of his usual conversation; it was difficult for us subalterns. He never took us into his confidence about company affairs, and we did not like asking him too much. His chief interests seemed to be polo and the regiment. He was most conscientious in taking his watch at night, a thing that the other company commanders did not always do. We enjoyed his food-hampers sent every week from Fortnum and Mason; we messed by companies when in the trenches. Our only complaint was that Buzz Off, who had a good nose for a hamper, used to spend more time than he would otherwise have done in the company mess. This embarrassed us. Thomas went on leave to England about this time. I heard about it accidentally. He walked about the West End astonished at the amateur militariness that he met everywhere. To be more in keeping with it he gave elaborate awkward salutes to newly-joined second-lieutenants and raised his cap to dug-out colonels and generals. It was a private joke at the expense of the war.

I used to look forward to our spells in trenches at Laventie. Billet life meant battalion mess, also riding-school, which I found rather worse than the Surrey-man had described it. Parades were carried out with peace-time punctiliousness and smartness, especially the daily battalion guard-changing which every now and then, when I was orderly officer, it was my duty to supervise. On one occasion, after the guard-changing ceremony and inspection were over and I was about to dismiss the old guard, I saw Buzz Off cross the village street from one company headquarters to another. As he crossed I called the guard to attention and saluted. I waited for a few seconds and then dismissed the guard, but he had not really gone into the billet; he had been waiting in the doorway. As soon as I dismissed the guard he dashed out with a great show of anger. "As you were, as you were, stand fast!" he shouted to the guard. And then to me: "Why in hell's name, Mr. Graves, didn't you ask my permission to dismiss the parade? You've read the King's regulations, haven't you? And where the devil are your manners, anyhow?" I apologized. I said that I thought he had gone into the house. This made matters worse. He bellowed at me for arguing; then he asked me where I had learned to salute. "At the depot, sir," I answered. "Then, by heaven, Mr. Graves, you'll have to learn to salute as the battalion does. You will parade every morning before breakfast for a month under Staff-sergeant Evans and do an hour's saluting drill." Then he turned to the guard and dismissed them himself. This was not a particular act of spite against me but the general game of "chasing the warts," at which all the senior officers played. It was honestly intended to make us better soldiers.

I had been with the Royal Welch about three weeks when the Nineteenth Brigade was moved down to the Béthune sector to fill a gap in the Second Division; the gap was made by taking out the brigade of Guards to go into the Guards Division which was then being formed. On the way down we marched past Lord Kitchener. Kitchener, we were told, commented to the brigadier on the soldier-like appearance of the leading battalion—which was ourselves—but said cynically: "Wait until they've been a week or two in the trenches; they will lose some of that high polish." He apparently mistook us for one of the new-army battalions.

The first trenches we went into on our arrival were the Cuinchy brick-stacks. The company I was with was on the canal-bank frontage, a few hundred yards to the left of where I had been with the Welsh Regiment at the end of May. The Germans opposite wished to be sociable. They sent messages over to us in undetonated rifle-grenades. One of these messages was evidently addressed to the Irish battalion we had relieved:

> We all German korporals wish you English korporals a good day and invite you to a good German dinner tonight with beer (ale) and cakes. You little dog ran over to us and we keep it safe; it became no food with you so it run to us. Answer in the same way, if you please.

Another message was a copy of the *Neueste Nachrichten,* a German army newspaper printed at Lille. It gave sensational details of Russian defeats around Warsaw and immense captures of prisoners and guns. But we were more interested in a full account in another column of the destruction of a German submarine by British armed trawlers; no details of the sinking of German submarines had been allowed to appear in any English papers. The battalion cared no more about the successes or reverses of our Allies than it did about the origins of the war. It never allowed itself to have any political feelings about the Germans. A professional soldier's job was to fight whomsoever the King ordered him to fight; it was as simple as that. With the King as colonel-in-chief of the regiment it was even simpler. The Christmas 1914 fraternization, in which the battalion was among the first to participate, was of the same professional simplicity; it was not an emotional hiatus but a commonplace of military tradition—an exchange of courtesies between officers of opposite armies.

Cuinchy was one of the worst places for rats. They came up from the canal and fed on the many corpses and multiplied. When I was here with the Welsh a new officer came to the company, and, as a token of his welcome, he was given a dug-out containing a spring-bed. When he turned in that night he heard a scuffling, shone his torch on the bed, and there were two rats on his blankets tussling for the possession of a severed hand. This was thought a great joke.

The colonel called for a patrol to go out along the side of the tow-path, where we had heard suspicious sounds on the previous night, to see whether a working-party was out. I volunteered to go when it was dark. But there was a moon that night so bright and full that it dazzled the eyes to look at it. Between us and the Germans was a flat stretch of about two hundred yards, broken only by shell-craters and an occasional patch of coarse grass. I was not with my own company, but lent to B, which had two officers away on leave. Childe-Freeman, the company commander, said: "You're not going out on patrol tonight, are you? It's almost as bright as day." I said: "All the more reason for going; they won't be expecting me. Will you please have everything as usual? Let the men fire an occasional rifle and send up a flare every half hour. If I go carefully they'll not see me." But I was nervous, and while we were having supper I clumsily knocked a cup of tea, and after that a plate. Freeman said: "Look here, I'll 'phone through to battalion and tell them it's too bright for you to go out." But I knew Buzz Off would accuse me of cold feet, so Sergeant Williams and I put on our crawlers and went out by way of a mine-crater at the side of the tow-path. There was no need that night for the usual staring business. We could see only too clearly. All we had to do was to wait for an opportunity to move quickly, stop dead and trust to luck, then move on quickly again. We planned our rushes from shell-hole to shell-hole; the opportunities were provided by artillery or machine-gun fire which would distract the sentries. Many of the craters contained corpses of men who had been wounded and crept in and died. Some of them were skeletons, picked clean by the rats. We got to within thirty yards of a big German working-party who were digging a trench ahead of their front line. Between them and us we could count a covering party of ten men lying on the grass in their great-coats. We had gone far enough. There was a German lying on his back about twelve yards away humming a tune. It was the *Merry Widow* waltz. The sergeant, who was behind me, pressed my foot with his hand and showed me the revolver he was carrying. He raised his eyebrows inquiringly. I gave him the signal for "no." We turned to go back; it was hard not to go back too quickly. We had got about half-way back when a German machine-gun opened traversing fire along the top of our trenches. We immediately jumped to our feet; the bullets were brushing the grass, so it was safer to be standing up. We walked the rest of the way back, but moving irregularly to distract the aim of the covering party if they saw us. Back in the trench I rang up the artillery and asked them to fire as much shrapnel as they could spare fifty yards short of where the German front trench touched the tow-path; I knew that one of the night-lines of the battery supporting us was trained near enough to this point. A minute and a quarter later the shells started coming over. We heard the clash of downed tools and distant shouts and cries; we reckoned the probable casualties. The next morning at stand-to Buzz Off came up to me: "I hear you were on patrol last night?" I said: "Yes, sir." He asked me for particulars. When I had told him about the covering party he cursed me for "not scuppering them with that revolver of yours. Cold feet," he snorted as he turned away.

One day while we were here the Royal Welch were instructed to shout across to the enemy and induce them to take part in a conversation. The object was to find out how strongly the German front trenches were manned at night. A German-speaking officer in the company among the brick-stacks was provided with a megaphone. He shouted: *"Wie gehts ihnen, kamaraden?"* Somebody shouted back in delight: *"Ah, Tommee, hast du den deutsch gelernt?"* Firing stopped and a conversation began across the fifty yards or so of No Man's Land. The Germans refused to say what regiment they were. They would not talk any military shop. One of them shouted out: *"Les sheunes mademoiselles de La Bassée bonnes pour coucher avec. Les mademoiselles de Béthune bonnes aussi, hein?"* Our spokesman refused to discuss this. In the pause that followed he asked how the Kaiser was. They replied respectfully that he was in excellent health, thank you. "And how is the Crown Prince?" he asked them. "Oh, b—r the Crown Prince," shouted somebody in English, and was immediately suppressed by his comrades. There was a confusion of angry voices and laughter. Then they all began singing the *"Wacht am Rhein."* The trench was evidently very well held indeed.

◆ ◆ ◆

This was the end of August 1915, and particulars of the coming offensive against La Bassée were beginning to leak through the young staff officers. The French civilians knew that it was coming and so, naturally, did the Germans. Every night now new batteries and lorry-trains of shells came rumbling up the Béthune-La Bassée road. There were other signs of movement: sapping forward at Vermelles and Cambrin, where the lines were too far apart for a quick rush across, to make a new front line; orders for evacuation of hospitals; the appearance of cavalry and new-army divisions. Then Royal Engineer officers supervised the digging of pits at intervals in the front line. They were sworn not to say what these were for, but we knew that they were for gas-cylinders. Scaling ladders for climbing quickly out of trenches were brought up by the lorry-load and dumped at Cambrin village. As early as September 3rd I had a bet with Robertson that our division would attack on this Cambrin-

Cuinchy sector. When I went home on leave on September 9th the sense of impending events was so great that I almost wished I was not going.

Leave came round for officers about every six or eight months in ordinary times; heavy casualties shortened the period, general offensives cut off leave altogether. There was only one officer in France who was ever said to have refused to go on leave when his turn came round—Cross of the Fifty-second Light Infantry (the Second Battalion of the Oxford and Bucks Light Infantry, which insisted on its original style as jealously as we kept our "c" in "Welch"). Cross is alleged to have refused leave on these grounds: "My father fought with the regiment in the South African War and had no leave; my grandfather fought in the Crimea with the regiment and had no leave. I do not regard it in the regimental tradition to take home-leave when on active service." Cross was a professional survivior and was commanding the battalion in 1917 when I last heard of him.

London seemed unreally itself. In spite of the number of men in uniform in the streets, the general indifference to and ignorance about the war was remarkable. Enlistment was still voluntary. The universal catchword was "Business as usual." My family were living in London now, at the house formerly occupied by my uncle, Robert von Ranke, the German consul. He had been forced to leave in a hurry on August 4th, 1914, and my mother had undertaken to look after it for him while the war lasted. So when Edward Marsh, then secretary to the Prime Minister, rang me up from Downing Street to arrange a meal, someone intervened and cut him off. The telephone of the German consul's sister was, of course, closely watched by the anti-espionage men of Scotland Yard. The Zeppelin scare had just begun. Some friends of the family came in one night. They knew I had been in the trenches, but were not interested. They began telling me of the air-raids, of bombs dropped only three streets off. So I said: "Well, do you know, the other day I was asleep in a house and in the early morning an aeroplane dropped a bomb next door and killed three soldiers who were billeted there, and a woman and child." "Good gracious," they said, looking at me with sudden interest, "what did you do then?" I said: "I went to sleep again; I was tired out. It was at a place called Beuvry, about four miles behind the trenches." They said: "Oh, but that was in France," and the look of interest faded from their faces, as though I had taken them in with a stupid catch. I went up to Harlech for the rest of my leave, and walked about on the hills in an old shirt and a pair of shorts. When I got back, "The Actor," a regular officer in A Company, asked me: "Had a good time on leave?" I said: "Yes." He said: "Go to many dances?" I said: "Not one." "What shows did you go to?" "I didn't go to any shows." "Hunt?" "No!" "Slept with any nice girls?" "No, I didn't. Sorry to disappoint you." "What the hell *did* you do, then?" "Oh, I just walked about on some hills." "Good God," he said, "chaps like you don't deserve to go on leave."

On September 19th we relieved the Middlesex at Cambrin, and it was said that these were the trenches from which we were to attack. The preliminary bombardment had already started, a week in advance. As I led my platoon into the line I recognized with some disgust the same machine-gun shelter where I had seen the suicide on my first night in trenches. It seemed ominous. This was the first heavy bombardment that I had yet seen from our own guns. The trenches shook properly and a great cloud of drifting shell-smoke clouded the German trenches. The shells went over our heads in a steady stream; we had to shout to make our neighbours hear. Dying down a little at night, the racket began again every morning at dawn, a little louder each time. We said: "Damn it, there can't be a living soul left in those trenches." And still it went on. The Germans retaliated, though not very vigorously. Most of their heavy artillery had been withdrawn from this sector, we were told, and sent across to the Russian front. We had more casualties from our own shorts and from blow-backs than from German shells. Much of the ammunition that our batteries were using came from America and contained a high percentage of duds; the driving bands were always coming off. We had fifty casualties in the ranks and three officer casualties, including Buzz Off, who was badly wounded in the head. This was before steel helmets were issued; we would not have lost nearly so many if we had had them. I had two insignificant wounds on the hand which I took as an omen on the right side. On the morning of the 23rd Thomas came back from battalion headquarters with a notebook in his hand and a map for each of us company officers. "Listen," he said, "and copy out all this skite on the back of your maps. You'll have to explain it to your platoons this afternoon. Tomorrow morning we go back to Béthune to dump our blankets, packs, and greatcoats. On the next day, that's Saturday the 25th, we attack." It was the first definite news we had been given and we looked up half startled, half relieved. I still have the map and these are the orders as I copied them down:

FIRST OBJECTIVE.—*Les Briques Farm.*—The big house plainly visible to our front, surrounded by trees. To get this it is necessary to cross three lines of enemy trenches. The first is three hundred yards distant, the second four hundred, and the third about six hundred. We then cross two railways. Behind the second railway line is a German trench called the Brick Trench. Then comes the Farm, a strong place with moat and cellars and a kitchen garden strongly staked and wired.

SECOND OBJECTIVE.—*The Town of Auchy.*—This is also plainly visible from our trenches. It is four hundred yards beyond the Farm and defended by a first line of trench half way across, and a second line immediately in front of the town. When we have occupied the first line our direction is half-right, with the left of the battalion directed on Tall Chimney.

THIRD OBJECTIVE.—*Village of Haisnes.*—Conspicuous by high-spired church. Our eventual line will be taken up on the railway behind this village, where we will dig in and await reinforcements.

When Thomas had reached this point the shoulders of The Actor were shaking with laughter. "What's up?" asked Thomas irritably. The Actor asked: "Who in God's Name is originally responsible for this little effort?" Thomas said: "Don't know. Probably Paul the Pimp or someone like that." (Paul the Pimp was a captain on the divisional staff, young, inexperienced and much disliked. He "wore red tabs upon his chest, And even on his undervest.") "Between you and me, but you youngsters be careful not to let the men know, this is what they call a subsidiary attack. We'll have no supports. We've just got to go over and keep the enemy busy while the folk on our right do the real work. You notice that the bombardment is much heavier over there. They've knocked the Hohenzollern Redoubt to bits. Personally, I don't give a damn either way. We'll get killed anyhow." We all laughed. "All right, laugh now, but, by God, on Saturday we've got to carry out this funny scheme." I had never heard Thomas so talkative before. "Sorry," The Actor apologized, "carry on with the dictation." Thomas went on:

The attack will be preceded by forty minutes' discharge of the accessory,* which will clear the path for a thousand yards, so that the two railway lines will be occupied without difficulty. Our advance will follow closely behind the accessory. Behind us are three fresh divisions and the Cavalry Corps. It is expected we shall have no difficulty in breaking through. All men will parade with their platoons; pioneers, servants, etc., to be warned. All platoons to be properly told off under N. C. O.'s. Every N. C. O. is to know exactly what is expected of him, and when to take over command in case of casualties. Men who lose touch must join up with the nearest company or regiment and push on. Owing to the strength of the accessory, men should be warned against remaining too long in captured trenches where the accessory is likely to collect, but to keep to the open and above all to push on. It is important that if smoke-helmets have to be pulled down they must be tucked in under the shirt.

The Actor interrupted again. "Tell me, Thomas, do you believe in this funny accessory?" Thomas said: "It's damnable. It's not soldiering to use stuff like that even though the Germans did start it. It's dirty, and it'll bring us bad luck. We're sure to bungle it. Look at those new gas-companies (sorry, excuse me this once, I mean accessory-companies). Their very look makes me tremble. Chemistry-dons from London University, a few lads straight from school, one or two N. C. O.'s of the old-soldier type, trained together for three weeks, then given a job as responsible as this. Of course they'll bungle it. How could they do anything else? But let's be merry. I'm going on again:

* The gas-cylinders had by this time been put into position on the front line. A special order came round imposing severe penalties on anyone who used any word but "accessory" in speaking of the gas. This was to keep it secret, but the French civilians knew all about it long before this.

Men of company: what they are to carry:

Two hundred rounds of ammunition (bomb-throwers fifty, and signallers one hundred and fifty rounds).

Heavy tools carried in sling by the strongest men.

Waterproof sheet in belt.

Sandbag in right coat-pocket.

Field dressing and iodine.

Emergency ration, including biscuit.

One tube-helmet, to be worn when we advance, rolled up on the head. It must be quite secure and the top part turned down. If possible each man will be provided with an elastic band.

One smoke-helmet, old pattern, to be carried for preference behind the back where it is least likely to be damaged by stray bullets, etc.

Wire-cutters, as many as possible, by wiring party and others; hedging-gloves by wire party.

Platoon screens, for artillery observation, to be carried by a man in each platoon who is not carrying a tool.

Packs, capes, greatcoats, blankets will be dumped, not carried.

No one is to carry sketches of our position or anything likely to be of service to the enemy.

"That's all. I believe we're going over first with the Middlesex in support. If we get through the German wire I'll be satisfied. Our guns don't seem to be cutting it. Perhaps they're putting that off until the intense bombardment. Any questions?"

That afternoon I repeated it all to the platoon and told them of the inevitable success attending our assault. They seemed to believe it. All except Sergeant Townsend. "Do you say, sir, that we have three divisions and the Cavalry Corps behind us?" he asked. "Yes," I answered. "Well, excuse me, sir, I'm thinking it's only those chaps on the right that'll get reinforcements. If we get half a platoon of Mons Angels, that's about all we will get." "Sergeant Townsend," I said, "you are a well-known pessimist. This is going to be a good show." The next morning we were relieved by the Middlesex and marched back to Béthune, where we dumped our spare kit at the Montmorency Barracks. The battalion officers messed together in a big house nearby. This billet was claimed at the same time by the staff of a new-army division which was to take part in the fighting

next day. The argument was settled in a friendly way by the division
and battalion messing together. It was, someone pointed out, like a
caricature of The Last Supper in duplicate. In the middle of the long
table sat the two pseudo-Christs, the battalion colonel and the
divisional general. Everybody was drinking a lot; the subalterns
were allowed whisky for a treat, and were getting rowdy. They
raised their glasses with: "Cheero, we will be messing together
tomorrow night in La Bassée." Only the company commanders were
looking worried. I remember C Company commander especially,
Captain A. L. Samson, biting his thumb and refusing to join the
general excitement. I think it was Childe-Freeman of B Company
who said that night: "The last time the regiment was in these parts it
was under decent generalship. Old Marlborough knew better than to
attack the La Bassée lines; he masked them and went round."

The G. S. O. 1 of the new-army division, a staff-colonel, knew the
adjutant well. They had played polo together in India. I happened
to be sitting next to them. The G. S. O. 1 said to the adjutant, rather
drunkenly: "Charley, do you see that silly old woman over there?
Calls himself General Commanding. Doesn't know where he is;
doesn't know where his division is; can't read a map properly. He's
marched the poor sods off their feet and left his supplies behind,
God knows where. They've had to use their iron rations and what
they could pick up in the villages. And tomorrow he's going to fight a
battle. Doesn't know anything about battles; the men have never
been in trenches before, and tomorrow's going to be a glorious balls-
up, and the day after tomorrow he'll be sent home." Then he said,
quite seriously: "Really, Charley, it's just like that, you mark my
words."

That night we marched back again to Cambrin. The men were
singing. Being mostly from the Midlands they sang comic songs
instead of Welsh hymns: *Slippery Sam, When We've Wound up the
Watch on the Rhine,* and *I Do Like a S'nice S'mince Pie,* to concertina
accompaniment. The tune of the *S'nice S'mince Pie* ran in my head
all next day, and for the week following I could not get rid of it. The
Second Welsh would never have sung a song like *When We've*

Wound up the Watch on the Rhine. Their only songs about war were defeatist:

> I want to go home,
> I want to go home.
> The coal-box and shrapnel they whistle and roar,
> I don't want to go to the trenches no more,
> I want to go over the sea
> Where the Kayser can't shoot bombs at me.
> Oh, I
> Don't want to die,
> I want to go home.

There were several more verses in the same strain. Hewitt, the Welsh machine-gun officer, had written one in a more offensive spirit:

> I want to go home,
> I want to go home.
> One day at Givenchy the week before last
> The Allmands attacked and they nearly got past.
> They pushed their way up to the keep,
> Through our maxim-gun sight we did peep,
> Oh, my!
> They let out a cry,
> They never got home.

But the men would not sing it, though they all admired Hewitt.

The Béthune-La Bassée road was choked with troops, guns, and transport, and we had to march miles north out of our way to get back to Cambrin. As it was we were held up two or three times by massed cavalry. Everything seemed in confusion. A casualty clearing-station had been planted astride one of the principal crossroads and was already being shelled. When we reached Cambrin we had marched about twenty miles in all that day. We were told then that the Middlesex would go over first with us in support, and to their left the Second Argyll and Sutherland Highlanders, with the Cameronians in support; the junior officers complained loudly at our not being given the honour of leading the attack. We were the senior regiment, they protested, and entitled to the "Right of the Line." We moved into trench sidings just in front of the village. There was about half a mile of communication trench between us and the trenches proper, known as Maison Rouge Alley. It was an hour or so past midnight. At half-past five the gas was to be discharged. We were cold, tired and sick, not at all in the mood for a battle. We tried to snatch an hour or two of sleep squatting in the trench. It had been raining for some time. Grey, watery dawn broke at last behind the German lines; the bombardment, which had been surprisingly slack all night, brisked up a little. "Why the devil don't they send them over quicker?" asked The Actor. "This isn't my idea of a bombardment. We're getting nothing opposite us. What little there is is going into the Hohenzollern." "Shell shortage. Expected it," answered Thomas. We were told afterwards that on the 23rd a German aeroplane had bombed the Army Reserve shell-dump and sent it up. The bombardment on the 24th and on the day of the battle itself was nothing compared with that of the previous days. Thomas looked strained and ill. "It's time they were sending that damned accessory off. I wonder what's doing."

What happened in the next few minutes is difficult for me now to sort out. It was more difficult still at the time. All we heard back there in the sidings was a distant cheer, confused crackle of rifle-fire, yells, heavy shelling on our front line, more shouts and yells and a continuous rattle of machine-guns. After a few minutes, lightly-wounded men of the Middlesex came stumbling down Maison Rouge Alley to the dressing-station. I was at the junction of the siding and the alley. "What's happened? What's happened?" I asked. "Bloody balls-up" was the most detailed answer I could get. Among the wounded were a number of men yellow-faced and choking, with their buttons tarnished green; these were gas cases. Then came the stretcher cases. Maison Rouge Alley was narrow and the stretchers had difficulty in getting down. The Germans started shelling it with five-point-nines. Thomas went through the shelling to battalion headquarters to ask for orders. It was the same place that I had visited on my first night in the trenches. This group of dug-outs in the reserve line showed very plainly from the air as battalion head-quarters, and should never have been occupied on the day of a bat-tle. Just before Thomas arrived the Germans put five shells into it. The adjutant jumped one way, the colonel another, the regimental sergeant-major a third. One shell went into the signals dug-out and destroyed the telephone. The colonel had a slight wound on his hand; he joined the stream of wounded and was carried as far as the base with it. The adjutant took charge. All this time A Company had been waiting in the siding for the rum to arrive; the tradition of every attack was a double tot of rum beforehand. All the other com-panies got it except ours. The Actor was cursing: "Where the bloody hell's that storeman gone?" We fixed bayonets in readiness to go up to the attack as soon as Thomas came back with orders. The Actor sent me along the siding to the other end of the company. The stream of wounded was continuous. At last Thomas's orderly appeared, saying: "Captain's orders, sir: A Company to move up to the front line." It seems that at that moment the storeman appeared with the rum. He was hugging the rum-bottle, without rifle or equip-ment, red-faced and retching. He staggered up to The Actor and said: "There you are, sir," then fell on his face in the thick mud of a sump-pit at the junction of the trench and the siding. The stopper of the bottle flew out and what was left of the three gallons bubbled on the ground. The Actor said nothing. It was a crime deserving the death-penalty. He put one foot on the storeman's neck, the other in the small of his back, and trod him into the mud. Then he gave the order "Company forward." The company went forward with a clatter of steel over the body, and that was the last heard of the storeman.

What had happened in the front line was this. At half-past four the commander of the gas-company in the front line sent a telephone message through to divisional headquarters: "Dead calm. Impossible discharge accessory." The answer came back: "Accessory to be discharged at all costs." Thomas's estimate of the gas-company's efficiency was right enough. The spanners for unscrewing the cocks of the cylinders were found, with two or three exceptions, to be misfits. The gas-men rushed about shouting and asking each other for the loan of an adjustable spanner. They discharged one or two cylinders with the spanners that they had; the gas went whistling out, formed a thick cloud a few yards away in No Man's Land, and then gradually spread back into the trenches. The Germans had been expecting the attack. They immediately put their gas-helmets on, semi-rigid ones, better than ours. Bundles of oily cotton-waste were strewn along the German parapet and set alight as a barrier to the gas. Then their batteries opened on our lines. The confusion in the front trench was great; the shelling broke several of the gas-cylinders and the trench was soon full of gas. The gas-company dispersed.

No orders could come through because the shell in the signals dug-out at battalion headquarters had cut communication both between companies and battalion headquarters and between battalion headquarters and division. The officers in the front trench had to decide on immediate action. Two companies of the Middlesex, instead of waiting for the intense bombardment which was to follow the forty minutes of gas, charged at once and got as far as the German wire—which our artillery had not yet attempted to cut. What shelling there had been on it was shrapnel and not high explosive; shrapnel was no use against barbed wire. The Germans shot the Middlesex men down. It is said that one platoon found a gap and got into the German trench. But there were no survivors of the platoon to confirm the story. The Argyll and Sutherland Highlanders went over too, on their left. Two companies, instead of charging at once, rushed back to the support line out of the gas-filled front trench and attacked from there. It will be recalled that the front line had been pushed forward in preparation for the battle; these companies were therefore attacking from the old front line. The barbed wire entanglements in front of this trench had not been removed, so that they were caught and machine-gunned between their own front and support lines. The leading companies were equally unsuccessful. When the attack started, the German N. C. O.'s had jumped up on the parapet to encourage their men. It was a Jaeger regiment and their musketry was good.

The survivors of the first two companies of the Middlesex were lying in shell-craters close to the German wire, sniping and making the Germans keep their heads down. They had bombs to throw, but these were nearly all of a new type issued for the battle; the fuses were lit on the match-and-matchbox principle and the rain had made them useless. The other two companies of the Middlesex soon followed in support. Machine-gun fire stopped them half-way. Only one German machine-gun was now in action, the others had been knocked out by rifle or trench-mortar fire. Why the single gun remained in action is a story in itself.

It starts like this. British colonial governors and high commissioners had the privilege of nominating one or two officers from their countries to be attached in war-time to the regular British forces. Under this scheme the officers appointed began as full lieutenants. The Governor-General of Jamaica (or whatever his proper style may be) nominated the eighteen-year-old son of a rich Jamaica planter. He was sent straight from Jamaica to the First Middlesex. He was good-hearted enough but of little use in the trenches. He had never been out of the island in his life and, except for a short service with the West Indian militia, knew nothing of soldiering. His company commander took a fatherly interest in Young Jamaica, as he was called, and tried to teach him his duties. This company commander was known as The Boy. He had twenty years' service in the Middlesex, and the unusual boast of having held every rank from "boy" to captain in the same company. His father, I believe, had been the regimental sergeant-major. The difficulty was that Jamaica was a full lieutenant and so senior to the other experienced subalterns in the company, who were only second-lieutenants. The colonel decided to shift Jamaica off on some course of extra-regimental appointment at the earliest opportunity. Somewhere about May or June he had been asked to supply an officer for the brigade trench-mortar company, and he had sent Jamaica. Trench-mortars at that time were dangerous and ineffective; so the appointment seemed suitable. At the same time the Royal Welch Fusiliers had also been asked to detail an officer, and the colonel had sent Tiley, an ex-planter from Malay, who was what is called a fine natural soldier. He had been chosen because he was attached from another regiment and had showed his resentment at the manner of his welcome somewhat too plainly. By September mortars had improved in design and become an important infantry arm; Jamaica was senior to Tiley and was therefore in the responsible position of commanding the company.

When the Middlesex made the charge, The Boy was mortally wounded as he climbed over the parapet. He fell back and began crawling down the trench to the stretcher-bearers' dug-out. He passed Jamaica's trench-mortar emplacement. Jamaica had lost his gun-team and was serving the trench-mortars himself. When he saw The Boy he forgot about his guns and ran off to get a stretcher-party. Tiley meanwhile, on the other flank, opposite Mine Point, had knocked out the machine-guns within range. He went on until his gun burst. The machine-gun in the Pope's Nose, a small salient opposite Jamaica, remained in action.

It was at this point that the Royal Welch Fusiliers came up in support. Maison Rouge Alley was a nightmare; the Germans were shelling it with five-nines bursting with a black smoke and with lachrymatory shells. This caused a continual scramble backwards and forwards. There were cries and counter-cries: "Come on!" "Get back, you bastards!" "Gas turning on us!" "Keep your heads, you men!" "Back like hell, boys." "Whose orders?" "What's happening?" "Gas!" "Back!" "Come on!" "Gas!" "Back!" Wounded men and stretcher-bearers were still trying to squeeze past. We were alternately putting on and taking off our gas-helmets and that made things worse. In many places the trench was filled in and we had to scramble over the top. Childe-Freeman got up to the front line with only fifty men of B Company; the rest had lost their way in some abandoned trenches half-way up. The adjutant met him in the support line. "You ready to go over, Freeman?" he asked. Freeman had to admit that he had lost most of his company. He felt this keenly as a disgrace; it was the first time that he had commanded a company in battle. He decided to go over with his fifty men in support of the Middlesex. He blew his whistle and the company charged. They were stopped by machine-gun fire before they had passed our own entanglements. Freeman himself died, but of heart-failure, as he stood on the parapet. After a few minutes C Company and the remainder of B reached the front line. The gas-cylinders were still whistling and the trench full of dying men. Samson decided to go over; he would not have it said that the Royal Welch had let down the Middlesex. There was a strong comradely feeling between the Middlesex and the Royal Welch. The Royal Welch and Middlesex were drawn together in dislike of the Scots. The other three battalions in the brigade were Scottish, and the brigadier was a Scot and, unjustly no doubt, accused of favouring them. Our adjutant voiced the general opinion: "The Jocks are all the same, the trousered variety and the bare-backed variety. They're dirty in trenches, they skite too much, and they charge like hell—both ways." The Middlesex, who were the original Diehard battalion, had more than once, with the Royal Welch, considered themselves let down by the Jocks. So Samson with C and the rest of B Company charged. One of the officers told me later what happened to himself. It had been agreed to advance by platoon rushes with supporting fire. When his platoon had run about twenty yards he signalled them to lie down and open covering fire. The din was tremendous. He saw the platoon on the left flopping down too, so he whistled the advance again. Nobody seemed to hear. He jumped up from his shell-hole and waved and signalled "Forward." Nobody stirred. He shouted: "You bloody cowards, are you leaving me to go alone?" His platoon sergeant, groaning with a broken shoulder, gasped out: "Not cowards, sir. Willing enough. But they're all f—ing dead." A machine-gun traversing had caught them as they rose to the whistle.

Our company too had become separated by the shelling. The Surrey-man got a touch of gas and went coughing back. The Actor said he was skrim-shanking and didn't want the battle. This was unfair. The Surrey-man looked properly sick. I do not know what happened to him, but I heard that the gas was not much and that he managed, a few months later, to get back to his own regiment in France. I found myself with The Actor in a narrow trench between the front and support lines. This trench had not been built wide enough for a stretcher to pass the bends. We came on The

Boy lying on his stretcher wounded in the lungs and the stomach. Jamaica was standing over him in tears, blubbering: "Poor old Boy, poor old Boy, he's going to die; I'm sure he is. He's the only one who was decent to me." The Actor found we could not get by. He said to Jamaica: "Take that poor sod out of the way, will you? I've got to get my company up. Put him into a dug-out or somewhere." Jamaica made no answer; he seemed paralysed by the horror of the occasion. He could only repeat: "Poor old Boy, poor old Boy." "Look here," said The Actor, "if you can't shift him into a dug-out we'll have to lift him on top of the trench. He can't live now and we're late getting up." "No, no," Jamaica shouted wildly. The Actor lost his temper and shook Jamaica roughly by the shoulders. "You're the bloody trench-mortar wallah, aren't you?" he asked fiercely. Jamaica nodded miserably. "Well, your battery is a hundred yards from here. Why the hell aren't you using your gas-pipes on that machine-gun in the Pope's Nose? Buzz off back to them." And he kicked him down the trench. Then he called over his shoulder: "Sergeant Rose and Corporal Jennings, lift this stretcher up across the top of the trench. We've got to pass." Jamaica leaned against a traverse. "I do think you're the most heartless beast I've ever met," he said weakly.

We went on up to the front line. It was full of dead and dying. The captain of the gas-company, who had kept his head and had a special oxygen respirator, had by now turned off the gas. Vermorel-sprayers had cleared out most of the gas, but we still had to wear our masks. We climbed up and crouched on the fire-step, where the gas was not so thick—gas was heavy stuff and kept low. Then Thomas arrived with the remainder of A Company and, with D, we waited for the whistle to follow the other two companies over. Fortunately at this moment the adjutant appeared. He told Thomas that he was now in command of the battalion and he didn't care a damn about orders; he was going to cut his losses. He said he would not send A and D over until he got definite orders from brigade. He had sent a runner back because telephone communication was cut, and we must wait. Meanwhile the intense bombardment that was to follow the forty minutes' discharge of gas began. It concentrated on the German front trench and wire. A good deal of it was short and we had further casualties in our trenches. The survivors of the Middlesex and of our B and C Companies in craters in No-Man's-Land suffered heavily.

My mouth was dry, my eyes out of focus, and my legs quaking under me. I found a water-bottle full of rum and drank about half a pint; it quieted me and my head remained clear. Samson was lying wounded about twenty yards away from the front trench. Several attempts were made to get him in. He was very badly hit and groaning. Three men were killed in these attempts and two officers and two men wounded. Finally his own orderly managed to crawl out to him. Samson ordered him back, saying that he was riddled and not worth rescuing; he sent his apologies to the company for making such a noise. We waited for about a couple of hours for the order to charge. The men were silent and depressed. Sergeant Townsend was making feeble, bitter jokes about the good old British army muddling through and how he thanked God we still had a navy. I shared the rest of the rum with him and he cheered up a little. Finally a runner came with a message that the attack was off for the present.

Rumours came down the trenches of a disaster similar to our own in the brick-stack area, where the Fifth Brigade had gone over, and again at Givenchy, where it was said that men of the Sixth Brigade at the Duck's Bill salient had fought their way into the enemy trenches, but had been bombed out, their own supply of bombs failing. It was said, however, that things were better on the right, where there had been a slight wind to take the gas over. There was a rumour that the First, Seventh, and Forty-seventh Divisions had broken through. My memory of that day is hazy. We spent it getting the wounded down to the dressing-station, spraying the trenches and dug-outs to get rid of the gas, and clearing away the earth where trenches were blocked. The trenches stank with a gas-blood-lyddite-latrine smell. Late in the afternoon we watched through our field-glasses the advance of the reserves towards Loos and Hill 70; it looked like a real breakthrough. They were being heavily shelled. They were troops of the new-army division whose staff we had messed with the night before. Immediately to the right of us was the

Highland Division, whose exploits on that day Ian Hay has celebrated in *The First Hundred Thousand;* I suppose that we were
"the flat caps on the left" who "let down" his comrades-in-arms.

As soon as it was dusk we all went out to get in the wounded. Only
sentries were left in the line. The first dead body I came upon was
Samson's. I found that he had forced his knuckles into his mouth to
stop himself crying out and attracting any more men to their death.
He had been hit in seventeen places. Major Swainson, the second-in-
command of the Middlesex, came crawling in from the German wire.
He seemed to be wounded in the lungs, the stomach and a leg.
Choate, a Middlesex second-lieutenant, appeared; he was unhurt,
and together we bandaged Swainson and got him into the trench
and on a stretcher. He begged me to loosen his belt; I cut it with a
bowie-knife that I had bought in Béthune for use in the fighting. He
said: "I'm about done for." * We spent all that night getting in the
wounded of the Royal Welch, the Middlesex and those of the Argyll
and Sutherland who had attacked from the front trench. The Germans behaved generously. I do not remember hearing a shot fired
that night, and we kept on until it was nearly dawn and we could be
plainly seen; then they fired a few shots in warning and we gave it
up. By this time we had got in all the wounded and most of the
Royal Welch dead. I was surprised at some of the attitudes in which
the dead had stiffened—in the act of bandaging friends' wounds,
crawling, cutting wire. The Argyll and Sutherland had seven hundred casualties, including fourteen officers killed out of the sixteen that went over; the Middlesex five hundred and fifty casualties,
including eleven officers killed.

Two other Middlesex officers besides Choate were unwounded;
their names were Henry and Hill, second-lieutenants who had
recently come with commissions from, I think, the Artists' Rifles;
their welcome in the Middlesex had been something like mine in the
Royal Welch. They had been lying out in shell-holes in the rain all

---

* Major Swainson recovered quickly and was back at the Middlesex Depot
after a few weeks. On the other hand, Lawrie, a Royal Welch company
quartermaster-sergeant back at Cambrin, was hit in the neck that day by
a spent machine-gun bullet which just pierced the skin, and died of shock
a few hours later.

day, sniping and being sniped at. Henry, according to Hill, had dragged five wounded men into his shell-hole and thrown up a sort of parapet with his hands and a bowie-knife that he was carrying. Hill had his platoon sergeant with him, screaming for hours with a stomach wound, begging for morphia; he was dying, so Hill gave him five pellets. We always carried morphia with us for emergencies like this. When Choate, Henry and Hill arrived back in the trenches with a few stragglers they reported at the Middlesex headquarters. Hill told me the story. The colonel and the adjutant were sitting down to a meat pie when he and Henry arrived. Henry said: "Come to report, sir. Ourselves and about ninety men of all companies. Mr. Choate is back, unwounded, too." They looked up dully. The colonel said: "So you've come back, have you? Well, all the rest are dead. I suppose Mr. Choate had better command what's left of A Company, the bombing officer will command what's left of B (the bombing officer had not gone over but remained with headquarters), Mr. Henry goes to C Company, Mr. Hill to D. The Royal Welch are holding the front line. We are here in support. Let me know where to find you if I want you. Good night." There was no offer to have a piece of meat pie or a drink of whisky, so they saluted and went miserably out. They were called back by the adjutant. "Mr. Hill! Mr. Henry!" "Sir?" Hill said that he expected a change of mind as to the propriety with which hospitality could be offered by a regular colonel and adjutant to temporary second-lieutenants in distress. But it was only to say: "Mr. Hill, Mr. Henry, I saw some men in the trench just now with their shoulder-straps unbuttoned and their equipment fastened anyhow. See that this practice does not occur in future. That's all." Henry heard the colonel from his bunk complaining that he had only two blankets and that it was a deucedly cold night. Choate arrived a few minutes later and reported; the others had told him of their reception. After he had saluted and reported that Major Swainson, who had been thought killed, was wounded and on the way down to the dressing-station, he leaned over the table, cut a large piece of meat pie and began eating it. This caused such surprise that nothing further was said. He finished his meat pie and drank a glass of whisky, saluted, and joined the others.

Meanwhile, I had been given command of the survivors of B Company. There were only six company officers left in the Royal Welch. Next morning there were only five. Thomas was killed by a sniper. He was despondently watching the return of the new-army troops on the right. They had been pushed blindly into the gap made by the advance of the Seventh and Forty-seventh Divisions on the previous afternoon; they did not know where they were or what they were supposed to do; their ration supply had broken down. So they flocked back, not in a panic, but stupidly, like a crowd coming back from a cup final. Shrapnel was bursting above them. We noticed that the officers were in groups of their own. We could scarcely believe our eyes, it was so odd. Thomas need not have been killed; but he was in the sort of mood in which he seemed not to care one way or the other. The Actor took command of A. We lumped our companies together after a couple of days for the sake of relieving each other on night watch and getting some sleep. The first night I agreed to take the first watch, waking him up at midnight. When I went to call him I could not wake him up; I tried everything. I shook him, shouted in his ear, poured water over him, banged his head against the side of the bed. Finally I threw him on the floor. I was desperate for want of sleep myself, but he was in a depth of sleep from which nothing could shake him, so I heaved him back on the bunk and had to finish the night out myself. Even "Stand-to!" failed to arouse him. I woke him at last at nine o'clock in the morning and he was furious with me for not having waked him at midnight.

The day after the attack we spent carrying the dead down to burial and cleaning the trench up as well as we could. That night the Middlesex held the line while the Royal Welch carried all the unbroken gas-cylinders along to a position on the left flank of the brigade, where they were to be used on the following night, September 27th. This was worse than carrying the dead; the cylinders were cast-iron and very heavy and we hated them. The men cursed and sulked, but got the carrying done. Orders came that we were to attack again. Only the officers knew; the men were only to be told just beforehand. It was difficult for me to keep up appearances with the men; I felt like screaming. It was still raining, harder than ever. We knew definitely this time that ours was only a subsidiary night attack, a diversion to help a division on our right to make the real attack. The scheme was the same as before. At four P.M. the gas was to be discharged again for forty minutes, then came a quarter of an hour's bombardment, and then the attack. I broke the news to the men about three o'clock. They took it very well. The relations of officers and men, and of senior and junior officers, had been very different in the excitement of the attack. There had been no insubordination, but a greater freedom, as if everyone was drunk together. I found myself calling the adjutant Charley on one occasion; he appeared not to mind it in the least. For the next ten days my relations with my men were like those I had with the Welsh Regiment; later discipline reasserted itself and it was only occasionally that I found them intimate.

At four P.M., then, the gas went off again. There was a strong wind and it went over well; the gas-men had brought enough spanners this time. The Germans were absolutely silent. Flares went up from the reserve lines and it seemed as though all the men in the front line were dead. The brigadier decided not to take too much for granted; after the bombardment he sent out twenty-five men and an officer of the Cameronians as a feeling-patrol. The patrol reached the German wire; there was a burst of machine-gun and rifle fire and only two wounded men regained the trench. We waited on the fire-step from four to nine o'clock, with fixed bayonets, for the order to go over. My mind was a blank except for the recurrence of "S'nice smince spie, s'nice mince spie. . . . I don't like ham, lamb or jam and I don't like roley-poley. . . ." The men laughed at my singing. The sergeant who was acting company sergeant-major said to me: "It's murder, sir." "Of course it's murder, you bloody fool," I agreed. "But there's nothing else for it, is there?" It was still raining. "But when I see's a s'nice smince spie, I asks for a helping twice. . . ." At nine o'clock we were told that the attack was put off; we were told to hold ourselves in readiness to attack at dawn.

No order came at dawn. And no more attacks were promised us after this. From the morning of September 24th to the night of October 3rd I had in all eight hours of sleep. I kept myself awake and alive by drinking about a bottle of whisky a day. I had never drunk it before and have seldom drunk it since; it certainly was good then. We had no blankets, greatcoats, or waterproof sheets. We had no time or material to build new shelters, and the rain continued. Every night we went out to get in the dead of the other battalions. The Germans continued to be indulgent and we had few casualties. After the first day or two the bodies swelled and stank. I vomited more than once while superintending the carrying. The ones that we could not get in from the German wire continued to swell until the wall of the stomach collapsed, either naturally or punctured by a bullet; a disgusting smell would float across. The colour of the dead faces changed from white to yellow-grey, to red, to purple, to green, to black, to slimy.

On the morning of the 27th a cry was heard from No Man's Land. It was a wounded man of the Middlesex who had recovered consciousness after two days. He was close to the German wire. Our men heard it and looked at each other. We had a lance-corporal called Baxter and he was tender-hearted. He was the man to boil up a special dixie of tea for the sentries of his section when they came off duty. When he heard the wounded man cry out he ran up and down the trench calling for a volunteer to come out with him and bring the man in. Of course no one would go; it was death to put one's head over the trench. He came running to ask me. I excused myself as the only officer in the company. I said I would come out with him at dusk, but I would not go now. So he went out himself. He jumped quickly over the parapet, then strolled across waving a handkerchief; the Germans fired at him to frighten him, but he came on, so they let him come up close. They must have heard the Middlesex man themselves. Baxter continued towards them and, when he got up to the Middlesex man, he stopped and pointed to show the Germans what he was at. Then he dressed the man's wounds, gave him a drink of rum and some biscuit that he had with him, and told him that he would come back again for him in the evening. He did come back for him with a stretcher-party and the man eventually recovered. I recommended Baxter for the Victoria

Cross, being the only officer who had seen the thing done; but he only got a Distinguished Conduct Medal.

The Actor and I had decided to get in touch with the battalion on our right. It was the Tenth Highland Light Infantry. I went down their trench some time in the morning of the 26th. I walked nearly a quarter of a mile before seeing either a sentry or an officer. There were dead men, sleeping men, wounded men, gassed men, all lying anyhow. The trench had been used as a latrine. Finally I met a Royal Engineer officer. He said to me: "If the Boche knew what an easy job it was, he'd just walk over and take this trench." So I came back and told The Actor that we might expect to have our flank in the air at any moment. We turned the communication trench that made the boundary between the two battalions into a fire-trench facing right; a machine-gun was mounted to put up a barrage in case they ran. On the night of the 27th the Highlanders mistook some of our men, who were out in No Man's Land getting in the dead, for the enemy. They began firing wildly. The Germans retaliated. Our men caught the infection, but were at once told to cease fire. "Cease fire" went along the trench until it came to the H. L. I., who misheard it as "Retire." A panic seized them and they came rushing back. Fortunately they came down the trench instead of over the top. They were stopped by a sergeant of the Fifth Scottish Rifles, a territorial battalion now in support to ourselves and the Middlesex. He chased them back into their trench at the point of the bayonet.

On the 3rd of October we were relieved. The relieving troops were a composite battalion consisting of about a hundred men of the Second Royal Warwickshire Regiment and about seventy Royal Welch Fusiliers, all that was left of our own First Battalion. Hammer Jones and Frank Jones-Bateman had both been wounded. Frank had his thigh broken with a rifle-bullet while stripping the equipment off a wounded man in No Man's Land; the cartridges in the man's pouches had been set on fire by a shot and were exploding. We went back to Sailly la Bourse for a couple of days, where the colonel rejoined us with his bandaged hand, and then further back to Annezin, a little village near Béthune.

NOT AN INCH TO BE YIELDED

The British and French moved to the offensive in the winter and spring months of 1915. There was savage fighting and severe losses, but no breakthrough. Allied troops often failed to reach even the first line of German trenches.

The Allied generals seemed to regard their troops as little more than pawns in a chess game. They rarely bothered to visit the trenches to observe the conditions under which their troops fought. At many points in the British lines positions had been taken early in the war that were vulnerable to those of the Germans. Rather than withdraw to allow their troops to adopt new positions furnishing better protection, General Headquarters ordered, "Not an inch to be yielded." In consequence, the British front, ". . . like the last few inches of a high tide, was everywhere indented by little areas of high ground, or groups of buildings at road junctions, or other sorts of positions that offered unusual advantages to the enemy.*

"Throughout these bleak months the German artillery dominated the situation, making life a misery for the British troops who were obliged to hold the line in greater strength either than the enemy or the French, owing to their own shortage of guns. For whereas their allies could afford to make their front positions little more than outposts that could call up an immense weight of artillery fire at the least sign of any suspicious activity on the part of the enemy, the British were dependent on rifle fire to cope with marauding patrols and local attacks. This was due to two things: in the first place the eighteen-pounders used for direct support were few in number, and hesitated to expose themselves except in an emergency owing to the fact that the heavier guns needed to support them against German

* *The Donkeys*, by Alan Clark, p. 36.

counter-battery fire were almost entirely absent. Secondly, they were so starved of ammunition as to make it futile to reveal their position for the sake of throwing the meagre daily 'ration' of shells at the enemy. In actual fact for the entire B.E.F. there was in the field only about three-fifths of the regulation amount *calculated on the experience of the Boer War*, and really little more than a day's supply in modern battle.

"The fire-power of the men in the front line was also seriously diminished by the shortage—amounting in cases to non-existence— of trench-mortars and hand-grenades. Of the latter a number of extemporized missiles were tried out, the most notorious being the 'jam-pot,' the 'Battye bomb' and the 'hairbrush'. These were dangerous and difficult to construct, their ignition was chancy and impossible in wet weather, and in general it is likely that they caused as many casualties among the British as among the enemy. No 'Mills' hand-grenades were produced until the spring of 1915—by March only forty-eight had been delivered. The trench-mortar, an ultra-short-range howitzer, more or less portable, with which the Germans were making great destruction, was even more rare in the Expeditionary Force." *

It can be acknowledged that few commanding officers had ever fought in battles approaching the size of some of the ensuing operations. But it is hard to understand the reluctance to take up new weapons and to plan a proper defense against the use of new weapons by the enemy—weapons such as poison gas, intensive massive artillery support for attacking forces, and the machine gun. As late as April 14, 1915 Sir Douglas Haig said "The machine gun is a much over-rated weapon and two per battalion is more than sufficient." **

Even more puzzling is the behavior of the British commanding officers who upon learning on good authority that the Germans were going to use poison gas, did not choose to believe it, and did not issue warnings to the men in the sectors where the gas was expected.

The first gas attack occurred at the Ypres salient on April 22, 1915.

* Clark, pp. 38, 39.
** Clark, p. 163.

"Throughout that morning the Germans had been putting heavy shell, 8 in. and 17 in. howitzers, on Ypres and the roads leading out of the town, but during the afternoon all was quiet. The sun shone gently on the flat countryside, glinting on the *Beekes*, the deep drainage ditches that meandered across the fields, still swollen with the rains of winter. Everywhere the green shoots of spring struggled upwards through the filth and squalor of battle. Right up to the support lines the land was still under cultivation. For four months the salient had seen no serious fighting.

"And then at 5 p.m. a new and furious bombardment of the town and the villages in front and to the north of it began. The enemy artillery, that had ranged accurately on to all these targets in the morning, now searched them out in crippling strength, making movement almost impossible. Soon those observers who were on points of vantage saw two greenish-yellow clouds creeping out across No-Man's-Land in the French sector, on either side of Langemarck. These clouds spread laterally, joined up and, moving before a light wind, became 'a bluish-white mist, such as is seen over water-meadows on a frosty night.' Then, as the enemy artillery fire lifted, dense masses of fugitives came stumbling down the roads from the direction of Langemarck and Pilckem. Few of them could speak, none intelligibly, many were blue in the face, others collapsed choking by the side of the road. At the same time onlookers began to feel a tingling of the nose and throat, and a tightening of the chest. At this time the mob was composed about equally of Tirailleurs, civilians and French African troops, but it soon became thicker and more disordered as the first of the French artillery teams and wagons attempted to drive their way through those on foot." *

The British were forced to retire, losing the high ground and nearly "half the breadth of the salient. The rest, under fire from three sides, was untenable.

"Second Ypres was, for its size, one of the most murderous battles of the war. The total casualties, including those due to gas, exceeded 100,000, those of the Allies being slightly the greater. By using poison

* Clark, pp. 74-76.

gas in defiance of the convention, the Germans gained the biggest success of the year in the west. They reduced the Ypres salient to a flat curve just east of the city and secured all the commanding ground. Yet, because their action had been experimental and they had so slender a reserve, they missed a far greater victory before the effect of surprise wore off." *

After the Allied failure to break through the German defenses in the spring, the British were loath to consider any more large-scale attacks until 1916. But Joffre, with a much larger artillery concentration to back up his troops was bent on a large-scale attack in the area of Champagne. He managed to persuade the British to combine with him to launch the greatest attack of the war to date to begin on Sept. 25.

"The major effort was in Champagne. Here the Eastern Group of Armies of General de Castelnau attacked on a front of fifteen miles halfway between Reims and Verdun, with two armies (Pétain and de Langle de Cary). The Germans had available only twelve divisions in line or local reserve, little more than a third of the French resources. The highest hopes accompanied the enterprise. Here, and in Artois too, cavalry stood ready to exploit a breakthrough. Buses were parked at hand to carry infantry in support. The French were all out for victory. Cloud gas was used on a large scale.

"There was no breakthrough. Initial success was considerable, with progress up to a mile and three-quarters at one point. The Germans were shaken, and only the insistence of Falkenhayn—who had hurried back from the Eastern Front—stopped a precipitate retreat. It was the new German second line that decided the issue. For the first time the Germans exploited the principle of defense in depth, having withdrawn part of their artillery behind the second line before the attack began. Deadlock having been reached, the French broke off the offensive on September 28. Their Artois offensive by d'Urbal's Tenth Army, in the Northern Group of Foch, accomplished less. It began badly, though Crown Prince Rupprecht of Bavaria had little more than two divisions in first line to meet it. On September

* Falls, pp. 111, 112.

28 a determined and gallant attack reached the crest of Vimy Ridge. Then the weather broke and the venture ended." *

The British offensive, according to Alan Clark, ". . . came at a transitional stage in the development of the British armies in France." ** They were reluctant to launch a new attack so soon after their spring losses. But once the die was cast, it was agreed that they would attack on September 25 at Loos.

"The scheme that appealed to Haig at the present time was to attack behind a 'wave' of chlorine gas, projected from cylinders. He had attended, earlier, a convincing demonstration of the possibilities of this technique and it had, among others, the advantage that it allowed the widening of the front from a two- to a six-division assault.

"There was a danger in this plan, however. To be sure of an effective 'wave' of gas, the engineers needed the wind in a certain quarter—west-south-west—and for it to be of at least moderate strength. Failing this the gas would simply hang about their own trenches, poisoning the troops crowded there waiting for the assault, or at best drift over towards the enemy lines in irregular gusts and patches, disrupting the uniformity and cohesion of the attack.

"As some insurance against this Haig had an alternative, 'inner' plan for an attack on a two-division front if unfavorable weather should cause the larger scheme to founder at the last moment. But, again, this was already seriously compromised by the fact that he had spread his guns, in themselves hardly adequate to support an offensive on this scale, over the larger front, so that the concentrated attack would be starting with the fatal handicap of dispersed supporting fire.

"Other factors, on a broader strategic level, were working against the success of the 1st Army's attack. Notwithstanding his earlier encouragement Joffre had privately become convinced, in the few weeks immediately preceding the date fixed for the opening of the offensive, that the ground in the Loos-Lens area was most unfavourable to the attacker, and had been shifting the main

* Falls, p. 114.
** Clark, p. 144.

emphasis of his own armies to the southern stroke in Champagne. However, on 14th September he gave a final explanation of his plans at a conference at Chantilly, attended by the three army group commanders and by French. At this meeting Joffre declared that the time was 'particularly favourable for a general offensive', and expressed his 'confidence in a great and possibly complete victory'. The simultaneous attacks were 'a certain guarantee of success'.

"1st Army Headquarters, too, were by now infected with optimism. Those who had doubts wisely held their peace, for 'disloyalty' or 'lack of offensive spirit' did not go unnoticed or unpunished.

"It was generally felt that the gas would work wonders—a view which ignored the fact that although gas will poison men, regardless of nationality, only high explosives will destroy wire." *

LOOS: FIRST AND SECOND DAYS**

by Alan Clark

At a quarter past five on the morning of 25th September, after an uneasy night spent in constant consultation with Captain Gold, the R. F. C. meteorological officer, Haig gave the orders to 'Carry on'.

Ponderously, for he had suffered a mild attack of asthma the previous evening, he climbed up the stairs of his wooden tower, his staff at his heels. As the sound of the bombardment, which had been unimpressive even at its height, abated, they peered across No-Man's-Land at the flickering bracelet of fire caused by the exploding shells as they crept slowly from the leading to the secondary German

* Clark, pp. 145-46.
** From *The Donkeys*, by Alan Clark.

positions. So still did the air seem that, as the minutes passed, all became infected by the fear that the gas would simply hang about the British trenches. After a quarter of an hour Haig made one of his staff telephone to 1st Corps to enquire whether it was possible to stop the arrangements for the attack. The answer came that 'General Gough did not consider it practicable to get word in time to the front trenches'.

Nor were they the only ones in doubt about the wisdom of releasing the gas; in Horne's 2nd Division the officer in charge of the gas on the 2nd Brigade front declined to assume the responsibility of turning on the cylinders. On this being reported to Horne he ordered that 'the programme must be carried out *whatever* the conditions'. The reluctance of the corps and divisional commanders to sanction any last-minute alteration in the plan is all the harder to understand when one discovers the very complex and thorough arrangements that had been made to ensure a last-minute cancellation if this should prove necessary. Between the higher formations three routes were arranged, by telephone, telegraph and despatch-riders. To pass the order on to the gas units, officers, attended by runners, were stationed at special points. Each of these officers had ready twenty typewritten slips, 'Attack postponed, taps *not* to be turned on until further notice'.

However, in spite of definitely unfavourable conditions on several parts of the attack front, these precautionary measures were nowhere implemented and, at nine minutes to six, the taps were opened.

There was certainly no shortage of gas. Until zero-hour at 6:30 over 150 tons were discharged from 5,243 cylinders concealed in sandbagged bays in the fire-trench. As the greenish-yellow chlorine came hissing out it slowly built up into a cloud from thirty to fifty feet high that billowed sluggishly forwards into No-Man's-Land. Overhead the German distress Verys curved red and white in the lightening sky and their forward machine-guns in the sap-heads began to chatter, firing short warning bursts at alternating elevations.

As the sun rose the wind did not increase. There can have been few among the infantry, packed like animals along the narrow slippery communication trenches, sweating in their improvised talc and flannel 'respirators', who did not feel a sense of foreboding as they waited for the subaltern's whistle. Far from being 'in a panic' the Germans had already begun to open bursts of deterrent fire and the bullets were slapping into the sandbag parados just above the heads of the waiting assault troops. Soon mortar-fire was added to this and, further back, the enemy field artillery began to come to life.

In front of Loos and further north in the region of the Hohenzollern Redoubt the gas cloud carried fairly well over the German trenches and was to exert a marked influence on the advance of the 47th, 15th and 9th Divisions, only falling short of complete success because it moved too slowly and there was not enough of it. But at the southern end of the front of the vapour, after thirty-five minutes' flow, it was still short of the enemy parapet. And in the centre, on both sides of the Vermelles-Hulluch road, it drifted in the right direction at first; but towards the end of the discharge began to float back and into the British trenches, giving rise, in the words of the *Official History*, to 'great inconvenience and some loss'. In other places, particularly on the 2nd Division front, the discharge had to be discontinued at once and no gas reached the German trenches.

There was some surprise effect, but it quickly wore off. The official narrative of the German 6th Army reads: 'In general the physical effect on the men was trifling.'

The drizzle of rain had cleared, leaving a thin ground mist, when, at 6:30 A.M., the infantry clambered out of the trenches, and in the fog of gas and smoke, which made it difficult to pick up landmarks, began the advance across No-Man's-Land. They were in fighting dress—without greatcoat and pack, but cumbered with bombs, picks and shovels, and extra rations. All ranks wore the original pattern smoke helmet—a flannel bag—over their heads, but with the front rolled up, and had a second helmet in their haversacks. With the front down they could hardly see through the talc-covered eye-holes, and with the front up the rain caused the chemicals in the flannel to soak out and irritate the eyes.

Although casualties were heavy at every point these varied from mere decimation to whole battalions being virtually obliterated, as did their achievements vary from the substantial and heroic to the utterly negative. If the course of the battle, and the causes of the ghastly massacre of the following day, are to be properly understood, it is best to follow briefly the fortunes of each of 1st Army's six divisions, starting at the southern end of the attack front opposite Loos village itself.

The 47th Division, at the extreme southern end, broke cleanly through the German first line—the men of 1/18th London Regiment dribbled a football in front of them as they crossed No-Man's-Land —at a cost of some 1,200 casualties, or roughly 15 per cent, in the first hour. Unfortunately, however, the right and centre of the division halted at the German rear support trench, which they began to organize for defence, instead of pressing forward towards Cité St. Pierre. In the meantime the London Irish, on the left of the division, had entered the southern outskirts of Loos village and the 1/20th London, passing through the Irish, carried all before them, taking in quick succession the cemetery, the 'garden city', arriving still full of fight, though now sadly depleted, at the heavily defended 'Chalk Pit copse' by 8:30 A.M. An hour later they had fought their way into the pit itself but their numbers were too few to evict the Germans dug in round the copse and they suffered severely under enfilade fire from this quarter while their comrades looked on from the old German support trench some 800 yards away.

On the left of the 47th was the 15th Division, whose assault brigades were made up entirely of Highland regiments. At zero-hour their assault was seriously impeded by the obstinacy of the gas cloud which simply hung about the congested trenches. Many of the men lingered in the hope that it would disperse or drift away towards the German lines and there was much difficult to-and-fro traffic in the crowded fire-trench as platoons made their way to places clear of cylinder bays. The situation was saved, however, by the extraordinary heroism of Piper D. Laidlaw of 7th K. O. S. B., who rallied the men by marching up and down the parapet playing 'Scotland the Brave' on the pipes, regardless of gas and enemy fire. He

continued to play even after being wounded and was awarded the
V. C. Once the assault got going the Highlanders pressed it with
great vigour and complete disregard for losses. It took them less than
an hour to penetrate both German trench lines in front of Loos
village and by 8 A.M. they were enthusiastically digging the garrison out of the cellars at the point of the bayonet.

Unfortunately the enemy's fire, and the prospect of his rout in the
village itself, had drawn all the Scottish regiments into the maze of
trenches and connected cellars there, to the detriment of the broad
plan of advance. Thus the front of the divisional attack narrowed
from 1,500 to less than 600 yards and the 7th K. O. S. B. on the
extreme left, who had achieved the deepest penetration of all,
reaching the line of the Lens road by 9:15, were left in isolation,
suffering intermittent shellfire from their own artillery. In Loos itself
the Highland regiments were by now thoroughly intermingled. A
very large proportion of their officers had been killed and many of
the subalterns remaining did not like to assume the responsibility of
giving orders, believing that their superiors were still alive but
perhaps lost in the confusion. The men themselves—'a magnificent
Border rabble'—believed that it was all over bar the shouting and,
by half past eight, were streaming out of the eastern end of the
village in great spirits and starting the ascent of Hill 70 in a somewhat leisurely manner. They had, in the words of a battalion diarist,
'the appearance of a bank holiday crowd'. Furthermore, as they
advanced up the bare slopes of Hill 70, the German garrison in the
redoubt there, which was at that time no more than a few
maintenance men and engineers, took to their heels. The sight of
their enemy running away was too much for the Scots and with a
renewed cheer they pressed forward and over the crest.

But once they were on the downward slope the troops of the 15th
Division were in full view of the Germans waiting behind the wire of
their very strong second line, which had been built outside the range
of the eighteen-pounders. And after they had travelled some half
distance down the bare slope, fire was opened by the enemy. The
Scots were completely pinned down. With only a few inadequate
entrenching tools they could make little impression on the hard

chalky soil. Some of them tried repeatedly to rush the wire. Others attempted to make their way back over the crest. But of the nine hundred or so who had advanced from the redoubt scarcely one survived.

During the day the Germans were rapidly reinforced and by the afternoon they were counter-attacking in sufficient strength to recapture the redoubt. The remnants of the 46th Brigade, now reduced to a handful, were rallied by Second Lieutenant Johnstone,* R. E., and made five separate attempts to retake it but were beaten off in each case.

The casualties of the division in this one day's fighting were nearly 5,400—or about 60 per cent—and some battalions, in particular the 9th Black Watch, 8th Seaforth, 7th Cameron, 7th K.O.S.B. and 1st Highland Light Infantry, were virtually annihilated. All the same the 15th and 47th Divisions had, though checked now and sadly depleted, made substantial gains in the first few hours. But further north, for the 1st and 7th Divisions, the situation was very different.

The attack plan of the 1st Division was, from the outset, of doubtful promise. On their right, or southern, flank No-Man's-Land was very wide. The opposing trench lines ran along the slopes of the Grenay Ridge, unobserved by each other and separated by the blind hump of the Col de Grenay on which stood 'Lone Tree', the enormous flowering cherry that had blossomed that May.** In consequence artillery observation both for cutting the wire and demolishing advanced saps had been very difficult, as also patrolling by night to investigate results. It had, accordingly, been decided to

---

* Lieutenant Johnstone was awarded a V.C. for his part on that day. He was killed at Delville Wood, 1916.

** After the blossoms had fallen a young lieutenant in the Seaforths had led a night patrol there and, climbing to the upper branches, had attempted to fasten a Union Jack to the trunk. Unfortunately, although successful in this, he had been caught in a flare on the way down and machine-gunned. For several days his body had hung there. Two attempts to re-cover it on subsequent nights failed and finally divisional artillery were directed on to the tree in an attempt to bury him. As the days wore on all the branches had been blown off but the guns never scored a direct hit and the stump remained, standing some fifteen feet high. It flowered again in 1920.

leave this sector out altogether and to concentrate the attack along the axis of the Vermelles-Hulluch road in the north, with the 1st Brigade to lead the attack and the 3rd Brigade in close reserve behind it.

At a later stage, however, as the plan worked its way up to Corps and Army level, amendments were made. In particular it was ordered that the Division's 2nd Brigade should after all make an attack to the south of Lone Tree. These instructions had the effect of weakening divisional concentration along the main axis of advance and, as the two brigades were from the outset directed to advance on diverging lines, threatened to aggravate this condition later. (To 'fill' this gap a composite force—known as 'Green's Force' from Lieutenant-Colonel E. W. Green, its commander—was created by taking away a battalion from each of the 1st and 2nd Brigade, and putting them back into reserve.) In particular, the orders meant that the 2nd Brigade was doomed, in effect, to be 'expended', for it had been given a task that was almost impossible.

And, as it turned out, the attack was a complete failure. The men were late in jumping off, as they suffered particularly from their own gas in this sector, and were badly enfiladed by machine-guns in two sap-heads that the Germans had run forward into No-Man's-Land. By the time the leading battalion reached the wire they had suffered over 400 casualties including their commanding officer, Lieutenant-Colonel Sanderson. The wire itself was some ten yards across, firmly staked low in the ground, and virtually intact. Thus, within an hour after zero, the remnants of the 2nd Brigade found themselves pinned down in hopeless disconnected positions among the craters and depressions immediately in front of the main German position, their numbers being steadily reduced by short-range artillery fire and mortaring. From time to time little groups would attempt to clear a way through the obstacle with wire-cutters, but all were shot. By 7:45 the smoke and mist had cleared, for the British artillery fire had long since passed on to more distant objectives, and the prospects of an assault became still more hopeless.

At this point the Brigade may be said to have disintegrated. 'A few officers,' the *Official History* records, 'nevertheless rallied their men

for another effort; but the attackers had lost heart and, individually
and by groups, began to struggle or crawl back to their original
trenches.'

The setback here, and the influence that it exercised on the mind
of the British commanders, was to have very serious consequences
on the operations further north.

Initially the attack of the 1st Brigade, opposite Hulluch, had
prospered, although once again at tremendous cost.

There were two small copses in No-Man's-Land in this sector,
known as Bois Carré and La Haie. For many months the artillery of
both sides had passed over them reducing them to little clusters of
shattered scrub and 1st Army Intelligence had classified them as
'unoccupied'. But in the weeks immediately preceding the offensive
the Germans had run saps out and into the undergrowth here. The
preparatory bombardment began along a line further in advance,
and the machine-gun nests there escaped untouched. Their crews
might have been incapacitated by the gas if things had gone right
but, as it was, the cloud progressed so slowly that the three lines of
British infantry were all deployed, fifty paces between each, and
advancing in full view of the enemy, before the Germans smelt the
first whiffs of vapour. Thus fire from these positions caused very
heavy casualties before the attackers had even got to grips with the
enemy.

On the right of the Brigade front the Gloucesters were the
assaulting force. With extraordinary courage they forced their way
into three successive German positions, but by the time they had
penetrated the German support line and reached the maze of
communication trenches that lay behind they were, in the words of
the *Official History*, 'destroyed as a battalion'. The fighting was
desperately exhausting and there was the utmost difficulty in
keeping a proper cohesion to the attack. By the time that they
arrived at the German wire the attacking infantry had, in almost
every case, lost a proportion of their officers and N.C.O.s so that
many sections were without proper instruction. The barrier itself
was seldom penetrable along its entire length and platoons and
companies would become badly intermingled and the confusion

more serious as they searched for and passed through such gaps as existed. Once in the German lines it became even harder for those in command to keep a full control of their men. The enemy system was very intricate in this sector and the trenches, eight feet deep with a raised fire-step on their western side, turned back and forth every eighteen feet or so in a series of orderly, buttressed, right angles. At intervals steps would lead down under the parados to the dug-outs where little groups of unharmed Germans lurked ready to emerge with grenades and machine-guns after the first attacking wave had passed over, or where, more often, lay numbers of shell-shocked and badly wounded defenders suffocating from the gas that lingered there, inert and deadly.

In this evil-smelling maze the British infantry became still further dispersed, and it was only with great difficulty that they could be rallied and induced to clamber out over the parados and attack, once again over open fire-swept ground, the German support trenches that lay some eighty yards in the rear. None the less, within half an hour of first entering the trench, the subalterns of the Gloucesters managed to mount a second attack on the German positions beyond. This, too, was successful, though at a sad price. As the men advanced across the broken, cratered earth, whole platoons would be reduced to mere handfuls of individuals as the German machine-gunners scythed into them again and again. But at the last moment their extraordinary courage broke the spirit of the defenders who turned and fled down the communication trenches to Hulluch, leaving their guns silent and smoking on the parapet and the British to cover the last fifty feet unmolested. By now, though, the 10th Gloucestershire existed in name only; less than sixty, of all ranks, survived the first two hours of the assault.

On the left of the Gloucesters the attack fared as well, and was less extravagant in life. It had been rehearsed for weeks before by the Berkshires—the leading battalion—against replicas of the German trench system constructed behind the lines from aerial photos. The result of this thorough training was a clean break-through to 'Gun Trench' by 8 A.M.—a penetration of three-quarters of a mile. This was the cleanest break on the whole front of the offensive, and that most urgently requiring exploitation. Here on 'Gun Trench', a shallow, wandering communication trench that connected a series of mortar pits, but was of little defensive significance, the Berkshires halted while the reserve battalion, the Cameron Highlanders, came up. Through the smoke the poplar trees along the Lens-La Bassée road could be seen. Immediately in front of them the firing had abated. It must have seemed that they were nearly through.

On their arrival the Camerons continued the advance at a good pace and by nine o'clock their forward elements had actually entered the village of Hulluch by progressing up Alley 4, a long 'arterial' communication trench that ran from the outskirts of the village across the northern part of the Loos Valley to the gun positions that had lain immediately behind. The German troops in the forward positions, never numerous, had been killed or wounded —there were many gassed and lightly wounded infantry lying on the floor of Alley 4 as the Camerons picked their way along—and the remainder had withdrawn, in considerable confusion, through the village and well behind the 'Second Position' for which, in spite of its natural strength, there were not enough men at that time.

Thus it was that the Camerons found themselves passing through 'gates' in the German wire, which the defenders in their haste had omitted to close, and heard their footsteps ringing in the deserted streets undisturbed by anything more lethal than an occasional shell from their own artillery, that was meant to be 'bombarding' the village. At the far, or eastern, end two enemy machine-guns and some infantry discouraged too close a follow-up without reinforcement but even they, in the words of the Company report sent back by the Camerons to 1st Brigade at 9:10 A.M., 'appear to be retiring'.

Here then, three hours after the start of the assault, was the critical point on the Loos front. For this small mixed force of the 1st Division—the Berkshires and the Camerons, and the remnants of the Gloucesters—were astride the German 'Second Position' at its most vulnerable point—that is, where it was closest to the original front line—with the choice of rolling it up to the north or the south, depending upon the course of the battle in those areas.

It was now essential to make sure that this spearhead could be adequately, and promptly, reinforced. Immediately available were the reserve battalions of the 1st and 2nd Brigade (Black Watch and 2nd Royal Sussex) and, less than an hour away, Colonel Green's force and the 3rd Brigade in its entirety—a total of some 6,500 men of whom none had yet seen action that day. Such numbers were more than adequate to force a clean break through the confused and battered German elements that held on to the eastern end of Hulluch village, and open a way, at last, for the cavalry that stood patiently among the copse and scrub on the far side of the Grenay Ridge.

But speed was essential. With every minute that passed the German defenders had time to recover their composure; the reinforcements that had been directed there as early as the previous evening began to arrive; the guns were manhandled into their new emplacements; the infantry were assembled, given their orders, shown their field of fire.

For the attackers, this of all times was not one to worry about the flanks. Although, in fact, the extraordinary heroism of the attacking infantry had more or less secured these at every point except on the 2nd Brigade front on Lone Tree Ridge—which, anyway, it had originally been planned to omit from the attack plan on account of its strength. But it was, most unfortunately, this very position with which the 1st Division Commander, Major-General A. E. Holland, was preoccupied. It was incomprehensible to him that British infantry should be stopped dead, as the 2nd Brigade had been. He knew from Intelligence reports that the force opposing them must be a small one. It was now, furthermore, cut off from any prospect of help from either Loos (by the 15th Division's advance) or from Hulluch (by his own 1st Brigade). Another attack would surely bring about its surrender and the 1st Division's front would be 'clean'. With this in mind the two supporting battalions, instead of being directed to reinforce the 1st Brigade, were ordered up with instructions to clear the German position on Lone Tree Ridge and 'press on'.

As might have been foretold by anyone inspecting the situation on the spot, this second attack, made without any pretence of artillery support, in broad daylight, with no protection from smoke or gas, was cut to pieces. More serious was the fact that, on the assumption that it would be successful, Green's force had been ordered forward to fulfil their originally conceived—but now quite meaningless— role.

This had two results. In the first place the men opposite Hulluch village were deprived of the prospect of immediate tactical re- inforcement from the 2nd Brigade reserve and, secondly, they saw the only substantial force (other than divisional reserve) that could have rendered them decisive assistance diverted to an objective that was militarily quite futile.

As Green's force set off it found that it, too, was under very heavy fire after breasting Lone Tree Ridge, owing to the failure of the latest attack by the 2nd Brigade reserve. Unable to use the com- munication trenches, which were filled with gassed and wounded men going in the opposite direction, both battalions were com- pelled to approach over open country under intense fire from a quarter which they had been told had already been successfully attacked. Soon they began to come up with the remnants of the 2nd Brigade and they, also, found themselves pinned down in the long grass in front of the German wire, unable to go forward or retire.

In the meantime precious hours were slipping past for the 1st Brigade, as the troops that it needed so badly for reinforcement were thrown away in frontal attacks directed against an enemy position that had already been outflanked. Lieutenant-Colonel Graeme, in command of the 1st Cameron Highlanders, could hear intense firing well to his rear, as the successive 2nd Brigade attacks went in. He realized the possibilities of an advance down the axis of the Lens road to outflank the enemy instead of repeatedly assaulting this front, and sent a succession of messages urging this course as well as that of occupying and consolidating Hulluch. But without reinforce- ment it would obviously be dangerous to further disperse his small mixed force and so they held on anxiously to the straggling cobweb formed by captured German gun-pits and such improvised trenches that the exhausted infantry had scratched in the hard chalk since their arrival.

Opposite them, the first of the German reserves were already beginning to arrive and move into the defensive belt that stretched away to the north and south, empty and undamaged. On their side, too, there was considerable confusion; the 26th Regiment, ordered up from Pont à Vendin, reported at midday: 'There appear to be no German troops ahead on a front of about three miles, and the forward batteries have all been over-run. How far the enemy has advanced is not known. The battalion will advance till it meets the enemy and be prepared for any eventuality.' At intervals the men of the 1st Brigade would, from their advanced position, be presented with splendid targets as the enemy infantry, all unknowing, would march up in close order. At one moment the Camerons opened fire on a detachment estimated at over 300 that was proceeding down the road between Hulluch and Benifontaine, with great effect. But with each bout of firing it was plain that the enemy was becoming more numerous and the British ammunition less plentiful. The men were short of water, also, and gradually, as the hours slipped past without relief or contact with the units on their flanks, an ominous sense of isolation began to envelop them.

There were now only two units left on the divisional front that were available as reinforcement. These were the Brigade's own reserve battalion, the 1st Black Watch, and the divisional reserve of three battalions in the 3rd Brigade. If these forces had been sent up immediately their combined strength ought still to have been sufficient to 'prop open' the breach in the German 'Second Position' at least for the twelve hours or so that must elapse before the Army Reserve, the 11th Corps, could arrive on the scene.

At this point in the battle the situation for Brigadier-General Holland was, the *Official History* tactfully records, 'full of difficulty'. However, in spite of the open breaches to the north and south of the German position, he decided against any outflanking movement and ordered yet another frontal attack, committing the whole of the 3rd Brigade and with it the last hope for any substantial help for the men in Hulluch. These orders arrived two hours late, owing to the loss of three runners in No-Man's-Land, and Colonel Green read 'with horror' the clear instructions to put in one battalion on either side of Lone Tree, to attack once again over this stretch of ground where the corpses were so thick and the groaning and calling for stretcher-bearers so insistent that the sound was 'like the cattle market at Devizes'.

Although he realized, as did everyone on the spot, the ease with which the German position could be outflanked, the orders were quite definite and, in view of the delays that had already taken place, there was no time to refer the question back to General Holland. So, at one o'clock, the two leading battalions (London Scottish and 1/9th King's were sent over the top, the majority of them to certain death, for

'. . . the approach of another attack did not have the expected effect on the resisting power of the Germans. Before the advancing lines had reached the wire, still intact, they were greeted with a hail of bullets at close range. Every attempt to get into the enemy trenches was in vain, the men being shot as they endeavoured to cut a way through the wire.'

The situation was aggravated by the fact that, owing to the sparsity of troops to the north, and their forward situation, the Germans on the 2nd Brigade front were all the time gradually working their way forward and northward along the trench line that the Berkshires and Gloucesters had passed over earlier in the morning. By midday they had even got a machine-gun back into position in the Bois Carré, which had been left unguarded in spite of the profusion of British troops in that area, and this had the effect of drawing off the 1st Black Watch—the last available unit that could have reinforced the 1st Brigade at Hulluch—who were instructed to dig in and seal off the old German line at the junction of the 1st and 2nd Brigade fronts.

Thus, by the early afternoon, there was a state of deadlock along the whole of the 1st Division front. The offensive had lost all momentum; the men were exhausted, without reserves, had suffered fearful casualties and the strength of the Germans opposite them was increasing hourly.

At four o'clock the German force that had held up the 2nd Brigade, and all but destroyed it and Green's force, surrendered. But this was for reasons quite unconnected with the succession of frontal attacks to which they had been subjected during the morning. For the Germans had been taken at last—and quite accidentally—in the rear by a small group of the 2nd Welch from the 3rd Brigade that had been driven northwards by the fierceness of the fire and, finding themselves more or less lost in the wide shelving expanse of the Loos Valley, had worked their way down and back towards the sound of battle along the Germans' own communication trenches, taking the defenders by surprise.

By now, though, it was too late, for almost at the same moment a German counterattack was driving the remnants of the 1st Brigade out of Hulluch and, although it was not pressed in sufficient strength to compel a withdrawal further than the line of the Lens road, its success did mean that the enemy 'Second Position' had now been restored in its entirety.

As this last short engagement died down the noise of battle abated. Leaden clouds, heavy with the rain that was to fall that night, darkened the Loos Valley as the remnants of the 1st Division trudged their way forward, unmolested now, their backs to a No-Man's-Land of hideous memory. Only the howitzers, eight miles in the rear, kept up their rumbling fire as the first big raindrops broke on the packs and helmets of exhausted infantry.

◆ ◆ ◆

Behind the assaulting troops was the newly formed 11th Corps consisting of the 21st and 24th Divisions,* the first of Kitchener's volunteer 'New Armies', who had only arrived from England a fortnight previously. It was to this force, under General Haking

* In the 11th Corps there was also the reorganized Guards Division but it was situated further back and separate from the 21st and 24th Divisions.

(promoted to corps commander following the 'aggressive spirit' he had shown at Aubers Ridge), that Haig, now desperately short of troops, turned his eye.

They had spent the three nights prior to the battle moving up towards the line from their concentration area west of St. Omer and were in no condition to face immediate action. Moreover they were the only units in reserve behind the 1st Army front and Sir John French did not wish to see them used in the offensive. Nevertheless, as a result of Haig's urgent requests, the 21st and 24th were finally placed at his disposal.

Whether French intended them simply to consolidate the ground gained, serving as replacements for the enormous losses that had been suffered on the 25th, or whether they were to be used as an instrument with which to renew the offensive, is not clear. The real intentions of the two commanders have been obscured by the bitter controversy and recrimination that followed on the fate of the two divisions. But there is no doubt that Haig and French diverged at this point. Haig saw his offensive already stalled. Unclear orders, fumbling at brigade and divisional level, and the enormous casualties that had followed thereon had seriously impaired the balance and condition of the attacking forces. The most that Haig could hope for was that the Germans were in similar plight. Perhaps he felt another 'punch', thrown quickly, might still give him a chance to let loose his horses. The thought seems to have occurred to him that with these troops their very 'freshness' might be an advantage; with the enthusiasm of ignorance they would tear their way through the German line. Of them he wrote that 'having been so short a time in France they have not yet acquired the sedentary habits of trench warfare'. . . . At its crudest, they didn't know what they were up against.

But French seems to have been getting uneasy about the prospects of the attack even some days before its actual launching, and this may explain his half-hearted effort to keep the 11th Corps under his wing. On the 24th September he wrote: 'In view of the great length of line along which the Army is operating I feel it to be necessary that I should keep a strong reserve under my own hand.' Twice he resisted Haig's insistence on being granted absolute control of the 11th Corps, until finally he relented after visiting advanced H.Q. at Lillers at midday on the 25th.

Then, at the shortest notice, the 21st and 24th Divisions were ordered up from their billets—which were a considerable distance from the firing line—against a tide of congestion. As they made their way forward ugly rumours spread from mouth to mouth. Past them, in the opposite direction, the ambulances creaked and jolted in endless procession; among them, following the same routes and accorded priority,* were the convoys of fodder for the cavalry. It was not until nightfall that they began to get clear of the complex of roads and lanes that were still crammed to capacity with supply and medical echelon and now awash under the heavy rain, and began to deploy in their final assembly positions behind Lone Tree Ridge.

As the men were formed up in the darkness for their cross-country march to the Lens-La Bassée road the confusion was considerable. Neither division had had longer than two weeks in France and their total training period in England had been no more than four months. They had, moreover, only a slight leavening of regular officers and N.C.O.s. None of the divisional staffs were familiar with the ground and there had been no time to issue large-scale maps. The men were soaked to the skin and, as the kitchens had been left behind, there was no hot food available. Thus it is not surprising to find that their deployment was only three-quarters complete by daybreak. By this time the troops had been continuously on the move for over eighteen hours, with only the customary halt of ten minutes in the hour while on the road. Even more serious was the fact that a thick mist, hanging over the area at dawn, led to the divisional artillery getting into positions some half-mile ahead of that allotted to them, so that when it cleared they were in full view of the German batteries about Haines and Hulluch. Thus the guns were effectually neutralized from the start.

But in spite of the complete exhaustion of all ranks, their morale

---

* Owing to the short notice at which the 21st and 24th Divisions had been ordered forward, no marking tapes or other arrangements for directing them had been provided along the route.

was high. This was to be the division's first action, but they had been told that all that was required of them would be a long march in pursuit of a demoralized enemy. Both Haig and Haking, the corps commander, had assured them that they would 'not be put in unless and until the Germans are completely smashed and retiring in disorder'.

However, in contrast with his general assurance, Haig's *explicit* orders for the 26th were that the divisions were to continue the battle. These orders, issued from 1st Army H.Q. at 11:30 on the night of the 25th, while the wretched troops of the 21st and 24th Divisions were still stumbling about in the darkness on Lone Tree Ridge preparing for their cross-country march, emphasized the importance of the various 'attacks' that were to start in at 11 A.M. the following day.

At 9 A.M. Haig saw the three corps commanders concerned at his headquarters. He had breakfasted. He enlarged on the orders of the previous evening. The divisions were to push on through the German 'Second Position' and take the Haute Deule Canal, some five miles distant, as their objective. Such an advance, he said, might turn the whole enemy position to the south and even force the Germans to evacuate Lens itself.

If given in good faith this appreciation must be reckoned ludicrously optimistic. Nor did it square well with his assurances that the battle had entered a pursuit phase. No blame for Haig's mental confusion can be attached to Intelligence, who had accurately predicted the German dispositions. They had also sent a warning to 1st Army H.Q. that the German local reserves (a total of five divisions in the threatened sector) could begin to reach the battlefield within twelve hours of the alarm. In point of fact twenty-two additional battalions arrived in the battle area within twenty-four hours, so that by zero-hour on the 26th the German 'Second Position' was as strongly held as had been the front line at the time of the original assault the day before.

In contrast to the attack of the previous day—which had, at least, been preceded by a four-day artillery bombardment and a half-hour discharge of gas along the entire front, and had, moreover, been carried out by four selected divisions trained for the assault in every detail for weeks beforehand—the hapless 21st and 24th Divisions were expected to cross No-Man's-Land in broad daylight with no gas or smoke cloud to cover them, with no artillery support below divisional level, and attack a position as strongly manned as had been the front defences and protected by a formidable and intact barbed-wire entanglement.

The German 'Second Position' was in the form of a tall, shallow 'D'. Originally, in depth, it had consisted of an 'ID' with the village of Loos lying between the two letters, and the 'I' representing the first line. But this 'I' had been overrun in the previous day's fighting. The very strong enemy 'Second Position' followed the curve of the 'D', swinging round from the twin villages of Hulluch and Benifontaine in the north down to the Hill 70 Redoubt in the south, and giving terrible enfilade and cross-fire over the gently sloping Loos Valley. The bar of the 'D' was formed by the Lens road that stretched straight down from north to south, white with chalk dust, marked by an occasional leafless tree. Inside this area was a mass of small quarries and mineshafts, and a densely wooded copse, the Bois Hugo. These, as has been seen, were evacuated by the Germans during the fighting of the 25th but were reoccupied as reinforcements came up, and formed an excellent outpost line for machine-gunners and sharp-shooters. The diary of the 15th Reserve Regiment records:

'One battalion in particular had an excellent position along the edge of a disused quarry overgrown with thick bushes and scrub. They were well concealed from view, and yet had a perfect field of fire to front or flank. Four machine-guns were placed in position there, with the champion machine-gunner of the regiment at one of them.'

A tragic aspect of the situation lies in the fact that all of this area, and large stretches of the German 'Second Position', could have been taken for the picking the previous afternoon. A battalion of the German 26th Regiment, marching up from Annay to occupy the sector between Hulluch and the Bois Hugo, was told to make all haste as the British might already have entered it. So probable did this in fact seem that the battalion deployed half a mile from it just before dusk and advanced against it in extended order, only to find it empty. During the night many other opportunities had passed; two more battalions, of the 153rd Regiment, came up into the Bois Hugo sector of the second-line position south of the 26th Regiment and advanced into the wood itself at dawn, under cover of mist. As this cleared they attacked the outposts of the 63rd Brigade at the western end of the wood and drove them back, thereby enfilading the front position of the brigade immediately north of the wood and forcing them to retire back across the Lens road. As the morning wore on the Germans in the wood were reinforced by a battalion each of the 93rd and 165th Regiments and extended their line southwards, joining up with the reinforcements—a further six battalions strong—that had arrived to strengthen the position at Hill 70.

These, and other minor local counterattacks carried out by the Germans with the intention of improving their defensive position, must surely have given 1st Army H.Q., and to both Haig and Haking, ample warning that an unprepared attack by two untrained divisions was unlikely to succeed. But the question of revising the order in the light of the Intelligence reports does not seem to have been considered. And so the stage was set for a repetition—at a distance of sixty-one years, in slow time, under conditions of infinite squalor and magnified in scale a hundredfold—of the charge at Balaclava. For the set-piece attack of 11th Corps, that was to be launched in the broad light of an hour before noon on the 26th, was as futile, and as foredoomed, as that of the Light Brigade.

As the morning wore on the British perfected their order of battle. Theirs was a depressing situation. They had had to cross the No-Man's-Land of the previous day, that was littered with the corpses of the Devon and Highland Regiments, lying in long straggling rows as the German machine-guns had traversed along their ranks. Among these were still many wounded who called out piteously to the newcomers for water and assistance. As assembly points the two divisions were using the former German front line. To make access to this easier, engineers had cleared gaps in the wire at regular intervals, but no one had yet had time to remove the contorted, lifeless figures that still hung at so many points on the entanglement. In the trench itself, and in the adjacent dug-outs, were pockets of gas, and many German dead, hideously yellow and blue in colour. The stench was frightful.

But the spirit of the men was unshaken. The official historian records that: '. . . they were delighted at the prospect of getting at the enemy after the exertions and frustrations of the last few days, although they had had hardly any food, and no sleep for forty-eight hours.'

Just after 10 A.M. a desultory pattern of artillery fire, unworthy of the term 'bombardment', was thrown at the German positions. Without their own artillery the 21st and 24th were paying the price of Haig's 'flexible' distribution of guns for the first stage. Indeed the gunners could have no very clear idea of where the German emplacements were located and simply fired off patches of shells, assorted H.E. and shrapnel, at likely looking points. The Germans suffered no casualties and the wire remained intact. This fire lasted some twenty minutes, and then for half an hour the front was practically silent.

Punctually at eleven o'clock the British rose out of the ground. Peering across the shelving valley of rank grass, slag and white chalk craters, the German look-outs could see column after column moving up in close formation at the crest of Lone Tree Ridge, the officers on horseback, marshalling successive battalions as they rose out of the old German trenches and formed up in a dense mass.

At first the effect was unnerving. Not since the German attacks in the closing days of the first battle of Ypres had such dense masses of infantry deployed for a daylight assault. Sheer weight of numbers must, it seemed, carry the British through the thinly spread German outposts. The colonel of the 15th Reserve Regiment has described how he was walking in the main street of Hulluch when an experienced N.C.O. from the Machine Gun Company came running up to him and shouted out, 'Two divisions. . . we will be surrounded . . . we must retire. . . .' A number of men were following close behind, panic-stricken. But almost simultaneously another officer, who had been watching the situation from a housetop, came up and told him that the situation was not so serious. 'The machine-gun and rifle fire from our position is terrific and no enemy can possibly advance across the open against it.' Quickly, extra detachments were organized and sent into position. For fully ten minutes the Germans held their fire as the two divisions deployed in column of extended line and started obediently off on their progress down the gentle slope towards the Lens road. It was a tense moment for the enemy, watching in silence until, as the leading columns of the 24th Division passed under the south-east front of Hulluch, at a range of 1,000 yards, the order to fire was given.

The diary of the 15th Reserve Regiment records that:

'Ten columns of extended line could clearly be distinguished, each one estimated at more than a thousand men, and offering such a target as had never been seen before, or even thought possible. Never had the machine-gunners such straightforward work to do nor done it so effectively. They traversed to and fro along the enemy's ranks unceasingly. The men stood on the fire-steps, some even on the parapets, and fired triumphantly [jauchsend] into the mass of men advancing across the open grass-land. As the entire field of fire was covered with the enemy's infantry the effect was devastating and they could be seen falling literally in hundreds.'

As the British infantry advanced they started to come across little pockets of dead and dying from the detachments of the 2nd Brigade that had pressed too far the previous day.

Some of these, delirious, stood up and screamed at them to turn back, or to fetch stretcher-bearers, or to duck down and join them in an adjacent crater. But the discipline of the two divisions never wavered. Slightly in front of the lines walked the subalterns, shouting encouragement: 'Come on, me lads, we're nearly there.' 'It won't last long.' 'We'll soon be at 'em.' 'Show 'em what we are,' and so forth.*

* Corporal J. Woosnam of the 8th East Yorks of 62nd Brigade of 21st Division has told me: 'The Lieutenant leading our Company, Harris or Harrison I think he was called, kept on talking all the time that we were going forward. He said the same thing over and over again—"Come on, my lads, show them what we are." After we had been advancing for about ten minutes he was hit

And indeed a German diary noted with amazement:

'In spite of it [the intensity of the fire] the extended columns
continued their advance in good order and without interruption.
When they reached the Lens road one of our companies advanced
from the Hulluch trench in an attempt to divert the attack, but only
a small party of the enemy swung round to meet it, the mass took
no notice and went on regardless past the southern front [of the
village]. Here they came under the enfilade fire both of the troops
lining the position and of a battery of artillery concealed in the
village. Their losses mounted up rapidly and under this terrific pun-
ishment the lines began to get more and more confused. Nevertheless they went on doggedly right up to the wire entanglement.'

This barrier consisted of hard steel barbed wire, too thick to be cut
with the hand-clippers that had been issued to some sections, braced
and criss-crossed among pine stakes and pit-props driven thirty-five
centimetres into the earth. Its height was over four feet and its depth
across five metres, or nearly nineteen feet.

Desperate, the men hurled themselves at it in frenzy; some tried to
scramble over it as one might a thick yew hedge, others pulled at it
with their bare hands; still more ran up and down along its edge in
the hopes of finding a gap that might have been cut by shellfire, until
they were cut down. The German diary continues:

'Confronted by this hopeless impenetrable obstacle and faced by
continuous machine-gun and rifle fire the survivors began to turn
and retire in confusion, though scarcely one in ten that had come
forward seemed to go back again.'

On the right flank the 21st Division was being dashed to pieces in
like manner. The diary of the 153rd Regiment tells the same sort of
story as that of the 15th:

'. . . dense masses of the enemy, line after line, appeared over the
ridge, some of their officers even mounted on horseback and advancing as if carrying out a field-day drill in peacetime. Our artillery and
machine-guns riddled their ranks as they came on. As they crossed
the northern front of the Bois Hugo, the machine-guns there caught

---

by a burst of machine-gun fire in the stomach which lifted him right off the
ground. He was calling for water and we gave him some although he was
going to die, which he did in a few minutes' time.'

them in the flank and whole battalions were annihilated. The English made five consecutive efforts to press on past the wood and reach the second-line position, but finally, weakened by their terrible losses, they had to give in.'

For the troops attacking the western end of the wood and struggling up the bare slopes of Hill 70 conditions were, if anything, worse.

One of the German battalion commanders spoke later of the revolting and nauseating impression made on them all as they watched the slaughter; so much so that after the retreat had begun they ceased fire. Before them was the 'Leichenfeld [field of corpses] von Loos', and, as among them dozens of khaki-clad forms rose up once again and began to limp and crawl back to their own lines, 'no shot was fired at them from the German trenches for the rest of the day, so great was the feeling of compassion and mercy for the enemy after such a victory'.

There had been twelve battalions making the attack, a strength of just under ten thousand, and in the three and a half hours of the actual battle their casualties were 385 officers and 7,861 men. The Germans suffered no casualties at all.

In the late afternoon, as the remnants of the two divisions rallied once more on Lone Tree Ridge, General Haking, the corps commander, came down from his H. Q. and moved among them, asking 'What went wrong?' The answer that he got from all, according to the *Official History*, was 'We did not know what it was like. *We will do all right next time*.'

. . . Such was the spirit of those who had answered Kitchener's call 'Your Country needs you.'

For these men were volunteers. They were the flower of the richest, most powerful, nation on earth. Behind them stretched the ordered childhoods of Victorian Britain; decency, regularity, a Christian upbringing, a concept of chivalry; over-riding faith in the inevitable triumph of right over wrong; such notions were imbued in them. This had been their first time in action, but if these were the rules of the game, well then, they would conform.

THE YEAR OF KILLING

On the Western Front, there were two great land battles fought in 1916, at Verdun and the Somme. According to the military historian Cyril Falls, "For sheer horror no battle surpasses Verdun. Few equal it." *

As the year 1915 drew to a close, with both sides once again seemingly at stalemate, both Germany and the Allies planned full-scale offensives.

Joffre asked for a common effort from all the Allies to be launched at approximately the same time. Together with the growing British forces he would hurl their combined armies in the north along a front of sixty miles forming a T across the Somme River. But before they could attack, the Germans struck at Verdun in the south. There the French once again suddenly found themselves with their backs to the wall.

General Falkenhayn, the German commander, had ordered the heaviest concentration of artillery ever seen. He meant to attack the French strong point, draw as many French divisions into battle as would take the bait, and by the fury of the German attack obliterate the French armies. In a memorandum to the Kaiser, Falkenhayn said, "Within our reach behind the French sector of the Western Front there are objectives for the retention of which the French General Staff would be compelled to throw in every man they have. If they do so the forces of France will bleed to death—as there can be no question of a voluntary withdrawal—whether we reach our goal or not. If they do not do so, and we reach our objectives, the moral effect on France will be enormous."

In the first weeks of 1916 the Germans massed over 1,200 pieces of artillery on an eight-mile front before Verdun. By February 1, they

* Falls, p. 186.

were in position. "In the woods ringing Verdun there was hardly room for a man to walk between the massed cannon and ammunition dumps." * The Germans concealed most of their movements with great success. The thick woods that abounded the area and the winter mists furnished effective cover. Huge underground concrete shelters were built to house the German troops, while the German Air Force formed a protective umbrella over the area.

Verdun was reputed to be the world's strongest fortress. "On the ground, Verdun's defenses looked dreadfully impressive. Surrounding it on all sides were the steep Meuse hills whose unusual concentric pattern itself formed an immense natural fort, with a radius of five to ten miles. . . . The crest of each important hill or ridge in this great natural stronghold was itself studded with powerful forts. To the south of Verdun, but unconcerned in the great approaching battle, were still further clusters of forts. Of all, the most powerful, and indeed, the cornerstone, was Douaumont; which, from its 1,200-foot elevation, dominated the terrain at every point of the compass like a scaled-down Monte Cassino.

"From the time of Vauban, French engineers have led the world in the ingenuity of their fortifications, and Verdun was no exception. Each fort was so sited that its guns could dislodge any enemy appearing on the glacis of its neighbour. The guns themselves, sometimes either a heavy 155 mm. or twin short-barrelled 75s, were housed under heavy steel carapaces in retractable turrets, and were invulnerable to all but a a direct hit from the heaviest artillery. They were supplemented by equally well-protected machine-gun turrets and ingeniously placed block-houses containing flanking guns that could repel an attack on the fort from any direction. The bigger forts contained a company of infantry or more underground, and the more modern were armoured with reinforced concrete up to eight feet deep under a thick layer of earth. They were in fact like ranks of immobile, but apparently indestructible tanks, or a flotilla of unsinkable monitors. Furthermore, as the battle had receded in 1914, the outer line of the forts had been left with a protective cordon of trenches in the foothills between them and the Germans, two or

* From *The Price of Glory* by Alistair Horne, p. 43.

three miles deep; which the French had had a relatively undisturbed fifteen months to make as impregnable as might be." *

But since 1914 the French had lost faith in these stationary strongholds. The huge German guns had destroyed such strongholds in the North with ease. In consequence they had stripped many of the forts of their heavy guns and had moved the defending troops elsewhere as well. The local French commander had resisted to no avail these inroads on his defenses. Joffre continued to decimate the strength of Verdun. Then in late January the first news of the German buildup trickled into the Allied headquarters and alarm broke out. Reinforcements were rushed but there was no time to prepare positions. The storm broke on February 21.

"The bombardment was very violent and punctuated by the frightful explosions of 305-mm. and 420-mm. howitzers. In many places the trenches of the first position were obliterated. Some gas shell and a great deal of lachrymatory was mingled with the high explosive. Nevertheless, the assault launched at 5 P.M. was disappointing. Two divisions actually fell back to their starting line during the night. Yet the Germans gained a footing in the foremost trenches and annihilated one French regiment, which lost 1,800 men out of 2,000. French reserves were on the move, but only one division was close at hand. The French command awaited the morrow with deep anxiety.

"This proved justified. By February 24, the Germans had progressed all along their front to a maximum depth of three and a half miles. The second position had been captured. Worse still for the French, unsteadiness had appeared in a battalion of North African *tirailleurs*, who could not face the drumfire north of Louvemont in the center of the front. That day the commander of the central army group, General de Langle de Cary, decided to abandon the plain of the Woevre, which had not been attacked.

"Blacker still was February 25, a day as ignominious for the French as it was brilliant for the Germans. An unnecessary withdrawal occurred near the left flank, accompanied by indiscipline and even panic, though, as always happened in this battle, when some

* Horne, pp. 48, 49.

troops cleared out, others blocked the enemy before he could break through." *

But most ignominious of all was the coup at Fort Douaumont.

VERDUN:
THE FALL OF FORT DOUAUMONT**

by Alistair Horne

No unit of the German Army was more strongly imbued with regimental pride than the 24th Brandenburgers of General von Lochow's III Corps. With intense pride the regiment recalled Blücher's tribute from the Napoleonic Wars: 'That regiment has only one fault; it's too brave.' From the moment of joining the 24th, young ensigns had that drilled into them, plus a dictum of Frederick the Great which had become a regimental motto: 'Do more than your duty.' In 1914, the 24th had romped through Belgium, hit the British Expeditionary Force hard at Mons, then marched on to the Marne. As it goosestepped through France, swigging 'liberated' Champagne and lustily singing 'Siegreich wolln wir Frankreich schlagen,' there seemed no limit to the regiment's successes. Great had been its indignation when the order came to turn about on the Marne. In February 1916, the 24th had just returned from a victorious campaign in the Balkans where it had helped hurl the Serbs out of Serbia. Now, at Verdun, things had not gone brilliantly so far for the regiment. Stubborn French resistance in Herbebois had led to shaming delays, and

* Falls, p. 189.
** From *The Price of Glory*, published by St. Martin's Press.

administered a bloody nose to the 3rd Battalion, which, to a regiment accustomed only to success, seemed to be almost a disgrace; especially when at the other end of the line there were reports of how well the Westphalian reservists, mere farmers in uniform, had done. As the French line bent and cracked before them, the Brandenburgers strained at the leash after fresh laurels with which to redeem the setback. Ahead there now loomed ever closer the greatest laurel of all; Fort Douaumont. Ever since they had been in the line at Verdun they had had an eye on its great tortoise hump. You could not escape from it. Like a small rodent under the unblinking gaze of a hawk, it made you feel quite naked and unprotected. At the same time, it beckoned with an irresistible magnetism.

Then, to the 24th's intense fury, just when the great fort seemed only a couple of day's fighting away, Corps HQ placed it within the boundary of advance of the neighbouring regiment, the 12th Grenadiers. In their marching orders for February 25th, the Brandenburgers were to halt on an objective about half-a-mile short of the fort, eventually leaving it on their right for their bitter rivals. It was unspeakably unfair.

From whatever angle you approached Fort Douaumont it stood out imposingly, menacingly. Hardly a square yard of terrain lay in dead ground to its guns. To the tottering French, it gave the comfortable feeling of having a mighty, indestructible buttress at one's back. It was, as Marshal Pétain later described it, the cornerstone of the whole Verdun defensive system. It was also the strongest fort in the world at that time—on paper. Started in 1885 as part of the 'de Rivières Line', Douaumont had been modernised and strengthened in 1887, in 1889, and again as recently as 1913. The huge mass was constructed in the traditional polygon shape favoured by Vauban, and measured some quarter of a mile across. The outer edge of the fort was protected by two fields of barbed wire 30 yards deep. Behind them came a line of stout spiked railings, eight feet high. Below stretched a wide ditch, or dry moat, 24 feet deep, girdling the fort. At the northern corners were sited concrete galleries, facing into the moat, and at the apex was a double gallery, shaped like a flattened letter 'M'. These three were (supposedly) armed with light cannons or pom-poms, machine guns and search-lights, so that any enemy climbing down into the moat would be caught by a deadly enfilading fire from two corners. Each gallery was connected to the centre of the fort by a long underground passage, enabling it to be reinforced regardless of enemy fire. Next, on the north side, came the gradually sloping glacis, itself swept by the fort's machine gun turrets—should the flanking galleries some-how have been knocked out. Even if an enemy survived the traversing of the glacis and penetrated to the Rue de Rempart that ran from East to West across the middle of the fort, he could still be taken from the rear by the garrison emerging out of shelters deep below ground.

At the southern under-belly of the fort, the entrance was protected by an independent blockhouse, also with double flanking galleries. The southwestern approach was masked by a bunker, called a 'Casemate de Bourges', out of which fired two 75 mm field guns. Meanwhile, the whole of this side of Douaumont also came under cover of the guns of Fort Vaux and other neighbouring fortifications.

Inside, the fort was a veritable subterranean city, connected by a labyrinth of corridors that would take a week to explore. There was accommodation for the best part of a battalion of troops, housed in barracks on two floors below ground level. The barrack rooms had rifle embrasures in the thick concrete of the exposed, southern side, so that each could put up a spirited defence as an independent pill-box; if ever the enemy got that far. As a reminder to the garrisons of their duty, there was painted up in large lettering in the central corridor: 'RATHER BE BURIED UNDER THE RUINS OF THE FORT THAN SURRENDER.' But the real teeth of the fort lay in the guns mounted in its retracting turrets. There was a heavy, stubby-barrelled 155 that could spew out three rounds a minute; twin short 75s in another turret mounted in the escarpment to the north; three machine-gun turrets, and four heavily armoured obser-vation domes. For their epoch, the gun turrets were extraordinarily ingenious; their mechanism adopted, with little alteration, for the

Maginot Line thirty to forty years later. Forty-eight-ton counter-weights raised them a foot or two into the firing position; but the moment the enemy's heavy shells came unpleasantly close, the whole turret popped down flush with the concrete. Only a direct hit of the heaviest calibre on their carapace of two-and-a-half-foot thick steel could knock them out, and until they were knocked out they could exact a murderous toll on an approaching enemy. Though, under Joffre's purge of the forts in 1915, the guns in the flanking galleries and the *Casemate de Bourges* had been removed, these powerful turret guns were still in operation.

The whole fort lay under a protective slab of reinforced concrete nearly eight feet thick, which in turn was covered with several feet of earth. Unlike the great forts of Belgium that had caved in beneath the blows of the German 420s, the concrete roof of Douaumont had been constructed like a sandwich, with a four-foot filling of sand in beween the layers of concrete. The sand acted as a cushion, with remarkable effectiveness. Exactly a year before the Verdun offensive began, in February 1915, the Crown Prince had brought up a battery of 420s to try their hand at Douaumont. Sixty-two shots in all were fired, and German artillery officers noted with satisfaction 'a column of smoke and dust like a great tree growing from the *glacis* of Douaumont'. The fort guns remained silent, so the Germans assumed that Krupp's 'Big Bertha' had once again done its stuff. In fact, though the reverberations and concussion within the fort had been extremely unpleasant, the bombardment achieved little other than knocking away half the inscription, *DOUAUMONT,* over the main gate. (Why the fort's 155 never returned the fire was quite simple; its maximum range was just over 6,000 yards, which would not have carried as far as the French front lines.) In the bombardments of February 1916, again the German 420s had caused negligible damage. Thus, it seemed—contrary to the pessimism of Joffre and G. Q. G.—that Douaumont was virtually impregnable.

By February 25th, 1916, the attacking Germans had reason to assume that Fort Douaumont had been badly knocked about, but was still likely to prove a stubborn and prickly obstacle. Never could they have guessed that it was both undamaged and—through an almost unbelievable series of French errors—to all intents and purposes undefended!

The 24th Brandenburg Regiment's orders for February 25th were to capture Hassoule Wood, then halt on a line about 750 yards to the northeast of Douaumont. The usual annihilating bombardment had started at 9 A.M. and was to lift to the fort itself, when the attack would begin. The line-up was as follows: 2nd Battalion on the right, 3rd on the left, with the 1st in reserve. On the right flank the 12th Grenadiers (in whose line of march the fort now lay, but who were also to halt short of it), and on the left the 20th Regiment, were to advance simultaneously. But in one of those last minute upsets that occurred so frequently in the First War when runners and word-of-mouth took the place of 'Walkie-Talkie', neither regiment received its orders in time. So at zero hour as the barrage lifted, the 24th found itself advancing unsupported. Rather typically, it paid no attention and thrust forward with its usual impetuousness. As luck would have it, instead of finding itself in a nasty trap, the 24th burst into a vacuum left by the Zouaves that had melted away the previous day. The few remaining French in the Brandenburger's path scattered rapidly, in some disarray. Two hundred prisoners were taken, and then followed a wild pursuit after a fleeing enemy. Within less than 25 minutes, advanced detachments from the 2nd Battalion of the 24th had reached the objective, having progressed over three-quarters of a mile. It was just about a record for that war.

On the extreme left of the 2nd Battalion was a section of Pioneers, commanded by a Sergeant Kunze. Kunze at twenty-four was a regular soldier of Thuringian peasant stock; from his photograph one gets the impression of heavy hands and limited intelligence; from his subsequent action, one gets an impression of complete fearlessness, but perhaps of that variety of boldness that often reflects lack of imagination. Men like Kunze were the backbone of any German Army; they would go forwards in execution of what they held to be their orders, unquestioningly and unthinkingly, until at last a bullet dropped them. In the usual practice of the German Army, Kunze's section had been detailed to accompany the first wave of storm troops, to clear any wire or other obstacle that might hold them up. Aided by the land contours, it was on the objective well to the fore. Kunze himself had already had an eventful afternoon. In a captured machine-gun post he had stopped and given first-aid to a wounded French NCO, but the ungrateful gunner had somehow regained his weapon and reopened fire. Kunze hastily returned and dispatched the man with little compunction. At another enemy position, a few minutes later, Kunze saw a Frenchman raise his rifle, but he shot first. When at last he reached the objective his blood was thoroughly up; after the day's brief action he was, in that favourite but quite untranslateable German Army expression, *unternehmungslustig.* As he paused to recover his breath, he saw the great dome of Douaumont looming ahead, incredibly close to him, terrifying but at the same time irresistibly enticing. French machine guns were chattering away busily to the right, but the Fort seemed silent. Kunze now reconsidered the orders he had received that morning; to eliminate all obstacles in front of the advancing infantry. And here, just in front of him, was the biggest obstacle of all! Ignoring in the excitement of the moment the other order—not to go beyond the prescribed objective—and with little thought as to what he would do when (or if) he got there, he set off in the direction of the Fort. His section followed obediently. Ten men against the world's most powerful fortress! It seemed an act of the most grotesque lunacy.

Within a matter of minutes Kunze and his section reached the wire on the Fort glacis. Encouragingly enough, nobody had fired at them, but Kunze had noticed the 155 in the Fort shooting over their heads at some distant target. He also noticed troops on the right flank of the 24th being given a bad time by a French machine gun cunningly placed aloft the church spire in the village of Douaumont. Much of the heavy barbed wire had been torn up by the German bombardment, and—with the aid of their pioneer wire-cutters—the section soon made a way through the two entanglements. They reached the spiked railings some 50 yards east of the northern apex of the fort. It was now shortly after 3:30. There was absolutely no way of getting through or over the obstacle. Kunze now followed the railings, moving leftwards; his choice apparently dictated by the machine gun over to his right. He turned the north-east corner and there, just round it, to his delight was a gap about four feet wide that a shell had blasted in the railing. While contemplating how to get down into the 24-foot abyss of the moat, Divine Providence made up Kunze's mind for him, in the shape of a near-miss that wafted him over the edge. Temporarily stunned, but otherwise unhurt, Kunze now urged the rest of his section to join him. A corporal, convinced by now that the section leader was out of his mind, announced that he was pulling back, but—possibly persuaded by their own heavy shells which were still falling thickly on the exposed superstructure of the Fort—the remainder lowered each other down to where Kunze was standing.

The moat was deserted. Near the breach in the railings were what looked like some small windows and a closed steel door (they were in fact the orifices of the north-east Gallery), set high up in the face of the wall. The barrel of a small cannon could be seen protruding from one, so Kunze and his men rapidly took cover as best they could among the debris lying about in the moat. But there was no sign of life here either. Once again, without pausing to consider the possible hazards, Kunze set about getting into the gallery. The steel door, however, was stoutly barred, and the gun embrasures were over 12 feet from the bottom of the moat. Then Kunze suddenly remembered something from the tedious PT exercises of pre-war days. Quickly he ordered his men to form a human pyramid. Several times it collapsed in a tangle of limbs, but eventually Kunze was able to squeeze his body through an embrasure, pushing aside the unmanned revolver-cannon that stood there. The gallery was quite empty. After several efforts, he prized open the steel door, and exhorted his men to climb up into it. Faced though with this gaping, tenebrous mouth in the Fort exterior, and all the terrible unknown perils that might lie beyond it, Kunze's little troop now began to lose its nerve. Death under one's own shells was infinitely preferable! All but two melted away, abandoning the sergeant in his folly.

Still never hesitating, Kunze set forth down a long, inky-dark tunnel. After the ear-splitting din of the bombardment outside, the silence was oppressively eery. On and on plunged Kunze. The tunnel seemed endless. Where was it leading them? And where was the French garrison? At last came some stairs. Kunze climbed them, then found at the top that the passage branched. He could now hear what sounded like the dull boom of a heavy gun firing close at hand. Leaving his two companions to cover one passage, he followed the other towards the sound of the firing. Soon he was close enough to hear the clatter of ejected cartridge cases. Pistol in hand, the intrepid sergeant flung open a door, bellowing '*Händehoch!*' Four French gunners, faces blackened with powder, stood there in utter astonishment. Before they could collect their wits, they had been roughly hustled out of the turret. Single-handed Kunze had stopped the fire of the 155 mm gun, the biggest in the fort.

In the midst of this grim battle an interlude of almost Marx Brothers comedy now began. On emerging from the turret, Kunze must have taken the wrong turning in the Douaumont rabbit warren; he was unable to re-discover his two companions keeping watch in the passage. Instead, marching the four Frenchmen before him, Kunze saw daylight glimmering ahead and once again heard the noise of the bombardment. Soon they came out into the open (the south courtyard of the Fort), and suddenly the prisoners bolted. Quick as lightning they turned back into another opening in the fort. Kunze followed, and was about to fire when they disappeared into a doorway to the left. Kunze caught a rapid glimpse of a barrackroom where an elderly NCO appeared to be giving a lecture to a group of about twenty men. Once again Kunze shouted '*Händehoch!*' but at that instant a heavy shell exploding above blew out the candles inside the room. In the ensuing confusion, Kunze's immediate thought was, 'Now they will rush me.' Quickly he slammed the heavy door, and, as luck would have it, was able to lock it from the outside. For a while Kunze kept watch outside the barrackroom, but no new candidates for his bag appeared. Time began to grow heavy on his hands, and he resumed his reconnaissance in search of further exploits. Soon he ran into another unarmed French soldier, who in utter terror kept calling him '*mon Capitaine*'. Though not speaking a word of French, Kunze somehow made it plain that he wanted to know where the Fort's officers were.

Accordingly, his latest trembling captive led him into another barrackroom, evidently belonging to the officers' mess. The room was empty, but upon a table stood a large basket full of eggs, wine and other provisions. It was something Kunze had not seen for many a month. He had not had a square meal since the battle began, and only iron rations during the miserable weeks of waiting in the *Stollen*. Suddenly he felt ravenously hungry. In his simple peasant mind the instinct to eat and drink now overruled all other considerations. The prisoners locked up in the barrackroom, his presence alone in a hostile fort surrounded by the enemy, the very war itself, all was forgotten. Before the astounded eyes of his latest captive Kunze sat down and began to gorge himself.

But where, one might ask, was the main garrison of this mighty bastion during all these events?

At the beginning of the war, Douaumont had a permanent garrison of some 500 infantrymen. Then, in 1915, Joffre's order de-rating the forts had sent the garrison out into the line, leaving only the artillerymen manning the remaining turret guns (by a twist of Fate, Douaumont's first wartime garrison had been decimated fighting near the Bois des Caures in the first days of the battle, its commander severely wounded). Under the statutes governing French fortresses, those at Verdun came directly under the Governor of Verdun—now General Herr. The Corps Commander in whose sector they lay had no control over them. Thus when General Chrétien had paid a visit to Douaumont on first taking up his command, he had received an extraordinary rebuff. At the drawbridge he had been turned away by the elderly *Gardien de Batterie*, a mere Warrant Officer called Chenot, with the words: 'The fort opens only to the Governor of Verdun. I cannot allow anybody to enter without his order. I wasn't warned of your visit. I should have you arrested as a spy!' Thus after this humiliating episode Chrétien worried no more about the fort, assuming perhaps that if it could keep out a three-star General it had little to fear from the enemy; in any case, it was not *his* responsibility. When the battle began the occupants of Douaumont in fact consisted only of Sergeant-Major Chenot and his 56 Territorial gunners manning the 155 and 75 turrets that alone had kept their weapons after the Joffre purge. On the desperate day of the 24th, General Herr had actually dictated that all the Verdun forts be prepared for demolition; Douaumont's tenants had accordingly been increased by one Sapper sergeant, but the officer sent from Verdun to organise the mining disappeared *en route*. The mining was never carried out.

Meanwhile, the first two brigades of XX Corps had arrived on the scene and at Souville Chrétien was about to hand over his command to General Balfourier. Shortly before this took place, he had been rung up from Verdun by a frantic Herr and told to reoccupy 'the line of the forts' and 'defend them to the last'. As one of his last acts, Chrétien detailed his staff to pass this order on to the divisional commanders. On his arrival, Balfourier, exhausted from the long forced march, accepted without query Chrétien's assurance that the garrisoning of the forts was in hand, that there was nothing to worry about there. General Deligny, the commander of the two new brigades that were up in position on both sides of Douaumont, asked Chrétien whether he should not set up his HQ in the Fort. No, said Chrétien, the fort is taken care of, you can take over my HQ here when I pull out tomorow.

Under the stress of sustained battle, the best-regulated staffs sometimes break down. Errors that would otherwise be inconceivable arise. Such a one occurred now. Somebody on Chrétien's staff, perhaps a humble Corporal-Signaller, forgot to transmit the vital order for the reoccupation of the forts. Deligny, separated from Chrétien's HQ by just a partition, swears he never heard of the order until it was already too late the next day. Up at the front the two brigadiers concerned—comfortably assuming that Fort Douaumont lay between them as a solidly defended bulwark, while recalling the dreadful reputation forts had for attracting shell-fire—ordered the regiments under them to give it the widest possible berth.

While Kunze was sating his appetite within the Fort, from the wings without, three officers of the 24th were preparing their various appearances. Their names were Radtke, Haupt and von Brandis. In short succession, but quite independently of each other from their different points on the battlefield, they too had been seized by the intoxicating magnetism of Douaumont. Radtke was a twenty-four-year-old lieutenant in 6 Company, a reservist who with his rimless glasses and sloping shoulders reminds one more of a bank clerk or petty official than a Prussian officer. With his platoon he had followed more or less the same course as Kunze though the objective, and then on to the edge of the Fort's wire, creeping up under cover of a defile called Strawberry Ravine. When he emerged into the open again at the wire he was surprised not to find himself fired upon by the French in Douaumont village. His two worries were the heavy German bombardment coming down around him and the fact that there appeared to be no sign of the 12th Grenadiers on the right. Radtke fired off all his Very cartridges to get the guns to lift their barrage, but as often happened they were not noticed by the artillery. The nerves of some of his men were beginning to crack under the intense shelling, but Radtke urged them on. Like Kunze he easily found a way through the wire, and reached the Fort near the northern apex, but somewhat to the right of Kunze. To his great good fortune a heavy shell had in the meantime blown a new, and much larger gap in the railing near the apex. It had also blasted a hole in the edge, leaving a pile of debris in the moat immediately below, so that the actual drop was considerably reduced. Followed by about twenty men, Radtke clambered down into the moat; the first German officer to enter Fort Douaumont.

To some extent, Radtke's leap into the Douaumont moat must have required more real courage than Kunze's. About half an hour behind, he could not have seen Kunze enter the moat unchallenged, and as an officer he knew enough about fortifications to expect to be met by a murderous fire from the flanking galleries. As soon as he realised that these were in fact unmanned, he set up some heavy timber, discovered in the moat, against the breach to facilitate the entry of succeeding groups. Instead of breaking into a gallery like Kunze, Radtke and his men now moved forward up over the glacis, creeping on all fours because of the German shelling. Having reached the Rue de Rempart, they soon found an opening leading into the upper floor of the barracks. Here the corridors were lit by dimly flickering kerosene lamps. There was a sound of footsteps, the

Germans crouched back in the shadows, and Radtke made his first
bag of three unarmed and terrified Frenchmen. To his astonishment,
they told him there were only about sixty men in the Fort, and then
promptly led him to another group of five in a barrackroom.

On the floor below, Kunze had now finished his meal and decided
it was time to resume duty. Marching his single prisoner down the
corridor, he propelled him into the room where he had incarcerated
his other prisoners. But, *du lieber Gott,* the room was now empty! At
this very moment they were probably alerting the whole garrison.
The full significance of his dereliction began to dawn on Kunze.
How could he explain matters to his officer? As a final touch of
comedy, a relief crew of four French gunners had meanwhile
reached the 155 turret, utterly dumbfounded at finding no trace of
the crew they were to relieve. Nevertheless, with a Gallic shrug of
the shoulders, they took their posts and after an interruption of
about half an hour the gun once again started firing aimlessly into
the distance.

Captain Haupt now makes his appearance. Aged nearly forty, a
modest officer of long service, Haupt was the commander of the 7th
Company. Gathering as many of his company as he could, Haupt
moved towards the fort five minutes after Radtke. It was now
snowing heavily. When one of his subalterns objected that they had
already gone far beyond the halt line, Haupt replied, 'We are going
to storm the fort.' Approaching from a little further to the right,
Haupt's group came under heavy fire from the machine guns in the
spire of Douaumont Church, and a subaltern was mortally wounded.
Haupt pressed on, to find the north breach in the railings and
Radtke's conveniently placed timbers. Still the German heavy shells
rained down on the Fort, and with commendable bravery one of
Haupt's men now stood upright on the top of the Fort to wave a large
artillery flag, in hopes of stopping the fire. Entering the upper floor
of the barracks in much the same way as Radtke, Haupt almost
immediately ran into a French gunner, who, it transpired, had found
Kunze's twenty-six captives, and released them, some quarter of an
hour earlier. Demoralised by this encounter with a fresh set of
Germans, he quickly led them to the white-bearded Chenot himself,

evidently taking refuge from the bombardment on the lower level of the Fort. The poor man was almost overcome with distress when he realised that the fort had been invaded by only a handful of Germans.

Gradually, all the threads became knitted together. Radtke met up with Haupt; Kunze was re-discovered by his officer, Lieutenant Voigt, who had reached the Fort with Haupt, and to whom Kunze now gave only the most blurred account of his recent activities. Assuming command as the most senior officer present, Haupt quickly organised the defence of the Fort against a possible French counter-attack, and sent Radtke to winkle out the remnants of the garrison. Their extraordinary success made the Germans suspicious that a hidden time bomb would now blow the Fort and themselves to smithereens, so for double security the unhappy Chenot and his fellow captives were lodged in a room right above the magazines.

The arrival of Haupt and his capture of Chenot form the point at which Fort Douaumont passed from French to German hands. The whole day's fighting had cost the Brandenburg Regiment only thirty-two dead; not a shot had been fired in defence of the world's greatest bastion, the loss of which, in the estimation of one French divisional commander at Verdun, was to cost France a hundred thousand men.

It was now about 4:30, three-quarters of an hour after Kunze had landed in the moat.

There remains von Brandis and his somewhat equivocal role in the capture of Douaumont. Brandis was a twenty-seven-year-old regular *Oberleutnant* (the nearest equivalent rank in the British Army would be Captain) commanding 8 Company. Through his own writings he betrays some of the less attractive Prussian characteristics; bombast and the contempt of the *Übermensch* for the lesser European breeds. On marching to the Marne in 1914, he had noted scornfully the rustic untidiness of French farms, deducing that this was a true indication of the decadence of the race. War, in von Brandis' eyes, was a succession of demoralised Frenchmen, hands above their heads, murmuring *'Pardon, Camarades!'* On February 25th, Brandis' company had been on the extreme right of the battalion. Undoubtedly it had had the worst time that day. The non-appearance of the 12th Grenadiers and heavy machine-gun fire from Douaumont village had both slowed down his advance and caused him more casualties than any other company. Thus at 4:30 he was well behind Haupt's and Radtke's companies, and still out in the open. According to Brandis' story, at the moment when he, too, was seized with the impulse to move on the Fort he had no idea that anyone else had got there first. But a remark made to the Battalion Adjutant at this time reveals that he *had* in fact seen Haupt's group reach the fort, and it seems unlikely that at least someone in his company should not have noticed the large German artillery flag when it was waved from the top of the Fort at so short a distance away. In a swirling snow storm, he reached the north breach, strangely enough not fired upon by the French in the village, to whom he was of course closer than either Haupt or Radtke had been. He and his men clambered down the timbers that stood under the breach, without—supposedly—pausing to wonder who might so conveniently have placed them there, and without noticing the tracks made by the fifty-odd men who had reached the fort before him. Traversing the glacis, he entered the Fort interior through an opening at the east end, and descended to the lower floor, where behind a closed door French voices were heard. A soldier who had once been a waiter in France shouted out 'vous êtes prisonniers', and a lively debate ensued, with the French within querying how they would be treated. When told 'as soldiers', twenty-six territorial gunners came out (Brandis claimed 'between fifty and sixty'). All the French in the Fort had been rounded up, without a shot being fired. There were now just over ninety Germans on the scene. Shortly before 5, Brandis met Haupt, and as second in seniority was put in charge of external defence. A quarter of an hour later, in the gathering dusk, Brandis' men repulsed a weak French patrol approaching the Fort, the only attempt to retake it that day. At 5:25, Haupt sent Brandis back to report to the C. O. and bring up the rest of the battalion. This was the full extent of Brandis' part in the capture, though it was not the last that would be heard of Brandis.

Before leaving the actual seizure of Douaumont, two puzzling questions about the French defence need to be answered. Why had

Chenot not seen the Germans approaching, and why had he not brought his twin 75s to bear on them? Why had the French troops on either side of the fort apparently done so little to stop them?

The answer to the first question is a simple, and human one. Though none of the 420 shells had penetrated the Fort's concrete, the effect of the last three days' bombardment on the occupants had been demoralising. Each time a heavy shell landed above, lamps blew out, corridors were filled with dust and asphyxiating fumes, and the reverberations underground imparted a sensation of being inside an immense drum. Well might the elderly Territorials have feared that any moment the Fort would collapse about their ears. Consequently, Chenot and all the gunners not actually manning the 155 gun turret had taken refuge as far below surface as possible; on the cellar floor. After his capture, Chenot claimed in self-defence that the observation domes were destroyed. This was not so; they were simply unmanned. Isolated from the rest of the world, out of touch with the course of the battle, Chenot had no idea that the Germans had advanced at such fantastic speed during the past twenty-four hours. Therefore, he had seen no need to man the observation domes. The crew of the 155, encased in their turret, had merely been firing blind on computed positions; on targets which had long since moved on. Some warning that the Germans were nearer than anticipated had apparently reached Chenot about half an hour before his capture. He had still not ascended from the cellars to verify this himself, but had sent a crew to man the 75s for the first time. It was too late, Radtke was already in the Fort and apprehended the gunners *en route*.

The answer to the second lies in the last of the series of tragic French errors. It will be recalled that the two brigades on either side of Fort Douaumont, the first arrivals of Balfourier's 'Iron Corps', had been told that the fort could look after itself. On the 25th, the 95th Regiment was solidly occupying the village of Douaumont, with excellent observation to the northern approaches of the Fort. In the haste and confusion of its arrival, all it knew of neighbouring friendly forces was that somewhere on its right (i.e. covering the Fort to the North) was a regiment of Zouaves. During the afternoon, the machine guns in the church spire had kept up a brisk fire on the attacking Brandenburgers, about half a mile away. It was snowing hard and visibility was worsening rapidly. Suddenly a group of men appeared, well in advance of where the Germans had last been spotted, heading up the glacis of the Fort, and within a couple of hundred yards of the flanking French company. This company at once opened fire, but the supposed enemy neither returned the compliment, nor was fired upon from the Fort; moreover it was marching straight into its own heavy barrage. Straining his eyes in the grey of the blizzard, the French company commander now gave the order to cease fire; it was painfully clear to him that his company had been firing on their own side. He swore that he could now even distinguish their *Chéchias*, the characteristic headgear worn by Zouaves. Thus the detachments of Haupt and Brandis had been allowed to progress the last vital yards up the glacis and into the Fort virtually unchallenged by the French 95th. (Kunze and Radtke, it will be remembered, approached the Fort in covered ground, along a defile to the east.) What the French had mistaken for *Chéchias* must have been the German helmets with their spikes removed to facilitate passage through the dense Verdun thickets. Pericard and Durassié, the principal French witnesses to this event, incredulous that Douaumont could have been taken without recourse to some kind of Trojan Horse guile, insist to this day that the Germans were clad in captured Zouave uniforms. Alas, no sufficient evidence to corroborate the thesis of the 'false Zouaves' has ever come forward. Certainly none of the men Chenot saw that afternoon was dressed in anything but *Feldgrau*.

In Germany, scenes of great jubilation acclaimed the capture of Douaumont. It was, as a British war correspondent noted later, 'the highwater mark of German efforts on the Western Front', the most notable triumph there since the breakthrough to the Marne. Church bells were rung all over the country, and schoolchildren were given a special holiday. One German newspaper reported the evacuation of Bar-le-Duc and Ste. Ménéhould, twenty-five miles behind Verdun; another declared 'VICTORY OF VERDUN . . . THE COLLAPSE OF FRANCE . . .' Even hardened 'Easterners' on the General Staff began grudgingly to admit that maybe Falkenhayn had been right in his decision to attack in the West. At the Crown Prince's Stenay headquarters, the All-Highest arrived to express in person his appreciation of the Brandenburgers' feat.

To the victor, the spoils. Once the Germans had assured their tenancy within the Fort it remained only to hand out the medals for this outstanding exploit. To the reader it should be fairly evident who among the Brandenburgers were most deserving of reward. But often in the course of war the ribbon merited by one in fact goes to another. So it happened at Douaumont. It was *Oberleutnant* von Brandis who had been detailed by Haupt to carry the news of the capture of Douaumont back to Battalion HQ. Having given his account of it to the C. O., Major von Klüfer, Brandis then requested permission to convey the news back to Regimental HQ. On the basis of Brandis' account alone, the staff at Brigade that night recorded in the war diary that Douaumont had been '. . . stormed by 7 and 8 Companies of the 24th, led by Captain Haupt and *Oberleutnant* von Brandis. Both officers most conspicuously distinguished.' And so, in this form, the citation passed back along the line until it lay on the desk of the Crown Prince himself. Meanwhile, the next morning— before he could give an account of his part in the action—Radtke was seriously wounded in a French counterattack. For over a week he lay in a torpor in the fort sick-bay, then was transported to hospital in Germany. There he heard that Haupt and von Brandis had been awarded the *Pour le Mérite*, Germany's highest decoration, and he had received nothing (nor, for that matter, had Kunze). In vain Major von Klüfer tried subsequently to set the record straight, but the heir to the Hohenzollerns could admit no mistake. Besides, von Brandis, with the 'flashing eyes' the Crown Prince so admired in his legions, was manifestly more of the stuff that heroes are made of than the faintly unmilitary Radtke; the fact that he was a *von* and Radtke was not may also have had its influence.

The modest Haupt, thoroughly deserving of his high award, soon slipped back into anonymity. Not so Brandis. Rapidly he assumed the position of favourite with the Crown Prince; was given a gold cigarette case inscribed 'Wilhelm', photographed with him in his staff car, or with arms linked in the company of other heroes, like the great air ace, Oswald Boelcke. His book, *The Stormers of Douaumont*, which appeared the following year, full of bombast and relegating even Haupt to a lesser role, was an instant best-seller. Letters of hero-worship flooded in by the hundred from Germany, even offers of marriage. After the war, a village in Prussia was named after Brandis, whose inspiring lectures to schools on the capture of Fort Douaumont are recalled to this day by a later generation of Germans. For ten years von Brandis' role remained undisputed. Then the official *Reichs Archives* appeared, establishing for the first time that, second only to Haupt, Radtke had played the most important part in the capture. Next Radtke himself published his own account of the action. At last, Sergeant Kunze, now a police constable, provoked by this reopening of the discussion and evidently feeling that after the passage of so much time it might now not be too imprudent to admit the dereliction of nearly twenty years ago, contacted his old C. O., Major von Klüfer, and told him his whole story. On the eve of the Second World War when interest in who took Douaumont had all but disappeared, Klüfer's meticulously compiled account, representing years of research, appeared. Radtke's claim was confirmed and for the first time it was revealed that a Pioneer Sergeant, not a Prussian officer, had been the first to penetrate the Fort. Kunze was rewarded with accelerated promotion to Inspector; in belated compensation, Radtke received a signed photograph from the Crown Prince.

If in their exaltation at the capture of Douaumont the Germans had exaggerated a trifle, it was nothing by comparison to French efforts to play down the disaster. The propagandists of G. Q. G., abetted by 'Anastasie' the ugly old lady with the scissors who personified French censorship, rose nobly to the occasion. The first communiqué on the 26th was a masterpiece:

> A fierce struggle took place round Fort Douaumont which is an advanced work of the old defences of Verdun. The position carried by the enemy this morning, after several fruitless assaults which in-

volved them in very heavy losses, has since been reached and passed by our troops, all the enemy's endeavours having failed to drive them back.

Then when it was realised there was no hope of its recapture, communiqués concentrated on the desperate German losses; one report thus inspired spoke lyrically of a 'whole autumn of green-grey leaves fallen on the snow'. Finally it was allowed to 'leak out' that the fort had in fact been demolished by the prescient French sometime previously, and the Germans had merely occupied a useless ruin. To important neutral countries like the U. S. A., it was pointed out somewhat mysteriously that the French Army was employing a 'new system of war, for which Verdun was fully prepared', in which forts played no part. At the Elysée, the G. Q. G. attaché, 'April Smiles' Pénélon, blandly assured President Poincaré that the French bombardment would not allow the Germans to remain in Douaumont long; then told him that it had in fact been recaptured. But the world could not be deceived for long. When the truth became apparent, Poincaré, in his mild fashion, notes, that there was 'excitability' in the Chamber of Deputies that day. In fact, the shock experienced by all Frenchmen was as devastating as the impact in Britain of the fall of Tobruk in 1942; with the difference that Fort Douaumont was but 150 miles from the Arc de Triomphe.

On the battlefield itself, the impact of the fall of Douaumont was immediate and grave. The commander of the 37th African Division, the last of the units of XXX Corps still in the line, now did a disastrous thing. The battle had gone extremely badly for de Bonneval. On arriving at Verdun, he had seen his fine division promptly dismembered and fed piecemeal to the 51st and 72nd Divisions. Worse still, he had seen its crack colonial units falter and break, one after another, in an unheard of fashion. Though described by contemporaries as having 'the bearing of a great commander', by the afternoon of the 25th de Bonneval was thoroughly depressed. Suddenly from his command post on Froideterre Ridge he had spotted the German rockets fired from Fort Douaumont to halt the bombardment. A disastrous breakthrough must have taken place on the right! His battered division, now molding the vital spurs of Talou and Pepper Hill, would be trapped in a pincer movement with its back up against the flooded Meuse. Though he had not been attacked at all that day, he at once gave the order to withdraw in stages, first to Froideterre, then right back to Belleville Ridge. The important bridge at Bras was also blown up. Belleville was the last of the transverse Meuse spurs before Verdun, looking down into the very city itself, and within machine-gun fire of it. Retreat to Belleville Ridge meant the yielding of all the forts and entrenchments on the Right Bank; within a short space of time, it must inevitably mean the loss of Verdun too.

The Germans had been quick to capitalise on their triumph by scattering leaflets from planes over the French lines, announcing, 'Douaumont has fallen. All will soon be over now. Don't let yourselves be killed for nothing.' Something alarmingly like mass panic began to sweep through Verdun. At the front, Sergeant Dubrulle of the 8th Regiment, one of the new units hurled precipitately into the battle, noted in his journal 'the beginning of incoherent sentiments which pave the way to defeat. "We are lost! They have thrown us into the furnace, without rations, almost without ammunition. We were the last resources; they have sacrificed us . . . our sacrifice will be in vain." A melée of guns, wounded, and deserters was pouring back along all the roads.' A Zouave overheard a general remark, 'Even if I were Napoleon, I couldn't stop the defeat of this shower.' Battle-shocked remnants of the 51st Division took refuge in the barracks where they had been lodged, and refused to budge. But even in barracks out of the line, terror pursued the French troops. Down upon Marceau Barracks where Dubrulle and his regiment were quartered, on being relieved from the line, there suddenly rained a deluge of German long-range shells. A sickening carnage was executed on the horses tethered outside. Then the roof of one of the buildings crumpled, crushing some hundred or more men. Survivors rushed out into the night, only to be blown to pieces among the crazed and pitifully wounded horses. Eventually, the exhausted, demoralised troops were marched out of the death trap of the barracks back towards the front again, and ordered to dig trenches for themselves.

Human endurance had reached its limits. In Verdun itself a Lieutenant was arrested for running through the streets, shouting 'Sauve qui peut!' Seeing the Meuse bridges prepared for demolition and all the other signs of impending withdrawal, the civil populace began to abandon its houses. Shortly afterwards, an order was issued that all civilians were to evacuate Verdun, within a matter of hours. The pathetic flotsam of war that was to become so familiar a sight on French roads a generation later—the hopeless columns of refugees, painfully pushing mattresses and belongings in prams before them—now added to the chaos on the roads leading from the city. In their haste, some of the citizens of Verdun had left even the food out on the table; others had found time to drag barrels up from the cellars and puncture them in the streets. The gutters ran red with wine. A food depot near the Citadel was thrown open, and soldiers told to take what they could carry. Elsewhere in the city that invariable companion of military rout, pillage, took place. Frightened troops who had taken refuge in the cellars of evacuated houses got drunk on their contents, then looted the other floors. There were reports of gendarmes being strung up by drunk looters when they attempted to intervene.

February 25th was, in the view of one foremost French authority, General Palat, 'perhaps the darkest of the whole assault on Verdun'. That night nothing seemed to stand between the victorious Crown Prince and the conquest of France's mightiest bulwark. It was no exaggeration to say, as he later wrote in his memoirs 'We were, in fact, within a stone's throw of victory!' Would he deny Falkenhayn the opportunity of trying out his 'bleeding white' experiment? There did indeed seem a possibility that the victim would die of shock before that sinister process could do its work.

WAR ON THE HIGH SEAS

Before World War I British naval strategy dictated that the size of her fleets should be equal to the aggregate of any other two naval powers. For decades the British Royal Navy had ruled the high seas. The mere arrival of a few British ships had been sufficient to dampen the ardor of revolts in countries with coastal cities dependent on naval commerce. Such a position of authority had not gone unnoticed by the Kaiser, nor could his ego allow another power to be superior to Germany. His army was the world's best and most feared. Germany's tradesmen needed little convincing by the Kaiser to back his plans for a navy at least as powerful as Britain's, because it would help protect their mushrooming overseas trade. For the first years of the 20th century the Germans laid keel after keel.

While the British could maintain their superiority by building at an equal or better rate, new weapons such as the self-propelled torpedo and the submarine had become available to all nations. These two weapons in combination substantially reduced the overwhelming impact of the battleship.

The British decided to take a long gamble. They fitted out a new battleship with bigger guns and turbine engines which increased the battleship's speed, maneuverability and fire power. The success of the British in creating their new Dreadnought battleships gave them another commanding lead. Germany and the other naval powers were forced to turn to this prototype to keep up. The more heavily gunned ships of the British were meant to coincide with their strategy of "hit first, hit hard and keep hitting."

In contrast, the role of the new German navy was more defensive, because their fleet was intended to range only so far as the North Sea. They were willing to give up some of their armament but worked to develop better armor protection and to give their ships the quality of "unsinkability."

When war was declared in 1914 the main British Fleet took position in Scapa Flow in northern Scotland where it could exercise dominance over the routes of German merchant shipping to the Atlantic from the North Sea. A blockade was now established against the Germans and imports via sea were cut off. Germany knew she could not survive indefinitely without relief.

However, month after month went by without the German fleet sallying forth to challenge the British. The Kaiser and some of his naval advisers had decided that their armies would win the war quickly; furthermore, the Germans hoped the British would bring the battle to them along the German North Sea coast, where their subs and mine fields would give the British trouble.

The British held fast, wanting to engage in open waters. Also their crews aboard the new Dreadnought battleships needed more training and gunnery practice. The direction of a line of battleships in combat is complex and difficult to master. Captain Douglas Macintyre says, "To bring all guns of the battleships into action, it was necessary to form them into a single line to avoid some being blanketed by others. When cruising or during the approach to battle, such a formation had many disadvantages. A column of twenty-four battleships in single line in the closest possible formation was more than six miles long. To pass a simple flag signal to all ships could take eight minutes or more. Eight minutes to alter the course or speed of the fleet! Furthermore, a single line ahead made the ideal target for a submarine and was impossible to screen by destroyers.

"The fleet in cruising order, therefore, steamed in columns in line ahead of four ships each, the columns abreast of each other or, in naval jargon, 'disposed abeam,' thus forming a rectangle. In this formation all ships could hope to be able simultaneously to read a flag signal hoist in the fleet flagship leading one of the centre columns. A signal by searchlight could similarly be passed out to the leaders of the columns. . . .

"Something like ten seconds would elapse after the order to the helmsman before the ship would ponderously begin to turn. Once begun, the swing would only be checked by application of opposite rudder for a similar period.

"As for their motion through the water, if the engines were stopped when moving at a speed of fifteen knots, the great steel mass would carry its way for another mile and a half before coming to rest. If the engines were reversed, the distance might be reduced to half a mile." *

In addition, the German strategy was to fight the British only when they could be sure of superiority of numbers and guns. It was necessary then to somehow divide the British fleet so the numbers which could be brought to bear in any one area would suit their tactics. Toward the end of 1914 high speed raids by small groups of German ships shelled British coastal towns. While damage was usually negligible the British public clamored for part of the fleet to be stationed further south to protect their coast. The British Admiral of the Fleet Sir John Jellicoe refused to fall prey to this argument.

In 1915, the Germans unleashed their U-Boats against the Allied merchant shipping approaching England. Parts of the British Grand Fleet were sent to patrol the coastal waters, as well as most of their destroyers and smaller armed vessels. While the U-boats were waging a successful campaign the German Admiral von Pohl did not venture out into the North Sea, spending his time in target practice in the Baltic. For most of 1915 the North Sea might have been a British pond.

Meanwhile the British Grand Fleet continued to build its strength. At the same time more and more pressure against the unrestricted U-Boat warfare was placed on the Kaiser by neutral nations whose shipping was destroyed. Relations between Germany and the United States worsened and the Kaiser, to keep the U. S. pacified, recalled the U-Boats which had been harrying the British coast.

Then in early 1916, Admiral Scheer, the new German naval commander, came on scene. He believed in aggressive warfare. He adopted the earlier German strategy of attempting to divide the British Grand Fleet and bringing just a part of it under his guns. Raids were conducted once again on the British coast with the result that again there were cries from the public to have part of the fleet

* From *Jutland*, by Captain Douglas Macintyre, Published by W. W. Norton, pp. 52, 53, 54.

sent south to guard the coastal towns. Before Jellicoe gave in, however, Admiral Scheer decided on a different ruse to draw the British out to battle.

THE BATTLE OF JUTLAND*

by Hanson Baldwin

It was two o'clock in the afternoon watch, May 31, 1916. A rusty tramp—the *N. J. Fjord*—with the flag of Denmark painted large upon her sides and splotches of red lead showing on her weather-beaten plates, steamed slowly across the North Sea. On the far horizon the top hamper of a ship rapidly took shape: the light cruiser *Elbing* of the Imperial German Navy. There came the peremptory orders of the sea, "Heave to!" The *N. J. Fjord* stopped. "Her steam blowing off shot skyward in a cotton-white jet which mixed with her funnel smoke to spread into a listless cloud visible for miles against the leaden atmosphere." German destroyers nosed alongside—boarding and search, the routine procedure of wartime.

Aboard H. M. S. *Galatea*, flying the broad pennant of Commodore Alexander-Sinclair, the white steam of the *Fjord* was sighted. The light cruiser, far on the wing of Beatty's Battle Cruiser Fleet then turning away to the northward, stood on to investigate. At 2:18 she signaled to the fleet: "Enemy in sight!"

The rusty *N. J. Fjord* had lifted the curtain on "the greatest drama of modern naval warfare." *Der Tag* had come.

The operation of May 31, 1916—a sortie resulting from the more aggressive German naval policy of 1916—had been planned

* From *Sea Fights and Shipwrecks,* published by Garden City Pub. Co.

originally as a raid on Sunderland on the British coast. But because of unfavorable weather Scheer's Zeppelins were unable to scout ahead of the High Sea Fleet and protect the Germans from surprise. Scheer therefore had abandoned the dangerous Sunderland operation and substituted for it a sweep to the north toward the Skagerrak, in hopes of luring the British Grand Fleet into submarine-infested waters, and of inflicting injuries upon detached and isolated portions of that fleet.

From the efficient British Intelligence Service Jellicoe knew that the Germans were planning some considerable movement, and the Grand Fleet actually had put to sea before the Germans left the Jade. Vice-Admiral Sir David Beatty, with the Battle Cruiser Fleet from Rosyth, had been ordered to scout to the east toward the Skagerrak before turning northward to join the main body of the Grand Fleet. At the same time Scheer, cruising northward off Denmark, had sent Hipper well ahead of his main body.

The opposing fleets, groping toward each other through the mists of the North Sea, were disproportionate in physical strength but not in courage, seamanship, or professional skill.

The Great Britain of 1916, with the Empire—Upon-Which-The-Sun-Never-Set—had passed its golden age; Jellicoe, who commanded the greatest battle fleet that ever put to sea, epitomized Quintus Fabius, the cautious Roman, rather than the dash and daring of Drake and Hawkins and Nelson. He understood his position of towering responsibility as the "only man who could lose the war in an afternoon"; but he had an almost unreasoning respect for enemy mines and the torpedoes of German U-boats and destroyers. Unlike his famous predecessors, he felt, in his own words, that he could not leave *anything to chance in a fleet action, because our Fleet was the one and only factor that was vital to the existence of the Empire.*

The gods of war never smile upon those who do not pay obeisance at the shrine of fortune, but the Admiralty—and, indeed, the British Government—endorsed the "to have and to hold" caution of Jellicoe.

Scheer was an admiral of different stripe, bearing different responsibilities and representing a German nurtured on nationalism, weaned on Bismarck's "blood and iron," eager to acquire. Scheer knew his fleet was far inferior to Jellicoe's; he was pursuing a policy of attrition; he hoped by his sorties—and by luck—to entice elements of the Grand Fleet to destruction.

And so the fleets—by far the mightiest of their era—stood forth to battle, neither anticipating the clash of arms that shook the world.

From Scapa Flow in the Orkneys and from Invergordon and Rosyth in Scotland, the British Grand Fleet that sortied to sea numbered twenty-eight battleships and nine battle-cruisers, mounting twelve-inch, thirteen-and-one-half-inch, fourteen-inch and fifteen-inch guns. Jellicoe also commanded eight armored cruisers, twenty-six light cruisers, and seventy-eight destroyers and destroyer flotilla leaders. Scheer's High Sea Fleet that stood out from the Jade counted twenty-two battleships (some obsolescent) and five battle-cruisers, armed with eleven- and twelve-inch guns, eleven light cruisers, and sixty-one destroyers and flotilla leaders. The British advantage in weight of broadside was large, in numbers of ships less so, in armor there was little difference, save that the British battle-cruisers had defects in design which cost them heavily during the battle. Frost estimates that the British had a material superiority in strength of about 8 to 5.

The battle that ensued, fought entirely in the sullen, heaving cockpit of the North Sea, was naturally divided by circumstance and tactics into four principal phases. Beatty, who commanded the British scouting force, built around the battle-cruisers, and Hipper, who commanded the German screen, had been sent ahead of the main fleets, each feeling for the enemy. The first phase of the battle ensued when Beatty and Hipper made contact and dueled with their battle-cruisers as Hipper led Beatty southward toward the bulk of the German High Sea Fleet, hidden in the mists. When the German main body was encountered Beatty turned north and steamed toward his own main fleet, with the Germans coming hard after him and the great guns echoing over the waters. The third phase was the brief encounter of the main bodies, when Scheer with the High Sea Fleet steaming in column met the Grand Fleet "crossing them" or steaming at a right angle across Scheer's course. The final phase, after the Germans turned away back toward port was a sprawling, inchoate night action, chiefly between the light forces.

But it was units from the scouting forces of both fleets, both investigating the smoke of the *N. J. Fjord*, that made the first contact of the battle of Jutland. Beatty and Hipper opened the ball.

H. M. S. *Galatea*, steaming at twenty-eight knots, fired the first ,gun of the battle; its unexpected concussion almost blew a surprised officer who had been basking in the sun down a fo'c'sle ladder. The Germans drew first blood: an enemy shell struck the *Galatea* below the bridge but did not explode; a cockney seaman came upon it and tried to pick it up; he jumped back, wringing his scorched fingers: "Crikey, the blighter's hot!"

As *Galatea* felt out the enemy, a strange-looking, awkward vessel, H. M. S. *Engadine*—just over the horizon from the Germans—stopped dead in the water, swung out a boom, launched a seaplane. The *Engadine*'s seaplane made a fifty-two-minute flight (interrupted by one landing on the sea due to a broken petrol pipe—repaired with a rubber tube); sighted the German battle cruisers, reported their course, position and numbers by W/T (radio), and became immortal in the annals of naval history, even though her report never reached Beatty. It was the first plane to participate in a naval battle; a quarter century later in the Pacific the history of the world was to be decided by *Engadine*'s descendants.

By 3:48 the battle was fairly begun, and within five minutes the *Tiger* was struck, and Beatty's flagship *Lion*. Shells made geysers alongside the speeding ships; dead fish floated belly up, killed by the detonations. The sun—shining through a gray haze—dazzled the eyes of the German gunners, but the wind rolled the battle smoke toward the British line. From the turret ports, or through the slits in the armored conning towers, men saw the red-black bursts of shells on steel.

At four sharp, the *Lion* took its fourth hit from the *Lützow;* and Major Harvey of the Royal Marines won his posthumous V. C. in the shambles of Q turret. The shell had penetrated the turret amidships and exploded with horrible effect, killing the turret crew, jolting open the breech plug of a loaded gun, and igniting the powder bags. Harvey, in the officers' booth at the rear, had both legs severed from his body by the explosion; but he sent his wounded sergeant to Flag Captain Chatfield to report Q turret out of action, and dragging himself to a voice tube ordered his handling-room crew to flood the magazines; the flash of flame met a rising tide of water, and the *Lion* was saved.

At 4:03, after two rapid salvos from the *Von der Tann*, the *Indefatigable* was finished. She disappeared in a great sheet of flame and smoke; boats, debris, armor plate, and bodies mushroomed two hundred feet into the sky—and she was gone, with a thousand British seamen.

Flames rose from the decks of stricken ships; below decks, mattresses and shores plugged shell holes against the water; surgeons with bloody scalpels bent above the wounded; the acrid odor of cordite smoke seeped into every casemate, and burned men screamed in agony.

Only the *New Zealand* escaped the raging hail of steel plunging now all along the British line—and she was a lucky ship. Her Old Man, Captain Green, with Admiral Pakenham beside him, wore a Maori war mat through all the heat and flame and fury of Jutland. It was called a *piu-piu* and resembled a kilt of black and white. It had been given to the ship with the admonition that the captain wear it when the *New Zealand* cleared for action. Below-decks thought it lucky, and it was; the *New Zealand* was hit only once that day, and lost no men.

To port—from the British line—the scene of battle looked "red, lurid, and beastly." Shell splashes cascaded foaming water across the splintered decks. Fair between the lines, with screeching death from turret guns arching high above her, lay a full-rigged merchant ship in ghostly beauty, like the *Flying Dutchman*, a portent of death and destruction. At 4:06 Evan-Thomas coming hard from the northwest with his four splendid battleships (which were operating with Beatty's battle-cruisers), opened fire at nineteen thousand yards. A fifteen-inch shell from the *Barham* sliced through the *Von der*

Tann's armor, and six hundred tons of water sluiced into the German ship. The tempo of battle speeded up; Hipper stood southward at twenty-three knots, leading the British battle-cruisers and Evan's battleships into the jaws of the German fleet.

The *Lion* was a moving pillar of smoke and flame; the German gunnery was good and Beatty took heavy losses. At 4:26 came the *Queen Mary*'s end. She was struck near Q turret, again and again and again. Terrific yellow flame spurted from the broken decks; then smoke hid her from the speeding ships. When it had been blown clear, the *Queen Mary* was on her beam-ends; great fluttering clouds of paper were blowing from her after hatch; black specks that were men were clambering about the slimy bilge keel, and at her stern, lifted clear of the cold North Sea water, her propellers were still turning futilely as if to speed her to her grave. A second explosion shook the torn hulk. Long later, when the battle had passed, a little midshipman and eight others were rescued from the sea: only survivors of the crew of 1,275 men.

Beatty, his cap cocked at a rakish angle, his hands thrust into the pockets of his "non-reg" uniform coat, stood on the *Lion*'s exposed bridge—a bridge shredded by flying steel splinters, shaken by concussion and explosion, and coolly charted the course of battle. He had seen his two ships go, and to port through the wreathing smoke watched the German battle-cruisers pounding the British line. *Lion* was on fire; *Tiger* was badly hit; only *New Zealand* had escaped. A German salvo struck the *Princess Royal*; a signalman on the *Lion*'s bridge, seeing the burst of impact and the licking flame, mistakenly reported: "*Pricess Royal* blown up, sir."

Beatty turned his keen blue eyes and jutting jaw toward his flag captain: "Chatfield, there seems to be something wrong with our bloody ships today. Turn two points to port" (toward the enemy).

H. M. S. *Nestor*—Commander the Hon. E. B. S. Bingham, V. C.— was waiting for her end. Of what was in store for her there was now no doubt. The *Nestor*, the *Nomad* and others of the 13th Destroyer Flotilla had made a mad dash toward the German battle-cruisers, as Beatty and Hipper dueled. They had launched torpedoes; but the *Nomad* had taken a shell in the engine room and the *Nestor* was soon disabled and unable to steam. Drifting, wrecked, they lay in the oily swells full in the path of the German High Sea Fleet steaming up from the south.

The German battleships of Scheer's High Sea Fleet were first sighted at 4:33 from light cruiser *Southampton,* well in the van of the British battle-cruisers. The destroyer recall signal was hoisted from *Lion* in ten minutes, and by 4:50 Beatty had his battle-cruisers —reduced now to four—turned away to the north and pounding hard to lead Scheer and Hipper into the guns of Jellicoe.

But *Nestor* and *Nomad* were done; as the British disappeared to the northward the disabled destroyers lay square between the lines of the mighty German battleships.

The *Nomad* took it first. Commander Bingham saw her smothered in clouds of smoke and columns of spray, as scores of German guns riddled her. She died game; she fired her final torpedo at two thousand yards and sank at last under the fire of the oncoming German battleships.

The *Nestor* was next. While her crew was waiting Commander Bingham threw overboard the lead-backed signal books, saw the boats filled with biscuits and water, and hoisted out the Carley floats. Then, to keep the men busy and their minds from the British fleet vanishing to the north and the German columns approaching from the south, he had the cables ranged on deck.

The van of the German column—twenty-two battleships, surrounded by a swarm of destroyers and cruisers—looked larger and larger. The Germans opened fire at five miles, far beyond the range of the *Nestor's* popguns; but Bingham fired his last torpedo before it was too late. By that time shells had made sieves of the light steel decks; spray from the splashes alongside were pattering on stacks and masts. The crew was decimated; the ship had filled and was starting to sink.

"Abandon ship!" Men climbed into the motor boat and the Carley floats. Commander Bingham looked at his wrecked command and turned to Lieutenant M. J. Bethell.

"Now where shall we go?"

"To heaven I trust, sir." Bethell, "that gallant spirit," turned aside

"to attend to a mortally wounded signalman, and was seen no more."
The *Nestor* sank, her crew singing "God save the King." 5:30 P.M.

At the Admiralty in London deft-fingered men work in guarded
rooms with coding boards and signal books. Radio direction finders
are trained on the German High Sea Fleet. Messages from Scheer to
Hipper are intercepted, the ciphers are broken, the code is translated
from a code book captured earlier in the war, and Jellicoe—steaming
hard to Beatty's assistance with the whole British Grand Fleet—is
informed at 5:45 of the exact position of the German main body as of
4:30. The British Intelligence Service is "amazingly efficient"; not so
the Admiralty's judgment: Tyrwhitt, champing at the bit, is kept
useless in harbor with the powerful Harwich force, until *Der Tag* is
almost done.

At the Admiralty in Berlin German naval officers bend stiffly
above charts—tense and waiting. In imagination they can hear the
thunder of the guns above the North Sea; shell bursts obscure the
rumble of traffic in the Wilhelmstrasse. . . . Germany's challenge
for sea power is come to fruition at last; the doctrines of Mahan are
translated into the voices of the guns. But they know less of the
course of battle than the British; the deciphering unit at Neumünster
has but little luck. And the German public knows nothing of the
North Sea action; they face the Western Front, where for months the
Crown Prince had been battering at Verdun, gateway to Paris.

The sun was low and the mists were gathering before the main
fleets met at last, about 6:15 on that day of battle.

From about 5 to 6 P.M. the British battle-cruisers, screened by
their light craft, drove to the north towards Jellicoe's battleships
steaming southwestward to join them. Evan-Thomas' four 25-knot
battleships—*Barham, Valiant, Malaya, Warspite*—attached to
Beatty's command brought up the rear in the "Run to the North,"
and were blanketed with heavy straddling salvos from the guns of
five German battle-cruisers and seven dreadnoughts in the German
column. The four British battleships got "the full hate of the German
Fleet, which was far from pleasant." The British ships were hit

repeatedly—particularly *Malaya*, the rear ship—but they gave better than they received, and the tender-skinned German battle-cruisers—already badly damaged by fire from the *Lion, Tiger, Princess Royal* and *New Zealand*—were struck many times. All of *Von der Tann's* guns were out of action; she stayed in line and surged on to the north—a floating target, her deck a shambles.

By 6 P.M. *Lützow, Derfflinger*, and *Seydlitz* were seriously damaged; *Seydlitz* was afire; *Derfflinger's* flooded bow was dropping low in the water; the German stokers—stripped to the waist, sweating and exhausted—scooped coal furiously into the boilers, to keep up the steam. Hipper—now well ahead of Scheer's main body—had pursued Beatty and Evan-Thomas almost into the jaws of the Grand Fleet, and the dying afternoon put him at a serious disadvantage. The British ships—except for gun flashes on the horizon—were hidden in the mists; "the low slanting rays of the setting sun made impossible any effective German reply" (Frost). Hipper turned away, and about the same time—in *Iron Duke*—Jellicoe hoisted the signal for deployment. The two fleets came together—torpedo craft, cruisers, battle-cruisers, battleships—as the darkness crawled above the sea. It was "Windy Corner"—a melee of stabbing gun flashes, of white froth upon the sea, of speeding ships and dying men—the confused chaos of battle.

The destroyer *Shark*, Commander Loftus Jones, R. N., with three others of the 4th Flotilla, *Acasta, Ophelia, Christopher*, tiny pawns in a titanic struggle, were assigned to Hood's Third Battle Cruiser Squadron. The great guns of the battle-cruisers roared above the destroyers' mast tips; *Invincible, Inflexible, Indomitable* were firing at the German light cruisers, *Wiesbaden, Pillau, Frankfurt*. Bödicker, the German, turned away from Hood's smothering salvos, fired his torpedoes at the giant British ships, ordered his destroyers to the attack. The white wake of the "tin fish" streaking underwater towards the battle-cruisers warned Hood; he too turned away and sent Loftus Jones and his four destroyers dashing madly in the foam-flecked sea to parry the German thrust.

Yellow cordite smoke bellied and eddied between the fighting lines; ripples of fire burst in shining flashes from the mist-hidden ships on the dark horizon. Their propellers lashing a frothy wake, the *Shark*, the *Acasta*, the *Ophelia*, and the *Christopher* raced towards the enemy.

It was a brief Armageddon. "Right ahead and close aboard" of the racing British destroyers were the *Regensburg* and two columns of "nine or ten" German destroyers on either hand. Farther off—half-hidden in the smoke and mist—were Bödicker's cruisers, their guns still flashing, but this time at Loftus Jones and his four ships. The British attacked at close range with torpedoes and guns, firing to port and starboard at the destroyers, launching their torpedoes at the cruisers, their screws working at top speed before annihilation.

The spitting flashes of crimson stained the horizon to west and southwards; the little *Shark* and her sisters, tearing along at 30 knots, careened and shivered as shell splashes geysered high alongside and roaring waters cascaded down upon their decks. It was only a question of time. . . .

The *Shark* lived for perhaps ten minutes in this, her last mad dash. Loftus Jones on the bridge kept her headed west and slightly southwards, where streamers of smoke bannered across the misty sky. Far on the horizon dim shapes began to form out of the haze and gun smoke; the *Shark* was speeding towards the whole German fleet. But Jones had more modest aims; the *Regensburg* was his target; he brought the *Shark* into firing position, launched a torpedo —and turned to go. But the enemy had found his range and salvos were straddling the straining ship. A shell struck her amidships; roaring steam wreathed above her in a pall of white; "the pipes to her oil suction were damaged"; a greasy slick oozed from the tortured steel and spread across the swells. The *Shark* slowed down. A shell struck the forward four-inch; the entire crew was killed; the gun dismounted. Flying splinters of steel shredded the bridge structure; Jones was wounded; another shell tore away the steering wheel, smashed the bridge. The *Shark* stopped . . . so slowly, her lifeblood spilling quietly on the waters, her panting breath steaming above her for all the fleet to see.

Loftus Jones, his blood staining the gold braid of his rank, staggered painfully aft across the broken and littered deck past the bodies of his men, mangled and torn. . . . The after and midship guns were still firing; the flag was still there.

Brief respite. The *Canterbury*, light cruiser, headed out of the battle smoke into the no-man's land between the fleets and drew the punishing fire of the *Regensburg*, the *Frankfurt*, other enemy light cruisers and the German destroyers. Quietly, the *Shark* waited for the coup de grâce. *Acasta*, Lieutenant-Commander John O. Barron, who had been with Loftus Jones in previous actions, pulled up alongside, wanted to tow. But Jones waved her away; he told Barron "not to get sunk for him."

"Soon afterwards" a number of enemy destroyers, probably of the 9th and 6th Flotillas, came up and "opened a heavy fire." The after gun was hit squarely, and its entire crew wiped out; Jones, who had been directing its fire, lost a leg at the knee. "But he continued to encourage his men," and lying there upon the deck among his dead and wounded, the blood swimming out upon the shattered deck plates, he noticed the White Ensign, the gaff shot away, drooping down the mast.

He asked "what was wrong with the flag and appeared greatly upset as he lay on the deck wounded. Twice he spoke of it." Seaman Hope, one of the only two men left unwounded, climbed the mast, unbent the ensign, and passed it down to Midshipman Smith, who hoisted it on the yardarm. "Commander Jones seemed then to be less worried when he saw the flag was hoisted again."

The enemy destroyers were closing down to the kill. The midship gun, manned by a crew of blood-stained, staggering spectres, was firing slowly as the *Shark* settled.

The British destroyer was on fire and dying fast; the flaming flashes of the enemy almost ringed her round. But still the lone gun spoke; its crew of wounded aimed it well; British shells crashed into the German V-48.

There came the end. Close by, a speeding enemy launched two torpedoes; one ran true and struck the battered *Shark* amidships near the funnel. The loud roar of the last explosion; the little destroyer lurching heavily. "She took a heavy list and sank," the

White Ensign flying from the mast, the midship gun still firing. "So, maintaining to the last the final traditions of the service, she came to her end, and it was in the heart of the battle she found it."

Vice-Admiral Reinhard Scheer in the *Friedrich der Grosse* had had little warning of the presence of the Grand Fleet; intent on pursuing Beatty, he had led his ships full into Jellicoe's overwhelming force. But he was a German General Grant, "direct and simple and cool as ice." He stood on into the jaws of death.

The Germans had had the best of the fight until now—even until 6:20 when German gunfire sank the *Defense*:

> . . . *in one sullen roar*
> *Of flame the furious incandescence tore*
> *Her symphony of steel to molten heat,*
> *And wrapped 900 men in one red sheet. . . .*

—the tide of battle had flowed their way.

But Jellicoe now crossed the German's T: before the path of Scheer lay England's mightiest ships—*King George V, Ajax, Iron Duke, St. Vincent, Temeraire Marlborough, Agincourt, Collingwood,* and a host of others bearing proud and ancient names and flying the cross of St. George.

The range, in the gathering dark, had closed to 11,000 to 16,000 yards; at long last the battle lines slugged toe to toe. The Germans could see little of their enemy except stabbing flashes ringing the horizon to the northward: the van of the German line was under concentrated fire. At 6:24 Von der Decker in the *Derfflinger* recorded, "*Lützow* heavily hit forward. Ship on fire. Much smoke." At 6:36 came the command *Gefechtskehrtwendung nach Steuerbord*, the famous simultaneous battle turn to starboard, to the reverse course. The Germans swung away from the destructive fire, the *König* flaming and smoking like a volcano and the *Lützow's* forecastle nearly under water—so badly damaged that Hipper ordered her home to Wilhelmshaven and transferred his flag. *Markgraf* and other ships were hit. The *Von der Tann's* heavy guns had not spoken for an hour; she was a shambles, turrets jammed, steel sides ripped, dead and wounded littering her decks. But again, just before the turn-away, Scheer drew blood, and the *Invincible*, with Hood her admiral—well beloved and efficient—went to join the *Indefatigable, Queen Mary,* and *Defense*.

The *Wiesbaden* was slowly sinking now. She had found her death wound in the thick of the fight, fair between the lines. Helpless, she had lain the target for ship after ship, replying with her puny guns as best she could; man after man killed, gun after gun dismounted. Lower she sank. The grimy stokers long since had drawn their fires; the grate bars, where the glowing coals had been, were under water. Her few survivors had seen the end of *Defense* and *Invincible;* had seen the *Gefechtskehrtwendung nach Steuerbord;* had watched in the gathering dusk while Scheer returned again to the fight, and the hell of battle screamed round them. Then, at last, while the cold North Sea lapped upward toward the slanted decks, Scheer had turned away. The battle flowed past them and the long hours under fire were over.

Out of the battered hulk, from behind the shattered plates the seamen crawled—what was left of them. They got the wounded up from below and waited, dead and dying and those soon to die, for the end. It was slow in coming, so a few of them sang while they waited, songs of the Fatherland. The *Wiesbaden* went with the long North Sea day. There was none there to see her passing when she slipped at last, slowly, slowly, into the darkness. The cold water took her crew one by one. Her only survivor, Chief Stoker Zenne, was rescued by a small steamer after thirty-eight hours in the rough and icy sea.

The first brief contact of the main fleets was quickly broken off as Scheer turned away. But at 6:55 the German admiral returned to the attack, partly to try to save the foundering *Wiesbaden* and the damaged *Lützow*. At 7:04 the battle fleets slugged again; again Jellicoe had the advantage of light and position; the broadsides of many of his ships bore upon the van of the German line, whereas only Scheer's leading ships could bear upon the British.

"The Germans were headed directly into the center of the Grand Fleet . . . in a regular death trap. . . ." (says Frost). "They were in the most unfavorable and dangerous situation imaginable. Jellicoe enjoyed the overwhelming advantages of position, visibility, and numbers, each in a very great degree." Scheer's attempt at surprise by unorthodox tactics might "prove to be one of the most colossal errors of all naval history."

From 7:12 on the leading German ships were blanketed in an "enormous concentration" of British salvos. It looked like the end. Here was a chance for annihilation; the God of Opportunity had knocked at the door of Jellicoe—he who might have been greater than Nelson. By 7:17 virtually all of the thirty-three remaining British capital ships were firing at the enemy—the first such concentration of the battle. Victory was in sight—God and St. George!

But it was not to be. Jellicoe was no Nelson; and Scheer the Bold quickly saw his mistake, and about 7:18 turned his battle line away, covered by a torpedo attack from his destroyers. To avoid the torpedoes, the British Grand Fleet—that fleet of the resounding names, blood and bone of British history—turned *away* from the enemy—not *towards* him—and opportunity had gone, to knock no more.

There was more scattered action in the waning day, and just after the sun set at 8:19 Beatty caught the oldest German battleships and the battered enemy battle-cruisers silhouetted against the afterglow, and in a few brief minutes registered seven hits and received only two. It was—though none could know it then—the last contact between heavy ships of the battle; indeed, the last capital ship action of World War I.

The rest was a sprawling chaos of night action between the light forces—as the German High Sea Fleet retired toward the Jade. The coup de grâce to cripples, the numbing surprise in contact in the dark, the crimson flare of guns and the stabbing beams of searchlights—the last act dragged on with all the props of drama. But the climax had passed.

The main fleets had lost contact in the darkness but all that night until well after dawn of June 1, when the German High Sea Fleet was safe at bases beyond Horn Reefs, a fierce melee between the light craft waxed and waned. Death struck many in the sudden flare of searchlights and the roar of guns at point-blank range. The *Elbing*, which helped to open the battle, did not quite live to see it end; she died in the night action, though most of her crew were saved. The *Frauenlob* sank in the dark with all her officers and men. The crew of her No. 4 gun, standing in water up to their waists, continued to fire to the last and just before she capsized those on board cheered for their Kaiser and the German Empire.

The *Tipperary's* crew, crowded on a tiny raft in the freezing water, sang "It's a Long Long Way to Tipperary," and died one by one.

Friend and enemy collided in the dark; friend crashed into friend. A British destroyer rammed a German cruiser and backed away with a crumpled bow and sixty feet of German plating. Her own masts and stacks and superstructure were swept clean by the blast of the German guns which could not be depressed sufficiently to hit. The *Lützow* sank; the *Seydlitz* was beached at the mouth of the Jade. The British drew last blood: the old battleship *Pommern* was sunk "with a tremendous roar of flame and sound" in a dawn torpedo attack, and at 5:20 A.M., June 1, the *Ostfriesland*, inward bound to the Jade, struck a mine and was seriously damaged.

The first of June drew on to an unpleasant day, with a cold raw wind and the sea making up. The battered British ships, working their way back to harbors, struggled with the sea, with fires and wreckage, and with the wounded. All over the North Sea, that day, the English were burying their dead:

> *We have fed our sea for a thousand years,*
> *And she calls us, still unfed—*

Creeping back to port the burned and blackened ships, with gaping decks and guns awry, were greeted with cheers by the dockyard workers at Invergordon and Rosyth. But the *Warrior* gave up the battle half-way home, and in the *Malaya*, the "smell of burnt human flesh remained for weeks."

Along Unter den Linden, Skagerrak was hailed as a glorious victory. The German Navy had come of age. The Kaiser with the withered arm—last of the Hohenzollerns—bestowed the Order *Pour le Mérite* on Scheer and Hipper and promoted them. Congratulatory telegrams from all over Central Europe sped to the German naval bases. But beneath the North Sea waters, or in plain coffins in the dock-yards, ranged row on row, lay 160 German officers and 2,385 German men—the price of "victory."

THE SOMME

After General Henri Pétain took over the defense of Verdun in late February, 1916, the French stiffened. The Germans continued to batter the French lines and gain ground, but Falkenhayn's strategy of attrition backfired, for German losses were almost as high as the French. By July 11, the German hammer blows had lost their force, and the French moved over to the offensive, retaking some of their lost ground.

Another factor forcing Falkenhayn to the defensive was the opening of the British bombardment at the Somme. German reserves, troops and guns, were rushed north to help stem the British thrust.

The Somme offensive was to be mainly a British effort (five French divisions were employed on the southern end of the British sector) with fourteen divisions in the front lines and four in reserve.

"Of the fourteen first-line divisions eleven came either from Kitchener's new armies or the Territorial force, two legions of amateurs about to engage a first-class army still leavened with professional, peace-trained soldiers. Here stood the flower of Britain, drawn from all classes of the community but on the average the best of all. Though the first universal service act was nearly six months old, these men were volunteers with hardly a conscript in their ranks. In some cases they had enlisted in groups of friends, so that here and there platoons were made up of men most of whom had known each other in civil life, bands of brothers. In such a case the talk in billets or dugouts might be of streets, of football fields, even of lanes and farmhouses, at home. They were in high spirits and inspired by high hopes. They were ready to give their lives. On the whole front of attack the German Second Army of General Fritz von Below had six divisions in line, with five more fairly close at hand.

There were three, in places four, lines of defense, to an average of five miles deep. The fortifications were very strong. The Germans, incomparably the hardest workers of any of the belligerent armies, had dug in the chalk excellent trenches and excavated numerous deep dugouts, proof against anything but a direct hit by an 8-inch shell." *

And Brian Gardner in *The Big Push*, says, "The German positions were well-nigh perfect. On a long crest, they were able to look down on the allied trenches in the dip below. The previous winter, when they had pumped water from their flooded dugouts, it had run down into the allied positions. This ridge was not a straight one but consisted of several spurs. The tops of these spurs had been turned into siege fortresses, stronger than any others on the whole Western Front. There were woods and villages on the spurs and they, also, had been heavily fortified. As there had been no serious fighting here since 1914, the Germans had occupied themselves by building what must have seemed to them an almost impregnable fort.

"The fortifications along the ridge and spurs had been constructed with great subtlety, so that there were few places where an attack would not come under crossfire. Subterranean passages had been constructed, leading to machine-gun emplacements in the side of spurs. Dugouts of thirty and even forty feet had been built. All this had been simplified by the chalk soil of the Somme valley.

"In the dugouts and deep trenches, there were electric light and washing apparatus, surgeries and hospital wards in bomb-proof cellars, pulleys, steel rails with trucks for ammunition, stairs with wired treads, air and escape shafts. The living-rooms, which had panelled walls, were decorated with cretonnes of the smartest Berlin patterns, and had neat bunks and furniture.

"Well behind the lines were many old caves and underground passages which had been made years before to gain chalk for building purposes. Now they provided excellent shelter for German reserves.

"The system consisted of two lines, each with several rows of

* Falls, p. 198.

trenches, and a third one in preparation. Before each was run an extremely formidable barrier of wire. This wire was in belts of twenty to thirty yards' thickness and had barbs as thick as a man's thumb. Staked down with iron posts, it already had its souvenirs, the stragglers of odd raiding parties, which hung on it like dilapidated scarecrows.

"Although the first German line could be seen or estimated from the forward British trenches, it was impossible to see the second line, or its wire. It was thus extremely difficult to tell how effective any barrage was in destroying that wire. These two trench systems were about two to three miles apart.

"The Germans, on the other hand, could see practically everything going on in the British lines, and behind them. They were able to see all the four roads leading from Albert to the front, and could shell them accurately.

"The British attempts at camouflage were ludicrously inadequate. The camouflage unit of the army, consisting of a few carpenters, painters, and artists, was not officially sanctioned until 22 March. They attempted to screen roads here and there by means of broad strips of canvas hung upon wires. Snipers' suits were made, and green and brown machine-gun covers. Artificial trees were prepared for observation posts or periscopes; but as the battlefield was soon to be made treeless, their possibilities were limited." *

The British began their bombardment on June 25, continuing through the 28th when it was decided because of bad weather to sustain the shelling until July 1. In the meantime, night raiding parties examined the results of the firing, even in the midst of the continuing bombardment. One thing was clear to all, the shelling was not effective as a wire-cutter. The rolls of barbed wire stood mostly intact as a barrier to the German lines. Brian Gardner says the leader of one such raiding party reported:

" 'When we did get started I soon discovered that cutting tangles of barbed wire in the dark in a desperate hurry is a job that needs ingenuity, even when your wire-cutters have rubber-covered handles and are fresh from the Army and Navy Stores. More than once we

* *The Big Push*, pp. 58, 59.

were driven in by shells which landed in front of our trench (some of them were our own dropping short); two men were wounded and some of the others were reluctant to resume work. In the first greying of dawn only three of us were still at it . . . but as the light increased I began to realise the unimpressive effect of the snippings and snatchings which had made such a mess of our leather gloves. We had been working three and a half hours, but the hedge hadn't suffered much damage, it seemed.'

"Later, on his own initiative, Sassoon went out to complete the job in broad daylight. 'It was', he later recorded in *Memoirs of an Infantry Officer*, 'rather like going out to weed a neglected garden after being warned that there might be a tiger among the gooseberry bushes.' Sassoon was, by all accounts, an astonishingly brave young officer. He was awarded the M. C. the day before the battle began.

"Every infantryman assembled his 'fighting order' and strapped himself up in it. This included: steel helmet, entrenching tool, rolled groundsheet, water bottle, haversack (with mess tin, towel, shaving kit, extra socks, message books, cheese, and preserved rations), two gas helmets, tear goggles, wire-cutters, field dressing and iodine, two bandoliers of small arms ammunition, and a rifle.

"The total equipment per man was meant to be about sixty-six pounds; in fact it was a good deal more, because of various odd articles which were distributed among them, such as picks, shovels (fifty to the leading companies), sand-bags, Mills grenades, carrier-pigeon boxes, telephones, and ladders. Officers and N. C. O.s also carried four flares each.

"Says the *Official History*:

'The total weight . . . made it difficult to get out of a trench, impossible to move much quicker than a slow walk, or to rise and lie down quickly. This overloading of the men is by many infantry officers regarded as one of the principal reasons for the heavy losses and failure of their battalions; for their men could not get through the machine-gun zone with sufficient speed.' " *

Then on July 1, at 6:25 A.M. ". . . there was an incessant earthquake of artillery fire. Shells screamed and whistled over the

* *The Big Push*, p. 67.

waiting troops. They burst, with great explosions, all along the German line, in No-Man's-Land, and even on the British trenches. It was almost impossible to talk, so great was the din. Some men half-heartedly cheered, believing this final blow must have finished what chance there was left of any opposition. Eight minutes before zero the mortars joined in, firing thirty rounds a minute each.

"The order was given: 'Fix bayonets.'

"The clinking of steel sounded down miles of narrow, twisting trench.

"The mines went off with dull thuds, or loud explosions, all adding to the deafening row. Men were breathing quickly, and swallowing often. Some shook hands. Some were sick. Seven-thirty showed on the dials of thousands of watches. Flasks appeared as if from nowhere. Suddenly the barrage lifted; there was a strange, uncanny silence. With cocked rifles slung over their right shoulders, an army of over a hundred thousand city clerks, farm hands, solicitors, miners, and barrow-boys went over the top.

"Along most of the eighteen-mile front, men were met with heavy machine-gun fire a few seconds after they had clambered up the ladders and swarmed over the parapets, through their own wire and into No-Man's-Land. It did not take long for the German gunners to scramble up from their dug-outs as soon as the barrage lifted to their rear at seven thirty. On some parts of the front the attackers were met by heavy artillery barrage as well as machine-gun fire.

"As they went over the top into the hailstorm of bullets, men mumbled prayers, stepped over corpses, pushed aside dead bodies of their comrades that fell back down the ladders, screamed out for 'stretcher bearers', and many knew already that it was going to be worse than any had expected. Bits of limbs flew about in the air. A leg, with puttee streaming behind it, landed in the wire. Some men could go no farther and sat down and wept.

"But all down the front the attack pushed on towards the German wire and the first enemy trench. As the soldiers fell, thousands more were incessantly pouring over to take their places. Steadily the decimated, always thinning line pressed on.

"In some places junior officers waved on their men with whistles jammed in their teeth piercing above the scream of battle. In other places, it had been ordered that 'strict silence' would be maintained during the advance and no whistles were to be blown.

"Once they had left the trenches and got through the British wire in single file, the remaining troops lined up shoulder to shoulder and walked on into the fire, carrying their useless rifles. Owing to the weight of equipment, at no point in the whole advance was any attempt made to run. Wincing and blinking, shouting and cursing, they stumbled on under the blazing sun." *

MAMETZ WOOD

There was to be no real breakthrough at the Somme. Instead the well-established process of attrition, of "nibbling," took over. Attacks were launched to knock out tenacious strong points but losses were so high in the achievement that the assaults stalled again and again.

"One of the most typical of the engagements taking place at this time was the struggle for the wood at Mametz, in which the British made almost as many difficulties for themselves as they received from the Germans. It was a thick wood, of hornbeams, limes, oaks, and a few beeches. The undergrowth was high, and there was much bramble. German machine-gunners and snipers had made some use of camouflage, and severe wire entanglements were knitted with the undergrowth. The way in which the British went about taking this wood, which was not in fact very heavily held, was clumsy in the extreme. The bombardment had made the wood, on a spur and with an area of about two hundred acres, into even more of a maze. It was

* *The Big Push*, pp. 72, 73, 74.

continually full of smoke, and sometimes partly on fire. Haig himself was particularly concerned with its capture. Rawlinson, however, told him that some of the senior commanders would have to be relieved of their commands before a successful assault on the wood could be launched. This was done.

"On 8 July, a corps order was issued at one forty P.M., directing the 38th Division to secure part of Mametz Wood. Reports were coming in that it was deserted (but other reports stated that patrols had been fired on when approaching it). Division ordered brigade to carry out the attack. Brigade ordered a battalion (the 14th Welch Fusiliers). Battalion ordered a platoon. The platoon commander, however, had to report that owing to confusion in the trenches, his platoon had found it impossible to reach the starting point of the attack. Mametz Wood was not taken that night; nor was it to be taken so casually.

"Another attack was ordered for the 10th—but on this occasion the whole division was to take part.

"To receive their instructions for the 10th, brigadiers had to trek to divisional headquarters, six miles behind the line. So it was nearly midnight when battalions got their orders for the attack the follow-ing day. Troops had to cover a thousand yards of open ground before they reached the edge of the wood, and nearly all this was uphill. The attack took place in early daylight and was immediately machine-gunned and decimated. Officers took over the groups nearest at hand. The British barrage was short and many men were killed by their own guns. The edge of the wood was reached by some units, which took shelter there.

"Patrols of the advanced units delved into the wood and reported the enemy was not there in great numbers. At some parts opposition ceased, and two battalion commanders asked for permission to go on. A further artillery barrage of the wood, however, had been arranged and it was found impossible to alter this. After a respite, the enemy thought better of evacuating the wood. Shelling had made the scene into a nightmare landscape. One who was there wrote: 'Limbs and mutilated trunks, here and there a detached head, forming splashes of red against the green leaves . . . one tree held in its branches a leg, with its torn flesh hanging down over a spray of leaf.' Swarms of flies, blackening the corpses, revolted many more than anything else they saw.

"When the second stage of the advance did at last take place, there was much wild shooting in the trees, and dreadful confusion. Telephone wires had been cut by enemy artillery or by British shells falling short, and practically all the runners were casualties (in one brigade all ninety-six of them were lost). Attempts to reorganize the confused mass of troops inside the wood were unsuccessful.

"Eventually, however, it was cleared to within forty yards of its northern edge. A decision for another attack, to clear it completely, was cancelled owing to the exhaustion of the troops. Mametz Wood was now ceaselessly shelled, the cracking of the wood and the explosions making a deafening noise, and there was some panicking.

"Next day another brigade relieved that which had spent a day and night fighting in Mametz Wood, and it was ordered to attack." *

UP TO MAMETZ**

by L. W. Griffith

At seven in the morning, Brigade Headquarters was to 'close down' at one place and to 'open' at another. This has a sound of the impossible in it, but it is easily resolved into a problem of telephone communication. If there is a telephone at the new headquarters, giving a means of speech backward to Divisional Headquarters and forward to Battalion Headquarters, the command of the brigade can

* *The Big Push*, pp. 103, 104, 105.
** From *Up to Mametz*, published by Faber & Faber, London.

be as well exercised from the new hole in the ground as from the old. For in this war, a telephone wire was not only the outward sign of command, but the life-blood of its existence; a General without a telephone was to all practical purposes impotent, a lay figure dressed in uniform, deprived of eyes, arms and ears.

All through the night the signallers had worked at their task of picking and choosing the right wire from the tangled mass of tendrils that wound round post and trench in this desperate jungle, following the wire across country, testing it in sections, until the welcome sound of the right voice in response brought an end to their search. A chance shell, or the unlucky stumble of a passer-by, might cut the wire and send weary men out again on their search.

In the stuffy darkness of the old German dugout an orderly lit a candle and roused us to say that it was half-past four. I swung my feet over the side of the wire-net mattress and stumbled up the stairs into the thin chill of the dawn, stupid and less than half awake, conscious chiefly of the difficulty of keeping my eyes from closing, and of a clammy, bitter-tasting thirst, a legacy from a short and too heavy sleep in a musty dugout. Shivering and stretching, stamping my feet on the duckboards, swinging my arms like a cab-driver, I walked along towards the sound of a crackling wood fire and its promise of a cup of tea. There was an unnatural stillness in the air. No guns were firing, no transport moving. A thin column of smoke was rising slowly, twisting and swaying idly in the thin light. The whole world seemed to have slackened its pace to the merest saunter through the sky, with no perceptible disturbance of the morning air, without song of bird or step of man. A vague unreality had taken the place of the visible and audible environment, concealing all the muddle and horrors of the day before, revealing nothing but a sleeping shape stretching out over the chalky downs, blackening the light greenish-grey of the landscape.

As the light grew stronger, this straggling trail of black hardened into its distinguishable components; wagons, dumps of ammunition and stores, battery after battery of guns, big and small. A little below the dugout, in the din between it and the ground rising up towards

Mametz, a string of guns squatted in a row, and from underneath a bivouac a gunner crept out, stretched himself, and walked through the line of guns to a stake in the ground. From this he removed a lamp. Other men followed him, appearing mysteriously from nowhere, and soon there was a bustle of life in this tiny village of nomads.

Far away to the South a shell burst in the empty air. Somewhere behind our hill a big gun fired, another followed it, and suddenly the battery below blasted a stuttering sentence of noises. The Devil had taken his seat at the keyboard to play the opening bars of his morning hymn; another day beginning, the last day for so many, a fine sunny day to devote to killing and bruising. Was it my last day? With a wise obstinacy, the mind refused to dwell on such a thought, and the signalman in my brain shunted such futile traffic into some siding, giving the right of way to the greater utility of a desire for a cup of tea. I found some biscuit and a tin of jam, and sat on an ammunition box near the fire, eating and drinking in silence. When I had finished I went down into the dugout for my shaving tackle, and as I descended the steps into a crescendo of foul stuffiness I wondered how I had dared to sleep in such a cesspool of smells, and hurried back to the trench to shave.

When I came back to the fire I found Taylor, the Brigade Signalling Officer, seated on a box and drinking his cup of tea. He was a man of forty, quietly carrying about him a reserved air of authority and competence, unhurried in movement and in speech. The technical nature of his work preserved him from interference, and he ruled over his kingdom of men with a certainty of control denied to an infantry officer. No Brigadier could dispute with him concerning the wisdom or unwisdom of his dispositions of men or material. His duty was to give others a means of speech, and as he never failed in his task, his competency was obvious to all.

This morning his face was as grey as his hair, and his eyes were dull and tired. I greeted him and sat down by his side.

'When did you finish your job?' I asked him.

'I've just come from there now, and I'm going back with some more men as soon as they have had a bite of food. It's a long tramp from here to Pommiers Redoubt, and I lost my way coming back. . . . Lost two men on the job already!'

'Killed?' I asked.

'No, both wounded—shrapnel in the leg. I had a terrible job to get them away. We were out on a line across country and I couldn't find a battalion or anybody likely to have stretcher-bearers. I tied them up as well as I could and went out on a search. I left my torch with them in case I couldn't find my way back in the dark. Just as I was giving it up and going back to them, a gun went off near me, a blaze of light and a hell of a noise. I was down on my face before you could say "knife", and I crept along till I got a bit nearer, and then I shouted. A gunner came out and yelled to me to come in quickly before they fired again. So I got some stretcher-bearers and got my lads away. Two good men, just when I most wanted them. Still, they are well out of it, poor devils, with a day like this in front of them.'

'What's it like at Pommiers Redoubt?' I asked.

'Just like any other hole in the ground. There's some heavy artillery headquarters there, and we may be glad of their lines before the day is out. . . . There's a lot of our fellows out there not buried yet. . . . You know old Evans the padre?'

'Yes, I know him.'

'I met him this morning, half an hour ago, just as it was getting light. He was going to do a bit of burying. I thought he looked queer . . . he was talking to himself, praying, maybe, when I walked along with him. It was in North Wales Welsh, and I couldn't make much of it. I got talking to him, and I asked him why he was up so early. He said he hadn't been to bed. He went towards Fricourt yesterday evening looking for a grave. Someone you knew, said I. . . . Yes, my own boy's grave, said he.'

'Good God, I knew young Evans well—he was in the ranks with me,' I answered.

'Well, Evans, poor chap, had heard yesterday evening that his boy was killed near Fricourt the day before, so he went off at once to try to find his grave. He walked about for hours, but couldn't find any one who knew where it was, nor could he find the padre who buried him. He walked till he could walk no more, got a cup of tea from some gunners, and had a rest, and then walked back here. And now he's out again. Going to bury other people's boys, he said, since he couldn't find his own boy's grave to pray over. . . . What could you say? I left him to turn up to this place . . . my Welsh isn't very good, as you know, but I managed to say to him, "I'm not a soldier now, padre; I'm taking off my hat to you." And so I did, I took off my tin helmet. . . . You couldn't talk English to a man who had lost his boy. . . .'

'No . . . not to a Welshman,' I replied.

'But there's a man for you, Griff . . . off to bury other men's boys at five in the morning, and maybe his own son not buried yet, a couple of miles away. There was some shrapnel overhead, but I saw him going up the slope as if he were alone in the world. If I come through this bloody business, I'd like to go to that man's church. The only thing he said that I could make out was that bit of a Welsh hymn—you'll know it, the one they sing at funerals to that tune that curdles your blood worse than the Dead March. . . . Well, this is no time to be talking of funerals, I'm going back to Pommiers Redoubt—are you coming with me?'

'I might as well,' I replied, 'I'm doing nothing here, but I'd better ask the Brigade Major first, in case he wants me.'

The Brigade Major, after some years in the East, was not at his best in the early morning, and in the minimum of words, told me that I could go.

Taylor was stuffing some biscuits into his haversack when I came back to him.

'You'd better do the same,' he said. 'You never know where you might land up to-day.'

'Cheer up, Taylor,' I answered. 'There are so many of us about to-day that you and I might well be booked for a through trip.'

I cut off a hunk of cheese and put it in my haversack with some biscuits, and filled my water-bottle: pipe, tobacco, matches, maps, note-book, orders—I made sure that these were on or about me.

We set off up the hill, passing the grey and red ruins of Mametz village on our left as we walked up towards Pommiers Redoubt. The guns were firing, and an occasional shell-burst crashed through the air with a venomous answer. Transport was crawling about in the distance, small groups of men were moving, dark against the white gashes in the chalk. Scattered equipment lying about underfoot, tangles of wire, small dumps of forgotten stores, all left behind in the advance. Other things were left behind in the advance, part of the purchase price of this downland, grim disfigured corpses rotting in the sun, so horrible in their discolour that it called for an act of faith to believe that these were once men, young men, sent to this degradation by their fellow men. One thought ran in and out of the mind like a shuttle in a loom; any one of the thousands of seconds in this July day might reduce Taylor or myself into a like travesty of living man, useless lumber best thrown away near some such heap of rubble as Mametz, 'where Ruin calls his brother Death'. There was some comfort in the thought that my wife did not know that this day held for me any fuller measure of danger than any other day of war, that for her there was no greater straining of the tense string that ran from hope to fear. And if I were killed, I would turn from man to memory in her heart without leaving a mutilated shell of flesh to haunt her eyes.

'I haven't seen anything of my young brother for some days,' I said to Taylor. 'I wonder what he is doing. He's such a kid, for all his uniform. He ought to be still in school, not in this bloody shambles.'

'He's all right,' replied Taylor. 'I saw him last night. The brigade called for two runners from each battalion, and he came as one of them—he's somewhere near that old German dugout we came from.'

'I wish I'd known. It was his birthday two days ago, and I've got a little present for him in my valise. I wonder if he'll ever see another birthday. . . . I don't know how I could face my mother if anything happened to him and I got through.'

'Well, he's got a chance, Griff—he might be in the line. What do you think of our job to-day?'

'The General was cursing last night at his orders. He said that only a madman could have issued them. He called the Divisional Staff a lot of plumbers, herring-gutted at that. He argued at the time, and asked for some control over the artillery that is going to cover us, but he got nothing out of them. We are not allowed to attack at dawn; we must wait for the show at Contalmaison, well away on our left.'

'We'll get a good view of that show from Pommiers Redoubt.'

'I dare say, but don't you think that it is a funny thing to keep us waiting in the lobby? We are going to attack Mametz Wood from one side, and Contalmaison is on the other side of the Wood—why shouldn't both attacks be made at the same time? It would spread out the German fire.'

'I suppose it would spread out ours too,' said Taylor, 'but if you are going to start asking "Why" about orders you'll soon be off the Staff or off your head. You might as well say, "Why attack the Wood at all?"'

'But I do say that, Taylor. Look at it now—it's a forest. What damage can our guns do to that place? If you had a good dugout near the edge of that wood, and a machine-gun, how many men would you allow to cross that slope leading up to the Wood? You'd mow them down as soon as they stood up.'

We had reached the high ground at Pommiers Redoubt, and, standing in a trench, scanning the Wood with our glasses, it seemed as thick as a virgin forest. There was no sign of life in it, no one could say whether it concealed ten thousand men or ten machine guns. Its edges were clean cut, as far as the eye could see, and the ground between us and the Wood was bare of any cover. Our men were assembled in trenches above a dip in the ground, and from these they were to advance, descend into the hollow, and cross the bare slope in the teeth of the machine-gunners in the Wood. On their right, as they advanced across the bullet-swept zone, they would be exposed to enfilade fire, for the direction of their advance was nearly parallel to the German trenches towards Bazentin, and it would be folly to suppose that the German machine-guns were not sited to sweep that slope leading to the Wood.

'I'm not surprised that the General cursed when he got his orders,' said Taylor. 'The truth about the Brigadier is that he's got too much sense. He was soldiering when some of the fellows above him were still playing marbles. I'm going to see my signallers. . . . I'll see you later.'

A little further along the trench a group of officers were engaged in a discussion over a map spread out on a box. I went up to speak to them, and found that this was the headquarters of a group of Heavy Artillery concerned in the bombardment of Contalmaison, and about to wipe it off the map, as I gathered.

Taylor came up out of a dugout. 'We're through to the old Brigade Headquarters, the Division, and to the battalions. How long we'll be through to the battalions is another story,' he said.

The General arrived with the Brigade Major and the Staff Captain, looked around him quickly, and turned to me.

'Have you found a good place for us?'

'Yes sir, there's room in the signallers' dugout, but this is a good place for seeing.'

'It's close on seven o'clock. Are we through to everybody, and have the battalions reported that they are in position?' he asked.

'Yes sir.'

'Then send out the report that Brigade Headquarters has opened here. You stay with me, and be ready to take down any orders or messages when the time comes.'

With this he went to consult with the Brigade Major. I stood on a step in the side of the trench, studying the country to the East and identifying the various features from the map. Our guns were quiet, and, although everybody within sight was moving, there was a weird stillness in the air, a brooding menace. Why was I standing here when men I knew were lined up in readiness to expose their bodies to a driving sleet of lead? The thought of the day's torment, doomed, as I thought, from its beginning, to bring no recompense, weighed like a burden of iron. The sound of a heavy bombardment, some distance away to our left, broke in upon the silence and grew to a storm of noise and smoke. Contalmaison was the target, prominent upon a hill until the smoke obscured the hill-top, turning it into a dark cloud hung between a blue sky and brown-pitted earth. Out of this cloud, at intervals of some minutes, an orange sheet of flame made an effort to escape, only to be conquered and smudged out by the all-pervading smoke. It did not seem possible that there could be guns enough in France to create such a fury as this, and my mind went back to the artillery fire of 1915 and early 1916. Our trench bombardments were things of no importance when contrasted with this, and I felt half ashamed to remember that they had frightened me.

At eight o'clock the artillery began its bombardment of the edge of Mametz Wood. A thousand yards away from where I stood, our two battalions were waiting. I read the orders again. The attack was to be carried out in three stages, beginning at half-past eight, reaching in succession three positions inside the Wood, under the protection of an artillery barrage. Smoke screens were to be formed here and there. Everything sounded so simple and easy.

A few minutes after eight, all our telephone wires to the battalions were cut by the enemy's reply to our fire. There was no smoke screen, for some reason never explained—perhaps someone forgot about it. This was the first departure from the simplicity of the printed word. Messages came through, a steady trickle of runners bringing evil news; our fire had not masked the German machine-guns in Mametz Wood, nor in the wood near Bazentin. The elaborate time-table suddenly became a thing of no meaning, as unrelated to our condition as one of Napoleon's orders; our artillery barrage was advancing in mockery of our failure, for we were two hundred yards away from the Wood.

A message arrived from the Division. In twenty minutes' time, the artillery would begin another bombardment of the edge of the Wood, and under cover of this we were to renew the attack— in twenty minutes. We were a thousand yards away from the battalions, with no telephone communication; there were maps at Divisional Headquarters, they knew where we were, they knew where the battalions were, and they knew that our lines were cut. A simple sum in arithmetic. . . . Our operation was isolated; no one was attacking on either flank of our Brigade, so that there was complete freedom of choice as to time. With all the hours of the clock to choose from, some master-mind must needs select the only hour to be avoided. He did not ask himself whether the order could reach its ultimate destination in time . . . the answer to that sum in arithmetic.

Every attempt to move near the Wood was met by a burst of frontal and enfilade machine-gun fire. Shells were falling, taking a steady toll of lives. Later, another order came from Divisional Headquarters. We were to attack again, to make a third effort to penetrate this wall of lead. The General gave some orders to his Brigade-Major, called me to accompany him, and we set out for Caterpillar Wood and to reach the battalions. Although the day was fine, the heavy rains of the preceding days had turned the chalky soil into a stiff glue. The hurry in our minds accentuated the slowness of our progress, and I felt as if some physical force was dragging me back. Haste meant a fall into a shell hole, for we had abandoned the attempt to move along the trench. Shrapnel was bursting overhead, and a patter of machine-gun bullets spat through the air. We passed through Caterpillar Wood, and in a disused trench on our left I saw an Artillery officer. I turned off to ask him whether his telephone was working, and learned that he was in communication with a Heavy Artillery Group somewhere beyond Pommiers Redoubt. I ran down the trench to rejoin the General, and we dropped down the bank into the nullah between Caterpillar Wood and Mametz Wood, passing a stream of 'walking wounded' making their way out.

There was a dugout in the bank, with scores of stretchers down on the ground in front, each stretcher occupied by a fellow creature, maimed and in pain. This was the Advance Dressing Station; twenty rounds of shrapnel would have made stretchers unnecessary. Along the bare ridge rising up to Mametz Wood our men were burrowing into the ground with their entrenching tools, seeking whatever cover they might make. A few shells were falling, surprisingly few. Wounded men were crawling back from the ridge, men were crawling forward with ammunition. No attack could succeed over such ground as this, swept from front and side by machine-guns at short range. Down in the nullah we were out of sight of the enemy, but fifteen minutes of shrapnel would have reduced the brigade to a battalion, and every minute that passed seemed to bring nearer the hour of our inevitable annihilation. We were caught in a trap, unable to advance, unable to withdraw without being observed. It must ever remain one of the many mysteries of the War why the enemy did not pound us with shell fire, for this was so obviously the only place of assembly.

The time was drawing near for the renewal of the attack, for another useless slaughter. Casualties in officers had been extremely heavy, and the battalions were somewhat disorganized.

'This is sheer lunacy,' said the General. 'I've tried all day to stop it. We could creep up to the edge of the Wood by night and rush it in the morning, but they won't listen to me. . . . It breaks my heart to see all this.'

'If I could get you through on the telephone, would you talk to them again?' I asked.

'Of course I would, but all the wires are cut, and there is no time to go back.'

'I know of a telephone to an Artillery Group, and they might get you through to the Division,' I answered.

'Find out at once whether I can get through,' he replied.

I hurried up to the trench where I had seen the Artillery officer and found that his wires were still uncut, and as I ran back to the General I prayed in my heart that they would hold; the lives of some hundreds of men depended upon it. It did not occur to me that words sent along that wire might fail in their object, that someone sitting far away would look at a map and say, 'No, you must reach that Wood at all costs.' Seen in its stark reality, our position was so hopeless that a dispassionate account of it must convince any one, even at a distance of six miles, that to remain where we were would be no less calamitous than to try to advance. The enemy had shown no desire to hold that exposed ridge with men, for his bullets were defence enough, and in a short space of time his artillery must realize that there was a magnificent target in that hollow between the ridge and the bank.

When I came back to the hollow, I could not find the General. I ran from one group of men to another, working my way up the ridge, until I found him organizing the defence of the position against any possible counter-attack. Shells did not seem to matter; my whole existence, up to that very minute, had been of no importance to the world, but my original conversation with that Artillery officer, so obviously prompted by what men call Destiny, could lead to the saving of hundreds of lives, and must not fail to do so. I knew that I had been 'chosen' for this. Ten minutes later I sat in the trench while the General spoke on the telephone, tersely describing the utter folly of any course of action other than a gradual withdrawal under cover of outposts, and quoting figures of our casualties. He was arguing with determination. There was opposition, but he won. As I jumped up to start on our way back to the ridge, he stopped me.

'Wait a minute. They are shelling this bank, and this message must get through. Give me a sheet of paper,' said he. He wrote down his order for the withdrawal and gave it to me. 'You go one way, and I'll go another way. Join me in the hollow. Go as fast as you can.' With this he went down the trench, and I ran and stumbled down the bank, still feeling perfectly safe in the hands of Destiny.

Two hours later the General and I were dragging our way from the nullah and back towards Pommiers Redoubt. We sat down in a trench to let a file of men pass by, and I suddenly noticed that his face was grey and drawn.

'Have you eaten anything since this morning?' I asked him.

'No . . . have you?' he replied. 'I feel whacked.'

'Will you wait here a few minutes—I'll be back soon,' I said.

I had seen a dug-out, and I went inside it. Some signallers were lighting a fire to boil a mess-tin full of water; they lent me an enamel cup, and in it I put a tablet of compressed tea. The brew was strong and the water was not boiling, but it was a warm drink, and I took it back to the General. It revived him, and we munched our biscuits as we walked along.

Back again to Pommiers Redoubt, but with a difference, in the flat greyness of approaching dusk. The noise of the guns had died down to a sullen scale-practice, with an occasional, and almost accidental chord, so different from the crashes of the day. Stretcher-bearers, bowed forward under their straps, were carrying their burdens of suffering across the ploughed and pitted slopes.

'How did you come to find that telephone?' asked the General.

'I happened to notice the Artillery officer on my way down, and I went to ask him if his line back was working. Don't you remember my leaving you?'

'No, I don't remember. . . . Well, it saved the lives of some hundreds of men, but it has put an end to me.'

'Why do you say that?'

'I spoke my mind about the whole business . . . you heard me. They wanted us to press on at all costs, talked about determination, and suggested that I didn't realize the importance of the operation. As good as told me that I was tired and didn't want to tackle the job. Difficult to judge on the spot, they said! As if the whole trouble hadn't arisen because someone found it so easy to judge when he was six miles away and had never seen the country, and couldn't read a map. You mark my words, they'll send me home for this: they want butchers, not brigadiers. They'll remember now that I told them, before we began, that the attack could not succeed unless the machine-guns were masked. I shall be in England in a month.'

He had saved the Brigade from annihilation. That the rescue, in terms of men, was no more than a respite of days was no fault of his, for there is no saving of life in war until the eleventh hour of the last day is drawing to an end. It was nearly midnight when we heard that the last of our men had withdrawn from that ridge and valley, leaving the ground empty, save for the bodies of those who had to fall to prove to our command that machine-guns can defend a bare slope. Six weeks later the General went home.

The next day brought no time for crying over spilt milk. The Staff Captain had become a casualty, and had been evacuated as a shell-shock case, so that it fell to my lot to do his work, poorly equipped as I was for the task. For the first time I realized that, battle or no battle, reports must be made, returns prepared, and administrative work must continue as if we were all in barracks. I did my best, but if there are lacunæ in the statistics, memoranda 'lost' and unanswered, mine must be the blame. The General and the Brigade Major were so concerned with matters of war that I could not in very shame intrude upon their consultations to ask advice on questions that appeared to me to lack fundamental importance. On paper, I promised where I did not perform, and, over the telephone, parried all demands from the Division.

The two remaining brigades of the Division were to attack Mametz Wood in the afternoon of the following day, and we were to be in reserve, ready to take over the defence of the wood if the attack succeeded. This venture was differently staged. A narrower front gave promise of greater support from the artillery, and the approach, bad as it was, did not make success impossible. Until we were called upon to fight, the brigade was to spend its time carrying and working for the others, in spite of our exhaustion in numbers and in strength. At the last moment, the attack was postponed for twelve hours, and it was not until dawn on the 10th July that the flower of young Wales stood up to the machine-guns, with a success that astonished all who knew the ground. Two of our battalions had become involved in the fighting in the Wood, and at five o'clock in the afternoon, our brigade was ordered to relieve the attacking brigades and to take over the responsibility for the defence of the sector against any counter-attacks. It was five o'clock in the morning before this relief was completed.

A little before dawn, the General and the Brigade Major went up to the Wood, leaving me to follow them at midday. At seven in the morning, as I was wrestling with some papers that I did not understand, a runner came in with a message from the General. The Brigade Major had been wounded, and I was to go up at once to join the General in the Wood. This, at any rate, was a man's job, and I left the papers in their disarray. A month ago, my military horizon was bounded by the limits of a company of infantry; now I was to be both Brigade Major and Staff Captain to a Brigadier-General in the middle of a battle. I consoled myself with the thought that if I could originate nothing, I could do what I was told to do.

I passed through two barrages before I reached the Wood, one aimed at the body, and the other at the mind. The enemy was shelling the approach from the South with some determination, but I was fortunate enough to escape injury and to pass on to an ordeal ever greater. Men of my old battalion were lying dead on the ground in great profusion. They wore a yellow badge on their sleeves, and without this distinguishing mark, it would have been impossible to recognize the remains of many of them. I felt that I had run away.

Before the Division had attempted to capture Mametz Wood, it was known that the undergrowth in it was so dense that it was all but impossible to move through it. Through the middle of the Wood a narrow ride ran to a communication trench leading to the German main Second Line of defence in front of Bazentin, a strong trench system permitting of a quick reinforcement of the garrison of the Wood. With equal facility, the Wood could be evacuated by the enemy and shelled, as it was not part of the trench system.

My first acquaintance with the stubborn nature of the undergrowth came when I attempted to leave the main ride to escape a heavy shelling. I could not push a way through it, and I had to return to the ride. Years of neglect had turned the Wood into a formidable barrier, a mile deep. Heavy shelling of the Southern end had beaten down some of the young growth, but it had also thrown trees and large branches into a barricade. Equipment, ammunition, rolls of barbed wire, tins of food, gas-helmets and rifles were lying about everywhere. There were more corpses than men, but there were worse sights than corpses. Limbs and mutilated trunks, here and there a detached head, forming splashes of red against the green leaves, and, as in advertisement of the horror of our way of life and death, and of our crucifixion of youth, one tree held in its branches a leg, with its torn flesh hanging down over a spray of leaf.

Each bursting shell reverberated in a roll of thunder echoing through the Wood, and the acid fumes lingered between the trees. The sun was shining strongly overhead, unseen by us, but felt in its effort to pierce through the curtain of leaves. After passing through that charnel house at the southern end, with its sickly air of corruption, the smell of fresh earth and of crushed bark grew into complete domination, as clean to the senses as the other was foul. So tenacious in these matters is memory that I can never encounter the smell of cut green timber without resurrecting the vision of the tree that flaunted a human limb. A message was now on its way to some quiet village in Wales, to a grey farmhouse on the slope of a hill running down to Cardigan Bay, or to a miner's cottage in a South Wales valley, a word of death, incapable, in this late century of the Christian Era, of association with this manner of killing. That the sun could shine on this mad cruelty and on the quiet peace of an upland tarn near Snowdon, at what we call the same instant of Time, threw a doubt upon all meaning in words. Death was warped from a thing of sadness into a screaming horror, not content with stealing life from its shell, but trampling in lunatic fury upon the rifled cabinet we call a corpse.

There are times when fear drops below the threshold of the mind; never beyond recall, but far enough from the instant to become a background. Moments of great exaltation, of tremendous physical exertion, when activity can dominate over all rivals in the mind, the times of exhaustion that follow these great moments; these are, as I knew from the teachings of the months gone by, occasions of release from the governance of fear. As I hurried along the ride in this nightmare wood, stepping round the bodies clustered about the shell holes, here and there helping a wounded man to clamber over a fallen tree trunk, falling flat on my face when the whistle of an approaching shell grew into a shrieking 'YOU', aimed at my ear, to paralyse before it killed, then stumbling on again through a cloud of bitter smoke, I learned that there was another way of making fear a thing of small account.

It was life rather than death that faded away into the distance, as I grew into a state of not-thinking, not-feeling, not-seeing. I moved past trees, past other things; men passed by me, carrying other men, some crying, some cursing, some silent. They were all shadows, and I was no greater than they. Living or dead, all were unreal. Balanced uneasily on the knife-edge between utter oblivion and this temporary not-knowing, it seemed a little matter whether I were destined to go forward to death or to come back to life. Past and future were equidistant and unattainable, throwing no bridge of desire across the gap that separated me both from my remembered self and from all that I had hoped to grasp. I walked as on a mountain in a mist, seeing neither sky above nor valley beneath, lost to all sense of far or near, up or down, either in time or space. I saw no precipice, and so I feared none.

Thus it was that the passing seconds dealt a sequence of hammer-blows, at first so poignantly sharp that the mind recoiled in unbelief, but in their deadly repetition dulling the power of response and reaction into a blind acceptance of this tragedy, and in the merciful end, pounding all sensibility into an atrophy that refused to link sight to thought. A swirl of mist within me had thrown a curtain to conceal the chasm of fear, and I walked on unheeding and unexpectant.

I reached a cross-ride in the Wood where four lanes broadened into a confused patch of destruction. Fallen trees, shell holes, a hurriedly dug trench beginning and ending in an uncertain manner, abandoned rifles, broken branches with their sagging leaves, an unopened box of ammunition, sandbags half-filled with bombs, a derelict machine-gun propping up the head of an immobile figure in uniform, with a belt of ammunition drooping from the breech into a pile of red-stained earth—this is the livery of War. Shells were falling, over and short, near and wide, to show that somewhere over the hill a gunner was playing the part of blind fate for all who walked past this well-marked spot. Here, in the struggle between bursting iron and growing timber, iron had triumphed and trampled over an uneven circle some forty yards in diameter. Against the surrounding wall of thick greenery, the earth showed red and fresh, lit by the clean sunlight, and the splintered tree-trunks shone with a damp whiteness, but the green curtains beyond could conceal nothing of greater horror than the disorder revealed in this clearing.

Even now, after all these years, this round ring of man-made hell bursts into my vision, elbowing into an infinity of distance the wall of my room, dwarfing into nothingness objects we call real. Blue sky above, a band of green trees, and a ploughed graveyard in which living men moved worm-like in and out of sight; three men digging a trench, thigh-deep in the red soil, digging their own graves, as it chanced, for a bursting shell turned their shelter into a tomb; two signallers crouched in a large shell hole, waiting for a summons to move, but bearing in their patient and tired inactivity the look of dead men ready to rise at the trump of a Last Judgment.

Other memories steal upon the screen of vision, growing imperceptibly from a dim remembrance of a part into a firmly-built unity of composition as the eye gains control over its focussing, but this image of war in its brutality flashes in an instant, sharp and clear in its uttermost detail. Then, at its first seeing, it was unreal, unrelated to my past, for the mist was within me, but now and for ever it must rise with every closing of my eyes into a stabbing reality that governs the future. So many things are seen more clearly now that the passing years have allowed the mud of action to settle at the bottom of the pool of life.

Near the edge of this ring I saw a group of officers. The Brigadier was talking to one of his battalion commanders, and Taylor, the Signals officer, was arguing with the Intelligence officer about the position on the map of two German machine-guns. The map itself was a sign of the shrinking of our world into a small compass: a sheet of foolscap paper bearing nothing but a large scale plan of Mametz Wood, with capital letters to identify its many corners, was chart enough for our adventure this day. 'What has happened to the Brigadier?' I asked Taylor. 'Why is his arm in a sling?'

'Shrapnel,' he answered. 'He got hit as he was coming up to the Wood, but he got the doctor to dress it for him. He says it doesn't hurt him, but I expect it will before the day is over.'

'Did you see the Brigade Major . . . was he badly hit?'

'Shrapnel in the leg—his gammy leg. The stretcher-bearers took him away, cursing everybody and damning his luck. Seems to me he doesn't know luck when he sees it. You'll have to get down to it now.'

'Yes. Tell me what has happened so far.'

'You never saw such a mess. Nobody knows where anybody is, the other brigades are still here—what's left of them—all mixed up.'

'Are your lines holding? Are you through to anybody?'

'Devil a soul,' answered Taylor. 'As soon as I mend a line the Boche breaks it. You can't keep a line up with that barrage across the bottom of the Wood. There's an artillery F. O. O. just behind you, in that shell hole; I don't know what the devil he's doing up here—he can't see twenty yards in front of him, and all his lines are gone. He might as well be in Cardiff.'

As soon as the battalion commander had gone I joined the Brigadier.

'Is this the Brigade Headquarters?' I asked.

'It is,' he replied. 'It's an unhealthy place, but we've got to be somewhere where we can be found by night as well as by day. Get your notebook and take down the position of affairs at the moment. We have been sent here to take over the line and to make secure against counter-attacks. There are four battalions of our brigade, and what is left of four other battalions. We are holding an irregular line about three hundred yards from the end of the Wood, bending back towards the West. The units are very mixed up, and I've just come back from trying to give them their boundaries. They are all straightening themselves out and digging in, but the undergrowth is so dense that it will be some hours before they are in their proper places.'

'Are we supposed to attack and clear the Wood?'

'No. Our orders last night were to take over the line. I've told the battalion commanders to reconnoitre and to push out where they can. We don't know whether the enemy is holding the far end in any great strength.'

'If we have to attack later on, how do you propose to do it?'

'By surprise,' answered the General. 'With the bayonet only. That's the only way to get through the Wood. If our artillery will keep quiet, we can do it. Here's my map—make a summary of what I've told you. It took me hours to get round our line.'

Runners came from the battalions giving news of progress in consolidation, and reporting that the enemy was in considerable strength on the Northern edge, with plenty of machine-guns. I sat down on a fallen tree-trunk and made a report of the situation, read it over to the General, and went in search of a runner to take it to the Division. Taylor was standing by a large shell hole, talking to his signallers.

'How can I get this to the Division?' I asked.

'Give it to me: that's my job. I've got a telephone down at Queen's Nullah, and if a runner can get out of the Wood and through the barrage, the message gets through.'

'Are the runners getting through?'

'Some don't, and some of those that do don't get back. . . . Don't give me any messages that are not absolutely essential and urgent. I'm getting short of men—seven down already this morning. I don't know what it will be like when the Boche wakes up. He's got us taped here. Look at those cross-rides—did you ever see such a butcher's shop?'

At this moment a signaller orderly came up to deliver a message. I opened it, glanced through it, and took it to the General. His face hardened as he read it. The Divisional Commander informed us that the enemy's trenches in front of Bazentin were being shelled, and that it was quite impossible that he had any strong force in Mametz Wood. The brigade was to attack and occupy the Northern and Western edges of the Wood at the earliest possible moment. Indeed, the Corps Commander strongly impressed the importance of clearing the Wood without delay.

While we were digesting this order, and drafting new orders to the battalions, a Staff Officer came up to join us. His red and black arm-band showed that he came from Army Headquarters, and he spoke with all the prestige native to a traveller from distant lands who had penetrated to within a few hundred yards of the enemy. He brought orders that we were to carry out an attack upon the two edges of the Wood. The Brigadier listened to him with the patience of an older man coldly assessing the enthusiasm of youth. When the Staff Officer had finished, the General spoke.

'I've just had orders from the Division to attack and clear the rest of the Wood, and to do it at once. The defence is incomplete, the units are disorganized, and I did not propose to attack until we were in a better position. My patrols report that the Northern edge is strongly held. I haven't a fresh battalion, and no one can say what is the strength of any unit.'

'What do you propose to do?' asked the Staff Officer.

'My intention is to take the remainder of the Wood by surprise, with the bayonet if possible; no artillery bombardment to tell him that we are coming. I want a bombardment of the main German second line when we have taken our objective, to break up any counter-attack. Do you know anything about the artillery programme?'

'No, I do not. Are you in communication with the Division or with any of the artillery groups?'

'No, except by runner, and that takes a long time. I'm issuing orders to the battalions to get ready to advance quietly at three o'clock, and I'm sending a copy of the order to the Division; if you are going back will you get in touch with them as soon as possible and tell them that I don't want a barrage?'

The Staff Officer left us, and we worked at the orders for the battalions. The enemy was shelling the Wood, searching it, as the gunners say, and there were intermittent bursts of machine-gun fire, with an occasional uneven and untidy rush of rifle fire. On our right a few bombs burst in a flat, cracking thud. At a quarter to three, while we were waiting for the hour, a sudden storm of shells passed over our heads, bursting in the Wood some two hundred yards ahead of us.

'Good God,' said the General. 'That's our artillery putting a barrage right on top of our battalion! How can we stop this? Send a runner down at once . . . send two or three by different routes . . . write the message down.'

Three men went off with the message, each by a different way, with orders to get to Queen's Nullah somehow or other. Our barrage had roused the enemy, and from every direction shells were falling in the Wood; behind us a devilish storm of noise showed that a heavy price must be paid for every attempt to leave the Wood.

The Brigadier sat on a tree-trunk, head on hand, to all appearances neither seeing nor hearing the shells.

'This is the end of everything . . . sheer stupidity. I wonder if there is an order that never reached me . . . but that Staff Officer ought to have known the artillery programme for the day. And if there is another order, they ought not to have put down that barrage until they got my acknowledgment. How can we attack after our own barrage has ploughed its way through us? What good can a barrage do in a wood like this?'

At twenty past three our own artillery was still pouring shells into the wood. None of the runners had returned. Taylor sent three more to try to rescue us from this double fire, but ten minutes later we were left with no worse burden than the enemy's shelling. Reports came through from the battalions that we had suffered severely. As the afternoon drew out into the evening, we nibbled away here and there with fluctuating fortune, but at the approach of night the enemy reinforced his line and kept us from the edge while he pounded away with his artillery.

It was nearing dusk when Taylor came up to me.

'I want to have a word with you,' he said, drawing me away. 'I've got bad news for you. . . .'

'What's happened to my young brother . . . is he hit?''

'You know the last message you sent out to try to stop the barrage . . . well, he was one of the runners that took it. He hasn't come back. . . . He got his message through all right, and on his way back through the barrage he was hit. His mate was wounded by the shell that killed your brother . . . he told another runner to tell us.'

'My God . . . he's lying out there now, Taylor!'

'No, old man . . . he's gone.'

'Yes . . . yes, he's gone.'

'I'm sorry . . . I had to send him, you know.'

'Yes, of course . . . you had to. I can't leave this place. . . . I suppose there's no doubt about his being killed?'

'None—he's out of it all now.'

So I had sent him to his death, bearing a message from my own hand, in an endeavour to save other men's brothers; three thoughts that followed one another in unending sequence, a wheel revolving within my brain, expanding until it touched the boundaries of knowing and feeling. They did not gain in truth from repetition, nor did they reach the understanding. The swirl of mist refused to move.

Within the unclouded portion of my being a host of small things took their place on the stage, drawing their share of attention, and passing on. More orders to draft, situation reports to send out, demands for more bombs, enemy trench-mortars to be shelled into silence, machine-guns wanted by everybody. The General put his hand on my shoulder. It began to grow dark. An order came from the Division to say that we would be relieved that night by a brigade from another Division, and that on completion of the relief we were to return to our bivouacs. More orders to the battalions. The wheel was still revolving, while the procession of mere events moved without a break.

I walked towards the large shell hole that served as a shelter for the signallers, carrying in my hand a sheaf of messages for delivery. From the background of bursting shells came a whistle, deepening into a menace, and I flung myself on my face. I remembered a momentary flash of regret that I was still two yards from the protection of that shell hole. A black noise covered everything. When my eyes opened I was lying on my back, further away from the hole. I got up on my hands and knees and crawled to the signallers, still clutching the crumpled messages, and spoke to them. There was no answer. The rim of another large shell hole nearly touched their shelter, and the three signallers were huddled together, dead, killed by the concussion, for there was no mark of a wound.

The wheel came to rest, and I do not remember much of what happened afterwards. The night came, within and without. I have a clear memory of walking up the ride towards the battalions, of tripping over a branch, and of a flash of anger because I hurt my shoulder when I fell. The General went forward to one battalion to make sure that the line was securely held to cover the relief, and I went to another battalion on the same errand. The night seemed to pass in a black film, broken only by the flashes of bursting shells. I am told that I found the battalion.

Some time later, a heavy storm of shell fire drove me into a little trench where I crouched with some men to shelter. We talked in Welsh, for they were Anglesey folk; one was a young boy, and after a thunderous crash in our ears he began to cry out for his mother, in a thin boyish voice, 'mam, mam. . . .' I woke up and pushed my way to him, fumbling in my pockets for my torch, and pulled him down to the bottom of the trench. He said that his arm was hurt. A corporal came to my assistance and we pulled off his tunic to examine his arm. He had not been hit, but he was frightened, still crying quietly. Suddenly he started again, screaming for his mother, with a wail that seemed older than the world, in the darkness of that night. The men began to mutter uneasily. We shook him, cursed at him, threatening even to kill him if he did not stop. He did not understand our words, but the shaking brought him back. He demanded his rifle and his steel helmet, and sat in the bottom of the trench to wait for the relief, talking rationally but slowly. English voices came out of the dark, enquiring for another battalion of our brigade; more men stumbled by in search of the posts they were to relieve. Our time was drawing to an end.

Dawn was breaking when I reached the clearing. The General had been waiting for me; another wave had passed over our brigade, and all the men of our battalions who were destined to leave the Wood were now on their way down to the bivouacs. He looked at me and asked me if I would like to sit down to rest, but I wanted to go on. We picked our way over the fallen timber and round the corpses, some sprawling stiffly, some huddled against the splintered tree-trunks, until we were clear of the Wood. I was afraid to look closely at them, lest I should recognize one of them.

Below the Wood, the enemy was still maintaining a barrage, but we were too tired to hurry. Our field-guns were pushing up towards the slopes, some were in position and were firing to support the attack on the German second line. With them was another brother of mine, a bombardier, but I did not know it. We walked in silence, until the General asked me if I had any food. I found some biscuits in my haversack, and realized that I had not eaten for twenty-four hours.

It was eight o'clock when we reached the old German dugout and drank a cup of tea. As we were finishing, a Staff Officer from the Division arrived to tell us that we were to get ready to move at short notice. Protest was useless; the battalions must be clear of the bivouacking ground by five o'clock the next morning, and we must march a distance of fourteen miles to another sector of the front.

The day passed in getting ready for the march, and in trying to write a letter to my father and mother to tell them what had happened. When at last I succeeded, I felt in some queer way that an episode was ended, that all feeling had been crushed out of existence within me. Night came, but I could not sleep. At two in the morning we set out to join the battalions, and as dawn was breaking over Bazentin, I turned towards the green shape of Mametz Wood and shuddered in a farewell to one, and to many. I had not even buried him, nor was his grave ever found.

ARRAS

Weather conditions since the end of the Battle of the Somme had been extremely bad. The mud in the British sector made a morass of the terrain. Very little significant offensive action took place after the Somme until early April, 1917. There was sporadic, sharp fighting but no major attacks launched by either side. In fact, the Germans had shortened their lines by twenty-five miles by withdrawing to prepared positions on the Hindenburg Line. Thirteen divisions were thus saved for a stronger reserve and for use elsewhere. The area between the originally held lines and the new front was laid waste by the Germans, causing the Allied armies endless supply difficulties until contact was once again made by the establishment of new Allied positions.

Some military historians claim that the early months of 1917 offered an opportunity for a negotiated peace. Another stalemate seemed at hand. The troops of both sides were exhausted and fed up with trench warfare, and Germany faced ever-increasing Allied forces. About four million Allied troops now fought two and a half million Germans.

However much the troops might hope and dream of their deliverance, there was as yet no sign of real understanding of the horrors of trench warfare on the part of their commanders or the home front. Discussion of a peace overture in England in November, 1916 helped bring about the fall of the government. The press of the day either didn't order their correspondents up to the front trenches, or newspapermen weren't permitted full access to the fighting. Haig particularly disliked the inquisitive press.

The Allied newspapers continued to serve up melodramatic stories of bloodthirsty Germans, and the German press was equally melodramatic in describing the Allied troops.

The insanity of frontal attacks on the opposing trenches continued.

In April the British launched their first full-scale attack of 1917 at Arras. "From April 9 to 24 on a fourteen-mile front, Sir Edmund Allenby's Third Army and a Canadian Corps (twelve divisions in the initial assault) drove hard against strong enemy resistance. Haig's answer to prior failures was more artillery; the preparatory bombardment lasted a week and during the battle about 88,000 tons of artillery and ammunition were expended. New contact fuses and new projectors for gas helped the attackers. Air superiority, ultimately won by the British helped after spectacular sky battles with Richtofen's "circus." The Canadians took and held Vimy Ridge, a dominating *terrain massif*, and this was an achievement of consequence a year later. But Arras in 1917 was again a limited victory—a two- to five-mile advance on a twenty-mile front, 18,128 Germans and 230 guns captured, 57,000 other enemy casualties at the cost of some 84,000 British casualties." *

The following narrative by Siegfried Sassoon describes life at the front at Arras.

A BOMBING PARTY**

by Siegfried Sassoon

A heavy snowstorm set in soon after we started. A snowstorm on April 11th was the sort of thing that one expected in the War, and it couldn't be classed as a major misfortune. Nevertheless we could

* Baldwin, *World War I*, p. 100.
** From *Memoirs of an Infantry Officer*, published by Faber & Faber.

have done without it, since we were marching away from all comfort and safety; greatcoats had been left behind and we had nothing but what we stood up in. As we slogged along narrow winding lanes the snow melted on the shiny waterproof sheets which kept the men uncomfortably warm. We were now in the devastated area; villages had been leveled to heaps of bricks; fruit-trees, and even pollard-willows, had been hacked down, and there was still a chance that we might be the victims of a booby trap in the shape of a dynamite charge under a causeway. A signpost pointed to Blairville; but a couple of inches of snow was enough to blot out Blairville. The next village was Ficheux (the men called it "Fish Hooks"—any joke being better than none in that snowstorm); but Ficheux wasn't there at all; it had vanished from the landscape.

The snow had stopped when, after marching eight miles, we bivouacked in the dregs of daylight by a sunken road near Mercatel, a place which offered no shelter except the humanity of its name. After dark I found my way into a small dug-out occupied by a Trench Mortar Sergeant-Major and two signalers who were working a field telephone. With Shirley (one of our Company officers) I considered myself lucky to be there, crouching by a brazier, while the Sergeant-Major regaled us, in omniscient tones, with rumors about the desperate fighting at Wancourt and Heninel, names which meant nothing to me. I dozed through the night without ever being unaware of the coke fumes from the brazier and the tick-tack of the telephone.

Daylight discovered us blear-eyed and (to abbreviate a contemporary phrase) "fed up and far from home." We got through the morning somehow and I issued some of my "emergency Woodbines." Rifle-cleaning and inspection was the only occupation possible. Early in the afternoon the Battalion moved on four miles to St. Martin-Cojeul. The snow had melted, leaving much mud which rain made worse. St. Martin was a demolished village about a mile behind the battle-line. As we entered it I noticed an English soldier lying by the road with a horribly smashed head; soon such sights would be too frequent to attract attention, but this first one was perceptibly unpleasant. At the risk of being thought squeamish or even unsoldierly, I still maintain that an ordinary human being has a right to be momentarily horrified by a mangled body seen on an afternoon walk, although people with sound common sense can always refute me by saying that life is full of gruesome sights and violent catastrophes. But I am no believer in wild denunciations of the War; I am merely describing my own experiences of it; and in 1917 I was only beginning to learn that life, for the majority of the population, is an unlovely struggle against unfair odds, culminating in a cheap funeral. Anyhow, the man with his head bashed in had achieved theoretical glory by dying for his country in the Battle of Arras, and we who marched past him had an excellent chance of following his example.

We took over an old German reserve trench (captured on Easter Monday). Company Headquarters was a sort of rabbit-hole, just wide enough to accommodate Leake, a tiny stove, and myself. Leake occupied himself in enlarging it with a rusty entrenching tool. When dusk was falling I went out to the underground dressing-station to get my festering fingers attended to. I felt an interloper for the place was crowded with groaning wounded. As I made my way back to our trench, a few shells exploded among the ruinous remains of brickwork. All this, I thought, is disgustingly unpleasant, but it doesn't really count as war experience. I knew that if I could get the better of my physical discomforts I should find the War intensely interesting. B Company hadn't arrived at the groaning stage yet; in fact, they were grimly cheerful, though they'd only had one meal that day and the next was to-morrow morning. Leake and I had one small slice of ration bacon between us; I was frizzling my fragment when it fell off the fork and disappeared into the stove. Regardless of my unfortunate fingers I retrieved and ate it with great relish.

The night was cold and sleep impossible, since there was no space to lie down in. Leake, however, had a talent for falling asleep in any position. Chiseling away at the walls by candlelight, I kept myself warm, and in a couple of hours I had scooped out sufficient space for the other two officers. They were a well contrasted couple. Rees was a garrulous and excitable little Welshman; it would be flattery to call him anything except uncouth, and he made no pretensions to being "a gentleman." But he was good-natured and moderately efficient. Shirley, on the other hand, had been educated at Winchester and the War had interrupted his first year at Oxford. He was a delicate-featured and fastidious young man, an only child, and heir to a comfortable estate in Flintshire. Rees rather got on our nerves with his table manners, and Shirley deprecated the way he licked his thumb when dealing the cards for their games of nap. But social incompatibilities were now merged in communal discomfort. Both of them were new to the line, so I felt that I ought to look after them, if possible. I noticed that Rees kept his courage up by talking incessantly and making jokes about the battle; while Shirley, true to the traditions of his class, simulated nonchalance, discussing with Leake (also an Oxford man) the comparative merits of Magdalen and Christ Church, or Balliol and New College. But he couldn't get the nonchalance into his eyes. . . . Both Shirley and Rees were killed before the autumn.

From our obsolete trench we looked toward the naked ground which rose to the ridge. Along that ridge ran the Hindenburg Line (a mile and a half away) from which new attacks were now being attempted. There was another attack next morning. Rees was detailed for an ammunition-carrying party, and he returned noisier than ever. It had been his first experience of shell-fire. Narrating his numerous escapes from hostile explosives, he continually invoked the name of the founder of his religion; now that it was all over he enjoyed the retrospective excitement, roaring with laughter while he told us how he and his men had flung themselves on their faces in the mud. Rees never minded making himself look ridiculous, and I began to feel that he was capable of taking care of himself. Shirley raised his eyebrows during the recital, evidently disapproving of such volubility and not at all sure that officers ought to throw themselves flat on their faces when shells burst. Later in the day I took him for a walk up the hill; I wanted to educate him in unpleasant sights. The wind had dropped and the sunset sky was mountainous with calm clouds. We inspected a tank which had got stuck in the mud while crossing a wide trench. We succeeded in finding this ungainly monster interesting. Higher up the hill the open ground was dotted with British dead. It was an unexpectedly tidy scene, since most of them had been killed by machine-gun fire. Stretcher-bearers had been identifying the bodies and had arranged them in happy warrior attitudes, hands crossed and heads pillowed on haversacks. Often the contents of a man's haversack were scattered around him. There were letters lying about; the pathos of those last letters from home was obvious enough. It was a queer thing, I thought, that I should be taking a young Oxford man for this conducted tour of a battlefield on a fine April evening. Here we were, walking about in a sort of visible fraction of the Roll of Honor, and my pupil was doing his best to behave as if it were all quite ordinary and part of the public school tradition. He was being politely introduced to the horrors of war, and he made no comment on them. Earlier in the day an attack on Fontaine-les-Croiselles had fizzled out in failure. Except for the intermittent chatter of machine-guns, the country ahead of us was quiet. Then, somewhere beyond the ridge, a huge explosion sent up a shapeless tower of yellow vapor. I remarked sagely that a German dump had probably been blown up. Shirley watched it intently as though the experience would be of use to him during future operations.

At five-thirty next morning our Brigade renewed the attack on Fontaine-les-Croiselles, but we remained in reserve. Enveloped by the din of the bombardment I leaned my elbows on the parapet and looked at the ridge. A glowering red sun was rising; the low undulant hills were gray-blue and deeply shadowed; the landscape was full of gun flashes and drifting smoke. It was a genuine battle picture, and I was aware of its angry beauty. Not much more than a mile away, on the further side of that menacing slope, lines of muttering men were waiting, strained to an intolerable expectancy, until the whistles blew and the barrage crept forward, and they stumbled across the open with the good wishes of General Allenby and the bad wishes of the machine-guns in the German strong-posts. Perhaps I tried to visualize their grim adventure. In my pocket I had a copy of a recent *communiqué* (circulated for instructive purposes)

and I may as well quote it now. "That night three unsuccessful
bombing attacks were made on the Tower at Wancourt. During the
Battalion relief the next night, the enemy opened a heavy bombardment on the Tower and its immediate vicinity, following it up with
an attack which succeeded, mainly owing to the relief being in
progress. A local counter-attack delivered by the incoming battalion
failed owing to the darkness, pouring rain, and lack of knowledge of
the ground. It was then decided that nothing could be done till
daylight." The lesson to be drawn from this episode was, I think, that
lack of Artillery preparation is a mistake. . . . The Wancourt Tower
was only a couple of miles away on our left, so I felt vaguely
impressed by being so close to events which were, undoubtedly, of
historic importance in the annals of the War. And any one who has
been in the front line can amplify that *communiqué* for himself.

♦ ♦ ♦

On Saturday afternoon the order to move up took us by surprise.
Two days of stagnation in the cramped little trench had relaxed
expectancy, which now renewed itself in our compact preparations
for departure. As usual on such occasions, the Company-Sergeant-
Major was busier than anybody else. I have probably said so before,
but it cannot be too often repeated that C. S. M.'s were the hardest
worked men in the infantry; everything depended on them, and if
anyone deserved a K. C. B. it was a good C. S. M.

At 9 P.M. the Company fell in at the top of the ruined street of St.
Martin. Two guides from the outgoing battalion awaited us. We
were to relieve some Northumberland Fusiliers in the Hindenburg
Trench—the companies going up independently.

It was a gray evening, dry and windless. The village of St. Martin
was a shattered relic; but even in the devastated area one could be
conscious of the arrival of spring, and as I took up my position in the
rear of the moving column there was something in the sober twilight
which could remind me of April evenings in England and the Butley
cricket field where a few of us had been having our first knock at the

nets. The cricket season had begun. . . . But the Company had left
the shell-pitted road and was going uphill across open ground.
Already the guides were making the pace too hot for the rear
platoon; like most guides they were inconveniently nimble owing to
their freedom from accouterment, and insecurely confident that they
knew the way. The muttered message "pass it along—steady the
pace in front" was accompanied by the usual muffled clinkings and
rattlings of arms and equipment. Unwillingly retarded, the guides
led us into the deepening dusk. We hadn't more than two miles to
go, but gradually the guides grew less authoritative. Several times
they stopped to get their bearings. Leake fussed and fumed and they
became more and more flurried. I began to suspect that our progress
was circular.

At a midnight halt the hill still loomed in front of us; the guides
confessed that they had lost their way, and Leake decided to sit
down and wait for daylight. (There were few things more un-
comfortable in the life of an officer than to be walking in front of a
party of men all of whom knew that he was leading them in the
wrong direction.) With Leake's permission I blundered experi-
mentally into the gloom, fully expecting to lose both myself and
the Company. By a lucky accident, I soon fell headlong into a
sunken road and found myself among a small party of Sappers who
could tell me where I was. It was a case of "Please, can you tell me
the way to the Hindenburg Trench?" Congratulating myself on my
cleverness, I took one of the Sappers back to poor benighted B
Company, and we were led to our Battalion rendezvous.

The rendezvous took some finding, since wrong map references
had been issued by the Brigade Staff; but at last, after many delays,
the Companies filed along to their ordained (and otherwise ana-
thematized) positions.

We were at the end of a journey which had begun twelve days
before, when we started from Camp 13. Stage by stage, we had
marched to the life-denying region which from far away had
threatened us with the blink and growl of its bombardments. Now
we were groping and stumbling along a deep ditch to the place
appointed for us in that zone of inhuman havoc. There must have

been some hazy moonlight, for I remember the figures of men huddled against the sides of communication trenches; seeing them in some sort of ghastly glimmer—(was it, perhaps, the diffused whiteness of a sinking flare beyond the ridge?) I was doubtful whether they were asleep or dead, for the attitudes of many were like death, grotesque and distorted. But this is nothing new to write about, you will say; just a weary company, squeezing past dead or drowsing men while it sloshes and stumbles to a front line trench. Nevertheless that night relief had its significance for me, though in human experience it had been multiplied a million-fold. I, a single human being with my little stock of earthly experience in my head, was entering once again the veritable gloom and disaster of the thing called Armageddon. And I saw it then, as I see it now—a dreadful place, a place of horror and desolation which no imagination could have invented. Also it was a place where a man of strong spirit might know himself utterly powerless against death and destruction, and yet stand up and defy gross darkness and stupefying shell-fire, discovering in himself the invincible resistance of an animal or an insect, and an endurance which he might, in after days, forget or disbelieve.

Anyhow, there I was, leading that little procession of Flintshire Fusiliers many of whom had never seen a front-line trench before. At that juncture they asked no compensation for their efforts except a mug of hot tea. The tea would have been a miracle, and we didn't get it till next morning, but there was some comfort in the fact that it wasn't raining.

It was nearly four o'clock when we found ourselves in the Hindenburg Main Trench. After telling me to post the sentries, Leake disappeared down some stairs to the Tunnel (which will be described later on). The Company we were relieving had already departed, so there was no one to give me any information. At first I didn't even know for certain that we were in the front line. The trench was a sort of gully, deep, wide, and unfinished looking. The sentries had to clamber up a bank of loose earth before they could see over the top. Our Company was only about eighty strong and its sector was fully 600 yards. The distance between the sentry-posts made me aware of our inadequacy in that wilderness, I had no right to feel homeless, but I did; and if I had needed to be reminded of my forlorn situation as a living creature I could have done it merely by thinking of a Field Cashier. Fifty franc notes were comfortable things, but they were no earthly use up here, and the words "Field Cashier" would have epitomized my remoteness from snugness and security and from all assurance that I should be alive and kicking the week after next. But it would soon be Sunday morning; such ideas weren't wholesome, and there was a certain haggard curiosity attached to the proceedings; combined with the self-dramatizing desperation which enabled a good many of us to worry our way through much worse emergencies than mine.

When I had posted the exhausted sentries, with as much cheeriness as I could muster, I went along to look for the Company on our left. Rather expecting to find one of our own companies, I came round a corner to a place where the trench was unusually wide. There I found myself among a sort of panic party which I was able to identify as a platoon (thirty or forty strong). They were jostling one another in their haste to get through a cavernous doorway, and as I stood astonished one of them breathlessly told me that "the Germans were coming over." Two officers were shepherding them downstairs and before I'd had time to think the whole lot had vanished. The Battalion they belonged to was one of those amateur ones which were at such a disadvantage owing to lack of discipline and the absence of trained N. C. O's. Anyhow their behavior seemed to indicate that the Tunnel in the Hindenburg Trench was having a lowering effect on their *morale*.

Out in No Man's Land there was no sign of any German activity. The only remarkable thing was the unbroken silence. I was in a sort of twilight, for there was a moony glimmer in the low-clouded sky; but the unknown territory in front was dark, and I stared out at it like a man looking from the side of a ship. Returning to my own sector I met a runner with a verbal message from Battalion H. Q. B Company's front was to be thoroughly patrolled at once. Realizing the futility of sending any of my few spare men out on patrol (they'd been walking about for seven hours and were dead beat), I lost my temper, quietly and inwardly. Shirley and Rees were nowhere to be seen and it wouldn't have been fair to send them out, inexperienced as they were. So I stumped along to our right-flank post, told them to pass it along that a patrol was going out from right to left, and then started sulkily out for a solitary stroll in No Man's Land. I felt more annoyed with Battalion Headquarters than with the enemy. There was no wire in front of the trench, which was, of course, constructed for people facing the other way. I counted my steps; 200 steps straight ahead; then I began to walk the presumptive 600 foot steps to the left. But it isn't easy to count your steps in the dark among shell-holes, and after a problematic 400 I lost confidence in my automatic pistol, which I was grasping in my right-hand breeches pocket. Here I am, I thought, alone out in this god-forsaken bit of ground, with quite a good chance of bumping into a Boche strong-post. Apparently there was only one reassuring action which I could perform; so I expressed my opinion of the War by relieving myself (for it must be remembered that there are other reliefs beside Battalion reliefs). I insured my sense of direction by placing my pistol on the ground with its muzzle pointing the way I was going. Feeling less lonely and afraid, I finished my patrol without having met so much as a dead body, and regained the trench exactly opposite our left-hand post, after being huskily challenged by an irresolute sentry, who, as I realized at the time, was the greatest danger I had encountered. It was now just beginning to be more daylight than darkness, and when I stumbled down a shaft to the underground trench I left the sentries shivering under a red and rainy-looking sky.

There were fifty steps down the shaft; the earthy smell of that triumph of Teutonic military engineering was strongly suggestive of appearing in the Roll of Honor and being buried until the Day of Judgment. Dry-mouthed and chilled to the bone, I lay in a wire-netting bunk and listened to the dismal snorings of my companions. Along the Tunnel the air blew deathly cold and seasoned with mephitic odors. In vain I envied the snorers; but I was getting accustomed to lack of sleep, and three hours later I was gulping some peculiar tea with morose enjoyment. Owing to the scarcity of water (which had to be brought up by the Transport who were eight miles back, at Blairville) washing wasn't possible; but I contrived a refreshing shave, utilizing the dregs of my tea.

By ten o'clock I was above ground again, in charge of a fatigue party. We went half-way back to St. Martin, to an ammunition dump, whence we carried up boxes of trench mortar bombs. I carried a box myself, as the conditions were vile and it seemed the only method of convincing the men that it had to be done. We were out nearly seven hours; it rained all day and the trenches were a morass of glue-like mud. The unmitigated misery of that carrying-party was a typical infantry experience of discomfort without actual danger. Even if the ground had been dry the boxes would have been too heavy for most of the men; but we were lucky in one way; the wet weather was causing the artillery to spend an inactive Sunday. It was a yellow corpse-like day, more like November than April, and the landscape was desolate and treeless. What we were doing was quite unexceptional; millions of soldiers endured the same sort of thing and got badly shelled into the bargain. Nevertheless I can believe that my party, staggering and floundering under its loads, would have made an impressive picture of "Despair." The background, too, was appropriate. We were among the débris of the intense bombardment of ten days before, for we were passing along and across the Hindenburg Outpost Trench, with its belt of wire (fifty yards deep in places); here and there these rusty jungles had been flattened by tanks. The Outpost Trench was about 200 yards from the Main Trench, which was now our front line. It had been solidly made, ten feet deep, with timbered firesteps, splayed sides, and timbered steps at intervals to front and rear and to machine-gun emplacements. Now it was wrecked as though by earthquake and eruption. Concrete strong-posts were smashed and tilted sideways; everywhere the chalky soil was pocked and pitted with huge shell-holes; and wherever we looked the mangled effigies of the dead were our *memento mori*. Shell-twisted and dismembered, the Germans maintained the violent attitudes in which they had died. The British had mostly been killed by bullets or bombs, so they looked more resigned. But I can remember a pair of hands (nationality unknown) which protruded from the soaked ashen soil like the roots of a tree turned upside down; one hand seemed to be pointing at the sky with an accusing gesture. Each time I passed that place the protest of those fingers became more expressive of an appeal to God in defiance of those who made the War. Who made the War? I laughed hysterically as the thought passed through my mud-stained mind. But I only laughed mentally, for my box of Stokes-gun ammunition left me no breath to spare for an angry guffaw. And the dead were the dead; this was no time to be pitying them or asking silly questions about their outraged lives. Such sights must be taken for granted, I thought, as I gasped and slithered and stumbled with my disconsolate crew. Floating on the surface of the flooded trench was the mask of a human face which had detached itself from the skull.

◆ ◆ ◆

Plastered with mud and soaked to the skin, the fatigue-party clumped down the steps to the Tunnel. The carrying job was finished; but a stimulating surprise awaited me, for Leake was just back from Battalion H. Q. (somewhere along the Tunnel) and he breezily informed me that I'd been detailed to take command of a hundred bombers in the attack which had been arranged for next morning. "Twenty-five bombers from each Company; you're to act as reserve for the Cameronians," he remarked. I stared at him over my mug of reviving but trench-flavored tea (made with chlorinated water), and asked him to tell me some more. He said, "Well, they're a bit hazy about it at Headquarters, but the General is frightfully keen on our doing an underground attack along the Tunnel, as well as along the main trench up above. You've got to go and discuss the tactical situation with one of the Company commanders up in the front line on our right." All that I knew about the tactical situation was that if one went along the Tunnel one arrived at a point where a block had been made by blowing it in. On the other side one bumped into the Germans. Above ground there was a barrier and the situation was similar. Bombing along a Tunnel in the dark. . . . Had the War Office issued a textbook on the subject? . . . I lit my pipe, but failed to enjoy it, probably because the stewed tea had left such a queer taste in my mouth.

Ruminating on the comfortless responsibility imposed on me by this enterprise, I waited until nightfall. Then a superbly cheerful little guide bustled me along a maze of waterlogged ditches until I found myself in a small dug-out with some friendly Scotch officers and a couple of flame-wagging candles. The dug-out felt more like old times than the Hindenburg Tunnel, but the officers made me feel incompetent and uninformed, for they were loquacious about local trench topography which meant nothing to my newly-arrived mind. So I puffed out my Military Cross ribbon (the dug-out contained two others), nodded my head knowingly, and took an acquiescent share in the discussion of the strategic situation. Details of organization were offered me and I made a few smudgy notes. The Cams. didn't think that there was much chance of my party being called on to support them, and they were hoping that the underground attack would be eliminated from operation orders.

I emerged from the desperation jollity of their little den with only a blurred notion of what it was all about. The objective was to clear the trench for 500 yards while other battalions went over the top on our left to attack Fontaine-les-Croiselles. But I was, at the best of times, only an opportunist officer; technical talk in the Army always made me feel mutely inefficient. And now I was floundering home in the dark to organize my command, put something plausible on paper, and take it along to the Adjutant. If only I could consult the Doctor, I thought; for he was back from leave, though I hadn't seen him yet. It seemed to me, in my confused and exhausted condition, that I was at a crisis in my military career; and, as usual, my main fear was that I should make a fool of myself. The idea of making a fool of oneself in that murderous mix-up now appears to me rather a ludicrous one; for I see myself merely as a blundering flustered little beetle; and if someone happens to put his foot on a beetle, it is unjust to accuse the unlucky insect of having made a fool of itself.

When I got back to Leake and Rees and Shirley I felt so lost and perplexed that I went straight on to Battalion H.Q.

The Tunnel was a few inches higher than a tall man walking upright; it was fitted with bunks and recessed rooms; in places it was crowded with men of various units, but there were long intervals of unwholesome-smelling solitude. Prying my way along with an electric torch, I glimpsed an assortment of vague shapes, boxes, tins, fragments of broken furniture and frowsy mattresses. It seemed a long way to Headquarters, and the Tunnel was memorable but not fortifying to a fatigued exploder who hadn't slept for more than an hour at a stretch or taken his clothes off since last Tuesday. Once, when I tripped and recovered myself by grabbing the wall, my tentative patch of brightness revealed somebody half hidden under a blanket. Not a very clever spot to be taking a nap, I thought, as I stooped to shake him by the shoulder. He refused to wake up, so I gave him a kick. "God blast you, where's Battalion Headquarters?" My nerves were on edge; and what right had he to be having a good sleep, when I never seemed to get five minutes' rest? . . . Then my beam settled on the livid face of a dead German whose fingers still clutched the blackened gash on his neck. . . . Stumbling on, I could only mutter to myself that this was really a bit too thick. (That, however, was an exaggeration; there is nothing remarkable about a dead body in a European War, or a squashed beetle in a cellar.) At Headquarters I found the Adjutant alone, worried and preoccupied with clerical work. He had worked in an office, at accountancy, I believe, before the War; and now most of his fighting was done in writing, though he had served his apprenticeship as a brave and indefatigable platoon commander. He told me that the underground attack had been washed out by a providential counter-order from Division, and asked me to send my organization scheme along as soon as possible. "Right-O!" I replied, and groped my way back again feeling the reverse of my reply. By a stroke of luck I discovered Ralph Wilmot, sitting by himself in a small recessed room— his dark hair smoothly brushed and his countenance pensive but unperturbed. He might conceivably have been twiddling a liqueur glass in a Piccadilly restaurant. Unfortunately he had no liquid refreshment to offer, but his philosophic way of greeting me was a consolation and in him I confided my dilemma. With an understanding air he assumed his monocle, deliberated for a while, snuffed the candle wick, and wrote out an authoritative looking document headed "Organization of F. F. Parties." The gist of it was "15 Bombers (each carrying 10 bombs) and Rifle Grenadiers (each carrying 5 grenades). 5 Carriers (also act as bayonet men). 1 Full Rank." There wasn't much in it, he remarked, as he appended "a little bit of skite about consolidation and defensive flanks." It certainly looked simple enough when it was done, though I had been at my wits' end about it.

While he was fixing up my future for me I gazed around and thought what a queer refuge I'd found for what might possibly be my final night on earth. Dug-out though it was, the narrow chamber contained a foggy mirror and a clock. The clock wasn't ticking, but its dumb face stared at me, an idiot reminder of real rooms and desirable domesticity. Outside the doorless doorway people were continually passing in both directions with a sound of shuffling feet and mumbling voices. I caught sight of a red-capped Staff Officer, and a party of sappers carrying picks and shovels. The Tunnel was a sort of highway and the night had brought a considerable congestion of traffic. When we'd sent my document along to the Adjutant there was nothing more to be done except sit and wait for operation orders. It was now about ten o'clock.

As evidence of my own soldierly qualities I would like to be able to declare that we eagerly discussed every aspect of the situation as regards next morning's attack. But the truth is that we said nothing at all about it. The thing had to be attempted and there was an end of it (until zero hour). The Brigadier and his Staff (none too bright at map-references) were hoping to satisfy (vicariously) General Whincop (who'd got an unpopular bee in his bonnet about the rum ration, and had ordered an impossible raid, two months ago, which had been prevented by a providential thaw and caused numerous deaths in a subsequently sacrificed battalion).

Whincop was hoping to satisfy the Corps Commander, of whom we knew nothing at all, except that he had insulted our Colonel on the Doullens Road. The Corps Commander hoped to satisfy the Army Commander, who had as usual informed us that we were "pursuing a beaten enemy," and who had brought the Cavalry up for a "breakthrough." (It is worth mentioning that the village which was now our Division's objective was still held by the Germans eight months afterwards.) And the Army Commander, I suppose, was in telephonic communication with the Commander-in-Chief, who with one eye on Marshal Foch, was hoping to satisfy his King and Country. Such being the case, Wilmot and myself were fully justified in leaving the situation to the care of the military caste who were making the most of their Great Opportunity for obtaining medal-ribbons and reputations for leadership; and if I am being caustic and captious about them I can only plead the need for a few minutes' post-war retaliation. Let the Staff write their own books about the Great War say I. The Infantry were biased against them, and their authentic story will be read with interest.

As for our conversation between ten o'clock and midnight (when my operation orders arrived from the Adjutant) I suppose it was a form of drug, since it was confined to pleasant retrospections of peace. Wilmot was well acquainted with my part of the world and he'd come across many of our local worthies. So we were able to make a little tour of the Kentish Weald and the Sussex border, as though on a couple of mental bicycles. In imagination we cycled along on a fine summer afternoon, passing certain milestones which will always be inseparable from my life history. Outside Squire Maundle's park gate we shared a distinct picture of his angular attitudes while he addressed his golf-ball among the bell-tinklings and baa-ings of sheep on the sunny slopes above Amblehurst (always followed by a taciturn black retriever). Much has been asserted about the brutalized condition of mind to which soldiers were reduced by life in the front line; I do not deny this, but I am inclined to suggest that there was a proportionate amount of simple-minded sentimentality. As far as I was concerned, no topic could be too homely for the trenches.

Thus, while working-parties and machine-gunners filed past the door with hollow grumbling voices, our private recess in the

Hindenburg Tunnel was precariously infused with evocations of rural England and we challenged our surroundings with remembrances of parish names and farmhouses with friendly faces. A cottage garden was not an easy idea to recover convincingly. . . . Bees among yellow wall-flowers on a warm afternoon. The smell of an apple orchard in autumn. . . . Such details were beyond our evocation. But they were implied when I mentioned Squire Maundle in his four-wheeled dog-cart, rumbling along the Dumbridge Road to attend a County Council Meeting.

"*Secret.* The Bombing Parties of 25 men will rendezvous at 2:30 A.M. to-morrow morning, 16th inst. in shafts near C Coy. H. Q. The greatest care will be taken that each separate Company Party keep to one side of the Shaft and that the Dump of Bombs be in the trench at the head of these shafts, suitably split. The necessity of keeping absolute silence must be impressed on all men. These parties (under 2nd Lt. Sherston) will come under the orders of O. C. Cameronians at Zero minus 10. Lt. Dunning and 2 orderlies will act liaison and report to O. C. Cameronians at ZERO minus 5. While the parties are in the shaft they must keep a free passage way clear for runners, etc."

Such was the document which (had I been less fortunate) would have been my passport to the Stygian shore. In the meantime, with another two hours to sit through, we carried on with our world without end conversation. We were, I think, on the subject of Canterbury Cricket Week when my watch warned me that I must be moving on. As I got up from the table on which we'd been leaning our elbows, a blurred version of my face looked at me from the foggy mirror with an effect of clairvoyance. Hoping that this was an omen of survival, I went along to the rendezvous-shaft and satisfied myself that the Bombing Parties were sitting on the stairs in a bone-chilling draught, with my two subordinate officers in attendance.

Zero hour was at 3 A.M. and the prefatory uproar was already rumbling overhead. Having tightened my mud-caked puttees and put my tie straight (there was no rule against wearing a tie in an attack), diffidently I entered the Cameronian H. Q. dug-out, which was up against the foot of the stairs. I was among strangers, and Zero minus 10 wasn't a time for conversational amenities, so I sat self-consciously while the drumming din upstairs was doing its utmost to achieve a reassuring climax. Three o'clock arrived. The tick-tacking telephone-orderly in a corner received a message that the attack had started. They were over the barrier now, and bombing up the trench. The Cameronian Colonel and his Adjutant conversed in the constrained undertones of men who expect disagreeable news. The Colonel was a fine-looking man, but his well-disciplined face was haggard with anxiety. Dunning sat in another corner, serious and respectful, with his natural jollity ready to come to the surface whenever it was called for.

At the end of twenty minutes' tension the Colonel exclaimed abruptly, "Good God, I wish I knew how they're doing!" . . . And then, as if regretting his manifestation of feeling, "No harm in having a bit of cake, anyhow." There was a large home-made cake on the table. I was offered a slice, which I munched with embarrassment. I felt that I had no business to be there at all, let alone helping to make a hole in the Colonel's cake, which was a jolly good one. I couldn't believe that these competent officers were counting on me to be of any use to them if I were required to take an active part in the proceedings upstairs. Then the telephone-orderly announced that communication with Captain Macnair's headquarters had broken down; after that the suspense continued monotonously. I had been sitting there about two and a half hours when it became evident that somebody was descending the steps in a hurry. H. Q. must have kept its cooking utensils on the stairs, for the visitor arrived outside the doorway in a clattering cascade of pots and pans. He was a breathless and disheveled sergeant, who blurted out an incoherent statement about their having been driven back after advancing a short distance. While the Colonel questioned him in a quiet and controlled voice I rose stiffly to my feet. I don't remember saying anything or receiving any orders; but I felt that the Cameronian officers were sensitive to the delicacy of my situation. There was no question of another slice of home-made cake. Their unuttered comment was, "Well, old chap, I suppose you're for it now."

Leaving them to get what satisfaction they could from the sergeant's story, I grinned stupidly at Dunning, popped my helmet on my head, and made for the stairway. It must have been a relief to be doing something definite at last, for without pausing to think I started off with the section of twenty-five who were at the top of the stairs. Sergeant Baldock got them on the move at once, although they were chilled and drowsy after sitting there for over three hours. None of them would have been any the worse for a mouthful of rum at that particular moment. In contrast to the wearisome candle-light of the lower regions, the outdoor world was bright and breezy; animated also by enough noise to remind me that some sort of battle was going on. As we bustled along, the flustered little contingent at my heels revived its numbness. I had no idea what I was going to do; our destination was in the brain of the stooping Cameronian guide who trotted ahead of me. On the way we picked up a derelict Lewis gun, which, I thought, might come in handy, though there was no ammunition with it. At the risk of being accused of "taking the wrong half of the conversation" (a favorite phrase of Aunt Evelyn's) I must say that I felt quite confident. (Looking back on that emergency from my armchair, I find some difficulty in believing that I was there at all.) For about ten minutes we dodged and stumbled up a narrow winding trench. The sun was shining; large neutral clouds voyaged willingly with the wind; I felt intensely alive and rather out of breath. Suddenly we came into the main trench, and where it was widest we met the Cameronians. I must have picked up a bomb on the way, for I had one in my hand when I started my conversation with young Captain Macnair. Our encounter was more absurd than impressive. Macnair and his exhausted men were obviously going in the wrong direction, and I was an incautious newcomer. Consequently I had the advantage of him while he told me that the Germans were all round them and they'd run out of bombs. Feeling myself to be, for the moment, an epitome of Flint-shire infallibility, I assumed an air of jaunty unconcern; tossing my bomb carelessly from left hand to right and back again, I inquired, "But where *are* the Germans?"—adding, "I can't see any of them." This effrontery had its effect (though for some reason I find it difficult to describe this scene without disliking my own behavior). The Cameronian officers looked around them and recovered their composure. Resolved to show them what intrepid reenforcements we were, I assured Macnair that he needn't worry any more and we'd soon put things straight. I then led my party past his, halted them, and went up the trench with Sergeant Baldock—an admirably impassive little man who never ceased to behave like a perfectly trained and confidential man-servant. After climbing over some sort of barricade, we went about fifty yards without meeting anyone. Observing a good many Mills bombs lying about in little heaps, I sent Baldock back to have them collected and carried further up the trench. Then, with an accelerated heart beat, I went round the corner by myself. Unexpectedly, a small man was there, standing with his back to me, stock-still and watchful, a haversack of bombs slung over his left shoulder. I saw that he was a Cameronian corporal; we did not speak. I also carried a bag of bombs; we went round the next bay. There my adventurous ardor experienced a sobering shock. A fairhaired Scotch private was lying at his side of the trench in a pool of his own blood. His face was gray and serene, and his eyes stared emptily at the sky. A few yards further on the body of a German officer lay crumpled up and still. The wounded Cameronian made me feel angry, and I slung a couple of bombs at our invisible enemies, receiving in reply an egg-bomb, which exploded harmlessly behind me. After that I went bombing busily along, while the corporal (more artful and efficient than I was) dodged in and out of the saps—a precaution which I should have forgotten. Between us we created quite a demonstration of offensiveness, and in this manner arrived at our objective without getting more than a few glimpses of retreating field-gray figures. I had no idea where our objective was, but the corporal informed me that we had reached it, and he seemed to know his business. This, curiously enough, was the first time either of us had spoken since we met.

The whole affair had been so easy that I felt like pushing forward until we bumped into something more definite. But the corporal had a cooler head and he advised discretion. I told him to remain where he was and started to explore a narrow sap on the left side of the trench. (Not that it matters whether it was on the left side or the right, but it appears to be the only detail I can remember; and when all is said and done, the War was mainly a matter of holes and ditches.) What I expected to find along that sap, I can't say. Finding nothing, I stopped to listen. There seemed to be a lull in the noise of the attack along the line. A few machine-guns tapped, spiteful and spasmodic. High up in the fresh blue sky an aeroplane droned and glinted. I thought what a queer state of things it all was, and then decided to take a peep at the surrounding country. This was a mistake which ought to have put an end to my terrestrial adventures, for no sooner had I popped my silly head out of the sap than I felt a stupendous blow in the back between my shoulders. My first notion was that a bomb had hit me from behind, but what had really happened was that I had been sniped from in front. Anyhow my foolhardy attitude toward the Second Battle of the Scarpe had been instantaneously altered for the worse. I leant against the side of the sap and shut my eyes. . . . When I reopened them Sergeant Baldock was beside me, discreet and sympathetic, and to my surprise I discovered that I wasn't dead. He helped me back to the trench, gently investigated my wound, put a field-dressing on it, and left me sitting there while he went to bring up some men.

After a short spell of being deflated and sorry for myself, I began to feel rabidly heroical again, but in a slightly different style, since I was now a wounded hero, with my arm in a superfluous sling. All my seventy-five men were now on the scene (minus a few who had been knocked out by our own shells, which were dropping short). I can remember myself talking volubly to a laconic Stokes-gun officer, who had appeared from nowhere with his weapon and a couple of assistants. I felt that I must make one more onslaught before I turned my back on the War, and my only idea was to collect all available ammunition and then renew the attack while the Stokes-gun officer put up an enthusiastic barrage. It did not occur to me that anything else was happening on Allenby's Army Front except my own little show. My over-strained nerves had wrought me up to such a pitch of excitement that I was ready for any suicidal exploit. This convulsive energy might have been of some immediate value had there been any objective for it. But there was none; and before I had time to inaugurate anything rash and irrelevant Dunning arrived to relieve me. His air of competent unconcern sobered me down, but I was still inflamed with the offensive spirit and my impetuosity was only snuffed out by a written order from the Cameronian Colonel, who forbade any further advance owing to the attack having failed elsewhere. My ferocity fizzled out then, and I realized that I had a raging thirst. As I was starting my return journey (I must have known then that nothing could stop me till I got to England) the M. O. came sauntering up the trench with the detached demeanor of a gentle botanist. "Trust him to be up there having a look round," I thought. Within four hours of leaving it I was back in the Tunnel.

FLANDERS AND THE YPRES SALIENT

According to Cyril Falls, "Arras had a wonderful start. The blow dealt on April 9 was a triumph for British arms. None of the successes won later were comparable to it. The depth gained was about five miles on the greater part of the front. . . . The conclusion must be that, though the British had made a considerable improvement in tactical skill since the Battle of the Somme, the infantry were better at a set piece than at improvising." *

But in the south, at the 2nd Battle of the Aisne, the French suffered a heavy defeat, a disaster only too common on the Western Front. Approximately a mile and a half was gained at the expense of 187,000 French casualties as against German losses of 163,000.

This battle had unexpected repercussions for the French. General Nivelle, who had displaced Joffre as Commander-in-Chief in December, 1916, went ahead with the Aisne offensive even though many fellow officers objected. When the battle ended, Nivelle was relieved and General Pétain was appointed Commander-in-Chief. But the French soldier had reached the breaking point; mutinies sprang up within small units, then spread to whole divisions. Falls says, "The French army cracked under the tensions to which it was exposed; disappointment, disillusion, losses, the weakness of the agitators, the flood of rumor, (and) the Russian Revolution." **

Pétain rectified some of the miserable conditions of the French soldiers, by increasing their time of leave and personally visiting the men to listen to their complaints. In his first month as Commander-in-Chief, he visited ninety divisions. His mere presence seemed to have an ameliorating effect on the French infantrymen. They respected him more than any other French General. However, the French armies had been so grievously hurt by the internal strife that

* Falls, p. 275.
** Falls, p. 279.

they could not launch a large-scale attack again until 1918. Curiously, the news of the mutinies never reached the Germans until long after they had been brought under control.

The British now took over the reins of attack. Haig wanted to strike in Flanders, his objective to open a flank on the German lines and seize the channel ports of Ostend and Zeebrugge. The Flanders terrain was, however, appalling for infantry operations.

"The fields of Flanders are mostly flat, flatter than the plains of Kansas, flatter than the lowlands of Hungary. On such terrain a ten-foot rise is a military prize worth fighting for. This was once a land of grassy, tree-filled, primeval swamps. Even after three years of war its scrubby desolation still gave the impression of a forest clearing. The plain is part of the one that runs from the Pyrenees to Russia, the only gateway into France which bypasses formidable mountains and plateaus.

"During the rainy season the rivers cannot discharge their waters because of the faintness of the gradient. Most of them flood once or more yearly. When they do, they spread their waters far and wide. Because of the impervious clay, the rain cannot escape and tends to stagnate over large areas. Unable to soak through, it forms swamps and ponds, and sluggishly spreads toward one of the already swollen rivers or canals. The ground remains perpetually saturated. Water is reached at an average depth of eighteen inches and only the shallowest of puddly trenches can be dug by the troops, reinforced by sandbag parapets. When the topsoil dries during fair weather, it cracks open. The next rain floods the fissures. Then the clay blocks slide upon themselves, causing little landslides.

"Everywhere by 1917 the water was contaminated, and the delivery of fresh water was a major operation. The filthy surface wash was locked in by the clay. Rivers and canals were polluted by refuse from the flooded land, and even the artesian wells had become poisoned. The decay and refuse of millions of men, alive and dead, sank into the soil and were carried by the blackened waters throughout the inland plain. These conditions were most severe on the maritime strip west of the Yser, where the land is lower than sea level at high tide. If not for the drains and dikes some sections would be ten feet under water, and, in fact, this had become the precise situation after the Belgians inundated the area in 1914.

"In October of that year the salient was formed, after two great offensives hurled at each other simultaneously and ending in stalemate. Next year the Germans won the entire ridge, though not Ypres itself, which now lay in a protruding pocket held stubbornly by the British, who did not realize that in time it would become a suicide trap half surrounded by Germans on the heights above them. For over two years the lines had remained stationary. But the fighting never ended, and innumerable were the tiny battles waged henceforth, mainly for meager topographical advantages. By the spring of 1917 the salient that curved roughly from the Wytschaete-Messines portion of the ridge to Boisinghe was as rigid in its contours as a portrait in stone, feared and hated like death itself by soldiers of the Empire everywhere in the world. Already a fourth of all the British killed on land or sea since the beginning of the war had died here.

"Other than that pertaining to war, all civilization had long ago left the salient. The last inhabitants had departed early in 1915. Only some stray dogs and cats stayed behind, wild and terrified, still roaming the land where their masters had once lived and played with them in quiet farms and cottages.

"Flanders lies at fifty-one degrees north latitude, about a hundred miles relatively north of the United States-Canadian border. Its average mean temperature is about forty-nine degrees. Rain falls on an average of every other day throughout the year. Fogs drift inland from the coast. Even during peace the climate is not inspiring. This was the countryside where the First and Second Battles of Ypres had been fought to a standstill, and where the Third Battle of Ypres would soon explode under the calm but relentless guidance of Sir Douglas Haig.

"When German cartoonists drew the salient during the war years they usually likened it to the mouth of a skull, the teeth of which were biting down on Ypres. For the British to push farther into the open mouth would leave them in danger of being swallowed up altogether. Plainly it was necessary first to capture the Messines-

Wytschaete lower jawbone, and then to proceed up the molars through Broodseinde, Passchendaele, and Westroosebeke. By June 1917 plans for the attack at Messines were completely and meticulously in readiness; and so was General Sir Herbert Plumer and his Second Army." *

THE TUNNELS AT MESSINES**

by Leon Wolff

Sir Herbert Plumer's hair had turned white during his two thankless years as warden of the salient. A heavy responsibility had been his, with no chance for glory, for there was hardly a point within the loop of ground held by his Second Army which German guns could not enfilade or fire into from behind—a state of affairs hardly calculated to improve the nerves of this commander of his troops. Nonetheless he had made of the salient a nut so hard to crack that the enemy had not tried to do so since 1915. An ideal officer to hold any position in bulldog fashion, Plumer was a prim little old man with a pink face, fierce white mustache, blue eyes, a little pot-belly mounted on tiny legs. As he walked, he panted and puffed. Only the dour cast to his mouth hinted at the essential stubbornness of his nature. Yet he liked to give lifts to women and children in his staff car as he toured the Belgian roads behind the front; and he took childlike delight when troops of his own kind—Lancaster or London —accomplished anything useful in battle.

He was fortunate in possessing an extraordinary chief of staff, the cultured and wise Major General Sir Charles ("Tim") Harington—

* *Flanders Field*, by Leon Wolff, pp. 81, 82, 83, 84, 86.
** From *Flanders Field*, published by the Viking Press.

also a cautious planner, but with, perhaps, an extra dash of imagination and verve. He was tall and thin, nervous, had a card-index mind and a sense of humor. The combination of the two men had proved outstanding in the war to date; and now they hoped to prove that they could storm an objective as well as hold one. Surely they had been allotted more than enough time to get ready. During the long, lean years while they had hung on, improving their defenses, not looking for trouble, they had studied their terrain with microscopic thoroughness. Of Plumer it was said that "he knew every puddle in the salient." Plans for capturing the Messines-Wytschaete ("White Sheet") flank of the ridge had been endlessly cast and recast in conference after conference, order after order. By spring 1917 the operation had been worked out with an intensity unmatched in the war thus far.

Plumer's trump card was a system of enormous land mines burrowed beneath the German front. This work had begun in 1915 with the construction of shallow galleries and small charges about fifteen feet underground. Next year the idea of concentrating on a deep mining offensive, with tunnels and charges nearly one hundred feet below the surface, was contemplated. But to penetrate secretly with galleries of substantial size the saturated, semiliquid layer that made up the Flanders subsoil was on the face of it quite impossible. Might there be another way?

The problem was studied by Lieutenant-Colonel T. Edgeworth David, chief geologist of the BEF, and the engineer in chief, Brigadier-General G. H. Fowke, who analyzed sand and clay layers and the variations of water in each. Perhaps, they thought, the layer of heavy blue clay lying even farther down—between eighty and one hundred twenty feet—might be a practical medium for their purpose. At that depth the tunnels and charges could not be blown up, accidentally or otherwise, by mortar fire or shallow countermines; and the sound of digging would be so muffled that secrecy might be possible. Under the harried conditions of war, with the time element so important, and specialized heavy equipment so scarce, was it possible to construct such shafts, to lay gigantic charges accurately under the key German frontline positions, within a reasonable time, and without being detected? Though the odds were not good, it was decided to try.

By January 1916 six tunnels had been started (the signs above them read "Deep Wells"); and during the next year twenty of the largest mines in the annals of warfare were in place or in process of being placed. Twenty underground communities came into being. From the sandbagged openings wooden stairs led down to sleeping quarters. Below these, planked passages slanted to headquarters posts and thence to the actual three-by-six galleries. In these bowels of the earth, the molelike character of the war was fantastically intensified. The hum of pumping engines never ceased. The thousands of men who worked here with picks and shovels, coughing in the dampness, white of skin, shoved their tunnels a pitiful ten or fifteen feet forward each day under the glare of electric lamps; and as each gallery was completed a mine was laid in place (sometimes two) containing charges of ammonal up to ninety-five thousand pounds. Some tunnels were almost half a mile in length. By June 7 the total had come to a million pounds of explosive and almost five miles of gallery.

Meanwhile the Germans were also mining toward the British lines, but in a smaller way and much more shallowly, for they had neither the equipment nor the plan for deep works possessed by their enemy. Yet in places they did venture to considerable depths— sometimes nearly sixty feet down—and many was the time when the British, listening with microphones at the forward, boarded-up faces of their galleries, heard with dismay a German tunnel approaching their own. Early in 1917 the enemy had dug within eighteen inches of the British at the northern corner of the ridge.

A colonel came to Harington with the news and recommended that the mine be blown. Harington thought for a moment, walked to Plumer's door, knocked, and entered.

" 'Mines' says we must blow the Hill Sixty mines today."

"I won't have them blown," snapped the General. "Good night."

Work stopped, the British evacuated the tunnel, and by chance the Germans veered away.

The enemy knew that the ridge would soon be attacked. Preparations above ground were obvious, and they had captured many prisoners who had talked. One specifically told them on May 29 that the assault would begin June 7 after eight days of bombardment. But what about the mines, the only element of real surprise? The Boches had their suspicions. While they did not greatly fear the small, shallow charges they had become apprehensive concerning deep mining. They sent out many raiding parties primarily to bring back not prisoners but samples of the soil thrown up by diggings. On April 9 one of these parties returned with blue clay. While this was a sure sign that the British were constructing at least one mine at great depth, the Germans reacted inconsequentially, assuming evidently that the shaft was only an isolated one (if it existed at all), and that, since the attack was so imminent, little further mining could be accomplished by the British in the brief time remaining.

To the British it seemed doubtful that their opponents could not know of the twenty deep mines. Certainly, they thought, some prisoners had disclosed them by now. (Not one had done so.) Surely the Germans had been able to hear the work going on, despite many soundproofing measures. (They had not, due to the inferiority of their microphones.) For once even Sir Douglas Haig seems to have been troubled by nervousness. His greatest fear was that the enemy might abandon his front lines just before the attack, a suggestion in fact made by Lieutenant General von Kuhl, Crown Prince Rupprecht's chief of staff, early in May. But this projected withdrawal was rejected by Rupprecht. The blow to morale would be too great, he estimated, if such an outstanding defensive sector were to be discarded without a fight. It could and would be held. As for British mining, the Germans had rather decided by May that it had ended, except for small efforts of no importance. Only at Hill 60 was it definitely known that the British were still digging in earnest, and here, according to the German officer in charge, their work had been hopelessly damaged by countermining. Thus misled by faulty Intelligence, the Crown Prince could not see how the clear and aboveboard preparations of the enemy could possibly succeed.

Accordingly on June 1 he caused the XIX Army Corps to issue an order concerning Wytschaete and Messines:

> These strong-points must not fall even temporarily into the enemy's hands. . . . They must be held to the last man even if the enemy has cut them off on both sides, and threatens them from the rear.

Furthermore, the German troops were told that they need have no fear of a breakthrough. Reserves were already in place and would move in swiftly to seal off any gaps that might occur. In these orders and reassurances the opposing high command clearly showed the value they placed on the east and south ridges of their precious encirclement.

So Haig's one great worry was baseless; the Germans would stay put and make their stand. Not knowing this, he recommended in a conference on May 30 that all mines be exploded before zero day; next the troops would occupy the ground; and later they would try to cross over the crest of the ridge. He also suggested moving the target date forward a day or two. Plumer begged to reject these last-minute changes, and Haig agreed to let matters go forward on schedule.

The trepidation of the British is understandable. The greatest series of simultaneous explosions in history was about to take place (it would triple the former record set in New York during subway construction late in the 1800s). Hundreds of thousands of men had been working toward this one day for over two years. The immensity, the importance of the operation was incalculable. And it all hung on the feeblest of threads. One British private soldier taken prisoner could have nullified it. German detection devices could have been alert to the entire plan for months. Airplane observation might have detected any number of blue-clay diggings, despite efforts to camouflage them as they were hauled to the rear. How much did the Germans know? From Haig on down, the British would have sold their souls for an answer.

The very fact that German countermining continued was noteworthy, even though most of these efforts were at shallow levels. In one place the Germans were known to be digging along a line that was bound to intersect the British gallery. Again this was near (or rather under) Hill 60, where the most spectacular mining, countermining, and mine fighting took place. The state of affairs was later described:

> . . . on May 9th the enemy was so near that work was stopped, and the branch gallery was loaded with 1600 lbs. of ammonal. The Germans had evidently completed their shaft and were driving a gallery past the end of the branch gallery. As, however, there was only a month to go, and the *camouflet* (a small defensive charge which ruins the enemy tunnel but does not open the surface of the ground) might detonate the great mine, or at least cause the Germans to probe vigorously, it was decided that the safest course was to accept the risk involved in letting the enemy work on, and not to fire the mine unless he touched the actual timbers of the branch gallery. . . . The Germans could now be heard putting in timber, working a truck, walking, and even talking. On May 25th in some other workings they fired a mine whose position was "dangerously correct" directly above the Hill 60 gallery. It crushed in the junction of the galleries and entombed two listeners. One, Sapper Earl, in the Hill 60 gallery, coolly went on listening and heard a German walk down an enemy gallery apparently directly over the great mine. . . . The listeners had to be withdrawn, and from then onwards the staff could only trust that the enemy would not reach the British workings before the mine was fired.

At Petit Douve, near Messines, one mine, already laid and electrically charged, was discovered by the Germans. They blew a *camouflet*, wrecked the main British gallery, and the mine had to be abandoned. This left nineteen. It was a race against time at Spanbroekmolen, where the major in charge of the tunneling company scribbled in pencil a note to division headquarters on June 6 that it was "almost" definite that his mine would explode the following morning of the attack.

It had indeed been a tense two years of underground digging and fighting, and the records of the period recall the strangeness of it all, and the peril:

> Captain Woodward and Lieutenant Clinton . . . heard the enemy "hard at work" and earth falling within twenty feet of them. The gallery commander . . . ordered the nearest part of the gallery to

be at once silently loaded. While the charge—2500 lbs. of ammonal —was being put in, the Germans could easily be heard "with the naked ear." So close were they working that the vibration kept shaking down flakes of clay on to the tin containers of the ammonal, which had therefore to be covered with sandbags. Woodward reported the situation "critical," and . . . when the Germans were probably ten feet away, the charge was fired.

Sapper Sneddon, having clearly heard the Germans boring and then charging the bore-hole, temporarily withdrew his men. As no "blow" followed, Major Henry suggested that means might be devised of simulating work while the gallery was empty, so that the enemy might fire his charge uselessly. Before this was done, however, early on April 7th the Germans fired their mine, crushing the rickety gallery and killing Sapper Sneddon, who was listening there.

. . . he had been working underground for nearly two years in the dark saps pierced under the German lines, and running very close to German saps nosing their way, and sometimes breaking through, to ours, so that the men clawed at each other's throats in these tunnels and beat each other to death with picks and shovels.

So the digging went on, and the never-ending pumping out of water; and seldom it was that men could last in this work for even a few months without a breakdown of nerve and health. "Listeners all a bit windy," one Captain Avery reported. Replacements flowed into the diggings, and as time went on the fighting infantry were relieved by labor battalions. Every tunnel had a name—the Newcastle shaft, the Snout, the Sydney, the Perth, the Hobart, the great Brisbane. One started from over two hundred yards behind the British lines, descended to ninety feet, and, the men said solemnly, would in time lead to Berlin. It was called the Berlin Sap. By late evening, June 6, these nineteen mines were in place and charged, their shafts were tamped down, and the only remaining question was how many of them—especially the old ones that had been laid down as long as six months ago—would actually explode next morning.

The mines were to be only a curtain-raiser. Because they were an unknown factor to a large degree—nobody really knew how many would go off, whether each lay in exactly the right position, and how much damage they would do to men, trenches, and guns many yards above—the greatest artillery mass of the war had been arrayed against enemy lines between Ploegsteert ("Plug Street") Wood and Observatory ridge, about a mile northeast of Hill 60. Over 2,400 guns and howitzers were to participate, fully a third of which were heavy pieces: one gun to every seven yards of front.

Other than the mines, as we have seen, there would be no surprise at all (except possibly for the precise moment of zero hour itself, and this was not officially told to the troops until the 5th); and the artillery preparations were unusually brazen. In single file the heavies were hauled directly to the frontal area from the rear towns and assembly points. Behind them jostled the little field guns, galloping up without the slightest caution, a wild noisy collection followed closely by their ammunition wagons. They were emplaced wheel to wheel, with no attempt to hide them. From May 18 to 30 the guns rumbled forward, and on the latter day they began shelling in earnest the enemy's wire entanglements, his roads, camp areas, supply dumps, and in particular the routes and points where it was known that water and food were being delivered to troops up front.

In the final days gas shells were thrown in vast numbers to force the enemy to don masks and lose sleep. And, further to confuse him, the bombardment was twice increased to pre-attack intensity, and twice the Germans reacted spasmodically to false alarms. By the morning of the 7th the British gunners were thoroughly rehearsed, every gun was registered on its target, and the Germans were weary and on edge. All that remained was the final performance, the efficiency of which was a near certainty from an artillery standpoint.

Tanks, too, were in readiness—seventy-two Mark IVs that assembled a few miles southwest of Ypres and waited under camouflaged shelters for the signal to proceed toward the front. The night of the 6th they emerged, throbbing and clattering, and approached their starting points under the cover of airplanes which flew back and forth to drown out their noise. It was the first appearance in battle of these new models. While their best speed on battle terrain with a crew of eight was only about three miles per hour, their plating was impervious to German armor-piercing

244 THE TUNNELS AT MESSINES

bullets, and it was hoped that they would be able to help the infantry overcome strong points.

Three hundred planes of the II Brigade Royal Flying Corps went into action late in May, mostly to assist the artillery by observation and photographs.

The attack itself was to be a straightforward operation along a ten-mile front toward a final objective two miles away at most, known as the Green Line, or Oosttaverne Line, running slightly to the east of that former village in a nearly straight line that formed a chord across the base of the German salient. Three corps (IX, X, and II Anzac) would participate with three divisions each, and each corps would have one division in reserve, ready to leapfrog through upon signal. About 80,000 infantry would go over the top at dawn, at which moment the mines would be detonated and the artillery barrage would commence with every operable gun along the Second Army Front.

During the long months of working, waiting, and suffering almost helplessly under the guns of their tormentors ringed round them on the slopes, the British troops had practiced their great freeing operation. Behind each of the three corps, training areas had been constructed. Roughly similar to the terrain that would be met June 7, they were marked with colored flags and tape lines designating ravines, woods, strong points, and other objectives. In full battle dress, infantrymen and artillerymen rehearsed their attack six times. A model of the entire ridge was laid out in a field about the size of a tennis court, and here all officers studied the slopes up and down which they would soon lead their men. Various of the twelve divisions, too, made clay tabletop replicas of their sectors.

As training progressed, and while the guns and supplies moved in opposite the German ridge-salient, commanders from Plumer down visited the front daily and saw to it that the movements of troops as small as corporals' sections were understood by the men and coordinated with the larger plan. Patrols increased their activity, seeking new information. Major General Monash, leader of the 3rd Australian Division, distributed circulars among his men telling how Australian prisoners had been nearly starved by their captors in a dungeon after the battle of Bullecourt; whether this tactic fed the ferocity of his assault brigades is doubtful, though the tale was true.

The men waited, worked, and trained. For once, in World War I, they approached zero hour with a sense of optimism, though they understood what they faced. "The enemy will fight his hardest for the Messines ridge," said an officer. "He has stacks of guns against us."

And another, who knew the salient perhaps too well, peered at the German-held ridges, lofty and arrogant in the hazy distance, flaming with guns, webbed with row after row of sandbagged trenches, peppered with thousands of machine-gun emplacements, pillboxes, and sharpshooters' nests. He turned to a newspaper man and murmured, "It's a Gibraltar." The mines would have to do their job.

Major-General Harington opened his advance press conference with these words: "Gentlemen, I don't know whether we are going to make history tomorrow, but at any rate we shall change geography."

Let us examine now the German side of the coin.

The Messines-Wytschaete portion of the ridge had been in the past manned by a total of four divisions. When in January 1917 Ludendorff became aware of the growing danger there, he placed two more in reserve. In February it was noticed that new British batteries were moving into position. On April 29 a spy advised the German high command that the British would attack the ridge two weeks after stopping their main effort on the Arras front—an estimate which was very nearly correct.

At about the same time, aerial observation disclosed that British movement on the roads and railways behind the salient was reaching alarming proportions, far greater than that which had preceded the assault farther south under Allenby a few weeks previously. After weighing these and other Intelligence reports Crown Prince Rupprecht decided that the Arras attack was merely a large-scale feint and that the Messines ridge was Haig's true objective. From this moment on, for the next five weeks, the Germans reinforced their positions substantially opposite Plumer's army.

But five German weeks were not equal to five British months. In those five weeks the German air arm covering the salient was driven out of the sky, and the former's batteries were nearly crushed by counter-bombardment. A few figures tell the story, and in reading them one can sense the intensity of this greatest of all counter-battery operations, and the despair of the defenders who helplessly watched the shattering of their artillery shield. By early June almost half the German howitzers, light and heavy, were out of action. Hardly one captured Russian gun remained operable. The Third Bavarian Division faced the coming attack with the astonishing total of only nineteen field guns; the Second division up north had lost fifteen of their eighteen medium and heavy howitzers.

Under such conditions, German infantry could expect only trivial support during the coming fight. Ominously, they had already been driven from at least one strong point even before June 7 and had been forced to take refuge out in open trenches. British gas shelling on an unprecedented scale had indeed accomplished its purpose of keeping the enemy awake for days, and the disruption of food supply had further demoralized him. The night before the attack a lucky British hit exploded a great ammunition dump near Menin, and gas quickly spread throughout the area. Many civilians who still inhabited the outskirts of this section of the rear zone were killed, as well as an undetermined number of corralled mules and horses. So shaken were the Germans by British shelling to which they could not effectively reply that five divisional replacements had to be consummated during the first week of June. One of these, as we shall see, was actually in progress during the morning of the 7th.

Too late it dawned on the Crown Prince that he was in trouble, and during the last few days he worked feverishly to save his position. More small bodies of infantry were hustled into action. Artillery was added, especially on the flanks of the threatened sector; more planes, pioneers, and machine guns were thrown into the pre-attack fighting. On June 3 thirteen thousand gas shells were poured into the Australians around Ploegsteert Wood. On June 6, knowing that the attack was due next day or the day after, Rupprecht ordered an even heavier gas barrage, in an attempt to smother the enemy artillery and catch troops on their approach march to the jumping-off line.

These last-minute measures embarrassed the British but failed to hamper them to any large extent, except in the case of General Monash's 3rd Australians, five hundred of whom were gassed en route. For once, the forty-eight-year-old Bavarian Prince, field marshal of the northern armies on the Western Front, descendant of the Stuart kings of Britain, brother-in-law of the Belgian queen, world traveler, and gifted military commander, had been too late with too little, outwitted underground, outmanned and outgunned on the ground, and overpowered in the skies above. The battle of Messines was lost by the Germans before it began.

During the evening the men marched silently in columns of fours like groping tentacles toward the communication trenches, and thence to the front, where white jumping-off tapes lay on the soft wet ground of No Man's Land. They were troubled and wearied by the need for wearing their masks, for gas shells were plopping all about them, laying low the unwary and careless as well as many pack animals gasping and heaving in the poisoned air. It was warm that night. Fog lay on the salient like a heavy caress, and in it not a breeze stirred. Overhead forked lightning played, accompanied by the mutter of thunder. At midnight a sharp thundershower broke. It lasted only a few minutes, and after it passed, a three-quarter moon floated regally in a nearly clear sky. Now brilliant flashes against the enemy slopes could be seen, and the steady whamming of the big guns sounded perceptibly louder as the blanket of fog melted away.

A half-hour before zero hour the British guns stopped firing, and the night became so still that one could hear nightingales singing in the nearby woods. The men fixed bayonets and removed their gas masks. Some of them dozed. Officers changed to enlisted men's tunics and kept peering at their wrist watches. Zero hour would be 3:10.

At 2:52 the Germans threw up yellow and green flares, calling for artillery fire—a disconcerting sign. How much did they know? At

2:57 heavy bursts of shrapnel swept segments of the British front; but quickly it ceased.

At 3:05 the first streaks of dawn filtered over the Messines ridge. On Mount Kemmel the cocks began to crow. Two green star-flares burst directly in front of the New Zealand division at 3:06, then machine guns and another flare. Had this unit been discovered? (Some of their assembly trenches had been dug dangerously forward in No Man's Land during the early evening.) But at 3:09 the German guns stopped chattering. For one minute absolute silence saturated the air, while at whispered orders the troops crawled over their parapets and lay flat in front of the tapes.

A few seconds before 3:10 some of the heavy guns rearward began to fire. Then each of the nineteen land mines exploded almost in unison. The earth quaked, tumbling and staggering the British soldiers as they rose in awe to see the rim of the hated ridge burst skyward in a dense black cloud, beneath which gushed nineteen pillars of flame that lit the salient with the red glare of hell. The pillars fused into greater mushrooms of fire that seemed to set flame to little clouds above. Then, a moment or two later, the long roar of nineteen explosions blended and reverberated into one long blast that stunned even the British troops, awakened the countryside, rolled through Flanders and northern France, hurtled the Channel, and was heard in London by Lloyd George, awake in his study at Number 10 Downing Street.

From the German positions yellow flares soared imploringly high into the sky, the pathetic prayers of doomed men crying for help. As the villages of Messines and Wytschaete disappeared into oblivion, the heaviest of all artillery barrages struck the German front, and the British assault brigades scrambled over the top.

Plumer and his staff had breakfasted at 2:30, after which everybody went to the top of Cassel Hill near Second Army headquarters, a few miles deep in the salient, to see the mines go up—all but Plumer, who returned to his room and knelt at his bed in prayer. When the first news of the infantry advance came, he burst into tears. It was quite clear that his Second Army was winning as planned, and with greater ease than had been expected. So swift and thorough was the British success that subsequent fighting came as an anticlimax.

The enemy was in a state of near shock when the British fell upon them. They surrendered en masse, weeping, waving handkerchiefs, grasping the ankles of their captors. Thousands lay beneath the ground, to be forever entombed there. Some of the mine craters were three hundred feet across and seventy feet deep. The wreckage of their front left many Germans cringing in derelict shelters "like beaten animals" while the British walked along throwing Mills bombs at unresisting clusters of men too dazed to surrender. One Australian lieutenant reported how they "made many fruitless attempts to embrace us. I have never seen men so demoralized." Another distraught prisoner said that only two men in his section of the line had survived the blast. A captured officer reported that of his two-hundred-man company only thirty were alive when the British foot soldiers arrived. The 3rd Bavarian Division was relieving the 24th Saxons precisely when the explosions and the attack burst; both relieved and relievers were decimated, and most of the balance were made prisoners.

While the British dug in near the crest of the ridge, German defenses began to tighten. Machine guns took a heavy toll of these farthermost troops and of those moving up in support. By 11 o'clock appreciable enemy infantry reinforcements were seen to be approaching the eastern slopes. Soon afterward, sporadic counterattacks developed. Small bodies of Germans stubbornly holding out at isolated points throughout the area redoubled their fire. It was at this stage that hundreds of British were killed and wounded by their own batteries and fellow infantrymen; for as they descended the western slopes of the ridge after being relieved they were mistaken again and again for German counterattackers. At other sectors along the front of advance, errors in direction were committed; some companies got temporarily lost; others were held up by the great mine craters. Yet, all in all, the general sweep forward proceeded on schedule.

During the middle of the afternoon, following the first long pause, all three reserve divisions plunged forward with their tanks and brushed aside secondary German defenses. From a previous line running some six hundred yards west of the final goal the new assault lapped toward the little village of Oosttaverne, captured it within an hour, and reached the entire Green Line by dusk.

For the next few days advance posts were established by the victors, the new line was consolidated, the Germans continued to counterattack feebly; but in line with previous plans no attempt was made by the British to exploit their success. The battle of Messines ridge was over and would stand on its merits. The south flank of the great salient at Ypres no longer existed, and now British troops stood astride that portion of the ridge from which they had been murdered wholesale since early in the war. The front had been pushed back two miles at the farthest point. Seventy-three hundred prisoners were taken, and the Germans had suffered almost 20,000 other casualties. These figures apply to the period from June 1 to 10. During the same time British casualties came to something under twenty-four thousand. So, "counting heads," the difference between the losses in men on both sides was, after all, disturbingly small, though the achievement as a whole was (or seemed to be at the time) beyond question. Certainly the operation had been, in the words of one writer, a "siege-war masterpiece," one "in which the methods employed by the command completely fitted the facts of the situation," a triumph of engineers in what was essentially an engineers' war.

In his memoirs von Hindenburg admits:

> The moral effect of the explosions was simply staggering. . . . The 7th of June cost us dear, and, owing to the success of the enemy attack, the price we paid was very heavy. . . . It was many days before the front was again secure. The British army did not press its advantage; apparently it only intended to improve its position for the launching of the great Flanders offensive.

RAIN AND MUD AT YPRES

It would be six weeks from the success at Messines until the larger strike at the Ypres salient was made, six weeks of good summer weather when the miserable Flanders terrain was at its best for offensive tactics. By then the Germans were looking for an attack and had moved troops up from the south in front of the French lines to strengthen their defenses.

"The Germans had put into force the defensive system introduced in the Battle of Arras, with an outpost zone to cushion the shock, and behind it a deeper battle zone. They had sown the ground with little concrete forts, some containing several chambers and impervious to any shell up to a direct hit with an 8-inch. Their counterattack divisions were ready to strike in the dangerous period apt to occur when an attacker reached his objective but before he had consolidated it and repaired the confusion." *

The British bombardment began on July 18 but the British did not go over the top until the 31st. "The assault nevertheless began well, but hard counterattacks robbed it of much of its gains, so that the maximum advance . . . was about two miles. That evening heavy and persistent rain fell. It was heartbreaking. The ground absorbed the wet like a sponge but kept it close to the surface. The shell holes, already close together though not yet lip to lip as they were to be later, filled with mud and water. Urgent though it was to maintain the pressure, there was nothing for it but to await better weather. The rain lessened, but the ground dried only to a small degree. Worse still, the second phase, the Battle of Langemarck, postponed to August 16 and undertaken in dry weather, was on balance a grievous failure. Very little ground was won and that only in the

* Falls, pp. 300-301.

centre. From August 15 onward the Canadian Corps fought a long and fierce diversionary action near Lens, which ended successfully.*

"The weather in August, and still more in late October and early November, is the chief factor in the horrible reputation which hangs about Third Ypres. The second is a belief that the offensive was mere blind bashing. This is not the case. Tactics were never more skillful. The gunners caught on to the German methods of counterattack and with the cooperation of the R. F. C. so plastered all hidden ground that on several occasions German divisions were either pinned down or were so depleted and exhausted when they got within striking distance that they failed utterly. In many cases the infantry tackled the forts—pillboxes, as they called them—with skill, working round them under cover of Lewis gunfire and then killing the defenders at close quarters with rifles and grenades. However, even with good tactics, the human body is lucky to prevail over ferroconcrete, and many brilliant attacks failed, with nothing to show but a few corpses sprawled about the strong points.

"It is hoped that the foregoing brief account will make it clear that popular verdicts on this battle, and on the British commander-in-chief's conduct of it, are too much simplified. The subject is one calling for constant qualifications. This applies particularly to his decision to continue the battle after the weather had broken. Most of the hostile judgments have come from those ignorant of the atmosphere on the German side. At the start the Germans often outfought the British. Toward the end the British could count on winning if they could get to close quarters. And it was largely the churning of the ground into a morass by their own artillery that held them up.

"Those who saw it will never forget that battlefield in the wet: as far as the eye could see a vision of brown mud and water, with a mixture of both spouting to extraordinary heights when heavy shells exploded in the ground; patient men trudging along the 'duckboards,' bent a little forward by the loads on their backs; equally patient horses and mules plodding and slipping under the weight on

* Falls, p. 301.

their packsaddles. It called for nerve and endurance, which were not wanting." *

And Leon Wolff says, "So desolate, so meaningless were these August struggles that the record of them in histories and memoirs fills one with a certain weariness. Listlessly the men assemble at the jump-off tapes. Behind the same familiar barrage they advance through the same narrow porridge-like strip of ground. The same hidden machine guns greet them; the same whiz-bangs open up at them. Here and there a strong point is captured, a new outpost is reached, to which a few riflemen forlornly cling. Some of these are held, and occasionally the line is advanced a few hundred yards. Brownish masses of German troops slog forward and everywhere nasty hand-to-hand encounters take place. The men on both sides are lacerated and punctured, bleed and die, in numbers that baffle the imagination. Nameless new beings take their place, but nothing else changes.

"Gaunt, blackened remnants of trees drip in the one-time forests. The shells of countless batteries burst deafeningly and without surcease; the dank smell of gunpowder, wet clay, poison gas, and polluted water spreads over the battleground and drifts eastward. The men hardly know what they are doing or how affairs in general are progressing. By mid-August they were told even less than soldiers are usually told: Move up there. Start walking that way. Occupy those shell holes. Wait near the barn. Surround that pillbox. Relieve those chaps (you can't see them from here) behind the canal and wait for further word. After two weeks such was the status of Haig's grand offensive which was to have burst out of the salient, bounded across the ridge, released the prancing cavalry steeds, and with flying banners captured the Channel ports.**

* Falls, pp. 304, 305.
** Wolff, pp. 143, 144.

THE THIRD BATTLE OF YPRES*

by Frank Richards

The third Battle of Ypres commenced on July 31st and our Divison were sent to the Belgian coast. We travelled by train and barge and arrived at Dunkirk. A little higher up the coast was a place named Bray Dunes, where we stayed about a week, and the architect and I went for many a long swim in the sea. We moved closer to the line along the coast and arrived at a place which the majority of inhabitants had only just evacuated. In July a British division had relieved the Belgian troops around this part. Ever since November 1914 the people had been living in peace and security in the towns and villages in this area, but as soon as the British troops took over the enemy began shelling these places and the people cleared out. In one place we were in the people were in the act of leaving and complaining very bitterly because the arrival of British troops had caused a lot of shelling and forced them to leave their homes. In one pretty village by the sea there hadn't been enough of shells exploded in it to have frightened a poll parrot away, yet there wasn't a soul left there now. They were evidently not such good stickers as the French people who worried less about their lives than about their property and hung on to the last possible minute.

At Bray Dunes I got in conversation with a Canadian officer who was in charge of some men building a light railway. He said it was a good job that the States came in the War as the French were ready

* From *Old Soldiers Never Die*, published by Faber & Faber.

to throw the sponge up. A few days later two of our signallers overheard a full colonel of the Staff telling our Colonel that he did not know what would have happened if the United States had not come in when they did. It was common knowledge among the Staff that the whole of the French Army were more or less demoralized, and the States coming in had to a great extent been the means of restoring their morale. We got wind that our Division and another had been sent up the coast to try and break through the German Front and capture Ostend. This was freely discussed by the officers, but no break through was attempted owing to so little progress being made on the Ypres front.

One of the largest concentration prison camps I ever saw was erected in this area. It was estimated to hold between ten and fifteen thousand prisoners, but all I saw in it were two solitary prisoners who must have been very lonely in so large a place.

On the night the Battalion went in the line I went on leave. It was eighteen months since I had the last one and as usual I made the most of it. I didn't spend the whole of it in pubs: I spent two days going for long tramps in the mountains, which I thoroughly enjoyed after being so long in a flat country. I was presented with a gold watch, in recognition of winning the D. C. M., which I still have, but it has been touch-and-go with it several times since the War. Probably if there hadn't been an inscription on it I should have parted with it. This time every man of military age that I met wanted to shake hands with me and also ask my advice on how to evade military service, or, if they were forced to go, which would be the best corps to join that would keep them away from the firing line. They were wonderfully patriotic at smoking concerts given in honour of soldiers returning from the Front, but their patriotism never extended beyond that.

When I landed back at Boulogne I came across the man who had been shot through his cheeks at Bois Grenier in April 1915. If anything, that bullet had improved his appearance. He now had a nice little dimple on each side of his face. We had a chat. I asked what he was doing now and he said that he had a Staff job, as a military policeman around the Docks. He told me very seriously that if it was possible, and he had the name and address of the German that shot him, he would send him the largest parcel he could pack and a hundred-franc note as well. He was having the time of his life on his present job and had one of the smartest fillies in Boulogne, who was the goods in every way. As I left him I could not help thinking how lucky some men were and how unlucky were others.

When I arrived back I found that the Division had left the coastal area on short notice. All returning leave men of the Division were in a little camp outside Dunkirk. One night some German planes came over bombing and one of our searchlights kept a plane in its rays for some time. Anti-aircraft guns, machine-guns and Lewis guns, and we with our rifles were all banging at him, but he got away with it. Whilst everyone was busy firing at that one, his friends were busy dropping their bombs on Dunkirk. It was very rare that a plane flying at any height was brought down by anti-aircraft guns or rifle-fire but we lost a lot of planes on the Somme by rifle-fire when they came down very low, machine-gunning the enemy before our troops attacked. German planes used to do the same thing and seldom got away with it either.

I rejoined the Battalion in a village near Ypres and guessed that we would soon be in the blood tub. Ricco and Paddy had been made full corporals but Paddy had taken a lot of persuading before he consented to be made an N. C. O. He was sent back to Division Headquarters for a special course of signalling and was lucky enough to miss the next show we were in. Our Colonel went on leave and missed the show too. The name of our Acting-Colonel was Major Poore. He was not an old regimental officer but had been posted to us some six months before from the Yeomanry, I believe. He was a very big man, about fifty years of age, slightly deaf, and his favourite expression was "What, what!" He was a very decent officer. A tall, slender young lieutenant who had just returned from leave was made Assistant-Adjutant for the show. I believe he was given that job because he was an excellent map-reader. As we were marching along the road, Sealyham asked him if he had come across Mr. Sassoon during his leave. He replied that he hadn't and that he had spent a good part of his leave trying to find out where he was

but had failed to get any news at all. This young officer had joined
the Battalion about the same time as Mr. Sassoon and we old hands
thought he was a man and a half to spend his leave looking for a pal.
His name was Casson. I wrote it down first here as Carson, but an
old soldiering pal tells me that I had it wrong. Mr. Casson was said
to be a first-class pianist, but trench warfare did not give him much
opportunity to show his skill at that. If he was as good a pianist as he
was a cool soldier he must have been a treat to hear.

During the night we passed through a wood where a Very-light
dump had been exploded by a German shell. It was like witnessing a
fireworks display at home. We stayed in the wood for the night. Our
Brigade were in reserve and ready to be called upon at any moment.
Orders were given that no fires were to be lit. September 26th, 1917,
was a glorious day from the weather point of view and when dawn
was breaking Ricco and I who were crack hands at making smoke-
less fires had found a dump of pick-handles which when cut up in
thin strips answered very well. We soon cooked our bacon and made
tea for ourselves and the bank clerk and architect, and made no more
smoke than a man would have done smoking a cigarette. We had at
least made sure of our breakfast which might be the last we would
ever have.

At 8 A.M. orders arrived that the Battalion would move off to the
assistance of the Australians who had made an attack early in the
morning on Polygon Wood. Although the attack was successful they
had received heavy casualties and were now hard pressed themselves. Young Mr. Casson led the way, as cool as a cucumber. One
part of the ground we travelled over was nothing but lakes and
boggy ground and the whole of the Battalion were strung out in
Indian file walking along a track about eighteen inches wide. We
had just got out of this bad ground but were still travelling in file
when the enemy opened out with a fierce bombardment. Just in front
of me a half dozen men fell on the side of the track: it was as if
a giant Hand had suddenly swept them one side. The Battalion had
close to a hundred casualties before they were out of that valley. If
a man's best pal was wounded he could not stop to dress his wounds
for him.

We arrived on some rising ground and joined forces with the Australians. I expected to find a wood but it was undulating land with a tree dotted here and there and little banks running in different directions. About half a mile in front of us was a ridge of trees, and a few concrete pillboxes of different sizes. The ground that we were now on and some of the pillboxes had only been taken some hours previously. I entered one pillbox during the day and found eighteen dead Germans inside. There was not a mark on one of them; one of our heavy shells had made a direct hit on the top of it and they were killed by concussion, but very little damage had been done to the pillbox. They were all constructed with reinforced concrete and shells could explode all round them but the flying pieces would never penetrate the concrete. There were small windows in the sides and by jumping in and out of shell holes attacking troops could get in bombing range: if a bomb was thrown through one of the windows the pillbox was as good as captured.

There was a strong point called Black Watch Corner which was a trench facing north, south, east and west. A few yards outside the trench was a pillbox which was Battalion Headquarters. The bank clerk, architect and I got in the trench facing our front, and I was soon on friendly terms with an Australian officer, whom his men called Mr. Diamond. He was wearing the ribbon of the D. C. M., which he told me he had won in Gallipoli while serving in the ranks and had been granted a commission some time later. About a hundred yards in front of us was a bank which extended for hundreds of yards across the ground behind which the Australians were. Our chaps charged through them to take a position in front and Captain Mann, our Adjutant, who was following close behind, fell with a bullet through his head. The enemy now began to heavily bombard our position and Major Poore and Mr. Casson left the pillbox and got in a large shell hole which had a deep narrow trench dug in the bottom of it. They were safer there than in the pillbox, yet in less than fifteen minutes an howitzer shell had pitched clean in it, killing the both of them.

During the day shells fell all around the pillbox but not one made a direct hit on it. The ground rocked and heaved with the bursting shells. The enemy was doing their best to obliterate the strong point that they had lost. Mr. Diamond and I were mucking-in with a tin of Machonochies when a dud shell landed clean in the trench, killing the man behind me, and burying itself in the side of the trench by me. Our Maconochie was spoilt but I opened another one and we had the luck to eat that one without a clod of earth being thrown over it. If that shell had not been a dud we should have needed no more Maconochies in this world. I had found eight of them in a sandbag before I left the wood and brought them along with me. I passed the other six along our trench, but no one seemed to want them with the exception of the bank clerk and architect who had got into my way of thinking that it was better to enter the next world with a full belly than an empty one.

The bombardment lasted until the afternoon and then ceased. Not one of us had hardly moved a yard for some hours but we had been lucky in our part of the trench, having only two casualties. In two other parts of the strong point every man had been killed or wounded. The shells had been bursting right on the parapets and in the trenches, blowing them to pieces. One part of the trench was completely obliterated. The fourth part of the strong point had also been lucky, having only three casualties. Mr. Diamond said that we could expect a counter attack at any minute. He lined us up on the parapet in extended order outside the trench and told us to lie down. Suddenly a German plane swooped very low, machine-gunning us. We brought him down but not before he had done some damage, several being killed including our Aid Post Sergeant.

A few minutes later Dr. Dunn temporarily resigned from the Royal Army Medical Corps. He told me to get him a rifle and bayonet and a bandolier of ammnuition. I told him that he had better have a revolver but he insisted on having what he had asked me to get. I found them for him and slinging the rifle over his shoulder he commenced to make his way over to the troops behind the bank. I accompanied him. Just before we reached there our chaps who were hanging on to a position in front of it started to retire back. The doctor barked at them to line up with the others. Only Captain Radford and four platoon officers were left in the Battalion and the Doctor unofficially took command.

We and the Australians were all mixed up in extended order. Everyone had now left the strong point and were lined up behind the bank, which was about three feet high. We had lent a Lewis-gun team to the 5th Scottish Rifles on our right, and when it began to get dark the Doctor sent me with a verbal message to bring them back with me, if they were still in the land of the living. When I arrived at the extreme right of our line I asked the right-hand man if he was in touch with the 5th Scottish. He replied that he had no more idea than a crow where they were, but guessed that they were somewhere in front and to the right of him. I now made my way very carefully over the ground. After I had walked some way I began to crawl. I was liable any moment to come in contact with a German post or trench. I thought I saw someone moving in front of me, so I slid into a shell hole and landed on a dead German. I waited in that shell hole for a while trying to pierce the darkness in front. I resumed my journey and, skirting one shell hole, a wounded German was shrieking aloud in agony; he must have been hit low down but I could not stop for no wounded man. I saw the forms of two men in a shallow trench and did not know whether they were the 5th Scottish or the Germans until I was sharply challenged in good Glasgow English. When I got in their trench they told me that they had only just spotted men when they challenged. The Lewis-gun team were still kicking and my journey back with them was a lot easier than the outgoing one.

I reported to the Doctor that there was a gap of about one hundred yards between the 5th Scottish Rifles and us; and he went himself to remedy it. The whole of the British Front that night seemed to be in a semi-circle. We had sent up some SOS rockets and no matter where we looked we could see our SOS rockets going up in the air: they were only used when the situation was deemed critical and everybody seemed to be in the same plight as ourselves. The bank clerk and I got into a shell hole to snatch a couple of hours rest, and although there were two dead Germans in it we were soon fast asleep. I was woke up to guide a ration party to us who were on their way. Dawn was now breaking and I made my way back about six hundred yards, where I met them. We landed safely with the rations.

Major Kearsley had just arrived from B Echelon to take command of the Battalion. The Brigadier-General of the Australians had also arrived and was sorting his men out. It was the only time during the whole of the War that I saw a brigadier with the first line of attacking troops. Some brigadiers that I knew never moved from Brigade Headquarters. It was also the first time I had been in action with the Australians and I found them very brave men. There was also an excellent spirit of comradeship between officers and men.

We were moving about quite freely in the open but we did not know that a large pillbox a little over an hundred yards in front of us was still held by the enemy. They must have all been having a snooze, otherwise some of us would have been riddled. Major Kearsley, the Doctor and I went out reconnoitering. We were jumping in and out of shell holes when a machine-gun opened out from somewhere in front, the bullets knocking up the dust around the shell holes we had just jumped into. They both agreed that the machine-gun had been fired from the pillbox about a hundred yards in front of us. We did some wonderful jumping and hopping, making our way back to the bank. The enemy's artillery had also opened out and an hour later shells were bursting all over our front and in the rear of us.

A sapping platoon of one sergeant and twenty men under the command of The Athlete were on the extreme left of the bank, and the Major and I made our way towards them. We found the men but not the officer and sergeant, and when the Major inquired where they were they replied that they were both down the dug-out. There was a concrete dug-out at this spot which had been taken the day before. I shouted down for them to come up, and the Major gave the young officer a severe reprimand for being in the dug-out, especially as he knew our men had just started another attack. Our chaps and the 5th Scottish Rifles had attacked on our right about fifteen minutes previously. The Major gave The Athlete orders that if the pillbox in front was not taken in fifteen minutes he was to take his platoon and capture it and then dig a trench around it. If the pillbox was captured during that time he was still to take his platoon and sap around it. I felt very sorry for The Athlete. This was the first real action he had been in and he had the most windy sergeant in the Battalion with him. Although The Athlete did not know it, this sergeant had been extremely lucky after one of his Arras stunts that he had not been court-martialled and tried on the charge of cowardice in face of the enemy.

We arrived back at our position behind the bank. We and the Australians were in telephone communication with no one; all messages went by runners. Ricco, the bank clerk and the architect were running messages, the majority of our Battalion runners being casualties. Sealyham was still kicking and Lane was back in B Echelon; it was the first time for over two years he had been left out of the line. The Sapping-Sergeant came running along the track by the bank and informed the Major that The Athlete had sent him for further instructions as he was not quite certain what he had to do. The Major very nearly lost his temper and told me to go back with the Sergeant and tell him what he had to do. Just as we arrived at the sapping-platoon we saw some of our chaps rushing towards the pillbox, which surrendered, one officer and twenty men being inside it.

C and D Companies were now merged into one company. They advanced and took up a position behind a little bank about a hundred yards in front of the pillbox. I informed The Athlete that he had to take his platoon and sap around the pillbox, and that this was a verbal message which Major Kearsley had given me for him. I left him and the Sergeant conferring together and made my way back by a different route.

The enemy were now shelling very heavily and occasionally the track was being sprayed by machine-gun bullets. I met a man of one of our companies with six German prisoners whom he told me he had to take back to a place called Clapham Junction, where he would hand them over. He then had to return and rejoin his

company. The shelling was worse behind us than where we were
and it happened more than once that escort and prisoners had been
killed making their way back. I had known this man about eighteen
months and he said, "Look here, Dick. About an hour ago I lost the
best pal I ever had, and he was worth all these six Jerries put
together. I'm not going to take them far before I put them out of
mess." Just after they passed me I saw the six dive in one large shell
hole and he had a job to drive them out. I expect being under their
own shelling would make them more nervous than under ours. Some
little time later I saw him coming back and I knew it was impossible
for him to have reached Clapham Junction and returned in the time,
especially by the way his prisoners had been ducking and jumping
into shell holes. As he passed me again he said: "I done them in as I
said, about two hundred yards back. Two bombs did the trick." He
had not walked twenty yards beyond me when he fell himself: a
shell splinter had gone clean through him. I had often heard some of
our chaps say that they had done their prisoners in whilst taking
them back but this was the only case I could vouch for, and no doubt
the loss of his pal had upset him very much.

During the afternoon the Major handed me a message to take to A
Company, which consisted of the survivors of two companies now
merged into one under the command of a young platoon officer.
They had to advance and take up a position about two hundred
yards in front of them. The ground over which I had to travel had
been occupied by the enemy a little while before and the Company
were behind a little bank which was being heavily shelled. I slung
my rifle, and after I had proceeded some way I pulled my revolver
out for safety. Shells were falling here and there and I was jumping
in and out of shell holes. When I was about fifty yards from the
Company, in getting out of a large shell hole I saw a German pop up
from another shell hole in front of me and rest his rifle on the lip of
the shell hole. He was about to fire at our chaps in front who had
passed him by without noticing him. He could never have heard me
amidst all the din around: I expect it was some instinct that made
him turn around with the rifle at his shoulder. I fired first and as the
rifle fell out of his hands I fired again. I made sure he was dead

before I left him. If he hadn't popped his head up when he did no doubt I would have passed the shell hole he was in. I expect he had been shamming death and every now and then popping up and sniping at our chaps in front. If I hadn't spotted him he would have soon put my lights out after I had passed him and if any of his bullets had found their mark it would not have been noticed among the Company, who were getting men knocked out now and then by the shells that were bursting around them. This little affair was nothing out of the ordinary in a runner's work when in attacks.

The shelling was very severe around here and when I arrived I shouted for the officer. A man pointed along the bank. When I found him and delivered the message he shouted above the noise that he had not been given much time; I had delivered the message only three minutes before they were timed to advance. During the short time they had been behind the bank one-third of the Company had become casualties. When I arrived back I could only see the Major. All the signallers had gone somewhere on messages and the Doctor was some distance away attending wounded men whom he came across. He seemed to be temporarily back in the R. A. M. C.

The Major asked me how my leg was. I replied that it was all right when I was moving about, but it became very stiff after I had been resting. During the two days many pieces and flying splinters of shells and bullets must have missed me by inches. But when a small piece of spent shrapnel had hit me on the calf of the leg I knew all about it. I thought at the time that someone had hit me with a coal hammer. I had the bottom of my trousers doubled inside the sock on the calf and also my puttee doubled in the same place which, no doubt, had helped to minimize the blow. If it had not been a spent piece it would have gone clean through the calf and given me a beautiful blighty wound, which I don't mind admitting I was still hoping for.

Ricco in returning from running a message to Brigade had come across the ration party of another battalion who had all been killed, and he had brought back with him a lovely sandbag full of officers' rations. There were several kinds of tinned stuffs and three loaves of bread. The bank clerk, architect and Sealyham had also arrived back

and we all had a muck in. The way the bank clerk and architect got a
tin of cooked sausages across their chests made me wonder whether
their forefathers had not been purebred Germans. The officers who
the bag of rations were intended for could never have enjoyed them
better than we did.

Just as we finished our feed Major Kearsley called me and told me
to follow him. I could see we were making our way towards where
we had visited the sapping-platoon, but I could not see any men
sapping around the pillbox and was wondering if they had been
knocked out. When we arrived at the concrete dug-out some of the
sapping-platoon were still outside it and some had become casualties, but The Athlete and the Sergeant were still down in the
dug-out. I shouted down and told them to come up and the Major
asked The Athlete the reason why he had not carried out his orders.
He replied that the shelling had been so intense around the pillbox
after it was taken that he decided to stop where he was until it
slackened. Then he had seen our troops advance again and he was
under the impression that the trench would not be needed. The
Major again gave him a severe reprimand and told him to take what
men he had left and sap around the pillbox as he had been ordered
at first.

Shortly after, the Major said he was going to visit the positions our
companies had lately taken. We set off on our journey and when we
passed through the Australians they started shouting, "Come back,
you bloody fools! They've got everything in line with machine-gun
fire." We took no notice and by jumping in shell holes now and again
we reached halfway there. We had only advanced a few yards
further when in jumping into a large shell hole an enemy machine-
gun opened out and the ground around us was sprayed with bullets.
The Major was shot clean through the leg just above the ankle. As I
dressed his wound we discussed the possibility of returning to the
bank. I said that it would be dusk in two hours' time and that we had
better wait until then. He replied that he could not do that as he
would have to hand over the command of the Battalion, and also
wanted to discuss matters with the Commanding Officer at the 5th
Scottish Rifles, and that we would make our way back at once. He

clambered out of the shell hole and I followed. He hopped back to the bank, taking a zig-zag course and I the same. How we were not riddled was a mystery: the machine-gun had been playing a pretty tune behind us.

We met the Doctor and Captain Radford, who had been sent for some time before, advancing along the bank. They had decided to shift Battalion Headquarters more on the left of the bank and they had just shifted in time. The spot where Battalion Headquarters had been was now being blown to pieces. Shells were bursting right along the bank and for a considerable way back and men were being blown yards in the air. The Major said that the Battalion would be relieved at dusk and he would try to stick it until then; but the Doctor warned him, if he did, that it might be the cause of him losing his leg.

He then handed over the command to Captain Radford, who said that he would much prefer the Doctor taking command, as he seemed to have a better grip of the situation than what he had. But the Major said he could not do that as the Doctor was a non-combatant, but that they could make any arrangements they liked when he had left. We made our way to the 5th Scottish Rifles and met their colonel outside a little dug-out. He mentioned that only three young platoon-officers were left in his battalion. They went in the dug-out to discuss matters and when we left the Major had a difficult job to walk. The Casualty Clearing Station was at Clapham Junction and all along the track leading down to it lay stretcher-bearers and bandaged men who had been killed making their way back. Many men who had received what they thought were nice blighty wounds had been killed along this track. The previous day the track, in addition to being heavily shelled had also been under machine-gun fire. As we were moving along I counted over twenty of our tanks which had been put out of action. Mr. Diamond, whom I had not seen since the previous day, passed us with his arm in a sling and said, "Hello. I'm glad to see you alive." He had been hit through the muscle of his arm. Shells were bursting here and there and we could sniff gas. We put our gas helmets on for a little while and it was twilight when we reached Clapham Junction.

The Major told me that the Battalion was going back to Dickiebusch after it was relieved and that I had no need to return. He wrote me out a note to take back to the transport. He then said that he would have liked to have remained with the Battalion until they were relieved but he thought it best to follow the Doctor's advice, especially when he said that he might lose his leg. I told him not to take too much notice of the Doctor, who would have made a better general than a doctor, and that I had seen worse bullet-wounds than what he had which had healed up in a fortnights' time. I hoped he would be back with the Battalion inside a couple of months. We shook hands and wished one another the best of luck and I made my way back to the transport.

The enemy bombed Dickiebusch that night but it was such a common occurrence around this area and I was so dead-beat that I took no notice of it. The following morning I rejoined the remnants of the Battalion and found that Ricco, the bank clerk, the architect and Sealyham were still kicking. They thought I had gone West and were as delighted to see me as I was them. We had lost heavily in signallers, but Tich was still hale and hearty.

THE DESERT WARFARE

After Gallipoli the Turks shifted elements of their army to the eastern part of their empire. Throughout 1916 they fought the Russians on the Caucasian front, and the British in Mesopotamia and the Suez Canal-Palestine sector. The fighting on both sides was conducted under almost insurmountable conditions. The few roads were not good, the railway system was inadequate, and the terrain itself was extremely difficult. For any larger undertakings, water often had to be supplied in the desert by freshly laid pipe lines. The heat of summer was so intense that campaigns were scheduled usually only for the spring and fall of the year.

By 1917 the British had secured the Suez Canal and pushed well into the Sinai peninsula, threatening Gaza. But in April they suffered a severe defeat. General Allenby, commander of the British Third Army on the Western Front, was sent to Cairo to take over the command of the Near East operations.

"Allenby asked and got reinforcements, and spent the summer in careful preparations. He was given two divisions from Salonika, formed another from bits and pieces in the theater, and by fall seven infantry and three cavalry divisions were ready. The Turks, too, were reinforced, but not strongly. Turkish divisions freed by the Russian collapse had been formed into the so-called Yilderim ("Lightning") Force under the German General von Falkenhayn, and some of these had reached the Gaza front. But the British had at least a two-to-one superiority.

"Allenby attacked the Beersheeba-Gaza position on October 31; Beersheeba was captured by dusk after a mounted cavalry charge by an Australian brigade, and Gaza fell on the night of November 6-7. It was victory, but incomplete; the Turks held tenaciously to the key communications junctions which covered their retreat. Both the retreat and the pursuit were governed by an arid land's most precious commodity—water.

"The way to Jerusalem was now open. From a defensive holding operation, the Palestine campaign had grown into a major offensive; Jerusalem had become a glittering political and psychological prize for the war-weary British people. Allenby had brought victory to a people starved for victory; on to Jerusalem!

"Supply and communications favored the British. The Turks depended upon a 1,300-mile railroad lifeline, with wood-burning locomotives; the British had organized well their land routes across Sinai, and above all, they possessed the inestimable advantage of command of the sea. The result was inevitable.

"On December 8, Allenby launched an assault with four divisions against Turkish positions which stretched from the Mediterranean, north of Jaffa, to angle back southward in the Judean Hills in front of Jerusalem. The Turkish lines bent and broke; on December 9 they retreated from Jerusalem; the Holy City was at last in British hands. In a few days the rains came, and the campaigning season was over.

"The Palestine campaign—fought by illiterate Turkish askars, Indian sepoys, rambunctious Australians, Oxford dons, and Prussian junkers, and supplied by man-back, donkeys, camels, mules, horses, railroads, pipelines, and ships—was aided by an Arab revolt, incited, inspired, and organized by British pounds and promises, and by the tortured genius of a young British archaeologist, T. E. Lawrence. During 1917 Lawrence and his Arab bands—mostly camel mounted —harried, cut off, and immobilized Turkish forces along the so-called Hejaz railroad in Arabia. During Allenby's advance into Palestine, Lawrence and his irregulars covered the British right flank, made raids and reconnoitered, and supplied invaluable information about Turkish dispositions." *

Lawrence believed in mobility and ubiquity resembling a naval striking force. He says in *Seven Pillars of Wisdom*, "Our tactics should be tip and run: not pushes, but strokes. We should never try to improve an advantage. We should use the smallest force in the quickest time at the farthest place.

"The necessary speed and range for distant war we would attain through the frugality of the desert men, and their efficiency on

* Baldwin, *World War I*, pp. 120-21.

camels. The camel, that intricate, prodigious piece of nature, in expert hands yielded a remarkable return. On them we were independent of supply for six weeks, if each man had a half-bag of flour, forty-five pounds in weight, slung on his riding-saddle.

"Of water we would not want to carry more than a pint each. The camels must drink, and there was no gain in making ourselves richer than our mounts. Some of us never drank between wells, but those were hardy men: most drank fully at each well, and carried a drink for an intermediate dry day. In summer the camels would do about two hundred and fifty miles after a watering; a three days' vigorous march. An easy stage was fifty miles: eighty was good: in an emergency we might do one hundred and ten miles in the twenty-four hours: twice the Ghazala, our greatest camel, did one hundred and forty-three alone with me. Wells were seldom a hundred miles apart, so the pint reserve was latitude enough.

"Our six weeks' food gave us capacity for a thousand miles out and home. The endurance of our camels made it possible for us (for me, the camel-novice in the army, 'painful' would be the fitter word) to ride fifteen hundred miles in thirty days, without fear of starvation; because, even if we exceeded in time, each of us sat on two hundred pounds of potential meat, and the man made camel-less could double-bank another, riding two-up, in emergency.

"The equipment of the raiding parties should aim at simplicity; with, nevertheless, a technical superiority over the Turks in the critical department. I sent to Egypt demands for great quantities of light automatic guns, Hotchkiss or Lewis, to be used as snipers' tools. The men we trained to them were kept deliberately ignorant of the mechanism, not to waste speed in action upon efforts at repair. Ours were battles of minutes, fought at eighteen miles an hour. If a gun jammed, the gunner must throw it aside and go in with his rifle.

"Another distinguishing feature might be high explosives. We evolved special dynamite methods, and by the end of the war could demolish any quantity of track and bridges with economy and safety. Allenby was generous with explosive." *

* *Seven Pillars of Wisdom* by T. E. Lawrence, published by Doubleday, Doran & Co., pp. 337 and 338.

BLOWING UP TRAINS*

by T. E. Lawrence

Quietly we regained our camels and slept. Next morning we returned on our tracks to let a fold of the plain hide us from the railway, and then marched south across the sandy flat; seeing tracks of gazelle, oryx and ostrich; with, in one spot, stale padmarks of leopard. We were making for the low hills bounding the far side, intending to blow up a train; for Zaal said that where these touched the railway was such a curve as we needed for mine-laying, and that the spurs commanding it would give us ambush and a field of fire for our machine-guns.

So we turned east in the southern ridges till within half a mile of the line. There the party halted in a thirty-foot valley, while a few of us walked down to the line, which bent a little eastward to avoid the point of higher ground under our feet. The point ended in a flat table fifty feet above the track, facing north across the valley.

The metals crossed the hollow on a high bank, pierced by a two-arched bridge for the passage of rain-water. This seemed an ideal spot to lay the charge. It was our first try at electric mining and we had no idea what would happen; but it stood to our reason that the job would be more sure with an arch under the explosive because, whatever the effect on the locomotive, the bridge would go, and the succeeding coaches be inevitably derailed.

The ledge would make an admirable position for Stokes. For the automatics, it was rather high; but the enfilade would be masterful

* From *Seven Pillars of Wisdom*.

whether the train was going up or down the line. So we determined to put up with the disadvantages of plunging fire. It was good to have my two British responsibilities in one place, safe from surprise and with an independent retreat into the rough: for to-day Stokes was in pain with dysentery. Probably the Mudowwara water had upset his stomach. So few Englishmen seemed to have been endowed by their upbringing with any organic resistance to disease.

Back with our camels, we dumped the loads, and sent the animals to safe pasture near some undercut rocks from which the Arabs scraped salt. The freedmen carried down the Stokes gun with its shells; the Lewis guns; and the gelatine with its insulated wire, magneto and tools to the chosen place. The sergeants set up their toys on a terrace, while we went down to the bridge to dig a bed between the ends of two steel sleepers, wherein to hide my fifty pounds of gelatine. We had stripped off the paper wrapping of the individual explosive plugs and kneaded them together by help of the sun-heat into a shaking jelly in a sand-bag.

The burying of it was not easy. The embankment was steep, and in the sheltered pocket between it and the hill-side was a wind-laid bank of sand. No one crossed this but myself, stepping carefully; yet I left unavoidable great prints over its smoothness. The ballast dug out from the track I had to gather in my cloak for carriage in repeated journeys to the culvert, whence it could be tipped naturally over the shingle bed of the watercourse.

It took me nearly two hours to dig in and cover the charge: then came the difficult job of unrolling the heavy wires from the detonator to the hills whence we would fire the mine. The top sand was crusted and had to be broken through in burying the wires. They were stiff wires, which scarred the wind-rippled surface with long lines like the belly marks of preposterously narrow and heavy snakes. When pressed down in one place they rose into the air in another. At last they had to be weighted down with rocks which, in turn, had to be buried at the cost of great disturbance of the ground.

Afterwards it was necessary, with a sand-bag, to stipple the marks into a wavy surface; and, finally, with a bellows and long fanning sweeps of my cloak, to simulate the smooth laying of the wind. The whole job took five hours to finish; but then it was well finished: neither myself nor any of us could see where the charge lay, or that double wires led out underground from it to the firing point two hundred yards off, behind the ridge marked for our riflemen.

The wires were just long enough to cross from this ridge into a depression. There we brought up the two ends and connected them with the electric exploder. It was an ideal place both for it and for the man who fired it, except that the bridge was not visible thence.

However, this only meant that someone would have to press the handle at a signal from a point fifty yards ahead, commanding the bridge and the ends of the wires alike. Salem, Feisal's best slave, asked for this task of honour, and was yielded it by acclamation. The end of the afternoon was spent in showing him (on the disconnected exploder) what to do, till he was act-perfect and banged down the ratchet precisely as I raised my hand with an imaginary engine on the bridge.

We walked back to camp, leaving one man on watch by the line. Our baggage was deserted, and we stared about in a puzzle for the rest, till we saw them suddenly sitting against the golden light of sunset along a high ridge. We yelled to them to lie down or come down, but they persisted up there on their perch like a school of hooded crows, in full view of north and south.

At last we ran up and threw them off the skyline, too late. The Turks in a little hill-post by Hallat Ammar, four miles south of us, had seen them, and opened fire in their alarm upon the long shadows which the declining sun was pushing gradually up the slopes towards the post. Beduin were past masters in the art of using country, but in their abiding contempt for the stupidity of the Turks they would take no care to fight them. This ridge was visible at once from Mudowwara and Hallat Ammar, and they had frightened both places by their sudden ominous expectant watch.

However, the dark closed on us, and we knew we must sleep away the night patiently in hope of the morrow. Perhaps the Turks would reckon us gone if our place looked deserted in the morning. So we lit fires in a deep hollow, baked bread and were comfortable. The common tasks had made us one party, and the hill-top folly shamed everyone into agreement that Zaal should be our leader.

Day broke quietly, and for hours we watched the empty railway with its peaceful camps. The constant care of Zaal and of his lame cousin Howeimil, kept us hidden, though with difficulty, because of the insatiate restlessness of the Beduin, who would never sit down for ten minutes, but must fidget and do or say something. This defect made them very inferior to the stolid English for the long, tedious strain of a waiting war. Also it partly accounted for their uncertain stomachs in defence. To-day they made us very angry.

Perhaps, after all, the Turks saw us, for at nine o'clock some forty men came out of the tents on the hill-top by Hallat Ammar to the south and advanced in open order. If we left them alone, they would turn us off our mine in an hour; if we opposed them with our superior strength and drove them back, the railway would take notice, and traffic be held up. It was a quandary, which eventually we tried to solve by sending thirty men to check the enemy patrol gradually; and, if possible, to draw them lightly aside into the broken hills. This might hide our main position and reassure them as to our insignificant strength and purpose.

For some hours it worked as we had hoped; the firing grew desultory and distant. A permanent patrol came confidently up from the south and walked past our hill, over our mine and on towards Mudowwara without noticing us. There were eight soldiers and a stout corporal, who mopped his brow against the heat, for it was now after eleven o'clock and really warm. When he had passed us by a mile or two the fatigue of the tramp became too much for him. He marched his party into the shade of a long culvert, under whose arches a cool draught from the east was gently flowing, and there in comfort they lay on the soft sand, drank water from their bottles, smoked, and at last slept. We presumed that this was the noon-day rest which every solid Turk in the hot summer of Arabia took as a matter of principle, and that their allowing themselves the pause showed that we were disproved or ignored. However, we were in error.

Noon brought a fresh care. Through my powerful glasses we saw a hundred Turkish soldiers issue from Mudowwara Station and make straight across the sandy plain towards our place. They were coming very slowly, and no doubt unwillingly, for sorrow at losing their beloved midday sleep: but at their very worst marching and temper they could hardly take more than two hours before they reached us.

We began to pack up, preparatory to moving off, having decided to leave the mine and its leads in place on chance that the Turks might not find them, and we be able to return and take advantage of all the careful work. We sent a messenger to our covering party on the south, that they should meet us farther up, near those scarred rocks which served as screen for our pasturing camels.

Just as he had gone, the watchman cried out that smoke in clouds was rising from Hallat Ammar. Zaal and I rushed uphill and saw by its shape and volume that indeed there must be a train waiting in that station. As we were trying to see it over the hill, suddenly it moved out in our direction. We yelled to the Arabs to get into position as quick as possible, and there came a wild scramble over sand and rock. Stokes and Lewis, being booted, could not win the race; but they came well up, their pains and dysentery forgotten.

The men with rifles posted themselves in a long line behind the spur running from the guns past the exploder to the mouth of the valley. From it they would fire directly into the derailed carriages at less than one hundred and fifty yards, whereas the ranges for the Stokes and Lewis guns were about three hundred yards. An Arab stood up on high behind the guns and shouted to us what the train was doing—a necessary precaution, for if it carried troops and detrained them behind our ridge we should have to face about like a flash and retire fighting up the valley for our lives. Fortunately it held on at all the speed the two locomotives could make on wood fuel.

It drew near where we had been reported, and opened random fire into the desert. I could hear the racket coming, as I sat on my hillock by the bridge to give the signal to Salem, who danced round the exploder on his knees, crying with excitement, and calling urgently on God to make him fruitful. The Turkish fire sounded heavy, and I wondered with how many men we were going to have affair, and if the mine would be advantage enough for our eighty fellows to equal them. It would have been better if the first electrical experiment had been simpler.

However, at that moment the engines, looking very big, rocked with screaming whistles into view around the bend. Behind them followed ten box-waggons, crowded with rifle-muzzles at the windows and doors; and in little sand-bag nests on the roofs Turks precariously held on, to shoot at us. I had not thought of two engines, and on the moment decided to fire the charge under the second, so that however little the mine's effect, the uninjured engine should not be able to uncouple and drag the carriages away.

Accordingly, when the front 'driver' of the second engine was on the bridge, I raised my hand to Salem. There followed a terrific roar, and the line vanished from sight behind a spouting column of black dust and smoke a hundred feet high and wide. Out of the darkness came shattering crashes and long, loud metallic clangings of ripped steel, with many lumps of iron and plate; while one entire wheel of a locomotive whirled up suddenly black out of the cloud against the sky, and sailed musically over our heads to fall slowly and heavily into the desert behind. Except for the flight of these, there succeeded a deathly silence, with no cry of men or rifle-shot, as the now grey mist of the explosion drifted from the line towards us, and over our ridge until it was lost in the hills.

In the lull, I ran southward to join the sergeants. Salem picked up his rifle and charged out into the murk. Before I had climbed to the guns the hollow was alive with shots, and with the brown figures of the Beduin leaping forward to grips with the enemy. I looked round to see what was happening so quickly, and saw the train stationary and dismembered along the track, with its waggon sides jumping under the bullets which riddled them, while Turks were falling out from the far doors to gain the shelter of the railway embankment.

As I watched, our machine-guns chattered out over my head, and the long rows of Turks on the carriage roofs rolled over, and were swept off the top like bales of cotton before the furious shower of bullets which stormed along the roofs and splashed clouds of yellow chips from the planking. The dominant position of the guns had been an advantage to us so far.

When I reached Stokes and Lewis the engagement had taken another turn. The remaining Turks had got behind the bank, here about eleven feet high, and from cover of the wheels were firing point-blank at the Beduin twenty yards away across the sand-filled dip. The enemy in the crescent of the curving line were secure from the machine-guns; but Stokes slipped in his first shell, and after a few seconds there came a crash as it burst beyond the train in the desert.

He touched the elevating screw, and his second shot fell just by the trucks in the deep hollow below the bridge where the Turks were taking refuge. It made a shambles of the place. The survivors of the group broke out in a panic across the desert, throwing away their rifles and equipment as they ran. This was the opportunity of the Lewis gunners. The sergeant grimly traversed with drum after drum, till the open sand was littered with bodies. Mushagraf, the Sherari boy behind the second gun, saw the battle over, threw aside his weapon with a yell, and dashed down at speed with his rifle to join the others who were beginning, like wild beasts, to tear open the carriages and fall to plunder. It had taken nearly ten minutes.

I looked up-line through my glasses and saw the Mudowwara patrol breaking back uncertainly towards the railway to meet the train-fugitives running their fastest northward. I looked south, to see our thirty men cantering their camels neck and neck in our direction to share the spoils. The Turks there, seeing them go, began to move after them with infinite precaution, firing volleys. Evidently we had a half-hour respite, and then a double threat against us.

I ran down to the ruins to see what the mine had done. The bridge was gone; and into its gap was fallen the front waggon, which had been filled with sick. The smash had killed all but three or four and had rolled dead and dying into a bleeding heap against the splintered end. One of those yet alive deliriously cried out the word typhus. So I wedged shut the door, and left them there, alone.

Succeeding waggons were derailed and smashed: some had frames irreparably buckled. The second engine was a blanched pile of smoking iron. Its driving wheels had been blown upward, taking away the side of the fire-box. Cab and tender were twisted into strips, among the piled stones of the bridge abutment. It would never run again. The front engine had got off better: though heavily derailed and lying half-over, with the cab burst, yet its steam was at pressure, and driving-gear intact.

Our greatest object was to destroy locomotives, and I had kept in my arms a box of gun-cotton with fuse and detonator ready fixed, to make sure such a case. I now put them in position on the outside cylinder. On the boiler would have been better, but the sizzling steam made me fear a general explosion which would sweep across my men (swarming like ants over the booty) with a blast of jagged fragments. Yet they would not finish their looting before the Turks came. So I lit the fuse, and in the half-minute of its burning drove the plunderers a little back, with difficulty. Then the charge burst, blowing the cylinder to smithers, and the axle too. At the moment I was distressed with uncertainty whether the damage were enough; but the Turks, later, found the engine beyond use and broke it up.

The valley was a weird sight. The Arabs, gone raving mad, were rushing about at top speed bareheaded and half-naked, screaming, shooting into the air, clawing one another nail and fist, while they burst open trucks and staggered back and forward with immense bales, which they ripped by the rail-side, and tossed through, smashing what they did not want. The train had been packed with refugees and sick men, volunteers for boat-service on the Euphrates, and families of Turkish officers returning to Damascus.

There were scores of carpets spread about; dozens of mattresses and flowered quilts; blankets in heaps, clothes for men and women in full variety; clocks, cooking-pots, food, ornaments and weapons. To one side stood thirty or forty hysterical women, unveiled, tearing their clothes and hair; shrieking themselves distracted. The Arabs without regard to them went on wrecking the household goods; looting their absolute fill. Camels had become common property. Each man frantically loaded the nearest with what it could carry and shooed it westward into the void, while he turned to his next fancy.

Seeing me tolerably unemployed, the women rushed, and caught at me with howls for mercy. I assured them that all was going well: but they would not get away till some husbands delivered me. These knocked their wives off and seized my feet in a very agony of terror of instant death. A Turk so broken down was a nasty spectacle: I kicked them off as well as I could with bare feet, and finally broke free.

Next a group of Austrians, officers and non-commissioned officers, appealed to me quietly in Turkish for quarter. I replied with my halting German; whereupon one, in English, begged a doctor for his wounds. We had none: not that it mattered, for he was mortally hurt and dying. I told them the Turks would return in an hour and care for them. But he was dead before that, as were most of the others (instructors in the new Skoda mountain howitzers supplied to Turkey for the Hejaz war), because some dispute broke out between them and my own bodyguard, and one of them fired a pistol shot at young Rahail. My infuriated men cut them down, all but two or three, before I could return to interfere.

So far as could be seen in the excitement, our side had suffered no loss. Among the ninety military prisoners were five Egyptian soldiers, in their underclothes. They knew me, and explained that in a night raid of Davenport's, near Wadi Ais, they had been cut off by the Turks and captured. They told me something of Davenport's work: of his continual pegging away in Abdulla's sector, which was kept alive by him for month after month, without any of the encouragement lent to us by success and local enthusiasm. His best helpers were such stolid infantrymen as these, whom I made lead the prisoners away to our appointed rallying place at the salt rocks.

◆ ◆ ◆

Blowing up trains was an exact science when done deliberately, by a sufficient party, with machine-guns in position. If scrambled at it might become dangerous. The difficulty this time was that the available gunners were Indians; who, though good men fed, were only half-men in cold and hunger. I did not propose to drag them off without rations on an adventure which might take a week. There was no cruelty in starving Arabs; they would not die of a few days' fasting, and would fight as well as ever on empty stomachs; while, if things got too difficult, there were the riding camels to kill and eat; but the Indians, though Moslems, refused camel-flesh on principle.

I explained these delicacies of diet. Ali at once said that it would be enough for me to blow up the train, leaving him and the Arabs with him to do their best to carry its wreck without machine-gun support. As, in this unsuspecting district, we might well happen on a supply train, with civilians or only a small guard of reservists aboard, I agreed to risk it. The decision having been applauded, we sat down in a cloaked circle, to finish our remaining food in a very late and cold supper (the rain had sodden the fuel and made fire not possible) our hearts somewhat comforted by the chance of another effort.

At dawn, with the unfit of the Arabs, the Indians moved away for Azrak, miserably. They had started up country with me in hope of a really military enterprise, and first had seen the muddled bridge, and now were losing this prospective train. It was hard on them; and to soften the blow with honour I asked Wood to accompany them. He agreed, after argument, for their sakes; but it proved a wise move for himself, as a sickness which had been troubling him began to show the early signs of pneumonia.

The balance of us, some sixty men, turned back towards the railway. None of them knew the country, so I led them to Minifir, where, with Zaal, we had made havoc in the spring. The re-curved hill-top was an excellent observation post, camp, grazing ground and way of retreat, and we sat there in our old place till sunset, shivering and staring out over the immense plain which stretched map-like to the clouded peaks of Jebel Druse, with Um el Jemal and her sister-villages like ink-smudges on it through the rain.

In the first dusk we walked down to lay the mine. The rebuilt culvert of kilometre 172 seemed still the fittest place. While we stood by it there came a rumbling, and through the gathering darkness and mist a train suddenly appeared round the northern curve, only two hundred yards away. We scurried under the long arch and heard it roll overhead. This was annoying; but when the course was clear again, we fell to burying the charge. The evening was bitterly cold, with drifts of rain blowing down the valley.

The arch was solid masonry, of four metres span, and stood over a shingle water-bed which took its rise on our hill-top. The winter rains had cut this into a channel four feet deep, narrow and winding, which served us as an admirable approach till within three hundred yards of the line. There the gully widened out and ran straight towards the culvert, open to the sight of anyone upon the rails.

We hid the explosive carefully on the crown of the arch, deeper than usual, beneath a tie, so that the patrols could not feel its jelly softness under their feet. The wires were taken down the bank into the shingle bed of the watercourse, where concealment was quick; and up it as far as they could reach. Unfortunately, this was only sixty yards, for there had been difficulty in Egypt over insulated cable and no more had been available when our expedition started. Sixty yards was plenty for the bridge, but little for a train: however, the ends happened to coincide with a little bush about ten inches high, on the edge of the watercourse, and we buried them beside this very convenient mark. It was impossible to leave them joined up to the exploder in the proper way, since the spot was evident to the permanent way-patrols as they made their rounds.

Owing to the mud the job took longer than usual, and it was very nearly dawn before we finished. I waited under the draughty arch till day broke, wet and dismal, and then I went over the whole area of disturbance, spending another half-hour in effacing its every mark, scattering leaves and dead grass over it, and watering down the broken mud from a shallow rain-pool near. Then they waved to me that the first patrol was coming, and I went up to join the others.

Before I had reached them they came tearing down into their prearranged places, lining the watercourse and spurs each side. A train was coming from the north. Hamud, Feisal's long slave, had the exploder; but before he reached me a short train of closed box-waggons rushed by at speed. The rainstorms on the plain and the thick morning had hidden it from the eyes of our watchman until too late. This second failure saddened us further and Ali began to say that nothing would come right this trip. Such a statement held risk as prelude of the discovery of an evil eye present; so, to divert attention, I suggested new watching posts be sent far out, one to the ruins on the north, one to the great cairn of the southern crest.

The rest, having no breakfast, were to pretend not to be hungry. They all enjoyed doing this, and for a while we sat cheerfully in the rain, huddling against one another for warmth behind a breastwork of our streaming camels. The moisture made the animals' hair curl up like a fleece, so that they looked queerly dishevelled. When the rain paused, which it did frequently, a cold moaning wind searched out the unprotected parts of us very thoroughly. After a time we found our wetted shirts clammy and comfortless things. We had nothing to eat, nothing to do and nowhere to sit except on wet rock, wet grass or mud. However, this persistent weather kept reminding me that it would delay Allenby's advance on Jerusalem, and rob him of his great possibility. So large a misfortune to our lion was a half-encouragement for the mice. We would be partners into next year.

In the best circumstances, waiting for action was hard. To-day it was beastly. Even enemy patrols stumbled along without care, perfunctorily, against the rain. At last, near noon, in a snatch of fine weather, the watchmen on the south peak flagged their cloaks wildly in signal of a train. We reached our positions in an instant, for we had squatted the late hours on our heels in a streaming ditch near the line, so as not to miss another chance. The Arabs took cover properly. I looked back at their ambush from my firing point, and saw nothing but the grey hill-sides.

I could not hear the train coming, but trusted, and knelt ready for perhaps half an hour, when the suspense became intolerable, and I signalled to know what was up. They sent down to say it was coming very slowly, and was an enormously long train. Our appetites stiffened. The longer it was the more would be the loot. Then came word that it had stopped. It moved again.

Finally, near one o'clock, I heard it panting. The locomotive was evidently defective (all these wood-fired trains were bad), and the heavy load on the up-gradient was proving too much for its capacity. I crouched behind my bush, while it crawled slowly into view past the south cutting, and along the bank above my head towards the culvert. The first ten trucks were open trucks, crowded with troops. However, once again it was too late to choose, so when the engine was squarely over the mine I pushed down the handle of the exploder. Nothing happened. I sawed it up and down four times.

Still nothing happened; and I realized that it had gone out of order, and that I was kneeling on a naked bank, with a Turkish troop train crawling past fifty yards away. The bush, which had seemed a foot high, shrank smaller than a fig-leaf; and I felt myself the most distinct object in the country-side. Behind me was an open valley for two hundred yards to the cover where my Arabs were waiting, and wondering what I was at. It was impossible to make a bolt for it, or the Turks would step off the train and finish us. If I sat still, there might be just a hope of my being ignored as a casual Bedouin.

So there I sat, counting for sheer life, while eighteen open trucks, three box-waggons, and three officers' coaches dragged by. The engine panted slower and slower, and I thought every moment that it would break down. The troops took no great notice of me, but the officers were interested, and came out to the little platforms at the ends of their carriages, pointing and staring. I waved back at them, grinning nervously, and feeling an improbable shepherd in my Meccan dress, with its twisted golden circlet about my head. Perhaps the mud-stains, the wet and their ignorance made me accepted. The end of the brake van slowly disappeared into the cutting on the north.

As it went, I jumped up, buried my wires, snatched hold of the wretched exploder, and went like a rabbit uphill into safety. There I took breath and looked back to see that the train had finally stuck. It waited, about five hundred yards beyond the mine, for nearly an hour to get up a head of steam, while an officers' patrol came back and searched, very carefully, the ground where I had been seen sitting. However the wires were properly hidden: they found nothing: the engine plucked up heart again, and away they went.

Mifleh was past tears, thinking I had intentionally let the train through; and when the Serahin had been told the real cause they said 'bad luck is with us.' Historically they were right; but they meant it for a prophecy, so I made sarcastic reference to their courage at the bridge the week before, hinting that it might be a tribal preference to sit on camel-guard. At once there was uproar, the Serahin attacking me furiously, the Beni Sakhr defending. Ali heard the trouble, and came running.

When we had made it up the original despondency was half forgotten. Ali backed me nobly, though the wretched boy was blue with cold and shivering in an attack of fever. He gasped that their ancestor the Prophet had given to Sherifs the faculty of 'sight', and by it he knew that our luck was turning. This was comfort for them: my first installment of good fortune came when in the wet, without other tool than my dagger, I got the box of the exploder open and persuaded its electrical gear to work properly once more.

We returned to our vigil by the wires, but nothing happened, and evening drew down with more squalls and beastliness, everybody full of grumbles. There was no train; it was too wet to light a cooking fire; our only potential food was camel. Raw meat did not tempt anyone that night; and so our beasts survived to the morrow.

Ali lay down on his belly, which position lessened the hunger-ache, trying to sleep off his fever. Khazen, Ali's servant, lent him his cloak for extra covering. For a spell I took Khazen under mine, but soon found it becoming crowded. So I left it to him and went downhill to connect up the exploder. Afterwards I spent the night there alone by the singing telegraph wires, hardly wishing to sleep, so painful was the cold. Nothing came all the long hours, and dawn, which broke wet, looked even uglier than usual. We were sick to death of Minifir, of railways, of train watching and wrecking, by now. I climbed up to the main body while the early patrol searched the railway. Then the day cleared a little. Ali awoke, much refreshed, and his new spirit cheered us. Hamud, the slave, produced some sticks which he had kept under his clothes by his skin all night. They were nearly dry. We shaved down some blasting gelatine, and with its hot flame got a fire going, while the Sukhur hurriedly killed a mangy camel, the best spared of our riding-beasts, and began with entrenching tools to hack it into handy joints.

Just at that moment the watchman on the north cried a train. We left the fire and made a breathless race of the six hundred yards downhill to our old position. Round the bend, whistling its loudest, came the train, a splendid two-engined thing of twelve passenger coaches, travelling at top speed on the favouring grade. I touched off under the first driving wheel of the first locomotive, and the explosion was terrific. The ground spouted blackly into my face, and I was sent spinning, to sit up with the shirt torn to my shoulder and the blood dripping from long, ragged scratches on my left arm. Between my knees lay the exploder, crushed under a twisted sheet of sooty iron. In front of me was the scalded and smoking upper half of a man. When I peered through the dust and steam of the explosion the whole boiler of the first engine seemed to be missing.

I dully felt that it was time to get away to support; but when I moved, learnt that there was a great pain in my right foot, because of which I could only limp along, with my head swinging from the shock. Movement began to clear away this confusion, as I hobbled towards the upper valley, whence the Arabs were now shooting fast into the crowded coaches. Dizzily I cheered myself by repeating aloud in English, 'Oh, I wish this hadn't happened.'

When the enemy began to return our fire, I found myself much between the two. Ali saw me fall, and thinking that I was hard hit, ran out, with Turki and about twenty men of his servants and the Beni Sakhr, to help me. The Turks found their range and got seven of them in a few seconds. The others, in a rush, were about me—fit models, after their activity, for a sculptor. Their full white cotton drawers drawn in, bell-like, round their slender waists and ankles; their hairless brown bodies; and the love-locks plaited tightly over each temple in long horns, made them look like Russian dancers.

We scrambled back into cover together, and there, secretly, I felt myself over, to find I had not once been really hurt; though besides the bruises and cuts of the boiler-plate and a broken toe, I had five different bullet-grazes on me (some of them uncomfortably deep) and my clothes ripped to pieces.

From the watercourse we could look about. The explosion had destroyed the arched head of the culvert, and the frame of the first engine was lying beyond it, at the near foot of the embankment, down which it had rolled. The second locomotive had toppled into the gap, and was lying across the ruined tender of the first. Its bed was twisted. I judged them both beyond repair. The second tender had disappeared over the further side; and the first three waggons had telescoped and were smashed in pieces.

The rest of the train was badly derailed, with the listing coaches butted end to end at all angles, zigzagged along the track. One of them was a saloon, decorated with flags. In it had been Mehmed Jemal Pasha, commanding the Eighth Army Corps, hurrying down to defend Jerusalem against Allenby. His chargers had been in the first waggon; his motor-car was on the end of the train, and we shot it up. Of his staff we noticed a fat ecclesiastic, whom we thought to be Assad Shukair, Imam to Ahmed Jemal Pasha, and a notorious pro-Turk pimp. So we blazed at him till he dropped.

It was all long bowls. We could see that our chance of carrying the wreck was slight. There had been some four hundred men on board, and the survivors, now recovered from the shock, were under shelter and shooting hard at us. At the first moment our party on the north spur had closed, and nearly won the game. Mifleh on his mare chased the officers from the saloon into the lower ditch. He was too excited to stop and shoot, and so they got away scathless. The Arabs following him had turned to pick up some of the rifles and medals littering the ground, and then to drag bags and boxes from the train. If we had had a machine-gun posted to cover the far side, according to my mining practice, not a Turk would have escaped.

Mifleh and Adhub rejoined us on the hill, and asked after Fahad. One of the Serahin told how he had led the first rush, while I lay knocked out beside the exploder, and had been killed near it. They showed his belt and rifle as proof that he was dead and that they had tried to save him. Adhub said not a word, but leaped out of the gully, and raced downhill. We caught our breaths till our lungs hurt us, watching him; but the Turks seemed not to see. A minute later he was dragging a body behind the left-hand bank.

Mifleh went back to his mare, mounted, and took her down behind a spur. Together they lifted the inert figure on to the pommel, and returned. A bullet had passed through Fahad's face, knocking out four teeth, and gashing the tongue. He had fallen unconscious, but had revived just before Adhub reached him, and was trying on hands and knees, blinded with blood, to crawl away. He now recovered poise enough to cling to a saddle. So they changed him to the first camel they found, and led him off at once.

The Turks, seeing us so quiet, began to advance up the slope. We let them come half-way, and then poured in volleys which killed some twenty and drove the others back. The ground about the train was strewn with dead, and the broken coaches had been crowded: but they were fighting under the eye of their Corps Commander, and undaunted began to work round the spurs to outflank us.

We were now only about forty left, and obviously could do no good against them. So we ran in batches up the little stream-bed, turning at each sheltered angle to delay them by pot-shots. Little Turki much distinguished himself by quick coolness, though his straight-stocked Turkish cavalry carbine made him so expose his head that he got four bullets through his head-cloth. Ali was angry with me for retiring slowly. In reality my raw hurts crippled me, but to hide from him this real reason I pretended to be easy, interested in and studying the Turks. Such successive rests while I gained courage for a new run kept him and Turki far behind the rest.

At last we reached the hill-top. Each man there jumped on the nearest camel, and made away at full speed eastward into the desert, for an hour. Then in safety we sorted our animals. The excellent Rahail, despite the ruling excitement, had brought off with him, tied to his saddle-girth, a huge haunch of the camel slaughtered just as the train arrived. He gave us the motive for a proper halt, five miles farther on, as a little party of four camels appeared marching in the same direction. It was our companion, Matar, coming back from his home village to Azrak with loads of raisins and peasant delicacies.

So we stopped at once, under a large rock in Wadi Dhuleil, where was a barren fig-tree, and cooked our first meal for three days. There, also, we bandaged up Fahad, who was sleepy with the lassitude of his severe hurt. Adhub, seeing this, took one of Matar's new carpets, and, doubling it across the camel-saddle, stitched the ends into great pockets. In one they laid Fahad, while Adhub crawled into the other as make-weight: and the camel was led off southward towards their tribal tents.

The other wounded men were seen to at the same time. Mifleh brought up the youngest lads of the party, and had them spray the wounds with their piss, as a rude antiseptic. Meanwhile we whole ones refreshed ourselves. I bought another mangy camel for extra meat, paid rewards, compensated the relatives of the killed, and gave prize-money, for the sixty or seventy rifles we had taken. It was small booty, but not to be despised. Some Serahin, who had gone into the action without rifles, able only to throw unavailing stones, had now two guns apiece. Next day we moved into Azrak, having a great welcome, and boasting—God forgive us—that we were victors.

THE WESTERN FRONT IN 1918

The United States had declared war on Germany in April, 1917. Once the declaration was made the country was anxious to fight, but hardly prepared for battle. The regular army could count only 92,000 men in uniform and 550 artillery pieces. Not until the last months of the war would American troops appear in numbers comparable to the British and French. Nor would they be fighting with arms manufactured in their own country. Other than the Springfield rifle made in America, all the artillery, planes and tanks were supplied by the British and French.

However, the mere presence of the first American troops in 1917 was a tonic to their weary allies. The Americans would have little time to train but nobody seemed to care; they were there to prove their mettle by fighting Germans.

In the beginning, Pershing and his staff vowed to keep the American troops together to form their own army. But some of the early divisions were given over to the French and British armies to bolster the lines where the Germans threatened breakthrough. Foch and his staff argued that it didn't matter what command the Americans fought under, just as long as they were gotten into the lines. Pershing was a stubborn battler, however. "How was it possible, he wondered, that (the British) could expect men to fight well in foreign ranks, so much cannon fodder under foreign brigadiers. The British had to keep their own cadres—wonderful ones too—as national entities; the Scottish battalions, the Canadian, Australian-New Zealand, and Irish could not have been brigaded into English regiments." *

Fully aware of the growing number of American troops, the Germans decided to launch a series of attacks in early 1918 designed

* From *The Doughboys* by Laurence Stallings, p. 46. Published by Harper and Bros.

to drive a wedge between the French and British and push the British into the sea. General Ludendorff, the German commander, planned a hammer stroke at the Somme front. His troops ". . . had been taught to forget all they had so painfully learned about trench warfare and to adapt themselves to mobility. Short intensive artillery preparations, a creeping barrage, bypassing of strong points, massive infiltration, and continued forward movement were the earmarks of the new tactics. Ludendorff hoped to crash through the British front, turn north toward the sea, and roll up the British armies.

"On a forty-four-mile front from La Bassée to La Fère the attack opened before dawn on March 21. The British batteries were drenched with gas and silenced, high explosives harried the trenches, and under cover of a fog, which handicapped the attack even more than the defense, the massive German assault made quick progress. . . .

"By March 24 the Germans thought the battle was won . . . the vital rail junction of Amiens was threatened, and the French and British were scraping up divisions from other sections of the front and hurrying them frantically toward the Somme. . . .

"A stalwart British stand on March 28 turned back the Germans and the Second Battle of the Somme died out by April 5, with Amiens still in Allied hands, and the breakthrough plugged with most of the available reserves. . . . The Germans had captured tremendous booty; they had re-established much of the old Noyon salient and were within seven miles of Amiens. But they had also forced what Allied deliberations had not been able to effect in four long years: an Allied unified command." *

On April 3, General Foch was appointed Supreme Commander-in-Chief of all the Allied forces in France. He had hardly assumed his exalted position when the Germans launched their second attack on April 9 with their objective the rail junction of Hazebrouck. The Germans again advanced, recapturing the Messines Ridge and the Ypres salient, as well. But by the end of April the German drive had still not split the British and French nor reached Hazebrouck. The British, however, were hanging on the ropes; reinforcements from

* Baldwin, pp. 140, 141, 142.

the fronts in Italy, Asia and Greece were recalled for the Western front.

"The Allies had lost at least 350,000 casualties in six weeks of fighting; the Germans not many less. Ludendorff determined to pin down the French and draw their reserves away from Flanders. The third great German blow—the Third Battle of the Aisne—struck the French (plus some British divisions resting in a 'quiet' sector) on May 27 on a twenty-five-mile-front with forty-two divisions, nineteen in the initial assault. The Chemin des Dames, so dearly bought, was wrenched from the French and the Germans were across the Aisne in a deep ten-mile penetration on the first day; by June 2–3 they had reached the Marne at Château-Thiérry, fifty-six miles from Paris. A salient about thirty-two miles deep at its maximum with a base of fifty miles had been hammered into the French lines.

"In the emergency General Pershing assigned the 2nd and 3rd U. S. divisions to the French. A machine gun battalion of the 3rd Division, under command of the French Sixth Army, assisted the French in repulsing German attempts to cross the Marne at Château-Thiérry. Two brigades helped the French to reduce German bridgeheads at Jaulgonne. The 3rd had never before been under fire, but it earned high French commendation. The 2nd Division, attacking throughout June and early July on the western flank of the salient's apex, took Vaux and Bouresches, and Belleau Wood in hard-fought, bloody actions. The Marine brigade, serving with the 2nd— its men known as "Leathernecks" or "Devil Dogs"—won its immortality in nineteen days of searing fighting. But the casualties were terrible: forty percent for many of the combat units. In the meantime, on May 28 in the first test of American combat effectiveness, the 1st U. S. Division took and held, in a neatly planned and executed operation, the strongly held village of Cantigny at the apex of the great Amiens salient.

"American arms had been bloodied; the test of battle had found them inexperienced, but brave and apt pupils. More important, these first appearances of American combat troops in "hot" sectors of the front (small numbers of medical, engineer, and air units had supported the British in the Somme and Lys battles) had brought renewed hope to the tired Allies. The Americans were big men; they marched proud and tall; and there were millions more behind them." *

In June, in an attempt to widen the Marne salient, the Germans attacked again without the desired success of the breakthrough. In July, they attacked once again.

"It was intended as a gigantic diversion to draw French forces away from the British front where the ultimate blow was to be struck. . . . The Germans tried with maximum strength—fifty-two divisions—in assaults east and west of Rheims, to extend the base of the Marne salient and to cross the Marne. . . . The Germans got nowhere. By the 18th the last great German drive had failed and the soldiers in the coal-scuttle helmets were moving north of the river again. Once again the river Marne, held by men who would not let them pass, had saved France."

"It was the final turning point. Pétain and Foch and Pershing had all foreseen that the first six months of 1918 would be the crucial days; by July, U. S. strength would be adequate to permit Allied offensives.

"By mid-July there were twenty-nine U. S. divisions in France or on their way, almost one million men. Some 85,000 Americans— three divisions—had been in action in the Second Battle of the Marne; a U. S. corps (the I Corps under General Hunter Liggett) was holding a section of the front, and U. S. units of various size from battalions to divisions were scattered along much of the front.

"From July 18, when Foch mounted his first riposte, throughout the rest of 1918, the Allies conducted an almost continuous offensive on the Western Front. The first hammer blows were directed at the great salients the Germans had driven into the Allied lines: the Aisne-Marne; the Amiens-Somme-Noyon; the Lys-Ypres; and St.-Mihiel. After the reduction of the salients, the final drives were aimed at breakthrough and triumph, which, it was felt, might not occur until 1919.

"Peppery General Mangin led the French Tenth Army in a hard

* Baldwin, pp. 143-144.

drive against the west flank of the Aisne-Marne salient on July 18. The 1st and 2nd American divisions under his command, drove deep into the enemy flank, south of Soissons." *

The 2nd Division had two regiments of U. S. Marines, and the next selection is the story of the 1st Battalion, Fifth Regiment, moving up to Soissons.

THE CHARGE AT SOISSONS**

by John W. Thomason

Company by company, the 1st Battalion passed on, and behind them the other battalions of the 5th Marines took the road and, after them, the 6th. "None of the wagons, or the galleys—don't see the machine-gun outfits, either," observed the lieutenant of the 49th Company, looking back from the crest of the first low hill. Here the battalion was halted, having marched for half an hour, to tighten slings and settle equipment for the real business of hiking. "They may get up to-night, chow an' all—wonder how far we came, an' where we're goin'. No, sergeant—can't send for water here—my canteen's empty, too. All I know about it is that we seem to be in a hurry."

The dust of the ride had settled thick, like fine gray masks, on the men's faces, and one knew that it was just as thick in their throats! Of course the canteens, filled at Croutte, were finished. The files swore through cracked lips.

* Baldwin, pp. 145, 146, 147.
** From *Fix Bayonets*, published by Charles Scribner's Sons.

The battalion moved off again, and the major up forward set a pace all disproportionate to his short legs. When the first halt came, the usual ten-minute rest out of the hour was cut to five. "Aw hell! forced march!" "An' the lootenant has forgot everything but 'close up! close up!'— Listen at him—"

The camions had set them down in a gently rolling country, unwooded, and fat with ripening wheat. Far across it, to the north, blue with distance, stood a great forest, and toward this forest the battalion marched, talkative, as men are in the first hour of the hike, before the slings of the pack begin to cut into your shoulders. . . . "Look at them poppies in the wheat."—"They ain't as red as the poppies were the mornin' of the 6th of June, when we went up to Hill 142—" "Yep! Beginnin' to fade some. It's gettin' late in the season." "Hi— I'm beginnin' to fade some myself—this guerre is wearin' on a man . . . remember how they looked in the wheat that mornin', just before we hit the Maxim guns?—red as blood—" "Pore old Jerry Finnegan picked one and stuck it in the buckle of his helmet—I seen it in his tin hat after he was killed, there behin' the Hill. . . . I'll always think about poppies an' blood together, as long as I live—" This last from little Tritt, the lieutenant's orderly.

"Long as you live—that's good!" gibed Corporal Snair, of the Company Headquarters group. "Don't you know by now how expendable you bucks are?"— The lieutenant heard, and remembered it, oddly enough, in a crowded moment the next day, when he lost the two of them to a hard-fought Maxim gun.

No wind moved across the lonely wheatland; the bearded stalks waved not at all, and the sun-drenched air was hot and dead. Sweat made muddy runnels through the thick white dust that masked the faces of the men. Conversation languished; what was said was in profane monosyllables. Clouds came up, and there were showers of rain, with hot sunshine between. Uniforms steamed after each shower, and thirst became a torture. The man who had the vin blanc in his canteen fell out and was quite ill. "Hikin'—in—a dam'—Turkish bath—"

After interminable hours, the column came to the forest and

passed from streaming sunshine into sultry shades. It was a noble wood of great high-branching trees, clean of underbrush as a park. Something was doing in the forest. Small-arms ammunition was stacked beside the road, and there were dumps of shells and bombs under the trees. And French soldiers everywhere. This road presently led into a great paved highway, and along it were more of the properties of war—row upon row of every caliber of shell, orderly stacks of winged aerial bombs, pile after pile of rifle and machine-gun ammunition, and cases of hand-grenades and pyrotechnics. There were picket-lines of cavalry, and park after park of artillery, light and heavy. There were infantrymen with stacked rifles.

Gunner and horseman and poilu, they looked amicably upon the sweating Marines, and waved their hands with naïve Gallic friendliness. The battalion came out of its weariness and responded in kind. "Say, where do they get that stuff about little Frenchmen? Look at that long-sparred horse soldier yonder—seven feet if he's an inch!"—"Them gunners is fine men, too. All the runts in the Frog army is in the infantry!"—"Well, if these Frawgs fights accordin' to their size, Gawd pity the old Boche when that cavalry gets after him—lances an' all!" "You said it! Them little five-foot-nothin' infantry, with enough on they backs, in the way o' tents an' pots an' pans, to set up light housekeepin' wit', and that long squirrel gun they carry, an' that knittin'-needle bayonet—! Remember how they charged at Torcy, there on the left—?"

The French were cooking dinner beside the road. For your Frenchman never fights without his kitchens and a full meal under his cartridge-pouches. They go into the front line with him, the kitchens and the chow, and there is always the coffee avec rhum, and the good hot soup that smells so divinely to the hungry Americans, passing empty. "When we goes up to hit the old Boche, we always says adoo to the galleys till we comes out again—guess the idea is to starve us so we'll be mad, like the lions in them glad-i-a-tor-ial mills the corp'ril was tellin' about."—"Hell! we don't eat, it seems—them Frawgs might at least have the decency to keep their home cookin' where we can't smell it!"

The highway led straight through the forest. Many roads emptied into it, and from every road debouched a stream of horses, men, and guns. The battalion went into column of twos, then into column of files, to make room. On the left of the road, abreast of the Marines, plodded another column of foot—strange black men, in the blue greatcoats of the French infantry and mustard-yellow uniforms under them. Their helmets were khaki-colored, and bore a crescent instead of the bursting bomb of the French line. But they marched like veterans, and the Marines eyed them approvingly. Between the foot, the road was level-full of guns and transport, moving axle to axle, and all moving in the same direction. In this column were tanks, large and small, all ring-streaked and striped with camouflage, mounting one-pounders and machine-guns; and the big ones, short-barrelled 75s.

The tanks were new to the Marines. They moved with a horrific clanging and jangling, and stunk of petrol. "Boy, what would you do if you seen one of them little things comin' at you? The big ones is males, and the little ones is females, the lootenant says. . . ." "Chillun, we're goin' into somethin' big— Dunno what, but it's big!"

The sultry afternoon passed wearily, and at six o'clock the battalion turned off the road, shambling and footsore, and rested for two hours. They found water and filled canteens. A few of the hardier made shift to wash. "Gonna smear soapsuds an' lather all over me—the Hospital Corps men say it keeps off mustard-gas!" But most of the men dropped where the platoon broke ranks and slept. Battalion H. Q. sent for all company commanders.

Presently the lieutenant of the 49th returned, with papers and a map. He called the company officers around him, and spread the map on the ground. He spoke briefly.

"We're in the Villers-Cotterets woods—the Forêt de Retz. At H hour on D day, which I think is to-morrow morning, although the major didn't say, we attack the Boche here"—pointing—"and go on to here—past the town of Vierzy. Eight or nine kilomètres. Three objectives—marked—so—and so. The 2d Division with one of the infantry regiments leading, and the 5th Marines, attacks with the 1st

Moroccan Division on our left. The Frog Foreign Legion is somewhere around too, and the 1st American Division. It's Mangin's
Colonial Army—the bird they call the butcher.

"The 49th Company has the division's left, and we're to keep in
touch with the French over there. They're Senegalese—the niggers
you saw on the road, and said to be bon fighters. The tanks will come
behind us through the woods, and take the lead as soon as we hit the
open.

"No special instructions, except, if we are held up any place, signal
a tank by wavin' a rag or something on a bayonet, in the direction of
the obstacle, and the tank will do the rest.

"No rations, an' we move soon. See that canteens are filled. Now
go and explain it all to your platoons, and—better take a sketch from
this map—it's the only one I have. Impress it on everybody that the
job is to maintain connection between the Senegalese on the left and
our people. Tritt, I'm goin' to catch a nap—wake me when we
move—"

It was dark when the battalion fell in and took the road again.
They went into single file on the right, at the very edge of it, for the
highway was jammed with three columns of traffic, moving forward.
It began to rain, and the night, there under the thick branches, was
inconceivably black. The files couldn't see the man ahead, and each
man caught hold of the pack in front and went feeling for the road
with his feet, clawing along with the wheels and the artillery horses
and machine-gun mules. On the right was a six-foot ditch, too deep
in mud to march in. The rain increased to a sheeted downpour and
continued all night, with long rolls of thunder, and white stabs of
lightning that intensified the dark. The picked might of France and
America toiled on that road through the Villers-Cotterets forest that
night, like a great flowing river of martial force. . . .

And after the 5th Marines have forgotten the machine-guns that
sowed death in the wheat behind Hill 142, and the shrapnel that
showered down at Blanc Mont, before St. Étienne, they will

remember the march to the Soissons battle, through the dark and the rain. . . .

As guns and caissons slewed sideways across the files, or irate machine-gun mules plunged across the tangle, the column slowed and jammed and halted on heavy feet; then went on again to plunge blindly against the next obstacle. Men fell into the deep ditch and broke arms and legs. Just to keep moving was a harder test than battle ever imposed. The battalion was too tired to swear. "I'm to where—I have to think about movin' my feet—! Plant—the left foot —an'—advance the right—an'—bring up the—left foot—an'—"

No battle ever tried them half as hard as the night road to Soissons. . . .

The rain ceased, and the sky grew gray with dawn. The traffic thinned, and the battalion turned off on a smaller road, closed up, and hurried on. Five minutes by the side of the road to form combat packs and strip to rifle and bayonet. "Fall in quickly! Forward!"

Overhead the clouds were gone; a handful of stars paled and went out; day was coming. The battalion, lightened, hastened. They perceived, dimly, through a mist of fatigue, that a cloudless day was promised and that the world was wonderfully new washed and clean —and quiet! Not a gun anywhere, and the mud on the road muffled the sound of hobnailed boots. "Double time! Close up! Close up, there!"

There had been fighting here; there were shell-holes, scarred and splintered trees. The battalion panted to a crossroads, where stone buildings lay all blasted by some gale of shell-fire. And by the road what looked like a well! The files swayed toward it, clutching at dry canteens— "Back in ranks! Back in ranks, you—!"

Then, barbed wire across the roadway, and battered shallow trenches to right and left, and a little knot of French and American officers, Major Turrill standing forward. The leading company turned off to the left, along the trenches. The 49th followed in column. "Turn here," ordered the major. "Keep on to the left until you meet the Moroccans, and go forward . . ." The 49th went beyond the trench, still in column of route, picking its way through the woods. The lieutenant looked back at his men as he went; their faces were gray and drawn and old; they were staggering with weariness— "Fix bayonets—" and the dry click of the steel on the locking-ring ran along the ragged column, loud in the hush of dawn.

◆ ◆ ◆

It was 4:35, the morning of July 18.

Miles of close-laid batteries opened with one stupendous thunder. The air above the tree-tops spoke with unearthly noises, the shriek and rumble of light and heavy shells. Forward through the woods, very near, rose up a continued crashing roar of explosions, and a murk of smoke, and a hell of bright fires continually renewed. It lasted only five minutes, that barrage, with every French and American gun that could be brought to bear firing at top speed. But they were terrible minutes for the unsuspecting Boche. Dazed, beaten down, and swept away, he tumbled out of his holes when it lifted, only to find the long bayonets of the Americans licking like flame across his forward positions, and those black devils, the Senegalese, raging with knives in his rifle-pits. His counter-barrage was slow and weak, and when it came the shells burst well behind the assaulting waves, which were already deep in his defenses.

The 49th Company, running heavily, sodden with weariness, was plunging through a line of wire entanglements when the guns opened. A French rifleman squatted in a hole under the wire, and a sergeant bent over him and shouted: "Combien—how far—damn it, how you say?—combien—kilomètre—à la Boche?" The Frenchman's eyes bulged. He did violent things with his arms. "Kilomèt'? *kilomètres?* Mon Dieu, cent mètres! Cent mètres!" Half the company, still in column, was struggling in the wire when, from the tangle right in front, a machine-gun dinned fiercely and rifle-fire ran to left and right through the woods.

It was well that the woods were a little open in that spot, so that the lieutenant's frantic signals could be seen, for no voice could have been heard. And it was more than well that every man there had been shot over enough not to be gun-shy. They divined his order, they deployed to the left, and they went forward yelling. That always remained, to the lieutenant, the marvel of the Soissons fight —how those men, two days without food, three nights without sleep, after a day and a night of forced marching, flung off their weariness like a discarded piece of equipment, and at the shouting of the shells sprang fresh and eager against the German line.

Liaison—to keep the touch—was his company's mission—the major's last order. To the left were only the smoky woods—no Senegalese in sight—and to the left the lieutenant anxiously extended his line, throwing out the last two platoons, while the leading one shot and stabbed among the first Boche machine-guns. He himself ran in that direction, cursing and stumbling in wire and fallen branches, having no time for certain Boches who fired at him over a bush. . . . Finally, Corbett, the platoon commander, leading to the left, turned and waved his arms. And through the trees he saw the Senegalese—lean, rangy men in mustard-colored uniforms, running with their bayonets all aslant. He turned back toward his company with the sweetest feeling of relief that he had ever known; he had his contact established; his clever and war-wise company would attend to keeping it, no matter what happened to him.

The battle roared into the wood. Three lines of machine-guns, echeloned, held it. Here the Forêt de Retz was like Dante's wood, so shattered and tortured and horrible it was, and the very trees seemed to writhe in agony. Here the fury of the barrage was spent, and the great trunks, thick as a man's body, were sheared off like weed-stalks; others were uprooted and lay gigantic along the torn earth; big limbs still crashed down or swayed half-severed; splinters and débris choked the ways beneath. A few German shells fell among the men—mustard-gas; and there in the wet woods one could see the devilish stuff spreading slowly, like a snaky mist, around the shell-hole after the smoke had lifted.

Machine-guns raved everywhere; there was a crackling din of rifles and the coughing roar of hand-grenades. Company and platoon commanders lost control—their men were committed to the fight—and so thick was the going that anything like formation was impossible. It was every man for himself, an irregular, broken line, clawing through the tangles, climbing over fallen trees, plunging heavily into Boche rifle-pits. Here and there a well-fought Maxim gun held its front until somebody—officer, non-com, or private—got a few men together and, crawling to left or right, gained a flank and silenced it. And some guns were silenced by blind, furious rushes that left a trail of writhing khaki figures, but always carried two or three frenzied Marines with bayonets into the emplacement; from whence would come shooting and screaming and other clotted unpleasant sounds, and then silence.

From such a place, with four men, the lieutenant climbed, and stood leaning on his rifle, while he wiped the sweat from his eyes with a shaking hand. Panting, white or red after their nature—for fighting takes men differently, as whiskey does—the four grouped around him. One of them squatted and was very sick. And one of them, quite young and freckled, explored a near-by hole and prodded half a dozen Boches out of it, who were most anxious to make friends. The other three took interest in this, and the Boches saw death in their eyes. They howled like animals, these big hairy men of Saxony, and capered in a very ecstasy of terror. The freckled Marine set his feet deliberately, judging his distance, and poised his bayonet. The lieutenant grasped his arm— "No! No! take 'em back —they've quit. Take 'em to the rear, I tell you!" The freckled one obeyed, very surly, and went off through the tangle to the rear. The lieutenant turned and went on.

To left and right he caught glimpses of his men, running, crawling, firing as they went. In a clearing, Lieutenant Appelgate, of the 17th Company, on the right, came into view. He waved his pistol and shouted something. He was grinning. . . . All the men were grinning . . . it was a bon fight, after all. . . .

Then little Tritt, his orderly, running at his side, went down, clawing at a bright jet of scarlet over his collar. The war became personal again—a keening sibilance of flesh-hunting bullets, ringing under his helmet. He found himself prone behind a great fallen tree, with a handful of his men; bark and splinters were leaping from the round trunk that sheltered them.

"You"—to a panting half-dozen down the log—"crawl back to the stump and shoot into that clump of green bushes over there, where you see the new dirt—it's in there! Everything you've got, and watch for me up ahead. Slover"—to Sergeant Robert Slover, a small, fiery man from Tennessee—"come on."

They crawled along the tree. Back toward the stump the Springfields crackled furiously. Somewhere beyond the machine-gun raved like a mad thing, and the Boches around it threw hand-grenades that made much smoke and noise. The two of them left the protection of the trunk, and felt remarkably naked behind a screen of leaves. They crawled slowly, stopping to peer across at the bushes. The lieutenant caught the dull gleam of a round gray helmet, moved a little, and saw the head and the hands of the Boche who worked the gun. He pushed the sergeant with his foot and, moving very carefully, got his rifle up and laid his cheek against the stock. Over his sights, the German's face, twenty metres away, was intent and serious. The lieutenant fired, and saw his man half-rise and topple forward on the gun.

Then things happened fast. Another German came into view straining to tear the fallen gunner off the firing mechanism. Slover shot him. There was another, and another. Then the bush boiled like an ant-heap, and a feldwebel sprang out with a grenade, which he did not get to throw. It went off, just the same, and the Marines from the other end of the tree came with bayonets. . . . Presently they went on. . . . "There's a squad of them bastards to do orderly duty for the corp'ral an' little Tritt," said the sergeant. "Spread out more, you birds."

Afterward, sweating and panting, the freckled one who had started back with prisoners caught up with the lieutenant. "Lootenant, sir!" he gasped, wiping certain stains from his bayonet with his sleeve. "Them damn Heinies tried to run on me, an' I jest natcherly had to shoot 'em up a few—" and he looked guilelessly into

the officer's eyes. "Why you— Hell! . . . fall in behind me, then, an'
come along. Need another orderly."

He pondered absently on the matter of frightfulness as he picked
his way along. There were, in effect, very few prisoners taken in the
woods that morning. It was close-up, savage work. "But speakin' of
frightfulness, one of these nineteen-year-olds, with never a hair to
his face—" A spitting gust of machine-gun bullets put an end to
extraneous musings.

Later, working to the left of his company, he was caught up in a
fighting swirl of Senegalese and went with them into an evil place of
barbed wire and machine-guns. These wild black Mohammedans
from West Africa were enjoying themselves. Killing, which is at best
an acquired taste with the civilized races, was only too palpably
their mission in life. Their eyes rolled, and their splendid white teeth
flashed in their heads. They were deadly. Each platoon swept its
front like a hunting-pack, moving swiftly and surely together. The
lieutenant felt a thrill of professional admiration as he went with
them.

The hidden guns that fired on them were located with uncanny
skill; they worked their automatic rifles forward on each flank until
the doomed emplacement was under a scissors fire; then they took
up the matter with the bayonet, and slew with lion-like leaps and
lunges and a shrill barbaric yapping. They took no prisoners. It was
plain that they did not rely on riflefire or understand the powers of
that arm—to them a rifle was merely something to stick a bayonet on
—but with the bayonet they were terrible, and the skill of their rifle
grenadiers and automatic-rifle men always carried them to close
quarters without too great loss.

They carried also a broad-bladed knife, razor-sharp, which
disembowelled a man at a stroke. The slim bayonet of the French
breaks off short when the weight of a body pulls down and sidewise
on it; and then the knives come out. With reason the Boche feared
them worse than anything living, and the lieutenant saw in those
woods unwounded fighting Germans who flung down their rifles
when the Senegalese rushed, and covered their faces, and stood

screaming against the death they could not look upon. And—in a lull, a long, grinning sergeant, with a cruel aquiline face, approached him and offered a brace of human ears, nicely fresh, strung upon a thong. "B'jour, Americain! Voilà! Beaucoup souvenir ici—bon! Désirez-vous? Bon—!"

Later, on the last objective, there was a dignified Boche major of infantry, who came at discretion out of a deep dugout, and spoke in careful English: "Und I peg of you, Herr leutnant, to put me under trusty guard of your Americans true-and-tried! Ja! These black savages, of the art of war most ignorant, they would kill us prave Germans in cold plood! . . . The Herr General Mangin, that"—here a poignant string of gutturals—"I tell you, Herr leutnant, der very name of Mangin, it is equal to fünf divisions on unser front!"

Back with his own men again, the company whittled thin! Was there no limit to the gloomy woods? . . . Light through the trees yonder!—

The wood ended, and the attack burst out into the rolling wheat-land, where the sun shone in a cloudless sky and poppies grew in the wheat. To the right, a great paved road marched, between tall poplars, much battered. On the road two motor-trucks burned fiercely, and dead men lay around them. Across the road a group of stone farm-buildings had been shelled into a smoking dust-heap, but from the ruins a nest of never-die machine-guns opened flanking fire. The khaki lines checked and swirled around them, and there was a mounting crackle of rifle-fire . . . and the bayonets got in. The lines went forward to the low crest beyond, where, astride the road, was the first objective; and the assault companies halted here to reform. A few Boche shells howled over them, but the Boche was still pounding the wood, where the support battalions followed. The tanks debouched from the forest and went forward through the infantry.

In a hollow just ahead of the reformed line something was being dealt with by artillery, directed by the planes that dipped and swerved above the fight. The shells crashed down and made a great roaring murk of smoke and dust and flickering flames of red and green. The lieutenant, his report to the major despatched, and his company straightened out, along with men from other units and a handful of Senegalese who had attached themselves to him, ran an expert eye along his waiting squads, and allowed his mind to settle profoundly on breakfast. "Let's see—it's July, an' in Texas they'll be havin' cantaloupes, and coffee, an' eggs, an' bacon, an'—" Second Lieutenant Corbett, beside him, groaned like a man shot through the body, and he realized that he had been thinking aloud. Then Corbett seized his arm, and gasped: "Lordy! Look at—"

The shelling forward had abated, but the smoke and murk of it still hung low. Into this murk ever man in the line was now peering eagerly. Advancing toward them, dimly seen, was a great body of Germans, hundreds upon hundreds, in mass formation—

Pure joy ran among the men. They took out cartridges, and arranged them in convenient piles. They tested the wind with wetted fingers, and set their sights, and licked their lips. "Range three-fifty— Oh, boy, ain't war wonderful! We been hearin' about this mass-formation stuff, an' now we gets a chance at it—!"

Then: "Aw, hell! Prisoners!" "The low-life bums, they all got their hands up!" "Lookit! One o' them tanks is ridin' herd over them—" It was the garrison of a strong point.

The artillery had battered them, and when it lifted, and they had come out of their holes, they found a brace of agile tanks squatting over their defenses with one-pounders and machine-guns. They had very sensibly surrendered, en masse, and were now ambling through the attacking lines to the rear.

The officers' whistles shrilled, and the attack went on. The woods fell away behind, and for miles to left and right across the rolling country the waves of assault could be seen. It was a great stirring pageant wherein moved all the forces of modern war. The tanks, large and small, lumbered in advance. Over them the battle-planes flew low, searching the ground, rowelling the Boche with bursts of machine-gun fire. The infantry followed close, assault waves deployed, support platoons in column, American Marines and Regulars, Senegalese and the Foreign Legion of France, their rifles slanting forward, and the sun on all their bayonets. And behind the infantry, straining horses galloped with lean-muzzled 75s, battery on battery—artillery, over the top at last with the rifles. On the skirts of the attack hovered squadrons of cavalry the Marines had seen the day before, dragoons and lancers, marked from afar by the sparkle and glitter of lance-heads and sabres.

And forward through the wheat, the Boche lines broke and his strong points crumbled; standing stubbornly in one place; running in panic at another; and here and there attempting sharp counter-attacks; but everywhere engulfed; and the battle roared over him. The Boche was in mixed quality that day. Some of his people fought and died fighting; a great many others threw down their arms and bleated "Kamaraden" at the distant approach of the attackers.

The rest was no connected story. Only the hot exaltation of the fight kept the men on their feet. Wheat waist-high is almost as hard to get through as running water, and the sun was pitiless. To the left of the battalion, and forward, machine-guns fired from the Chaudun farm; the 17th Company went in and stamped the Maxims flat. In a little hollow there was a battery of 105s that fired pointblank upon the Marines, the gunners working desperately behind their gun-shields. The Marines worked to right and left and beat them down with rifle-fire, and later a gunnery sergeant and a wandering detachment of Senegalese turned one of these guns around and shelled the Vierzy ravine with it—range 900 yards—to the great annoyance of the Boche in that place.

Further, a hidden strong point in the wheat held them, and a tank came and sat upon that strong point and shot it into nothing with a one-pounder gun. Another place, hidden Saxons, laired behind low trip-wires in high wheat, raked the line savagely. There was crawling and shooting low among the poppies, and presently hand-to-hand fighting, in which the freckled boy saw his brother killed and went himself quite mad among the wounded and the corpses with his bayonet. . . .

Then, without being very clear as to how they got there, the lieutenant and his company and a great many others were at the Vierzy ravine, in the cross-fire of the machine-guns that held it.

The ravine was very deep and very precipitous and wooded. A sunken road led into it and, while the riflemen stalked the place cannily, a tank came up and disappeared down the sunken road. A terrific row of rifles and grenades arose, and a wild yelling. Running forward, the Marines observed that the tank was stalled, its guns not working; and a gray, frantic mass of German infantry was swarming over it, prying at its plates with bayonets and firing into such openings as could be found. One beauty of the tank is that, when it is in such a difficulty, you can fire without fearing for your friends inside. The automatic-rifle men especially enjoyed the brief crowded seconds that followed. Then all at once the farther slope of the ravine swarmed with running Boches, and the Americans knelt or lay down at ease, and fired steadily and without haste. As they passed the tank a greasy, smiling Frenchman emerged head and shoulders and inquired after a cigarette. There were very many dead Germans in the ravine and on its slope when they went forward.

Wearily now, the exaltation dying down, they left the stone towers of Vierzy to the right, in the path of the Regulars of the 9th and 23d. On line northeast of it they halted and prepared to hold. It was a lonesome place. Very thin indeed were the assault companies; very far away the support columns. . . . "Accordin' to the map, we're here. Turn those Boche machine-guns around—guess we'll stay. Thank God, we must have grabbed off all their artillery, 'cept the heavies. . . ."

"Lootenant, come up here, for God's sake! Lord, what a slew o' Boches!" Beyond rifle-shot a strong gray column was advancing. There were machine-guns with it. It was not deployed, but its intention was very evident. . . . Here were thirty-odd Marines and a few strays from one of the infantry regiments—nobody in sight, flanks or rear—

But to the rear a clanging and a clattering, and the thudding of horse-hoofs—"Graves, beat it back an' flag those guns." Graves ran frantically, waving his helmet. The guns halted in a cloud of dust, and a gunner lieutenant trotted up, jaunty, immaculate. He dismounted, in his beautiful pale-blue uniform and his gleaming boots and tiny jingling spurs, and saluted the sweating, unshaven Marine officer. He looked with his glasses, and he consulted his map, and then he smiled like a man who has gained his heart's desire. He dashed back toward his guns, waving a signal.

The guns wheeled around; the horses galloped back; there was a whirl and bustle behind each caisson, and two gunners with a field-telephone came running. It all happened in seconds.

The first 75 barked, clear and incisive, and the shell whined away . . . the next gun, and the next. . . . The little puff-balls, ranging shots, burst very near the Boche column. Then the battery fired as one gun—a long rafale of fire, wherein no single gun could be heard, but a drumming thunder.

Smoke and fire flowered hideously over the Boche column. A cloud hit it for a space. When the cloud lifted the column had disintegrated; there was only a far-off swarm of fleeing figures, flailed by shrapnel as they ran. And the glass showed squirming heaps of gray flattened on the ground. . . .

The gunner officer looked and saw that his work was good. "Bon, eh? Soixante-quinze—!" With an all-embracing gesture and a white-toothed smile, he went. Already his battery was limbered up and galloping, and when the first retaliatory shell came from an indignant Boche 155, the 75s were a quarter of a mile away. The Boche shelled the locality with earnestness and method for the next hour, but he did not try to throw forward another column. . . . "Man, I jest love them little 75s! Swa-sont-cans bon? Say, that Frog said a mouthful!"

The lieutenant wrote and sent back his final report: ". . . and final objective reached, position organized at . . ." and stopped and swore in amazement when he looked at his watch—barely noon! Sergeant Cannon's watch corroborated the time— "But, by God! The way my laigs feel, it's day after to-morrow, anyway!—" "Wake those fellows up—got to finish diggin' in—No tellin' what we'll get here—" Some of his people were asleep on their rifles. Some were searching for iron crosses among the dead. A sergeant came with hands and mouth full. "Sir, they's a bunch of this here black German bread and some stuff that looks like coffee, only ain't—in that dugout—" And the company found that Kriegsbrot and Kaffee Ersatz will sustain

life, and even taste good if you've been long enough without
food. . . .

The shadows turned eastward; in the rear bloated observation
balloons appeared on the sky-line. "Them fellers gets a good view
from there. Lonesome, though . . ." "Wonder where all our planes
went—don't see none—" "Hell! Went home to lunch! Them birds,
they don't allow no guerre to interfere with they meals. Now, that's
what I got against this fighting stuff—it breaks into your three hots a
day." "Boy, I'm so empty I could button my blouse on the knobs of
my spine! Hey—yonder's a covey o' them a-vions now—low—strung
out—Boche! Hit the deck!"

They were Boche—sinister red-nosed machines that came out of
the eye of the sun and harrowed the flattened infantry, swooping one
after another with bursts of machine-gun fire. Also they dropped
bombs. Some of them went after the observation balloons, and shot
more than one down, flaming, before they could be grounded. And
not an Ally plane in sight, anywhere! To be just, there was one, in
the course of the afternoon; he came from somewhere, and went
away very swiftly, with five Germans on his tail. The lieutenant
gathered from the conversation of his men that they thought the
Frenchman used good judgment.

That afternoon the Boche had the air. He dropped bombs and
otherwise did the best he could to make up, with planes, for the
artillery that he had lost that morning. On the whole, he was
infinitely annoying. There's something about being machine-gunned
from the air that gets a man's goat, as the files remarked with
profane emphasis. Much futile rifle-fire greeted his machines as they
came and went, and away over on the right toward Vierzy the
lieutenant saw one low-flying fellow crumple and come down like a
stricken duck. This plane, alleged to have been brought down by a
chaut-chaut automatic rifle, was afterward officially claimed by four
infantry regiments and a machine-gun battalion. Late in the afternoon the French brought up anti-aircraft guns on motor-trucks and
the terror of the air abated somewhat; but, while it lasted, the lieutenant heard—

"There comes—" (great rending explosion near by) "God-damighty! 'nother air-bomb?"

"Naw, thank God! That was only a shell!"

As dusk fell, the French cavalry rode forward through the lines. The lieutenant thoughtfully watched a blue squadron pass— "If spirits walk, Murat and Marshal Ney an' all the Emperor's cavalry are ridin' with those fellows. . . ."

In the early dawn of the next day the cavalry rode back. One squadron went through the company's position. It was a very small squadron, indeed, this morning. Half the troopers led horses with empty saddles. A tall young captain was in command. They were drawn and haggard from the night's work, but the men carried their heads high, and even the horses looked triumphant. They had, it developed, been having a perfectly wonderful time, riding around behind the German lines. They had shot up transport, and set fire to ammunition-dumps, and added greatly to the discomfort of the Boche. They thought they might go back again to-night. . . . They did.

The night of the 19th the galleys got up, and the men had hot food. Early the morning of the 20th the division was relieved and began to withdraw to reserve position, while fresh troops carried the battle on. The 1st Battalion of the 5th Marines marched back, in a misty dawn, across the ground they had fought over two days before. In the trampled fields, where the dead lay unburied, old French territorials were mowing the ripe wheat and shocking it up. The battle was far away. . . .

The battalion entered the woods and turned off the road toward the blue smoke of the galleys, from which came an altogether glorious smell of food. One of the company officers ran ahead of the 49th to find a place to stack arms and pile equipment. Presently he beckoned, and the lieutenant led his people to the place—a sort of clearing, along one side of which lay a great fallen tree. Under an outthrust leafy branch something long and stiff lay covered with a blanket.

"Stack arms . . . fall out!"

Graves, the officer who had gone ahead, was standing by the

blanket. "Do you know who's under this?" he said. The lieutenant stooped and looked. It was little Tritt. . . .

After breakfast, some of the men enlarged the pit where the machine-gun had been and tidied it up. . . . They wrapped the body in a blanket and two German water-proof sheets that were handy, and buried the boy there.

". . . But before he got it, he knew that we were winning." The men put on their helmets and went away, to look for others who had stopped in the woods . . . to gather souvenirs.

"Well, he's where he ain't hungry, an' his feet don't hurt from hikin', an' his heavy marchin' order won't never cut into his shoulders any more. . . ." "No, nor no damn Boche buzzards drop air-bombs on him—"

"Wonder where we'll hit the old Boche next—"

THE TIDE TURNS

The bulge around Soissons diminished slowly under the combined attacks of British, American and French troops. "The battle ended with two U. S. corps in line, Soissons recaptured, and the Vesle [River] reached. The successful counteroffensive spoiled Ludendorff's plans for another blow at the British and convinced some in Berlin that 'all was lost.'" *

Foch went on the offensive, his targets the salients the Germans had pushed into the Allied lines along the Western Front. Fierce attacks were launched at the Amiens-Somme-Noyon bulge, and although the Germans fought stubbornly, they were forced to withdraw, abandoning the salients at Lys-Ypres and Somme-Noyon and retreating to their prepared defense in the Hindenburg Line, "back where they had started from in the hopeful spring months." **

As new American divisions arrived in Europe, the Allies' superiority in numbers over the Germans grew. On August 10, Pershing announced the formation of the American First Army, consisting of fourteen American divisions, and three French. Anxious to show what the Americans could do in a unit as large as this, Pershing asked Foch for the task of eliminating the St.-Mihiel salient, a bulge in the trench system dating back almost to the beginning of the war. The St.-Mihiel salient protected important iron mines and railroads, the capture of which would seriously hurt the Germans. Foch agreed to Pershing's plan but Pershing hardly had time to set up his headquarters when Foch wanted to limit the objectives of the American assault; once the salient was reduced he would split the American forces in two, handing each separate objectives under French command in different sectors of the front.

This new plan resulted from Haig's proposal for an all-out assault

* Baldwin, p. 147.
** Baldwin, p. 148.

on the Hindenburg Line in front of the British. Haig hoped that a converging attack by the armies to the south and his British armies in the north would exert great pressure on the Germans and make his own task easier for the breakthrough. Foch, always agreeable to the grand attack at multiple points of the front, now proposed that a new Franco-American army be formed under a French commander to attack between the Argonne Forest and the Meuse River. To Pershing, this meant once again that American divisions would be taken from him, reducing and weakening the American effort. He rejected Foch's plan.

After heated argument, a compromise was agreed to. The American army was to be left intact, but Pershing had agreed to launch two great attacks on battlefields sixty miles apart, within two weeks of each other—at St.-Mihiel and then the Argonne forest. This would mean that Pershing could not shift his divisions from St.-Mihiel in time to use them in the Argonne sector, and green troops would have to be thrown into the Argonne-Meuse attack.

Now Foch issued orders for "the grand assault"; it would begin September 26, with the Americans attacking in the Meuse-Argonne; in twenty-four-hour intervals, the British would attack at Cambrai and St. Quentin; the French would assault the center, and also on the Americans' left flank; later Foch added the Flanders sector, and gave the task to the British Second Army, which included French and Belgian divisions.

The St.-Mihiel assault was to begin after a four-hour bombardment on September 12. The U. S. First and Fourth Corps were to drive into the salient from the south, the U. S. Fifth Corps from the north. The German positions were lightly held, due partly to their being undermanned in face of the French and British pressures in the north, and also because the Germans had decided to pull back to shorten their lines. In consequence the American troops had a comparatively easy time; within twenty-four hours they had driven to the line Foch had set as the limit of their drive, taking fifteen thousand prisoners and 443 guns.

Now Pershing turned to the main objective Foch had handed him, the Meuse-Argonne sector.

According to Liddell Hart, the objective of the Meuse-Argonne attack "was more idealistic than realistic. . . . the Ardennes formed an impenetrable back wall to the great German salient in France, and that if the Allies could reach and close the exits east and west they would cut off the German armies in the salient. But the impassability of the Ardennes has been much exaggerated, especially in Haig's reports. Actually, the Ardennes were traversed by numerous roads, and several railways, so that though the severance of the routes east and west might complicate the German withdrawal, this would be imperiled only if the objective were attained very rapidly. As always in war, everything turned on the time factor.

"To reach the lateral railway from the Meuse-Argonne sector, the Americans would have to advance thirty miles. And, to be effective, they would have to advance more rapidly than from the St.-Mihiel sector, because their thrust would be aimed close to the main German armies instead of, like the St.-Mihiel thrust, close to the German frontier. The attempt, and hope, were fundamentally unreal. To cross these thirty miles of difficult country, they would first have to break through the German front, and then, some eight miles behind it, would meet the untouched defenses of the Kriemhilde section of the Hindenburg Line. Pershing might have confidence in the capacity of his untried army, but his faith, like that of the French in 1914 and 1915, was to founder on the rock of machine-guns. Pétain, if he underestimated the effect of other factors, was closer to reality when he predicted that the Americans might cover a third of the distance before the winter. That, roughly, was as far as their original attack reached, and there they stuck, until other factors, unforeseen by Pétain, intervened to relieve them.

"In the second place, the Meuse-Argonne attack did not fulfill its immediate aim—the Haig-inspired aim for which Pershing had sacrificed his own plan. For the left wing attack broke through the Cambrai-St. Quentin section of the Hindenburg Line, the strongest artificially, before the Meuse-Argonne attack had drawn off any German divisions from the British front.[*] Thus the result justified

* Cyril Falls has sketched in the action to the north of the American front:
"On September 27, twenty-four hours after the opening of the Franco-

American offensive, the British Third and First Armies launched an attack on a front of eighteen miles with the left flank on the Sensée Canal. It was to be a tremendous offensive, bigger even than the Meuse-Argonne. When the Fourth Army joined in on the twenty-ninth, forty-one divisions (including two American) would be advancing against forty-one German divisions, whereas in the Meuse-Argonne it was thirty-seven American and French against thirty-six German. Whereas the country was by nature the easier on the British front, indeed ideal, the obstacles were forbidding. They included the Canal du Nord and Canal de Saint-Quentin, and on the whole Fourth Army front the intact Hindenburg position, three powerful lines of defenses. It had the biggest task, and was allotted ten of the fourteen tank battalions available. So the first two days were only the prologue. Yet the swift passage of the Canal du Nord and the six-mile advance which brought the inner flanks of Byng's and Horne's armies virtually to the gates of Cambrai alarmed O.H.L. On the evening of the twenty-eighth Ludendorff told Hindenburg that a request for an armistice ought to be made.

"The alarm was heightened by the success of Rawlinson's Fourth Army. It crossed the Canal de Saint-Quentin—where this held water, the assault troops used collapsible boats, rafts, and 3,000 life belts borrowed from Channel packets—and breached the first and second Hindenburg systems. Rawlinson, a very good tactician, noting the obstinacy with which the enemy was now disputing the progress of the Third and First Armies, was convinced that by extending the breach northeastward he could clear their path. On October 4 he smashed a way through the third Hindenburg system. His expectations were fulfilled. The Germans drew back, not only on his front but on that of the Third, First, and even the Fifth Army in the now quiet country between Lens and Armentières. So three corps, one of which was American, cleared the front of three armies. The incident points to a flaw in Haig's masterful handling of the offensive: he parceled out divisions rather too evenly. This heavy punch on a narrow section of a long front was rarely to be repeated. We must recall, however, that Haig had allotted Rawlinson nearly all the British armor, without which the punch would have lacked its violence.

"The Flanders offensive began on September 28. The original forces allotted were ten British, twelve Belgian, and six French divisions. The Belgians had fought only one major battle since those of 1914. Since then 120,000 men, the majority refugees, had joined the army, which was now 170,000 strong.

"Despite heavy rain upon the Flanders clay, the first day was a great success. By evening most of the notorious Ypres ridge, wrung from the enemy in the prolonged and bloody struggle of 1917 and afterward perforce yielded without a battle, was in the hands of the Allies. By the following evening that could be said for it all, and at the Anglo-Belgian junction due east of Ypres the progress exceeded nine miles. The defense of the German Fourth Army was a thing of patches, and the infantry was generally ready to flee or surrender. For a moment the vision of a swift advance providing a chance to roll up the German right hung before the vision of the Allies.

"It was a mirage. Once again the Ypres plain lived up to its reputation. The conditions differed from those of 1917. The advance had stridden across the old battlefield into unspoiled country and reached firm ground. It was not now the troops who were bogged, but it came to the same thing, except that they were spared the miseries of a year ago. It was the transport that was caught by the rise of the water in the churned ground. The stoppage was most serious

Haig's confidence, but not his precaution, proving that his troops could break through without indirect help to ease their path. The strength of the defenses was nullified by the weakening morale of the defenders.

"The irony of the result was increased by the fact that while fifty-seven German divisions faced the left wing attack by Forty British and two American divisions, only twenty German divisions were present to oppose the right wing attack by thirteen American and thirty-one French divisions—the equivalent of at least sixty ordinary strength divisions. The difference of result may be explained, in part, by the differing degree of experience, and in part by the difference of conditions. The left wing attack opened with the British close on the edge of the Hindenburg Line, while on the right wing the Americans had to conquer a deep series of defenses before they could assault their section of the Hindenburg Line. And before they reached it their attack had lost its momentum.

"Thereafter, although stubborn American assaults at heavy cost caused the Germans to draw off, on balance, a further sixteen divisions from the French front, the strategic effect was small. For with shrewd strategic sense the French in the centre appreciated that decisive results depended on the rapid penetration and closing of the pincers, and so did not unduly hasten the retreat of the Germans facing them. In their skillful advance they usually kept a step in rear of their Allies on either flank, moving forward by successive bounds when the enemy had been shouldered back. For the first two years they had borne the main burden of the fighting. If their

---

behind the Belgians, the largest contingent. On October 2, 15,000 rations for Belgian and French troops were dropped by the Belgian Air Force, with some aid from the R.A.F. This hold-up came when the Allies stood facing the German Flanders position, had indeed pierced its foremost line, and when fresh German divisions had reached the scene. But for local actions, rarely successful, the offensive was hung up until October 14, while the assailants turned their energies to toil on roads and railways. The convergent operations which Haig had suggested and Foch had decreed were showing no signs of turning the enemy's flanks and meanwhile Haig's armies of the left center had burst into open country.

"Thus the plan was not working perfectly. On the other hand, the Allies were clearly marching to victory."—Cyril Falls, *The Great War*, pp. 409, 410 and 411.

commanders had been slow to learn how to economize life, they, and still more their men, had learnt it now.

"When the assault (by the Americans) was launched, at 5:30 A.M. on September 26, the V Corps, which had its flanks protected, made far less progress than its neighbors—although its left divisions, the 91st, was a happy exception. On the right of the V Corps, the 4th (Regular Division) penetrated deeply past the flank of Montfaucon, while the 80th and 33rd near the Meuse made good progress. On the left wing of the army, which had the most difficult task and ground, (there was) a good start. Thus the 35th Division neatly circumvented the formidable obstacle of Vauquois by an encircling advance, and then, with the 28th Division on their left, drove a wedge nearly four miles deep up the Aire Valley just east of the Argonne Forest. Through the forest itself moved the 77th Division, which had the difficult task of linking up with the French on the west side." *

THE LOST BATTALION

The 77th division was described by its leader, Major-General Alexander as "a group of hardy frontiersmen from the Bowery and the East Side." They were having their troubles meeting well-established German positions, "heavy machine guns echeloned in depth, each gun with traverse pins set to cover its captured neighbor. Outflanking such gun nests was beyond the capabilities of any but sacrificial units expert with grenades and Stokes mortars. Many Doughboys died as soon as they had overrun one of these chattering

* Liddell Hart, *The Real War*, pp. 461, 462, 464, 465.

assassins with its stovepipe water jacket, seven-point-six millimeter nose protruding through its flash screen and feedbelt cartridges glittering like a rattlesnake's back. No sooner had an attacker thrust his bayonet through the breast of the surviving gunner than a flanking gun, until then silent on the checkerboard of dense underbrush, killed him mercilessly in turn. Any man badly wounded and bleeding at its captured muzzle lost his life too, unless he lay still." *

General Alexander was an aggressive commander. According to Pierce Fredericks, he was a "thunderous chewer-outer." He "chewed out his brigadiers, the brigadiers gnashed the colonels at regiment, and the colonels walked hobnailed up and down the backs of their battalion commanders." ** When greater progress was demanded of the troops in the Argonne, orders were given on October 2 to get the drive going and let no obstacle stand in their way.

One of Alexander's attack battalions was the First, led by Major Charles Whittlesey. In support, the Second Battalion was led by Captain George McMurtry.

"They hit a valley running straight north and the sides were a cinch to be full of machine guns. Whittlesey looked it over and decided to go up the hill to the left, then changed his mind and asked permission to go up the hill to the right and received it. The regiment's 2nd battalion under McMurtry had closed up behind them while they waited. The two forces started up a draw on Hill 198.

"A lot of Germans had been pulled eastward that day to fill in the front; Whittlesey's men had stumbled on a hole left open in the German line. Over Hill 198 they went, down the slope to Charlevaux Brook, and across a wooden footbridge with long-range machine guns taking a whack at them as they advanced. They were in the bottom of a valley with a steep rocky bank ahead rising to an old Roman road running east and west. What with the bank before them and the trees on either side, no one could see much, but something told

---

* Stallings, p. 271.
** *The Great Adventure,* by Fredericks, published by E. P. Dutton, pp. 187, 188.

Whittlesey that it was the same old story; he was way out in front
and it was time to see whether he had any communications left." *

On their left, a unit from the French 4th Army had been slow to
move up. On Whittlesey's right, the 308th Battalion, plus the reserve
307th had got confused in their move forward and had not closed the
gap.

ALAMO OF THE ARGONNE**

by Richard Hanser and Hy Stockman

A chilly Autumn twilight was closing down as the men began
digging in for the night on the north slope which was steep, densely
wooded and covered with underbrush. The ground was hard and
stony, stubbornly resistant to entrenching tools. The road above
loomed over the position like a parapet, and the reverse slope on
which the men were holing in was considered an advantage since it
would offer protection against hostile artillery.

The various units were distributed in a rough oblong formation
about 300 yards long paralleling the road and 60 yards deep. A
machine-gun section was sited on both flanks, and *chaut-chaut* teams
were placed where they would do the most good. The *chaut-chaut*
was a French light automatic rifle similar to the B. A. R., and was
usually fired from the hip. Guards and lookouts were posted, and
when everything seemed secure, the order for chow was given.

* Fredericks, pp. 188, 189.
** From *True* magazine.

Now it was discovered that two companies had moved out so hurriedly that they had not been able to pick up their rations. Nobody, in fact, had brought along more than iron rations of hardtack and corn willy. Moreover, overcoats and blankets had been discarded at the start of the attack. Aside from weapons, the men were stripped of all equipment and supplies.

Those who had food shared it with those who didn't, and that went for smokes, too, mostly Bull Durham and Piedmonts. With nothing warm for the stomach, no coffee, no shelter or covering after a grueling and exhausting day, the men huddled in their shallow holes for the night, cursing and bitching. Well, *c'est la guerre,* as they had learned to say from the Frogs: "That's war." Things would be better tomorrow when the ration detail came up.

In the morning, as the men stamped and slapped themselves against the cold, there were no signs of rations, but morale got something of a boost when Capt. Nelson Holderman turned up with Company K of the 307th and reported to the major. Captain Holderman was a good man to have around any time and in any spot. He was all soldier and he relished campaigning as other men enjoy a good football game or boxing bout. He was born for combat, sought it, thrived on it.

He had made his way to Major Whittlesey's command along the chain of runner posts that had been dropped off every several hundred yards during yesterday's advance as a link to the rear. His arrival indicated that the runner chain was functioning and in good order. He and his men were dispatched to hold down the right flank of the position.

German artillery began coming over at about 8:30 A.M., but owing to the protection of the reverse slope it had little effect. Out on the left flank Lieut. "Red" Cullen sent a patrol from H Company to feel out conditions to the west—and suddenly things began to get ominous.

On the left there should have been units of French dismounted cavalry whose mission it was to move up level with Major Whittlesey's command and form a continuous line with it. But instead of Frenchmen, the patrol found the Boche threaded almost invisibly into the flanking thickets.

On the right Captain Holderman was making a similar reconnaissance. Out there, if all had gone according to plan, would be units of the 307th Infantry. But out there, also, was the Boche.

Now came reports from the rear that two of the runner posts had been fired on, and several of the runners either killed or captured. This was the gravest news yet, and Captain Holderman was immediately ordered to take his company and 20 scouts from 2nd Battalion Headquarters back across the marsh and to the ridge of the southern slope to re-establish the runner posts and re-open communications to the rear.

By noon Holderman was back with the battered remnants of his detachment. He had run into withering machine-gun and rifle fire from an enemy who had filtered around the flanks during the night and was now strongly entrenched in high ground to the rear of the position.

So it was a little after noon of October 3rd, a Thursday, when Maj. Charles Whittlesey definitely knew that his command was cut off and surrounded in the Argonne Forest.

In the shallow double funk hole where he had established his P. C., his Post of Command, he conferred with his next ranking officer, Captain McMurtry, who was an acting major. Between them they were responsible not only for the 550 Americans now trapped in a four-acre pocket of French soil but also for continuing to hold up their end of a decisive Allied offensive.

The contrast between the two men in the funk hole could hardly have been more pronounced if they had been chosen for their roles by a casting director. Whittlesey was austere, aloof, concealing an inner sensitivity behind a frigid exterior. McMurtry was bluff, hearty, a bulldog of a man who had quit Harvard to become a trooper with Teddy Roosevelt's Rough Riders in the Spanish-American War and jumped eagerly into this one at the first opportunity. If the troops respected Whittlesey, they adored George McMurtry.

The two men had no way of knowing that of the 50,000 troops who had attacked on the previous day, only their own had broken through to their objective, leaving flanking units a mile behind. Elsewhere along the line, the offensive was stalled. Major Whittlesey's premonition had come true: they were now in the sore-thumb position which he had foreseen and feared, ripe for chopping.

But neither man entertained for a moment the possibility of pulling back. The orders were clear: "Ground once captured must under no circumstance be given up."

Captain McMurtry took from his pocket a pad of field-message blanks and began scribbling. When he finished, he handed the sheet to the major, who read it and nodded: "That ought to do it."

Cpl. Walter Baldwin, who was in charge of the 1st Battalion runners, was summoned. "Have this delivered to all company commanders," he was ordered.

The message read: *"Our mission is to hold this position at all costs. Have this understood by every man in your command."*

The battalion was beyond the reach of telephone wire and only one way of communicating with the rear remained: carrier pigeons. The pigeons, seven of them, had been brought up in crates in charge of Pvt. Omer Richards, a little French-Canadian from New York State. The system was to write the messages on rice paper, insert them in a capsule attached to the bird's leg, and then release it for the flight back to the base loft at Division.

That morning the major sent back two pigeons with precise information on his command's location and condition, and requested artillery support. It was a primitive way of communicating in a modern mechanized war, but it worked—and the time was coming when a great deal would depend on it.

That day, the first in the pocket, was a generous and sufficient sampling of what the siege was going to be like before it was over, and no man could tell how long that would be. Machine-gun fire began to rake the area early, laced with sporadic but nerve-shattering sniper fire that could not be traced or silenced.

About noon the last bit of food was eaten. A couple of machine gunners on the left flank were lucky. Their final mouthful was a gulp of savory jam eaten with knives out of a can that their lieutenant, Marshall Peabody, shared with them.

From about 600 yards to the northwest a heavy *Minenwerfer*, a German mortar, opened up, its shells arriving with a great booming crash and spraying their whining shrapnel in all directions in search of human flesh. A patrol sent out to silence it was turned back by machine-gun fire and reported its emplacement too strong to assault. At 3 P.M. came the first organized attack on the pocket.

From the ridge above the position came a shower of German grenades which exploded like a string of gigantic firecrackers, blasting geysers of rock, debris and tree splinters all over the area. Behind the grenades the Boche infantry advanced, but brisk machine-gun fire from the periphery of the pocket and accurate shooting by the *chaut-chaut* gunners beat them back.

In some sections the battalion men were so close to the enemy that shouted German commands could clearly be heard. Toward evening another, and more violent, attack was heralded by a Boche roll call audible in the pocket:

"Müller?"

"*Hier!*"

"Kraus?"

"*Hier!*"

"Gottlieb?"

"*Zur Stelle!*"

And so on until, all being apparently present and accounted for, the command rang out:

"*Also—los!*" ("All right—let's go!")

There was a surge against the flanks of the pocket, coupled with another grenade attack from the ridge, but the defenders were alert and set, and they stopped the assault with accurate fire from all weapons. Some Germans fell near enough so that the bodies could be pilfered for food, spare rifles and ammunition.

But nothing stopped the *Minenwerfer* or the enemy machine-guns that kept up their lethal rattling from all sides, or the hidden snipers.

Major Whittlesey sent back another pigeon with a plea for ammunition, and listing his casualties. About a quarter of the effective strength of his command had been killed or wounded in the first 24 hours after reaching the position. The message ended: "Situation serious."

All bandages and medical supplies were used up that day, and there was nothing to cover the wounded against the excruciating chill of the night. A soldier with a bullet in his belly tried manfully to suppress his moaning. "It hurts like hell, Captain," he said, as McMurtry bent over him in the darkness. "But I'll try to shut up."

The groans and shrieks of the wounded could be heard by the Germans, and every noise in the pocket during the night drew fire.

Burial parties worked by night, little groups of exhausted men tottering from hunger and struggling to open up the cold, hard earth to receive their comrade dead. Sometimes, the dawn caught them still at their gruesome mission and the Hun machine-guns and snipers opened up, making work for further burial parties.

Water became the worst, the most desperate need. Some soldiers like Zip Cepeglia, the little runner from New York, became expert at wriggling, rolling and squirming to the water holes with strings of canteens and getting away with it. Others were picked off by snipers, who kept the water holes under surveillance all day, and machine-guns that sent blind bursts around the holes at erratic intervals all night.

On Friday, the 4th, the Germans made a great show of strength around the pocket, delivering torrents of machine-gun, mortar and rifle fire and making a commotion of movement on the flanks to give an impression of overwhelming numbers. They called out jeers and taunts and demands to surrender in English. There were enough Americans who spoke German to shout back insult and defiance.

The enemy fire was never too thick to prevent the major from loping, erect and stiff-legged, around the pocket, checking positions and giving his stern orders wherever he went. "Galloping Charlie," the men called him and they did what he told them to do. Captain McMurtry went lumbering from funk hole to funk hole, walking a little stiffly now from a wound in the knee caught in the previous day's fighting. He assured his men that everything was "practically O.K.," a favorite expression, and he bucked them up enormously.

Among the wounded, Lieutenant Peabody, with one of his own legs shattered, joshed and joked, a tower of strength until a sniper's bullet put him beyond helping and beyond help.

The men, burrowed deep into the underbrush, munched on twigs, and waited—and the empty waiting was the worst. They smoked dried leaves wrapped in yellow message paper and talked in desultory grunts:

"We *ever* goin' to get outta here?"

"Christ, I could eat a horse."

Sometimes when the wind was right, far to the rear, they could hear the distinctive crackety-crack-crack of the automatic rifles. Back there, somewhere, their own people were trying to fight forward. Would they break through? Would they come up in time?

Two pigeon messages went back that morning: "Need rations badly." And later: "Men suffering from hunger and exposure; wounded in very bad condition . . . Can not support be sent at once?"

About noon there was a lull in the German fire, and many of the men crawled from their holes to sit in the open for a breather. Suddenly the entire command was electrified by a series of explosions on the ridge to the southeast. By God—American artillery at last!

Slowly the barrage crept forward down the slope and across the marsh, increasing in intensity as it came. Roaring volcanoes of earth and trees and underbrush were being blown skyward, closer and closer and closer to the pocket.

From somewhere inside the position came a hoarse shout of horror and dismay, and then another and another, until a whole chorus of outrage and despair was raised within the greater tumult of the artillery. There was no longer any doubt: the barrage was falling in all its fury squarely on the pocket, and it was not moving on.

Down among the funk holes the big shells burst, blasting and killing and maiming. Trees and foliage were blown away all around, stripping the men of cover and leaving them naked to the fire of gleeful Germans who added their bullets to the American shells. The pocket became a howling holocaust.

The officers frantically struggled to hold down the panic. The major left his headquarters hold to go stalking about in the open, deadly grim but also grand in his complete indifference to the shelling. Captain McMurtry was in the thick of it, seeing to the mounting wounded and spreading his own steadiness with, "Take it easy, there. Take it easy. This won't last long. We'll be all right."

Corporal Baldwin was helping a wounded buddy toward better shelter when he was joined by Top Sgt. Ben Gaedeke, intent on reaching the command post where the major might want him. Into the center of the group, as it leaned against the shelling like sailors on a wind-swept deck, came a tremendous burst and roar. Baldwin's wounded man had his chest torn out and he himself was hurled away, deafened, gasping and semi-conscious. Sgt. Ben Gaedeke disappeared completely.

And the barrage thundered on.

Back in his P. C. hole, Major Whittlesey summoned Omer Richards and his pigeon crate. There was only one bird left, and its name was Cher Ami—"Dear Friend." The message from the major that was clipped to its leg read:

"We are along the road parallel 276.4 [the map co-ordinate]
Our own artillery is dropping a barrage directly on us.
For heaven's sake, stop it."

Omer Richards cupped the bird in his hands and tossed it skyward. It circled several times as all eyes followed its flight—and it came to rest on the broken branch of a blasted tree. There it sat serenely with the message that was the battalion's one hope of deliverance.

Richards and Whittlesey shouted and yelled and waved their helmets. They picked up small stones and threw them. Cher Ami sat there, imperturbable and immovable.

Omer Richards finally shinnied up the tree until he could grab the branch and shake it. Then Cher Ami took off and began circling again, preparatory to its homing flight.

The Germans had spotted the bird, and guessed that its message was of first importance to the men in the pocket. Mausers opened fire on Cher Ami as it went whirring off to the south.

While the bird was winging back, the shells kept dropping relentlessly and the casualties mounted until more than 30 men in the pocket were killed or wounded by what came to be known, with bitterest irony, as "the friendly barrage." When Cher Ami finally reached the Division loft, one leg was shot away, one eye was gone and its breastbone broken. But the message was intact and, after almost two calamitous hours, the barrage that had begun with an error in map co-ordinates was finally stopped because a wounded pigeon did its duty and kept flying. Cher Ami was awarded the Distinguished Service Cross, put on pension for the rest of its life and stuffed for the Smithsonian Institution when it died.

But no wounded bird or blundering barrage was needed to focus attention on the Argonne pocket. From the first day of Major Whittlesey's isolation, his plight became the "cause for most lively apprehension," in the words of Division and Army brass. It was realized that the men in the pocket were in desperate need of food and ammunition, that swift relief was both militarily and humanly urgent.

A general attack along the whole front of the 77th Division was accordingly launched, with emphasis on the left wing where the pocket was. But the extremely difficult terrain and the resistance of the Germans brought the assault to nothing. Other relieving attacks also failed and it was afterwards estimated that more men died trying to relieve the pocket than were isolated in it. These attempts at relief were at the same time part of the grand strategy to break the Hun decisively in the Argonne, and the hammering at the enemy lines never let up.

In those October days all the fronts were aflame and the war was blazing up toward its climax. The British were smashing successfully at Cambrai and in Berlin the Cabinet was falling. Frantic orders were going out to the German troops to fight with increased tenacity in order that the best possible terms could be obtained when the inevitable collapse came.

In the midst of these mighty events, a United Press war correspondent sent back to the States a short dispatch about the lone American detachment trapped in the Argonne. On the cable desk in New York an editor with a sure sense of the dramatic singled out that small story and played it up over the bigger and more significant news. And he wired back to his correspondent at the front: SEND MORE ON LOST BATTALION.

It was the first use of the name. Newspapers across the nation picked it up at once, set it in howling headlines, and it caught the imagination of the country. Millions of men were fighting along hundreds of miles of the Western Front, but for most Americans the greatest drama of this greatest of wars was concentrated in the "Lost Battalion" and its fate.

It made no difference that the name was a mistake. Major Whittlesey's men were not lost; they knew where they were and so did everyone else. They were not one battalion, but two, with elements of others. Yet—the "Lost Battalion" it became, not only for the headlines but for history.

Of the glamorous new name they had acquired, of the history and heroics that surrounded it, the men in the pocket knew nothing. Their only indication that anyone was aware of, or interested in, their plight came when planes of the 50th Aero Squadron tried to drop food and ammunition to them. Three two-seaters were lost in the attempts, but not a scrap of food fell into the pocket. It dropped all around and the Germans pounced upon it joyously and consumed it greedily. Some Battalion soldiers, half crazed with hunger, plunged recklessly into the thickets in search of it when it fell but were either killed or captured. Two U. S. airmen were posthumously awarded the C. M. H. for their part in the suicidal mission.

Now there were no longer any burial parties by night. The men were too weak to dig the frozen earth. The dead were simply covered over with branches and leaves, and the intolerable stench of human decay was added to the spreading misery of the pocket. Blood-crusted bandages were taken from the dead and transferred to the newly wounded. All through the nights the cries of the wounded never ceased—"Mama! Mama! Help me!" and "Turn me over. For Christ's sake, turn me over." A buddy pleaded deliriously with Corporal Baldwin to kill him and end his agony.

And on October 6th, Sunday, came the wildest, most tempestuous assault on the pocket. It was preceded by machine-gun fire that swept the area like a tornado, and it sounded to Captain McMurtry like "ten thousand bull whips cracking at once." When the assault came it was featured by a new barbarity—flame-throwers, three of them spouting hundred-foot bursts of fire whose physical effect was frightful and whose morale effect was devastating.

All around the flank where the flame-throwers were operating men screamed and sobbed and let off their guns blindly in wild response to the fresh horror that was being inflicted on them. The German assault crashed through the outposts of the pocket and captured some prisoners, all badly wounded, and two light machine-guns. Then accurate *chaut-chaut* fire dropped the flame-throwers, and a general rally repulsed the attack.

Afterwards the whole command sagged back as if some giant blow had knocked the collective wind out of it. Men shuddered and gasped uncontrollably, and across the mind of more than one officer from the major down a dread began to flicker. How much more of this could the men be expected to take? How much longer before flesh and blood reached, and passed, the last limit of endurance? Already some had gone over the hill to the Germans. Morale was wearing away, thinning out.

Overhead an aerial observer thought he saw the enemy moving about in the valley where the battalion was last sighted. He reported this, and at Division H. Q. it was believed that the battalion was wiped out and the Germans were mopping up. . . .

The Germans knew better.

Generalmajor Wellman of the I Reserve Korps knew that this, "the damned nest of Americans," was still a festering, gangrenous wound in his front. It continued to imperil his line and endanger the whole German position.

It was, besides, a maddening source of bafflement and irritation. Heaven knew the Germans were as tough as soldiers come, and they never gave in easily. But the common sense of war said that when a unit was surrounded, and hopelessly outnumbered, and without food and supplies—why, it surrendered. Yet here were these foolish Americans in exactly that situation and they wouldn't give up, and you couldn't shoot them into submission.

Perhaps a direct appeal to plain good sense and elementary humanity would work.

On the afternoon of October 7th, Pvt. Lowell R. Hollingshead of Company H came hobbling from the German lines into the pocket carrying a white flag. He had been wounded and captured, and now he was the bearer of a message.

It was addressed to "Commanding Officer, Second Battalion, 308th Infantry" and it read:

> ". . . it would be quite useless to resist any more in view of the present situation.
> "The sufferings of your wounded can be heard in the German lines and we are appealing to your humane sentiments.
> "A white flag shown by one of your men will tell us that you agree with these conditions. Please treat Private Lowell R. Hollingshead as an honourable man. He is quite a soldier, we envy you.
> THE GERMAN COMMANDING OFFICER"

Major Whittlesey and Captain McMurtry received the surrender demand at their P. C. As they read it over, Captain Holderman joined them. The three officers looked at each other and grinned. "They're begging us to quit," said McMurtry. "They're more worried than we are."

The Germans got no reply at all to their note, though legend has it that Major Whittlesey replied, "Go to hell!" and the phrase that was never uttered thrilled millions of Americans.

News of the surrender appeal swept the pocket like some bracing elixir. Men who a moment before were numb and apathetic, men who were painfully scrawling farewell messages or mumbling prayers, men half dead from hunger and exhaustion, sat up and began to check their rifles.

Wounded who hadn't been capable of movement for days inched from their holes and scrabbled about for cartridges. One man squirmed out into the bushes and gathered in the white airplane signal panels, lest they be mistaken for the white flag of defeat.

Around the edges of the pocket men shouted to the Germans: "Surrender? Come and get us, you Dutch bastards!"

The attack that came in the afternoon, bolstered this time by fresh troops from a special assault company, was sent reeling back with the bloodiest repulse of the entire siege. Out on the right flank, Nelson Holderman was a one-man battalion of his own. He had been wounded four times in previous actions and he met this one propped up on two rifles used as crutches, shooting with a pistol and whooping at every hit he scored. He was wounded again, but the German wave that rolled against his position broke and flowed back.

On the left "Red" Cullen made good his oft-repeated boast that "by order of General Pershing this territory is under the protection of American troops and is going to stay that way." It did, and so did the whole pocket.

But it was the last gasp.

When another night of cold and starvation began to close in, not many believed that there was any hope any longer. Only two of the original nine machine-guns were still in action, and there were no gunners left to feed them. Grenades were all gone. Rifle ammunition was virtually exhausted. No friendly planes had been sighted that afternoon.

At 7:07 P.M., Maj. Charles Whittlesey and Capt. George Mc-Murtry lay wearily in their funk holes, talking in low voices. The captain lay gingerly on his side. In his back was a jagged, clotted wound where the handle of a stick grenade had pierced his body.

There came a sudden rustle in the darkness as a runner scrambled down the slope through the underbrush.

"Major!" the runner panted in a strangled whisper. "Over on the right. There's an officer wants to see you. An American."

Over on the right was Lt. Richard Tillman with a patrol of the 307th Infantry.

The Lost Battalion had been found.

The repeated relieving attacks, which never wholly stopped, had finally jolted the Germans loose from their positions. Several companies of the 307th had managed to filter through gaps in the German wire and into the enemy line, forcing the Boche on the right to fold up and pull back.

There was no jubilation on the hillside, no cheering. Sunken-cheeked men rose slowly from their holes and stared blankly into the dark. Some staggered silently into each other's arms. Others stumbled over to the wounded to tell the news. They were utterly spent.

Crates of rations were rushed up, and the men wolfed canned meat and bread and molasses like animals. Many promptly vomited, unable to hold what they most desperately wanted. And all through that unforgettable night not a shot disturbed them. The Germans had withdrawn, and were retreating northward all along the front. The next morning, October 8th, long lines of ration bearers streamed into what had once been a pocket and was now being turned into a picnic ground. Ambulances came rolling along the Charlevaux road for the wounded. Efficient burial parties began their work.

Of the 550 men who had been cut off in the Argonne pocket, 107 were dead, 190 wounded and 63 missing. Those that were left, and could still walk, formed up to march down the valley to Regimental Headquarters.

Some of them swayed and faltered as they went, but their chins were up and their shoulders were back and something gripped the throats of those who stood aside and watched them go. Gaunt they were, and dirty and stinking, but a kind of glory went with them— clerks and bartenders and salesmen and plumbers from the Big City, and farmers and laborers from the West, and all of them soldiers when they had to be. Ghosts from the Alamo and the Little Big Horn kept cadence with them as they went. . . .

Maj. Charles Whittlesey, the Ivy League lawyer, watched them file past. His face was as impassive as ever behind his steel-rimmed spectacles, but he turned to Capt. George McMurtry, the Wall Street broker, and he said:

"George, as long as we live we'll never be in finer company."

THE ACES

The use of airplanes at the beginning of the war was largely for their psychological effect. "They frightened the enemy as they zoomed down out of the skies. If it were possible to drop a small bomb or two, so much the better, but a loud machine counted for so much more than actual destruction." * But soon the plane was being used for artillery observation and photographing the enemy's position. As the generals saw some real use in the contraption, a struggle developed between the adversaries for mastery of the air over No Man's Land. This led to sending along a "fighter" plane for escort, which provoked duels between the German and Allied pilots. By the end of the war, whole squadrons were fighting each other across the sky.

"To begin with, the best fighter was held to be the 'pusher,' that is, an aircraft with the propeller in the tail. In these machines the French generally took the lead. Then the Germans produced something startling. It was the Fokker, the name being that of its Dutch inventor. The first Fokker was a monoplane, still something of a rarity. It was also a 'tractor'—with the propellor in front—and had a gear which synchronized the flow of machine-gun bullets with the engine propulsion, so that they passed beween the propeller blades. The aircraft was fast and handy. It appeared in October, 1915, and was superior to all others until the following May. Synchronizing gear came into general use, but few British aircraft were fitted with it even during the Battle of the Somme in 1916.

"Tactically, the most striking combat-winning trick was the long-famous 'Immelmann turn.' Max Immelmann, finest of the Fokker pilots, observed that they seldom got a second chance because, having dived on their opponents, they maintained the dive if it had

* *The Aces,* by Frederick Oughton, p. 24.

failed, in order to avoid being attacked from above. His expedient was to make his aircraft rear up, as though to loop, turn sideways, and flatten out in the opposite direction, thus regaining height and reversing course simultaneously. Many victories were won by him and his imitators by this means.

"The young men of the air forces, national and racial characteristics apart, resembled each other closely. They returned from their expeditions to comfortable billets beside airfields in the heart of the countryside. For them the battlefields were not as depressing as for the land forces who slept there. The airmen were adventurous, high-spirited, and gay, though they passed through bad phases when the other side exploited superior aircraft. In general they suffered big losses in proportion to their numbers. Death being always so near, they tried to make the most of life. Life often meant for them *Wein, Weib, und Gesang* and parties ending with smashed glass, crockery, and furniture." *

The Germans had the first edge in overall quality of their fighters due to the headstart Anthony Fokker had given them with his modern designs. Their lead was overcome with the designs of the Nieuport and Spad for the Allied pilots and both proved superior to the Fokker. The Allies achieved mastery of the air until late 1916, when the Germans redressed the balance with their Albatros and Halberstadt.**

The American contribution to the air war was small in comparison to their Allies, but they did not join the battle until the last months of the war. In May 1918, the U. S. Army Air Service came into being. America's greatest advocate of air power, Billy Mitchell, had asked General Pershing to establish a separate service for air operations,

---

* Falls, pp. 105-106.
** According to Billy Mitchell, "German airplanes were very good in general, being turned out in production with not nearly the amount of work put into them that the French airplanes had. In the French airplanes, each piece of wood was drawn out from a single piece. It was then planed, sandpapered and even worked down by handrubbing. The Germans just sawed off their pieces and left them in the rough. They were just as strong and enduring, and since they were concealed under the fabric covering, I did not see that it made any difference." (From *Memoirs of World War I* published by Random House.)

but Pershing thought the fledgling air group should be a part of the regular army. He appointed Mitchell Chief of Air Service of the First Army Corps.

It should be noted that as early as 1916 a group of American volunteers had fought for the Allies. They were the members of the Lafayette Escadrille. The early pilots in this famous squadron had been freebooters, many of whom were already living in Europe when the war began. To join a foreign military service meant swearing allegiance to a foreign flag and giving up their American citizenship. To avoid this, Dr. Edmund L. Gros of the American Ambulance Service devised a plan by which Americans could join the French Foreign Legion (no oath of allegiance was required) and were then transferred to the French air force. Most of the volunteers could fly a plane but in 1916 they had had no experience in combat. Their record was never spectacular but their exploits endeared them to the American public. From the Lafayette Escadrille came experienced pilots to help form the nucleus of the new American air service in 1918, as well as one of the three leading American aces—Raoul Lufbery.*

Quentin Reynolds calls the pilots who flew the planes in World War I a "race of gallant men. . . . The pilots of that war are still better known today than the equally great—and more numerous—aces of World War II. But the unique development, and one which will probably never be repeated again, was the fact that the first war in the air unexpectedly returned the ancient concept of the duel to modern warfare, and along with it a code of conduct which had been considered obsolete for centuries. There was no more ghastly death than to be caught in a flaming machine of wires, wood and fabric at ten thousand feet, and each side respected the other because each faced the same destruction. But in spite of these horrors, the early pilots will still laugh when they tell of putting a stove lid under their cockpit seat for makeshift armor, or of the primitive little hammer they were issued to smash the tubes of their mysterious radio sets if they were forced down so the Germans could not reproduce them. Nor would there ever be another war in which a hero like

* The other two were Eddie Rickenbacker and Frank Luke.

Richthofen could name his successor in his will and have that wish respected by the High Command.*

One of the great Aces who fought for England was Edward Mannock, whose story follows.

MICK MANNOCK**

by Frederick Oughton

Edward Mannock was a quiet-mannered, smoldering Irishman who came of a poor family. His body developed on top of a pair of thin, twig-like legs, and throughout his life he wore a lugubrious expression which was totally misleading. Mannock grew up with an intimate knowledge of the army. Born on May 24, 1887, he never really knew his father, nor did he ever speak about him, except in the most superficial fashion. His father was an enigma, never quite understood, a mixture of rollicking good humor and sullen temper.

Mannock, the future ace, was a quiet, reserved, gawky boy, not at all quarrelsome, always thoughtful. He read book after book, any book and gradually suffered an impairment of vision. Even when he became totally blind, he did not whimper or cry. He always sat quietly, believing that he would soon be able to see properly. The blindness dragged on, month after month, and in the end he was able to make out dark objects in the house and the swaying trees that surrounded the hill station. Two months later he was completely

---

* *They Fought for the Sky,* by Quentin Reynolds, pp. 237-38, Rinehart & Co.

** A slightly condensed version of three chapters from *The Aces,* published by G. P. Putnam's.

blind again, and the trouble came and went for the rest of his life, including his time as an RFC pilot.

One of the remarkable sides to Mannock, the boy, was his hatred of killing for the sake of killing. He could never join other lads in the slaughter of a bird or animal. Even when he went poaching fish as a schoolboy at Canterbury, he made a special point of going to Confession as soon as possible afterward to atone for his "sins."

The Mannocks—two boys, three girls, the mother and the unpredictable father—sailed for South Africa soon after the start of the Boer War, returning later to Britian and the base at Shorncliffe, then on to Canterbury Cavalry Depot where Edward was sent off to school.

Quite suddenly, without giving any reason or even leaving a note behind him, Mannock senior packed his bags and left. Nothing more was heard of him until he unexpectedly turned up at Buckingham Palace to receive his dead son's decorations from King George V.

Edward's life was hard as granite. He had to stand by and watch his mother trying to make shift with any work she could get, for the lowest wages, supplemented with pennies earned by the elder children. Most of the time the family barely got by.

By this time he was finding new books to read and his mind was becoming livelier than ever. He told some friends: "I'm going to become a successful engineer, tea planter, or rancher. I feel it is the duty of every man to try and raise himself to whatever heights his ideals take him, whether they be spiritual or worldly. It only requires the determination to try."

It was this refinement of his father's spirit which took him to Turkey aboard a tramp steamer in the belief that something would turn up. Over there he talked himself into a job with an English telephone company at Constantinople. Within six months he was made district inspector, stationed at Istanbul. If he had trouble with his eyes, he did not mention the fact to anybody.

When the war started, Mannock was made a prisoner of war and managed to get only one letter, a Christmas greeting, through to his friends in England. On February 19, 1915, an inquiry made through official channels by his friends brought this reply: "Sir, The Embassy is in receipt of your inquiry of January 11th and in reply takes pleasure in informing you that Mr. Edward Mannock is still in Constantinople and in good health."

The depressing truth behind these few severe lines was that Mannock had been forced to work for the telephone company, which had now fallen into enemy hands. He tried to escape many times and was severely punished for being so rash. Thrown into a cell, he tried to eat the bread and water, but vomited and felt ill. He lost weight, broke out in septic sores.

Miss Florence Minter, also a prisoner at the same time, wrote the following about Mannock:

"I see that his comrades invariably spoke of him as a 'sport.' That he was always, and in the dark days of our internment and during that bad time when we were under arrest coming home, he was always cheerful and helpful, and kept the men 'British' all through; he was our philosopher, friend and guide."

At last the Turks decided to repatriate Mannock if only for the reason that he was a physical wreck, apparently good for nothing. In this condition he would only be a liability to the Allied powers. He looked so insignificant and broken that the Turks did not believe he would make a soldier. They despised him for his "soft" approach to life.

On the way home, still under arrest along with many more British nationals, Mannock again suffered a pain in his left eye. It gave him hours of agony. He needed proper medical attention, but it was not available.

As soon as he landed he went to report to his original RAMC Territorial company and was posted to Ashford, Kent. Given an immediate rank of sergeant, he was then sent to the transport section of the 3/2nd Home Counties Field Ambulance Company.

Soon after this, and no doubt after a lot of thought, he suddenly applied for a transfer. He wanted to be sent to the Royal Engineers. On April 1, 1916, he wrote: "I intend to become a Tunneling Officer and blow the bastards up. The higher they go and the more pieces that come down, the happier I shall be."

In training as a sapper he discovered that he lacked a textbook mind. He could not begin to understand the large number of orders which came his way, and developed an uneasy feeling that he was being cheated out of something, namely, the excitement of war. He remained good-humored, though it was sometimes a strain under the dull training routine. Then, one day when he could stand it no longer at Fenny Stratford camp, he demanded to see the adjutant. He wanted to be transferred to the RFC.

"For one thing," wrote his adjutant, "I thought he was too old—he was over thirty at the time—to adapt himself to the newest arm in warfare and the strange business of flying, especially as the prevailing opinion was that only young men were suitable for the job. Still, the novelty and excitement of flying must have appealed irresistibly to his adventurous spirit, and despite all opposition and the disadvantage of his age, he stuck grimly to his decision and eventually realized his ambition."

Mannock's first obstacle was his vision, still as bad as ever it was. The RFC medical order said: "An air pilot must have 100 per cent eyesight." He approached the examination with a great show of confidence and faced the doctor.

"Are your eyes good, Mannock?"

"Of course!" he exclaimed.

In August 1916, Second Lieutenant Mannock was officially transferred to the RFC. In his personal diary he wrote: "When the Adjutant sent for me today and informed me of my transfer to the RFC I could have kissed him, though he was the most repulsive mug of any man that I have ever met. Yes! I could have kissed it; such was my unbounded delight. Now for the Boche. I am going to strive to become a scout pilot like Ball. Watch me. I wonder what fate has in store. . . ."

He was sent to Reading No. 1 School of Military Aeronautics and worked his way through such subjects as map reading, rigging, mechanics, the theory of flight, machine gunnery and bombing. They called him "Mick," and most of them envied his almost fierce application to the job. It was different for him now. As a soldier he felt dull and stupid when it came to learning how to burrow through mud, but he was sprouting wings and the world was a wonderful place, war or no war.

He passed and went to Hendon, but the place was choked with airmen in training, and he barely managed to find a space to qualify. He received the Aero Club's Certificate No. 3895, after a stiff test. On December 5 he passed on to No. 19 Training Squadron at Hounslow, and on February 1, 1917, was commissioned flying officer attached to Hythe Gunnery School. After fourteen days there they sent him to Joyce Green Reserve Squadron where he realized that he was just beginning to learn something about flying.

Captain J. B. McCudden, another British ace, was also at Joyce Green, employed there as an instructor. "I reported to the Wing at Maidstone," McCudden wrote, "and was told to make my headquarters at Joyce Green for the time being. I was allotted a Bristol Scout for my work, but as it was not yet ready, I used a DH2, which I 'spun' regularly to the great consternation of the pupils there, who regarded the machine as a super death trap, not knowing that in its day it was one of the best machines in the RFC. . . ."

McCudden and Mannock became great friends and were almost brotherly in their affection for one another. Mannock's other friend was Captain Meredith Thomas, who shared quarters with him.

"I first met Micky in February 1917 when he came along from Hythe to No. 10 Reserve Squadron at Joyce Green to fly DH2s and FE8s.

"One particular incident regarding his flying training I well remember. That was his first solo flight on a DH2, when he was told, as all were told in those days, 'Don't turn below 2,000; if you do, you will spin and kill yourself.'

"Micky proved this wrong early one Sunday morning in March, when he accidentally got into a spin at about 1,000 feet over the munition factory—then just across the creek on the edge of the airfield—and came out extremely near the ground and the munition factory, and landed successfully in a small field which was too small to fly out from. He was accused of spinning intentionally, and after a rather unpleasant scene in the mess and later in the CO's office, was threatened with being turned down."

By the end of March he was a completely qualified pilot. He was eventually sent to No. 40 Squadron where he played his part in the war. The instrument on which he played his bloody concerto over the battlefields was a Nieuport Scout. From the very start he felt at one with it.

◆ ◆ ◆

Mannock went to No. 40 Squadron in great confidence, though some of the things he saw while in transit made a horrifying impression on his mind, and he knew that war was not all swings and merry-go-rounds. He was told that he would be sent on offensive patrols and bomber escort, both duties carrying the highest mortality rate in the combined air forces. His CO was Major Dallas, a bouncy Australian, who regarded the war as one long joke. He once took a pair of flying boots on a lone trip, and dropped them on a German airfield together with a note: *Ground officers—for the use of.* Banking over the enemy airfield, hiding in low clouds, he then descended to see if the boots had been found. A few Germans were clustered around them, reading the sardonic message. Dallas drew a bead on the gathering and fired, then fled for his life.

Mannock's mess mates were like Dallas, and included such distinguished names as Mulholland, Barwell, Blaxland, McElroy, Ellis, Todd, De Burgh, Bond, Keen and Gregory, practically all of them either decorated or recognized as aces after their deaths in combat.

It was an entirely new atmosphere for Mannock. All his previous experience had been acquired as a solitary man, but he had, of course, made one or two friends at various squadrons during his training period. At No. 40 Squadron he was suddenly thrown into the melee of the mess atmosphere and on his first entrance there invited to occupy the chair of an officer who had been shot down that same morning. He accepted, trying not to worry too much about false premonitions. The mess was in a more sober mood than usual. The battle of Arras stood somberly in the offing, and preparations for this conflict were costly in human lives. Thirty-one officers and seven other ranks appeared that day on the list of missing men. And this was only a softening-up of the Germans! He was shown reports of the day's activities. What he read made him realize that he was going to become embroiled in the real war at last. They said that the battle of Arras was only a prelude to the larger and more important fight by the French against the Germans at Chemin des Dames. As it happened, the latter was a fiasco and did not benefit the Allies.

On April 19, Mannock shook hands with death for the first time. He was due to carry out some firing and diving exercises in his Nieuport, and when he came down from a thousand feet he let his machine gather speed before testing his guns over the dummy target area. He was in the middle of the first few rounds when he heard a loud snapping sound. Before he could pull out of the dive he saw the right bottom wing smash to bits and fall away from the body of the machine. Using strength and a still-crude skill, he somehow managed to land, but the plane piled up. One of the riggers scrambled forward to see if he could drag Mannock out of the wreckage, and was amazed to find him strolling away in another direction. They met and Mannock looked very strict and stern, telling him off for fitting defective wing struts. It was the Irishman's idea of a joke. Everybody knew that the fault lay more with the French manufacturers than with the well-trained and efficient RFC riggers.

"One day," said Sergeant Bovvett, the NCO in charge of rigging on Mannock's flight, "he returned from a job and his plane had been set alight by tracers which he managed to extinguish by diving; calling the armorer over he demanded more tracers than usual in future. 'I'll give the bastards what for', he said. *And he did.* He was a man with plenty of nerve. When he became Flight Commander, he fixed a pair of silk stockings on his struts for streamers—where he got them from we don't know—more nerve, I suppose!"

For all this show of "nerve," Mannock was not entirely insensitive to the hazards of the job that was now occupying all his time. On March 20 he was over the lines when his engine cut out three times. He flew on, his heart in his mouth. "Now I can understand what a nervous strain flying is. However cool a man might be, there must always be more or less of a tension on the nerves under such trying conditions," he wrote. "When it is considered that seven out of ten forced landings are practically write-offs and fifty per cent are cases where the pilot is injured, one can quite understand the strain of the whole business." He knew even more strain when he got lost in the dark, thirty miles away from his airfield. He managed to get home all right, but admitted that he was scared to death by the experience.

By this time he had been made leader of his flight. In the air he set a difficult example, especially when it came to the younger pilots. On the ground he lectured them, telling them not to try and fly home at the first sign of trouble. He would lead them into all the trouble they could handle, he explained, and teach them how to fight. Next day a pilot did attempt to turn away from the flight as it arrowed toward the German lines. Mannock whipped around and fired ten tracer bullets over the coward's head. While he was banking to see what was happening ahead, he realized that some of his pilots were warding off an attack about to be made by German machines. With one eye on the would-be deserter, the other on the enemy, he fought brilliantly, bringing down two of the enemy within ten minutes.

After a squadron move from Aire to Auchel, he was detailed to act as escort to a photographic reconnaissance over Douai, home of the German aces. His diary reads:

"We were attacked from above over Douai. I tried my gun before going over the German lines, only to find that it was jammed, so I went over with a revolver only. A Hun in a beautiful yellow and green bus attacked me from behind. I could hear his machine gun cracking away. I wheeled around on him and howled like a dervish (although of course he could not hear me) whereat he made off toward old Parry and attacked him, with me following, for the moral effect! Another one (a brown-speckled one) attacked a Sopwith and Keen blew the pilot to pieces and the Hun went spinning down from 12,000 feet to earth. Unfortunately the Sopwith had been hit, and went down too, and there was I, a passenger, absolutely helpless not having a gun, an easy prey to any of them, and they hadn't the grit to close. Eventually they broke away, and then their Archie (anti-aircraft) gunners got on the job and we had a hell of a time. At times

I wondered if I had a tail-plane or not, they came so near. We came back over the Arras with two vacant chairs at the Sopwith Squadron mess! What is the good of it all?

"A week ago, the Germans posted a notice up in their trenches which read:

'For God's sake give your pilots a rest.'

"We sent three BEs along at once and machine-gunned the trench where the notice was. Such is war. . . ."

By May 1917 Mannock was suffering from a serious attack of nervous trouble which seemed beyond his personal control. While the German propagandists were building up their heroes, regardless of actual integrity, the British made only scant mention of the personalities who had to fly out and meet the Richthofen and Boelcke squadrons. Mannock believed this to be a good thing. He liked the near-anonymity of it all. There was nothing of the god about him and to be surrounded by what he considered to be the sickly aura of hero worship suggested to him something of the society set which he abhorred.

During that damp month of May he overcame his nerves because flying conditions were good and he wanted to get into the air. He used to go off on his own, looking for trouble, and often managing to find it. On May 13 he arranged to carry out an early-morning patrol with Glin, a friend of his. They took off at about quarter to five, rising with the dawn into a sky heavy with thick clouds. They were just approaching their agreed patrol height when Glin zoomed alongside, signaling that he was not too keen on the weather conditions. They would be better off if they turned back and had breakfast. This could not be a very fruitful patrol, because the Germans might not be flying at all. Mannock half agreed, but did not want to go home. Mechanics had serviced the machines, ground crews had filled the tanks. It seemed a pity to waste the efforts of so many men. He made a hand signal to the waiting Glin. He would not go home just yet, but Glin was free to do as he wished. Glin seemed to hesitate a moment, then waved farewell, leaving Mannock to his own devices.

Some time later Mannock was flying over the Lens-Arras area, dodging in and out of the cumulus cloud banks, wondering whether the Germans were going to come up for a bit of early-morning sport, the terrible death-dealing sport which both sides played all the time. He came gliding out of the clouds and went straight into a torrential rainstorm which drenched him within a few minutes. He was soon so wet that he no longer cared about keeping dry. The bottom of the cockpit was awash. Every time he banked, even slightly, there was a rush of water from one side to the other. It sloshed about over his feet, chilling his toes. A fight in this water-logged condition could lead to trouble, he knew, but he went on searching for Germans. There was no sign of a plane, and he was about to turn and go home for breakfast when an ominous sound told him something in his engine was broken. Before he could reach out for the controls, the engine coughed again, then stopped. He was high enough to have plenty of time to try and rectify the matter. He juggled with the stubborn throttle, wondering how long this was going to last. He was about to try and land behind German lines when the engine picked up and responded to his touch.

He was banking for a new bearing when he caught up with three triplanes, all of them from British squadrons. Trying to get rid of the cold water in his cockpit, he looped round and round the formation, letting the shower of water cascade over him. Leaving the triplanes after saluting them, he scooted through the skies until he could see the ground. He was trying to plot a course for home when German artillery started banging away at him. Cramming the map into a sleeve at the side of the cockpit, he went into a zigzag, noticing the course of the acrid black cordite puffs on his tail. They were not shooting very well this morning, perhaps because of the weather. The rain had stopped and he estimated that the night crews were still on duty and therefore tired of sitting about in the mud. He took one more chance, sweeping in close, almost at ground level where he knew they could not get at him. His engine was running sweetly now, but he did not want to take too many chances. As he pulled the stick back, feeling the machine rise under him, he could see the faces and helmets of the Germans and resisted a temptation to turn around and give them a dose of their sort of hell. They might be more alert next time, holding their rifles at the ready. One well-placed bullet could put an engine out of commission. He did not want to wind up as a burning corpse near a German artillery nest. He was always frightened of fire, from the first day he flew, and told friends that he preferred to shoot himself rather than go down in a burning plane.

He was back in the mess by six-thirty, eating his bacon and eggs and saying very little about his one-man patrol.

Mannock's reputation was a strange, incongruous one. While he was friendly with most of the other pilots, this did not stop them from spreading some scandal about him. His nerves, they alleged, were shaky. Fighter and scout pilots were not supposed to suffer from this complaint, and most of those who did so managed to cover up any tendency, especially when in the presence of senior officers. Mannock, however, did not try to cover anything up. He cheerfully told people that he often felt scared while flying in combat. It did not go down very well, especially among the veterans.

Captain G. L. Lloyd, Mannock's CO at No. 40 Squadron, wrote: "He was not actually called 'yellow', but many secret murmurings of an unsavory nature reached my ears. I was told that he had been in the squadron two months, and that he had shot down one single Hun out of control, and that he showed signs of being overcareful during engagements. He was further accused of being continually in the air practicing aerial gunnery as a pretense of keenness. In other words, the innuendo was that he was suffering from 'cold feet.'"

When Lloyd had a few words with him about it, Mannock said: "Of course, I've been very frightened against my will—nervous reaction. I have now conquered this physical defect, and having conquered myself, I will now conquer the Hun. Air fighting is a science. I have been studying it, and I have not been unduly worried about getting Huns at the expense of being reckless. I want to master the tactics first. The present bald-headed tactics should be replaced by well-thought-out ones. I cannot see any reason why we should not sweep the Hun right out of the sky."

Lloyd was satisfied that he was telling the truth and tried to kill the scandal which was being tossed about in the mess. It did not seem fair that Mannock, who was serious about the war, should be the victim of such gossip.

Mannock now assumed a different personality, that of a ruthless killing machine, a man with an unremitting grudge against the Germans. It is possible, he thought, that Lloyd might regrade him and stop him from flying. Pilots who could not make the grade were being sent back to England where they were remustered and posted to infantry units at the front. With distaste, Mannock remembered his days in the Royal Engineers and RAMC. He could not stand any of that again. Some idea of the new mentality which made him one of our most daring pilots may be obtained from the following entry in his personal log:

"2.6.17. A beautiful morning, with more than a handful of cold wind blowing from the northwest. Am standing by to escort Sopwiths over lines on photography. No sign of them yet, thank God.

"Had several exciting moments since writing the last notes. Led the patrol yesterday (five machines) and had a scrap. Emptied a full drum of rounds into a big colored two-seater Hun from about 25 yards. Must have riddled the bus, but nothing untoward happened. She put her nose down and went straight. 'Melbourne' Bassett got hit in the leg in this scrap. Made a good show by flying all the way back to the field and landing, and this with a shattered leg! It was just bad luck that this shot was the only one on the machine.

"I tried my hand on a balloon northeast of LaBassée just after the above scrap. Fired about 25 rounds of Buckingham, but couldn't set the darned thing alight. In the meantime clouds of Archie all round me, but managed to zigzag away. Later was Archied by our people at 7,000 feet. Felt very mad.

"MacKenzie came back from leave on the 1st and was promptly ordered to Home Establishment again. Lucky dog! . . . I had almost forgotten to record the visit of the GOC Army on the 28th last. He came specially to congratulate us on the success of the last balloon stunt. He was very pleased indeed, and advised us to shoot at the observers as well as the balloons. He shook hands with the ''eroes'. Our CO was very pleased, I imagine."

In June, however, he had a recurrence of the nervous trouble. Life moved very fast, and he was shaken when forced into a fight with five German machines, all controlled by crack enemy pilots. It happened north of Douai. Only twenty-four hours after that encounter, from which he barely escaped with his life, he nearly crashed his plane while landing. Like most pilots, he was in the habit of pushing his flying goggles up on his forehead just before landing, so that he could see better and make sure of bringing the machine in on an even keel. This time a piece of grit flew up from the ground and went straight into his right eye, nearly blinding him. He was landing at about 120 mph and only just managed to get down safely. He went at once to see the MO, who said that the foreign body seemed to be lodged quite deeply in the membrane of the eye. Mannock insisted that something be done right away. The MO gave him an injection of cocaine and dislodged the grit. "My eye feels like a bell tent," Mannock commented painfully.

It was not only such incidents and accidents as these but also the chaffing of his fellow pilots, who liked to pull his leg, that played up the nervous tension. At last, late in June, he wrote: "Feeling nervy and ill during the last week. Afraid I am breaking up. . . . Captain Keen very decent. Let me off flying for today. I think I'll take a book and wander into the woods this afternoon—although it rather threatens rain. Oh, for a fortnight in the country at home!"

A few days later he was granted leave. The only salient feature of it was a surprise visit to Hanworth to inspect some new machines. A few days earlier somebody introduced him to a sporting baronet. To an acquaintance at Hanworth he said that it was a pity such people as baronets mattered merely because they had handles to their names.

Less than a month later he had an historic encounter with a German machine, and described it in a letter to a friend:

". . . I was interrupted in this letter to get out after a Hun. That was yesterday morning at 9:50 A.M. At 10:20 A.M. I was lucky enough to get a big two-seater Hun down in our own lines. I shot the pilot in three places and wounded the observer in the side. The machine was smashed to pieces and a little black-and-tan dog which was with the observer (a captain) was also killed. The observer escaped death, although the machine fell about 9,000 feet. The pilot was horribly mutilated."

A day or two later he had the chance of examining the wreckage on the ground, but it was a nightmare journey and, like many other aces, he felt sickened to see the war in the trenches at such close quarters. "The journey to the trenches was rather nauseating—dead men's legs sticking through the sides with puttees and boots still on —bits of bones and skulls with the hair peeling off, and tons of equipment and clothing lying about. This sort of thing, together with the strong graveyard stench and the dead and mangled body of the pilot (an NCO) combined to upset me for days."

Mannock was now averaging one German per day. By way of recognition he was awarded the Military Cross in August 1917, and then promoted to the rank of captain. He still believed that his part in the war had yet to be fought.

◆ ◆ ◆

Mannock had now sustained so many blows that he knew the strain on his nerves to be almost more than he could stand. He had to acknowledge that his early and youthful ideal of the non-Germanic superman did not exist, could not exist, under such conditions as these. After flying three or four missions each day, every week, he knew the effect of this kind of living. The effort of taking off from his airfield more than twenty times a week was too much for even his strong reserves of energy and he was beginning to lack the primitive savagery which had taken him through so much of the war in the air. Apart from the muscular drag from which he now suffered, there was the terrible lack of sleep to contend with. He found himself feeling drowsy in the thin coldness of the upper air, and had to shake himself awake. He knew that attack could easily come when he was caught nodding over the controls. If it happened like that, he would not stand a chance. Members of all the crack German squadrons used high speeds to make their kills. Mannock had watched too many Allied planes going down in a plume of flame to want the same thing to happen to him. His long-standing fear of being "sizzled" was intensified when he dwelt on the horror of being trapped in a blazing machine which was plummeting into the mud and sludge. As a man of many phases, he finally did manage to pull himself together. On July 28, 1917—the "year of heroes," as it has been called by one author—he scored a new victory which made a big impression on his mind. His own report best describes what happened.

"Hostile machine observed at 3:10 P.M. crossing our lines south of Thelus.

"E. A. attempted to attack our balloon west of that point and descended to low altitudes for that purpose. Nieuport engaged E. A. at approximately 1,000 feet over Neuville St. Vaast and fired 70 rounds during the course of a close combat. The hostile aircraft was observed to be hit, a glow of fire appearing in the nacelle, and glided down under reasonably capable control south and east of Petit Vimy, landing downwind and turning over on touching the ground. Prisoner: Lieut. von Bartrap, sustained fracture of left arm and flesh wounds in right arm and leg, and was taken to hospital immediately on landing. Machine was in very good condition, although upside down, but was unfortunately affected by eventual hostile gunfire."

A few weeks later—weeks of hard, violent fighting in which he was nearly shot down several times—he had another momentous encounter, and in his log described it thus:

"5.9.17. The end of a fairly hard day. Went over to Petit Vimy and Thelus in a sidecar this morning in an endeavor to pick up some relics of the last victims, downed yesterday afternoon in flames. Regret that nothing remained of the machine. I met this unfortunate DFW at about 10,000 over Avion coming southwest, and I was traveling southeast. I couldn't recognize the black crosses readily (he was about 300 yards away and about 500 feet above me), so I turned my tail toward him and went in the same direction, thinking that if he were British he wouldn't take any notice of me, and if a Hun I felt sure he would put his nose down and have a shot (thinking I hadn't seen him). The ruse worked beautifully. His nose went (pointing at me), and I immediately whipped around, dived and zoomed up behind him, before you could say 'knife'. He tried to turn but he was much too slow for the Nieuport. I got in about 50 rounds in short bursts while on the turn and he went down in flames, pieces of wing and tail, etc., dropping away from the wreck. It was a horrible sight and made me feel sick. He fell down in our lines and I followed to the ground, although I didn't land. The boys gave me a great ovation.

"The same evening I got another one down east of Lens, confirmed by the A. A. people. Captain Keen had previously engaged it but broke off combat in order to renew the ammunition drum. I got quite close up and let him have a full drum, and he went nose-down east. Owing to the haze, I couldn't see him crash.

"Prior to that at 9:40 A.M. I had a beautiful running fight with another two-seater at 17,000 feet, from Bruay to east of Lens. This one got away, notwithstanding the fact that I fired nearly 300 rounds at close range. I saw the observer's head and arm lying over the side of the machine—he was dead, apparently—but the pilot seemed to be all right. He deserved to get away really, as he must have been a brave Hun. This fight was watched from the Advance Landing ground by the mechanics and caused great excitement. Anyhow, two in one day is not bad work, and I was today congratulated by the Colonel.

"Had a scrap this evening with six Hun scouts east of Lens, but had to retire early owing to gun trouble.

"This is the first gun trouble I've had for months.

"The CO bet me tonight ten to one . . . I don't bring down a two-seater tomorrow (if fine) on this side of the lines. I've taken him on, so I am going all out tomorrow to win my bet."

He got his two-seater and won his bet, but the sequel distressed him. It came in the shape of a note received when he was on leave in England.

To The British Flying Corps,
    The 4th of September I lost my friend Fritz Frech. He fell between Vimy and Lievin. His respectable and unlucky parents beg you to give any news of his fate. Is he dead? At what place found

he his last rest? Please to throw several letters, that we may found one.

Thanking before,
HIS FRIEND,
K. L.

P.S.: If it is possible, send a letter to the parents, Mr. Frech, Konigsberg 1, Pr. Vord Vorstadt 48/52.

Reading this plea, Mannock felt sickened by the war which seemed to create so much suffering. He immediately wrote to the parents, making special arrangements for the delivery of the letter. He himself often flew over the German lines with replies to notes from the Germans, notifying them of deaths, burials or imprisonments. When all is considered, there were similarities between Oswald Boelcke and Edward Mannock.

Now in his mid-thirties, Mannock's vigorous ability was at its height, but his combat duties were somewhat curtailed when he was seconded to duties which involved the training of young pilots newly arrived at the front. He was ready to complain about the tediousness of the work when he was awarded a bar to his Military Cross with a citation which read:

"October 14. He has destroyed several hostile machines and driven others down out of control. On one occasion he attacked a formation of five enemy aircraft singlehanded and shot one down out of control. On another occasion while engaged with an enemy machine, he was attacked by two others, one of which he forced to the ground. He has consistently shown great courage and initiative."

This marked the end of a chapter of his life, and he knew that sooner or later he would be sent on leave, his second since being posted to the front. Before it came, he was flying on January 1, 1918, when he happened to find a German two-seater. Unable to resist the bait, he went in to close with it. It was one of the shortest, sharpest and most decisive fights of his life, and the enemy exploded before his eyes. He could not make out what had happened to the pilot or observer in the tumult of the explosion as the fuel tanks erupted in a scarlet violence all their own. This was the twentieth time he had shot down a German machine, and he went on leave the next day to the sound of cheers of assembled mechanics and fellow pilots.

At home everybody knew how tired he was, and a gentle conspiracy sprang into being to keep him at home for a time. Despite his often angry endeavors to return to the front, he was detained in England for three months, resting and trying to curb his tongue when meeting the inevitable society lionizers. A month after leaving France, he was sent to the Wireless Experiment Establishment at Biggin Hill, but from the start he hated the atmosphere, the quietness of it all, and he longed to escape. When his outbursts became so loud that they could not very well be ignored, he was posted to No. 74 Training Squadron, London Colney, Hertfordshire. He arrived there wearing a threatening expression, but was quickly pacified on hearing that No. 74 Squadron would be going to France in February. His posting to the squadron was organized with a minimum of red tape; otherwise, as he himself threatened General Henderson, he would go straight back to France without official permission. He told Henderson that he would fly back, not follow the overland route, stealing a plane for the purpose if he had to. The authorities could do what they liked about it. Henderson was the one who capitulated and arranged for him to be sent to London Colney.

While with this squadron Mannock spent hours lecturing young pilots, giving them hints on the handling of the SE5, a machine about which he knew practically everything there was to know. He was able to talk the more imaginative fledglings out of the idea that they were mere "Fokker fodder."

By March 1 No. 74 Training Squadron was reorganized, becoming known as No. 74 Fighter Squadron, under the command of Major A. S. Dore, DSO, Mannock was promoted to flight commander of "A" Flight.

Over in France things were happening quickly. Before Mannock really had a chance to realize that he was in the thick of things once more, he was flying every day, engaging in some of the quickest aerial fights he had ever known. He had the double task of seeing that the newly qualified fighter pilots were sufficiently astute to act on their own responsibility and, for his own part, lifting his personal score, now standing at more than forty, even higher. The following extract from the diary of Lieutenant Ira Jones, himself an ace, will perhaps explain why Mannock was often short-tempered and intolerant when it came to the faults of others. Mannock was living faster than any other man at the front, both mentally and physically, and it was engagements such as this which made his temperament sometimes smolder, sometimes burst into violent flame. "Mick" was Edward Mannock.

"28.5.18. The C O saved Giles' life today. Giles very carelessly allowed a black Albatros to pounce on him while he was concentrating on the destruction of a silver-gray two-seater. Giles had his leg pulled unmercifully; we declare he was decoyed. Pilots hate admitting that they have been taken in as a sucker!

"Clements tells me that Mick saved his life tonight, too. Mick and Clements went up for a bit of fun after tea. They each got what they wanted. . . . Clements spotted a large formation of Huns obviously making a beeline for them. Clements put on full throttle . . . to catch up to Mick, who as usual was wasting no time in getting at his enemy. Mick had seen the Hun formation all the time . . . he turned west quickly and dived, the Huns following and firing. Mick saved Clements by losing height directly beneath them and so drawing them on to him, while Clements got clear. Clements says it was a rotten sight to see one SE being attacked by such a bunch, and that had it been anyone except Mick, he would have been anxious about his safety. (We all believe that no Hun will ever shoot down Mick.) One Pfalz following him very closely, and suddenly Mick went down apparently out of control; on his back—spinning— and doing everything imaginable from 8,000 feet to 4,000 feet. At 5,-000 feet, the Hun, completely fooled, flattened out to watch the crash. Mick then decided he had had enough, and flattened out too and made for our lines, diving hard. . . .

"29.5.18. Mick took Clements and me up at 7 P.M. . . . Mick spotted about a dozen Huns coming from the direction of Roubaix; we were then over Lille. As we had not too much time for a fight, having already been up for over an hour, he decided to go straight at them, as we had a slight advantage of height. The Huns, who were Albatros scouts, were of the stout variety, and they accepted our head-on challenge. Both Mick and the Hun leader opened fire at one another, as they approached from about 300 yards range, but nothing happened. This burst of fire was the signal for a glorious dogfight—as fine and as frightening a dogfight as I've ever been in. Friend and foe fired at and whistled past one another at a tornado pace . . . I have never been so frightened in my life. Of late I have been able to keep very cool during the actual fight, but tonight I became so flustered that occasionally I fired at my own pals in an effort not to miss a chance—thank God, my shooting was erratic. How terrible it would have been if I had, say, shot Mick down! The thought gives me the very creeps. . . . Mick sent two slate-blue Albatroses down out of control, and Clements crashed his first Hun. He is very bucked about it. It is wonderful how cheered a pilot becomes after he shoots down his first machine; his morale increases by at least 100 per cent. This is why Mick gives Huns away—to raise the morale of the beginner. . . ."

Analyzing tactics between combats, Mannock often wondered whether the extended course, which most of his pilots had taken at Ayr Fighting School prior to their transfer to France, was having effect. He believed there was far too much idiocy and clumsiness manifesting itself. There were also times when he had rows with Caldwell, the CO of No. 74 Squadron who replaced Dore. Before leaving for France Dore told him that he might not be going to France at all.

"Surely you don't mean to say you would rather stay at home on a staff job than be commanding this fighting squadron in France!" Mannock exclaimed.

"But I am going to be promoted," Dore said.

Mannock yelled: "What! That's worse than ever."

As it happened, Dore did stay at home, and Major Keith Caldwell, a New Zealander, was appointed the new CO. He called all airplanes "grids," had obtained his fighting experience with men like Albert Ball. VC, believed in *esprit de corps,* and decried the cult of the individualist which, he believed, was what led to the downfall of the German Air Force. Adjusting his own personality to that of Caldwell, Mannock found that he had to alter his attitude to the war itself, and immediately got down to the not inconsiderable job of merging with the other pilots, instead of being *the* Mannock. He never pretended that it was simple. Part of his private objection to Caldwell's dogmatic creed was carefully covered by bouts of jokes and leg-pulling. The New Zealander retaliated with grim humor about the way Mannock would "sizzle" when he was finally shot down. Mannock certainly did not relish the prospect, but nevertheless allowed Caldwell his bit of fun. He still had the same old black fear of being lapped by flames as his machine fell to pieces. It was one of the few things which he could hardly bring himself to face. In France on his second tour of duty, he seemed to pay much more attention to the fire hazards while he also subjugated his long-standing hatred of the Germans, though when news came of Richthofen's death he would not join in toasting the Red Baron's memory. He walked out of the mess in disgust. The only Germans he ever admired for their skill as pilots were Boelcke and Werner Voss.

The daily fight in the air had now become so commonplace that Mannock frequently forgot or omitted to report exactly what had happened after he returned from his sorties. For this reason, reports of his most memorable actions must come from others, including Van Ira, a South African member of No. 74 Squadron. Mannock was leading his fighters into battle and presently Van Ira witnessed a terrible sight.

"I saw a dogfight going on between a number of machines east of Merville at about 14,000 feet, so I went along to join in the fun, although I was at a lower altitude. As I was climbing toward the scrap, I suddenly saw a machine falling away from the whirling mob and come tumbling down in my direction. I awaited its approach with a considerable amount of anxiety, as I suspected a ruse, and that he was going to attack me. However, as he approached my level, the Pfalz, which was highly colored with a black body, white-tipped tail, silver and black checkered top surfaces, suddenly assumed a position on its back, and I noticed that the propeller was stopped. I flew close up to it, and to my horror, I saw the body of the pilot partially dangling out of the cockpit as if he were dead; in addition, the machine began to smoke badly."

Along with others, Van Ira was becoming concerned about the

grim blood lust which was again coming to the surface of Mannock's feelings. It was not a desirable trait in an Allied pilot because it betokened a loss of control. Mannock risked his life several times when he followed crippled German planes down to shoot them to bits as they lay on the ground. He was believed to be callous, coldblooded, and those who did not know him very well felt that he was exceeding the bounds. Caldwell, the CO of No. 74 Squadron, noted the following:

"Mannock and Dolan were up together, and on seeing British Archie bursting on our side of the lines, they chased along to see what could be done. They spotted a Hun two-seater beetling back toward the lines, and got down just in time to prevent this.

"The Hun crashed, but not badly, and most people would have been content with this—but not Mick Mannock, who dived half a dozen times at the machine, spraying bullets at the pilot and the observer, who were still showing signs of life. I witnessed this business, and flew alongside of Mick, yelling at the top of my voice (which was rather useless), and warning him to stop.

"On being questioned as to his wild behavior, after we had landed, he heatedly replied: "The swines are better dead—no prisoners for me!"

While still quite approachable and talkative, Mannock was reserving the greater part of himself for the battles in which he was engaged. He was shooting down an average of one German every day, and often led his followers deep behind the German lines. The German attitude to aerial warfare had altered. No longer did the Hun aces flaunt themselves over the front line, tempting the Allied airmen to come out and duel. After great setbacks on the ground and the deaths of many of their best pilots, they could only hang about over their own flying fields, hoping for easy victories. These places were Mannock's chief objectives. It often meant having to fly more than twenty miles before any engagement could be made. Mannock forced every fight, generally managing to shoot down his unwilling opponents in flames. He let off steam by coming back to the mess and shouting at the top of his voice: "Sizzle, sizzle, sizzle, wonk, woof!" as a sign that he had shot down another one. It was this eternal urge to hunt which started to fray his nerves. He expected the Germans to be up there, watching for him and preparing for the next fight, but it was not working out like that at all. They were badgers in holes. He disliked having to do all the spadework. Sometimes, when he was so bored that he could not stand being on the ground any longer, he gave orders to the ground crews to have his machine fueled and the drums of ammunition clipped in position, then went out by himself to pick a fight. Doing this was strictly against his better judgment, but he suffered from boredom and it was the only way out. He repeatedly told younger pilots that it was stupid to fly alone over the front because any victories gained lacked the necessary confirmation. He had a complicated way of blooding members of his flight, and often guided two of them straight into the heart of a fight which he himself started. He then flew away to the sidelines to watch developments. Conscious of his critical eyes fixed upon them, the youngsters generally did very well.

Major Caldwell told of one of Mannock's victories when flying alone. "The only time I can remember Mannock got a Hun when alone, happened when he attacked a Fokker scout just east of Ypres one afternoon in June. He attacked at short range, did a climbing turn to keep height in case the Hun zoomed, and never saw the Hun again. When he landed on the airfield he told me that he thought he could not very well have missed from such close range. So I rang up the Archie battery near Ypres and asked for a description of any combats between 7,000 feet and 10,000 feet just east of Ypres between 3 P.M. and 4 P.M. The reply came straight back that an SE5 had shot down a Fokker in a vertical dive at the time Mannock reported."

On May 21 Mannock shot down four German scout planes and a two-seater. This incident is described by Van Ira.

"In his first fight, which commenced at 12,000 feet, there were six Pfalz scouts flying east from Kemmel Hill direction. One he shot to pieces after firing a long burst from directly behind and above; another he crashed; it spun into the ground after it had been hit by a deflection shot; the other, a silver bird, he had a fine set-to with, while his patrol watched the Master at work. It was a wonderful sight. First, they waltzed around one another like a couple of turkey cocks, Mick being tight on his adversary's tail. Then the Pfalz half-rolled and fell a few hundred feet beneath him. Mick followed, firing as soon as he got in position. The Hun then looped—Mick looped too, coming out behind and above his opponent and firing short bursts. The Pfalz then spun—Mick spun also, firing as he spun. This shooting appeared to me a waste of ammunition. The Hun eventually pulled out; Mick was fast on his tail—they were now down to 4,000 feet. The Pfalz now started twisting and turning, which was a sure sign of 'wind-up'. After a sharp burst close up, Mick administered the *coup de grâce,* and the poor old fellow went down headlong and crashed.

"This was a really remarkable exhibition of cruel, cool, calculating Hun-strafing. A marvelous show. I felt sorry for the poor Hun, for he put up a wonderful show of defensive fighting. His effort reminded me of mine on April 12. The only difference was, that he was miles over his own lines and had a slower machine. Had he only kept spinning down to the ground, I think he would have got away with it.

"I asked Mick after he landed why he fired during the spin. He replied, 'Just to intensify his wind-up.' And a very good answer, too! This was the first occasion that I have ever seen a machine loop during a fight. It was obvious to us, watching, that to loop under such circumstances is foolish. Mick managed, however, to keep behind him, and did not lose contact with him, although it was obvious by his maneuvers after he came out of the loop that the Pfalz pilot was all at sea, for he twisted and turned his machine in a series of erratic jerks, just as if he was a dog stung on his tail. Mick says he only looped as well for a bit of fun, as he felt his opponent was 'cold meat'. He says what he should have done instead of looping was to have made a zooming climbing turn as the Pfalz looped, then half-rolled and come back on his tail as he came out of the loop. By this means he would have been able to keep the Hun in sight all the time, while he would not have lost control of his machine as the Hun did while coming out of the loop.

"Mick's other Hun was a two-seater, which he shot down after a burst at right angles. The old boy crashed into a tree near La Couranne, south of Vieux.

"Four in one day! What is the secret? Undoubtedly the gift of accurate shooting, combined with the determination to get to close quarters before firing.

"It's an amazing gift, for no pilot in France goes nearer to a Hun before firing than the CO, but he only gets one down here and there, in spite of the fact that his tracer bullets appear to be going through his opponent's body! Mick, on the other hand, takes an angle shot and—Hun in flames."

Famous pilots were being just as well lionized as well-known authors and actors. Some fliers were outrageous in lapping up the extravagant praise. Only after some painful experiences did Mannock learn to take it in his stride. He was generally bluff and hearty, quite unlike his usual rather taciturn self seen at the airfield. When all the adulation was over and done with, he was able to revert to his other, more businesslike, nature, glad to get away from the sycophancy. He was, however, trapped into meeting General Plumer, one of the more admired members of the General Staff, who was going the rounds of the front and thought to call in on the squadron to see the aces for himself.

"This afternoon General Plumer, who commands the Second Army, came and gave us a surprise," wrote Van Ira. "He is a quaint little man to look at, but very charming to speak to. He is about five-feet-eight in height, corpulent, has a pudgy red face, white hair and mustache, a twinkle in his eye, wears a monocle, and stands like the grand soldier he is, very stiff and erect. He flattered us with his praises of our fighting efforts, but I have suspicions that he did not approve of either the cleanliness or the mode of our dress. Naturally when off duty we are not particular about our dress, as we believe in being comfortable today, as tomorrow we may be dead.

"Mick, who had just landed, was the most disreputable of all. As he approached the group where the General stood, he was hatless, without a collar, his tunic open, his hair ruffled; in fact, he looked a typical bush-ranger!

"The General said, 'Which is Mannock?' Mick was duly pointed out to him. When he set eyes on him, I really thought he was going to pass right out. By a masterly effort, however, he pulled himself together and literally seemed to stagger up to Mick with his arm outstretched. Mick's dirty paw clutched the gloved hand and squeezed it in his usual hearty manner. Plumer's face twitched, and for a second I thought he was going to give a shout. 'Mannock,' he stammered, 'let me congratulate you on your DSO.'

"This was the first intimation of Mick's well-deserved award which we've been expecting for some days. Later he said to Mick: 'Further, let me congratulate you on your first day's work'.

"Mick replied: 'We expected that, sir,' meaning that, having a lot of good fellows in his flight, he naturally thought they would shoot down some Huns. But, of course, it did not sound like this to General Plumer, and he departed with a puzzled expression in his face, no doubt wondering what sort of fellow Mick might be, and possibly thinking that he is spoiled by success. Quite wrong."

Mannock generally managed to mix well with the others, rising to new heights as an after-dinner speaker. He was always the one chosen to voice the sentiments, and he always earned his applause. There was, of course, another side to him. In the early morning, shortly before dawn, he slipped out of his camp bed and put on his flying overalls after a cold-water sponge-down to liven himself up. Going into the mess, he put the gramophone on. It was always the same sad lament of *The Londonderry Air* which he played as he stood at the window, watching the mechanics pushing his machine into position. He never ate or drank anything and once said that he would like to die with an empty stomach if he had to die at all. As the song came to an end, he walked out to his plane, the last lingering notes sounding in his ear. An hour later he would be back after shooting down another German, sometimes more.

Often high-spirited, he liked to organize practical jokes and spoofs. He was responsible for an organized raid on No. 1 Squadron when a couple of hundred oranges were dropped as "bombs." Next day planes of No. 1 Squadron flew over in revenge and bombed Mannock's crowd with bananas, a fruit which seemed to make a more effective mess than the oranges. Peace was declared at a joint squadron dinner at Saint-Omer, where they converged on the George Robey cafe and drank together. That night Mannock was in great form.

Thoughts that he might become the victim of a violent roasting were never far from his mind. He was now having nightmares again about airplanes in flames, and was always saying to his close friends that he would blow his brains out rather than go down enveloped in fire. Evidence of the bad state of his nerves came when he somehow crashed two machines, one of them nose-diving into the earth, the other turning completely over on a bad run-in. That week other squadron pilots managed to write off seven of their own machines. One pilot smashed up as many British as he shot down German planes. Caldwell received a stiff note of reprimand from headquarters. Mannock felt angry that anybody had even noticed the write-offs at a time when a new phase of the war had to be fought and won, and he had an argument with Caldwell about it, but in the end conceded that he himself was probably in the wrong. Everybody knew that bad landings were usually the result of bad nerves. He was often in a state when he could hardly control the shaking of his arms and wrists after handling his machine in arduous combat. The immediate reaction to minutes of hectic warfare was too much for any nervous system, though he always insisted that it was his own frailty that was to blame. He promised to try and do better in future.

He now believed that the Germans were suffering from cold feet, and any similar trait in his own men sent him into spasms of anger. One young pilot who came up from a replacement pool did actually turn coward after Mannock had spent long hours instructing him in the kind of strategy which seemed best suited to squadron flying. He was so disgusted that he could not find any pity for the youngster. When the order came to send this man to a desk job in England he told his orderly to get hold of the pilot's jacket, rip off the wings and replace them with a scrap of yellow cloth. Certain officers viewed Mannock's attitude with distaste, but he insisted that his orders be carried out. While they were still shaking their heads over him he was cited in the *London Gazette* to receive a bar to his DSO. The citation said: "A fine example of marksmanship and determination to get to close quarters. As a patrol leader he is unequaled."

There was room for a man like Mannock to act as a morale booster, and he was selected to spend part of his time visiting various squadrons in the area. He tried to concentrate mainly on senior pilots, who would show an example to the younger members of the RFC. Although he was supposed to spend a lot of his time talking to them, he was in the habit of returning to his own flying field as soon as possible, so that he could get into the air. His machine was always kept at the ready. Once, when he came back too late to join the others, he went up with a seventeen-year-old fledgling, "Swazi" Howe, a South African and the youngest in the squadron. According to Van Ira it was an eventful flight.

"Mick came back in a furious temper from a patrol this morning. He had taken Swazi out on a private war to see if he could help him to get a Hun. At 11:20 A.M. he spotted half a dozen Albatroses flying in formation near Armentiéres and at the same time he noticed a flight of Camels patrolling near by, so he flew up to the leader and waggled his wings to attract his attention and to ask him to follow him, this being a recognized procedure. The Camels followed Mick while he maneuvered for position before attacking. Eventually he gave the signal to attack, and down he swooped on the completely surprised enemy. A dogfight immediately commenced, and when Mick had time to look around to sum up the situation he discovered that he and Swazi were alone and that some distance away was the Camel flight, flying away! Both Mick and Swazi eventually made a safe getaway after expending all their ammunition, but each of their machines much shot about, both the tires of Mick's machine were punctured, and as a result he turned a somersault on landing. He was so angered about the whole affair that he asked the CO to report the matter at once to Wing Headquarters. What apparently happened was, when the leader of the Camels commenced to dive with Mick, he saw another enemy formation approaching toward the fight from some distance away, so he thought he'd better go and intercept them. The result was that they sheered off and Mannock's fight was over before the Camels could return and join in the fray. They were, however, able to confirm that one of the Huns went down in flames. Mannock credited this victory to Howe."

On leave in England some time later Mannock was told that he had been promoted to major's rank and was being transferred to another squadron. On July 3, when returning to France and the front after a bad attack of influenza, he suddenly felt that he could not carry on much longer. He was stunned, remembering that he had told friends at the RFC Club in Bruton Street about premonitions of death in this, his third tour of duty. Even so, his new rank bucked him, though he did not want to leave No. 74 Squadron. He even cried over it in front of friends, who were embarrassed to see how low his spirits were sinking. They tried to cheer him up and he apologized for his weakness. Influenza left him debilitated. He frankly admitted that he was not in a fit condition to do much operational flying at present. On reaching France his temperament changed. No longer did he feel impelled to carry on his relentless private war against the Germans. He was doubtful whether he could shoot a Hun in cold blood as he often had done in the past. He began living a new routine. He combed his hair with great concentration; he had his batman clean and press his uniform and stitch on the row of decorations. His boots were shined, and he somehow subjugated his passionate, often fierce manner. He went on telling people that he felt himself to be coming to the end, but did not know whether he was going to die fighting or not.

He was in the depths of this mood when he had tea with some VAD nurses from a nearby hospital. In the party was a man called Donald Inglis, a shy new fighter pilot, only recently arrived at the front. Mannock was stirring his tea when he caught Inglis' eye. "Have you got a Hun yet, Inglis?"

Inglis colored. Mannock was one of his private gods. "No, sir," he answered quietly.

Mannock put down his tea untouched. "Well, come on out and we will get one." To his hostesses he apologized: "Excuse us for a few minutes, please."

Something went wrong with Inglis' plane and he could not take off. Mannock flew on alone, returning two hours later to admit that he had seen nothing of the enemy. He was tired and his face was etched with fatigue. It was as much as he could do to walk into the mess and sit down, still wearing his flying overalls.

His personal interest in Inglis did not lessen. Once more the ace was teaching the beginner. Early one morning he made a determined effort to get Inglis initiated. Those who knew Mannock of old wakened to hear *The Londonderry Air* playing on the gramophone.

Mannock and Inglis strolled out to their warmed-up machines and the dawn was split by the roaring of their engines. It was an excellent morning for killing Germans.

There can be no better witness to what happened than Inglis himself.

"My instructions were to sit on Mick's tail, and that he would waggle his wings if he wanted me closer. I soon found that I didn't have much chance of looking around, as Mick would waggle, and the only thing I could do was to watch his tail and stick tight, as he was flying along the lines at about thirty to fifty feet up and not straight for more than thirty seconds, first up on one wing tip, then the other. Suddenly he turned toward home, full out and climbing. A Hun, thought I, but I'm damned if I could find one; then a quick turn and a dive, and there was Mick shooting up a Hun two-seater. He must have got the observer, as when he pulled up and I came in underneath him I didn't see the Hun shooting. I flushed the Hun's fuel tank and just missed ramming his tail as I came up, when the Hun's nose dropped. Falling in behind Mick again we did a couple of circles around the burning wreck and then made for home. I saw Mick start to kick his rudder and realized we were fairly low, then I saw a flame come out of the side of his machine; it grew bigger and bigger. Mick was no longer kicking his rudder; his nose dropped slightly and he went into a slow right-hand turn around about twice, and hit the ground in a burst of flame. I circled at about twenty feet but could not see him, and as things were getting pretty hot, made for home and managed to reach our outposts with a punctured fuel tank.

" 'Poor old Mick!' All I could say when I got into the trench was

that the bloody bastards had shot my major down in flames."
Mannock died enveloped in flames, just as he feared he would.
The man who shot down seventy-two Germans was no more.
They never found his body. He had no known grave.

ASSAULT ON A GERMAN U-BOAT BASE

Britain's weapon against her continental enemies was the naval blockade; the world's greatest navy enabled her to starve an enemy into submission. In World War I, however, the Germans turned the tables on the British. The Kaiser instructed the U-boat skippers to attack merchantmen to prevent food and supplies from reaching British ports. This counter-blockade was extremely effective in 1917. The British countered with the convoy, an armed escort of large groups of merchant vessels. Losses were reduced but the battle went on.

The British Admiralty laid mine fields along the coastal exits used by the U-boats, but the German U-boat skippers were studying their latest instructions: " 'It is best and safest to pass through the Straits of Dover on the way to the Atlantic seaways. Pass through at night and on the surface . . . without being observed and without stopping. If forced to dive, go down to 40 metres and wait.' In this way, the average of 30 U-boats passed over the defenses every month, slipping easily between the high-standing buoys and across the drooping hawsers which supported the nets." *

Finally, a raid was planned for early 1918 which, if successful, would block the canals leading to one of the main U-boat bases at Bruges. The facilities at Bruges could take care of 30 subs and 35 torpedo craft or destroyers.

Bruges lay eight miles inland from the Belgian coast, connected by two canals, with Zeebrugge and Ostend at the mouth of each. Both Zeebrugge and Ostend were heavily defended by German guns. The weakest point to defend was the installation at Zeebrugge, whose canal lock lay just a half-mile in from the coast.

From the British coast to Zeebrugge the distance was approximately 65 miles. The British were wary of the approaches because

* *Zeebrugge,* by Barrie Pitt, published by Ballantine Books, p. 18.

of the sandbanks which continually shifted. The Belgian coast is only protected from deep erosion by long jetties built out into the sea, and beyond the limit of the jetties the tidal flow washes the sea bed into a thousand differing shapes, building banks and scouring hollows of ever-changing and inconsequent variety.

"Before 1914, survey vessels continually buoyed the channels and marked the banks, and a coastal pilot who took a month's leave would spend a week learning the new contours when he returned; but the German naval authorities, realizing that here they had a defensive ally requiring no supplies or maintenance, removed the main buoys or allowed them to drift, and restricted their own vessels in the neighborhood to those of shallow draught. They then sat back, snug and secure behind their own nature's defenses.

"It would certainly take much ingenuity to penetrate such a fastness." *

In front of the canal entry at Zeebrugge extended a huge Mole, the largest in the world. It was a nest of strong defenses, extending in a long arc out into the water for one and two-thirds miles. Once beyond it, the blockships had to navigate the harbor with its shifting sands, reach the mouth of the canal, and then execute difficult maneuvers to block it.

One of the most important missions was that of the ship to land troops on the Mole to assault its defenses. A ship was needed which could grapple to the Mole and hold her position "against both the fierce tideway and the surge which the ship would carry with her. Derricks were erected fore and aft, from which were suspended grappling irons to hook over the parapet." ** An outdated light cruiser, the *Vindictive*, was chosen.

The fleet would approach on a moonless night at high tide, so the lock ships could get into the canals safely. A rolling smoke screen would be used to protect the ships from early sighting. After careful planning, it was decided that the earliest proper time fell between the 9th and the 13th of April.

Twice the attack force set off, and each time the wind and weather

* *Zeebrugge*, p. 26.
** *Zeebrugge*, p. 46.

conditions changed, affecting the use of the smoke screen. Rather than wait until the following month, a decision was made to try at the next high tide, which fell in late April, even though there would be bright moonlight. On April 22nd, at 5 P.M., the attack force formed out in the English Channel and moved toward the Belgian coast, this time apparently with luck favoring them.

"At 11:30 P.M. *Warwick*, ten minutes ahead of the assault ships, steamed past an occulting light buoy five miles northwest of Zeebrugge Mole; parallel with her, Lieutenant Hill was roaring across the last minefields on his way into position from Dover. Like ants attacking a rotten apple, the head of the convoy split into component strands and led out towards the battle positions.

"The destroyer screens broke apart and fanned out; C. M. B. s 22B and 23B of Unit V with the youthful Lieutenant Welman in command sped forward to lay smoke directly under the barrels of the Mole guns and drape a blinding scarf around the observation posts in the lighthouse. Unit H (C. M. B. s 5 and 7) swung out in a wide circle which would take them into the bight of the Mole to carry out torpedo attacks on enemy destroyers moored alongside, and C. M. B. s 21B and 26B swung the other way, to lob their Stokes bombs over the Mole parapet.

"Gradually the already low visibility closed in. White metallic-tasting clouds of Brock smoke thickened and rose, and as each ship in turn nosed forward into the acrid fog, contact was lost between craft. Enveloping all, the clouds moved with them, renewed by the C. M. B. s, drifted in by the faintly perceptible northerly wind. Now every member of the fleet lived on borrowed time in a world of choking smoke and roaring engines, counting out the seconds until the enemy should react; but for a few more brief, expanding moments the night was theirs alone.

"Then lazily—whitely—a star-shell burst to seaward, making daylight beyond the screen, and searchlights poked inquiring fingers up into the sky.

"The German defenses awoke to danger. It was 11:50 P.M. The smoke was close inshore now, masking everything. Aboard the C. M. B. s an impudent excitement held everyone as the swift craft danced forward and back, in and out of concealment of their own smoke screens, inviting attack. . . . Then, with a baying roar which split open the last silence of the night, shore batteries fired blind, and heavy shells screamed overhead to plunge harmlessly into the sea far beyond the last units of the approaching fleet.

"Relief washed through the blood: at last there could be no more turning back.

"At 11:56—the most crucial moment of the approach—as though it grudged the help it had given and now sought satanically to undo it, the wind changed. During a few incredible seconds the night which had been black and dense turned greyly opaque, then crystal clear as the smoke moved solidly north. Metal tore up the surface of the water around the revealed *C. M. B. s*, the *M. L. s*, and the plunging destroyers as they circled back, smoke pouring from stacks, exhausts and canisters in an attempt to repair the gaps torn by the treacherous wind.

"Then, less than a quarter of a mile from the Mole end, shoulder-ing aside the remnants of the fog like a bull terrier coming out of long grass, the *Vindictive* suddenly appeared. She seemed to pause for a split second just clear of the receding cloud and blackly silhouetted against its now silvered screen; then on she came, gathering speed and weight for the attack.

"But however fast she moved, she had at least four minutes in the open sights of the Mole Extension guns. There were six of these— four 105-mm. and two 88-mm.—and at that range they could hardly miss. To those who watched it seemed that the whole operation was doomed. *Vindictive* could never reach the Mole."*

* *Zeebrugge,* pp. 86, 87.

ZEEBRUGGE*

by Barrie Pitt

For Carpenter—until the moment when *Vindictive* had burst from the smoke screen—the night had been one of continuous but expected strain and responsibility, coupled with a curious lack of excitement. Even when his ship entered the Brock smoke and visibility was cut to a few feet so that he could not see even the forecastle, there was no sudden jab of anxiety—certainly nothing of panic. Rosoman's voice came regularly and imperturbably every minute through the voice pipe from the conning-tower under the bridge, with the arranged routine question—"Are you all right, sir?" —and in the *Flammenwerfer* hut at the port end of the forebridge which gave an excellent view of the ship from bow nearly to stern, Carpenter could take due satisfaction from the smooth precision with which they had proceeded so far and which now would surely take them to a perfect landfall on the Mole.

There had been no shattering explosions to tell of shallow undiscovered mines or forewarn the enemy; no ominous shuddering of keelson over unknown and treacherous shoal. Perfect planning had been rewarded: faith had been justified.

Then in a second the whole position changed.

From being a potent hidden aggressor, *Vindictive* was stripped of her cloak and advantage by the wind, and reduced to a looming target beneath heavy guns. In the moment of revelation two thoughts exploded together in Carpenter's brain: first, their position,

* From *Zeebrugge*, published by Ballantine Books. Chapters 6, 7, 8 and 9 have been slightly condensed.

course and speed were exactly right, and second, unless he altered all three very quickly his ship would be reduced to a drifting hulk in a matter of minutes.

Years of training as a professional officer in a proud Navy told: with the promptness of a reflex action and the exactitude of a modern calculating machine he gave orders to conning-tower and engine-room which would close ship to Mole at a different angle and at full speed; then as *Vindictive* swung to starboard and the whole length of the Mole extension came into view, he waited, poised and watchful, for the inevitable. Deliberately the British guns remained silent until discovery was certain: his ship vibrated under him with the increased power.

There was a void in time while all aboard held their breath, then six yellow-white flowers bloomed at regular intervals along the Mole extension and the night was filled with screaming metal as every gun in *Vindictive*'s foretop and port battery replied. Infernal clangor stunned the senses—but the ship held course.

Shell after shell hurtled across the rapidly-narrowing gap between the ship and the Mole, and as she swung in on her new course, she presented to the German gunners a target which grew in size until it was half the length of the extension from which they fired, and nearly twice the height—it was literally true that they could not miss her. *Vindictive* was perhaps two hundred yards from the eastern-most gun when fire was opened on her and by the time she was abreast of number 6 at the western end, the range was down to fifty yards: heavy shell thudded into her, machine gun and rifle bullets streamed over like a driven cloud.

But still she steamed doggedly on, flames now shooting from her torn funnels, sparks and glowing steel fragments cascading from her upper works.

And now she had closed almost to safety—for this was the secret with which Carpenter had defeated the Mole artillerymen: this and their own lack of cool thought. The Germans were so sure that *Vindictive* was in their power that they had fired without pattern or plan, rightly certain that they could not miss. Every shell, every bullet, every bomb had hit her, but the targets had not been selective: men had died—but not the ship. Neither boilers nor steering gear were damaged during the first crucial hundred yards of closing spurt—and after that, every yard gained took them closer under the parapet until *Vindictive's* vitals were protected by the Mole itself. Her upper works were in ribbons, but she was still seaworthy—and now she was reaching the area where the Mole guns tended to mask each other.

She bumped against the Mole one minute late—at 0001 on St. George's Day.

But if *Vindictive* was only one minute late, she was sadly out of position. She was also rolling from side to side like a dinghy in a liner's wash, and every roll did further damage to the essential landing-brows. Her speed through shallowing water had built up an enormous surge, now trapped between her side and the concrete Mole, and thrashing to burst free. Up and down the waters leaped, forced up by the following undercurrent, dropping back into the void left as the surge bounced away from the base of the Mole; oiling up and spewing out again as *Vindictive* bucked and reared in the turmoil.

In an endeavor to edge back towards the correct position—for their speed had taken them far past the fortified zone at the Mole end—Carpenter rang engines astern. The huge screws churned, *Vindictive* rocked sideways like a baby's cradle, and anchor derricks and gangways ground themselves to pieces on the parapet. Carpenter could see over the top now, and identified a long, low shadow as number 3 shed. They were nearly a quarter of a mile too far westward, but time was pressing and the landing parties must go ashore. He ordered the starboard anchor to be let go and held the ship steady by alternately reversing engines until it grappled. By now the din had risen in a crescendo and he could not be certain that his orders had reached the cable-party through the voice-pipe. He had heard no reply from them and the ship still hung loose in the maelstrom. He ordered Rosoman below to investigate. Eastlake, in the hut with him, gave orders to switch on the flamethrower but just at that moment a piece of shrapnel neatly sliced off the nozzle: the lives of everyone in the immediate vicinity were only saved by the fact that the pipes bringing up fuel for the dreadful weapon had already been cut by shellfire.

Then news came from the cable-deck. The starboard anchor had been let go but was unaccountably jammed and nothing could budge it. Carpenter ordered the port anchor to be dropped at the foot of the wall, and rang the engines astern again until a hundred yards of cable had been veered out. When the cable was snubbed, *Vindictive* brought up sharp and swung away from the Mole. With helm to starboard she went in again, but her bows were now so tight to the Mole that her stern jutted clear and the remaining gangways failed to reach the parapet-top. Helm amidships put the ship parallel but with the gap so wide that the bows wouldn't reach at all—and with the helm to port she swung far out again. Every enemy gun within two miles had now found *Vindictive* and was endeavoring to hit her. Above the level of the parapet-top she was like a sieve, and from the hellish din she might have been trapped in the heart of a gigantic thunderstorm.

Then *Iris* chugged sedately along her starboard flank, and *Daffodil* arrived. The tow had parted nearly an hour previously and only by cutting a corner and flogging engines to bursting-point had they arrived now. An unlucky shot had hit *Daffodil*'s bridge and her captain was wounded in the head and half blind. Nevertheless, he put her blunt nose expertly against *Vindictive*'s starboard beam, and pinned her bodily to the Mole so that at last the two remaining serviceable gangways could be dropped on to the parapet. The landing parties came out from below *Vindictive*'s false deck and stormed across them.

These assault parties were now all led by the junior officers—for one simple and tragic reason. The men who had organized and trained them were dead, shot down as they stood waiting in too-exposed positions for the moment of attack.

One detachment commander alone remained—Lieutenant-Commander Bryan Adams—and he was the first man on the Mole, leading his Bluejackets of 'A' Company across a shuddering, heaving plank which rose and fell several feet at one end with the rocking of the ship, while the outboard end sawed back and forth across the parapet and frequently came near to sliding off and precipitating everyone thirty feet down towards certain death. The first arrivals set about securing the Mole anchors of the assault craft. Incredibly, despite the hail of fire which swept flatly over their heads, the Mole appeared deserted.

A hundred yards further west, the officers leading 'D' Bluejacket Company and 'A' Company of the Royal Marines were facing similar troubles. *Iris*, too, was rocking through nightmare angles; in addition the scaling ladders were too short. Lieutenant Claude Hawkins, R. N., balanced himself on the top of one of them—held upright by his men—grabbed the parapet-top as he swayed towards it, pulled himself up and scrambled astride until he could turn and secure the ladder. Enemy soldiers immediately attacked him and he was last seen defending himself with his revolver. In an endeavor to succeed where Hawkins had failed, Lieutenant-Commander G. N. Bradford climbed the port anchor derrick, judged his moment perfectly and jumped the gap, carrying the grappling-anchor with him. As he hooked it into position a stream of machine-gun bullets lifted him off the parapet-top and dropped him between *Iris* and the Mole—and with the deep loyalty of the Service, Petty Officer Hallihan gave his life trying to recover his body.

To the east, the Mole defenders were loath to approach *Vindictive* too closely. The fighting foretop was above the parapet and, despite the fact that it was now the principal target for enemy hostility, was still pouring out an accurate fire at every sign of life on the Mole itself and on the German destroyers which could now be seen moored on the inner side. The foretop was commanded by Lieutenant C. Rigby, R. M. A., Commander Osborne having turned it over to him when he went below to supervise the laying and firing of the remaining howitzers.

Rigby's instructions were to cover the landing party. He and his men engaged every enemy gun within range, switching targets continually, pinning the Germans down and destroying strongpoints: it was undoubtedly due to their efforts that for the first few minutes Adams and his men of 'A' Company were virtually undisturbed. Then two heavy shells crashed in and the foretop was reduced in a second to a tangled nest of smoking guns, exploding ammunition and blood-soaked, writhing bodies. From this chaos, one grimfaced, blackened, lantern-jawed figure clawed his way back to the rail, found a workable Lewis-gun, mounted it and took up the fight again: enemy machine gunners grown too presumptuous in the brief pause leaped back for cover and died if their reflexes were slow. Sergeant Norman Augustus Finch was demonstrating an essential indestructibility—even when another heavy shell blew his gun back off the rail on top of him and completed the wreck of the foretop, he retained sufficient hold on life and strength to find and carry the only other still-breathing occupant down tattered ladders and along crowded mess-decks to the sick bay. There he collapsed from his own wounds.

Meanwhile Wing-Commander Brock had decided that the time had come for him to collect his reward for the months of unremitting work and brilliant inventiveness. He had been somewhat disappointed that *Vindictive* had brought up so far from the Mole guns, for he had thus been unable to prove his assertion that his flamethrowers would deal with the German gunners unaided. Even more disappointing was the fact that when at last he had tried to switch on, all that happened was that thick and extremely inflammable oil flooded over the decks due to shrapnel smashing the ignition apparatus at the crucial moment. But that was now in the past: he had dealt effectively with the results and it was time for him to put a few of his other ideas into operation. There were some new phosphorus grenades he particularly wanted to see in action and there was also that matter of the sound-ranging apparatus on the Mole to investigate.

Handing over command of the pyrotechnics on board *Vindictive* to his chief assistant Graham Hewlett, and accompanied by one of his air-mechanics, Brock ran quickly over the plunging gangway and joined Adams on the Mole.

By now attempts to fix the grappling-irons had been abandoned. Despite several men sitting on top of the parapet (just the place in a night attack), despite also Rosoman's attempt to emulate Bradford's feat by climbing up the derrick, the grappling-anchors had proved too heavy to maneuver by hand, and eventually the foremost hoisting davit had been smashed against the Mole by one of *Vindictive*'s wilder lurches, and the steel prongs crashed down into the sea.

However, no further time could be spared, for the allocated duty for Adams and his men was to destroy the Mole Extension guns before the blockships arrived. It had been planned that they should be landed right on top of them, but they now had to make a 250-yard advance before they even reached their objective. The survivors of Adams's own company (half of them had become casualties on *Vindictive*) and some men of 'B' Company had now reached the Mole, and he led them swiftly eastward towards the guns. Forty yards past the stern of *Vindictive* they found a concrete observation post with what appeared to be a range-finding system rigged above it, and with the intense satisfaction of a man pursuing his hobby despite all minor distractions, Brock went forward to investigate. He allowed himself to be restrained long enough for a hand-grenade to be tossed in, then vanished through the entrance producing spanners and wrenches from his pockets with something of the air of an aggressive conjurer.

There was an iron ladder abreast of the concrete post and Adams sent some men down it to deal with enemy soldiers who were trying to escape from quarters below to the dubious security of the destroyers moored on the far side of the Mole. Some men he prudently left to guard the top of the ladder, then led the remainder in a rush further along the road towards the Mole guns: they were now reaching the fortified zone at the end of the Mole proper, which it had been intended to attack from inside.

He and his party were subject to heavy fire. In addition to the illumination supplied by explosions, star-shell and flares, one of the pyrotechnic party was firing off rockets through *Vindictive*'s stern portholes in order to silhouette the lighthouse for the approaching blockships. These burst brilliantly above the Mole—and the Bluejacket assault party advancing along the parapet roadway were as easy to spot as the targets in a well lighted shooting-gallery.

From behind constructed stone trenches machine-gun fire swept the roadway, a small party of the enemy who had been courageously advancing to meet them fired a concerted and well placed volley before retreating rapidly, and the machine guns and pom-poms of the enemy destroyers were now released for wider action by the elimination of Sergeant Finch from the contest. Adams's party dwindled sadly. At last the few gallant survivors went to ground and Adams himself returned to find reinforcements.

He found three new arrivals at the concrete post—Petty Officer Antell and two Lewis-gunners. Antell was in considerable pain due to multiple wounds of hand and arm and was firmly ordered back aboard the *Vindictive*. The two Lewis-gunners went forward, and in their advance were joined and then led by the huge, slightly-swaying figure of Lieutenant-Commander Harrison who had recovered consciousness aboard *Vindictive,* hurled himself across the gangway before anyone could stop him, and despite the physical torture and mental perplexity caused by a badly-fractured jaw and concussion, now arrived to take firm control. He listened to Adams's report, ordered him back to request Royal Marine reinforcements, then went forward and joined the remnants of the Bluejacket assault force.

He had successfully led too many assaults to allow his men to be trapped into a static position, and he had his party on their feet and racing forward again in a matter of seconds. Harrison had spirit and a good sense of tactics; unfortunately he lacked hitting-power and light automatic support fire. True, Able Seaman McKenzie was at his side, but a Lewis-gun is unhandy and its weight with sufficient ammunition to be really effective is crippling. Inevitably the rush lost momentum as withering fire cut down the numbers. They were on a brilliantly lit stage, and far enough from their objective for riflemen to take deliberate aim. At last Harrison fell, and McKenzie and Able Seaman Eaves went to ground—both badly-wounded but still determined.

McKenzie got his sights on the trench positions and swept up and down them until running figures burst from cover, then he shot them down as they ran. Eaves managed to hoist Harrison's body across his shoulders and tried to run back with him, but was repeatedly hit himself until he too fell, some way from the look-out post. He was eventually taken prisoner.

McKenzie managed to crawl back—still lugging his Lewis-gun, despite his wounds.

In the meantime, westward and abreast of the *Vindictive*, the Marines were in action. Their original tasks had been to drop down on top of the fortified zone at the far end of the Mole proper and from there cover the Bluejackets wrecking the Mole guns, then to advance westward out through the fortifications and down the Mole as protection for the demolition parties blowing up the sheds, cranes and all other dock installations within reach. Once more the position of the *Vindictive* complicated the tasks and a desperate shortage of manpower made matters worse. Nearly seven hundred officers and men of the R. M. L. I. had sailed with the convoy; of these the whole of 'A' company were virtually marooned in the *Iris,* and of the main body who had travelled in *Vindictive* far too many had died on the decks or been shot down as they debouched on to the Mole. Incredibly, during the entire debarkation, no one had been killed crossing the gangways, either by enemy fire or the far greater danger of toppling off the see-sawing planks and falling between ship and Mole.

Colonel Elliot and Major Cordner were dead, and command now devolved upon Major Weller, commanding 'C' Company from Plymouth. He decided that he must first secure the landward approaches to ensure that the essential line of communication and retreat to *Vindictive* remained open.

He sent Lieutenant T. F. V. Cooke with the men of number 5 platoon westwards along the parapet roadway, where they eventually reached a position some two hundred yards in front of *Vindictive*. They had silenced a party of snipers who had been only too effective from the end of number 2 shed, and now they provided covering fire for men of 9 and 10 platoons who had lowered themselves by ropes down on to the Mole proper. Under the leadership of Lieutenant C. D. R. Lamplough, these latter crossed the Mole in a storming rush, formed a strongpoint at the western end of number 3 shed which commanded the land approaches, thus securing the first objective and establishing a firm base for a possible assault on one of the enemy destroyers.

Now number 7 platoon under Lieutenant H. A. P. de Berry descended scaling ladders placed in position by Sergeant-Major Thatcher, joined Lamplough's men, and under over-all command of Captain Bamford began to form up for the second objective—an attack on the fortified position at the Mole end. By now Cooke's advance party had become the focus of enemy machine guns further on down the Mole and like the Bluejacket party to the east, were suffering dreadfully from the lack of cover. Cooke himself was hit twice and eventually lost consciousness, and Private Press, himself wounded, carried him back to the ship. With Lamplough's party now in position, there was no further necessity for this advance post. The survivors of number 5 platoon carried their wounded back to safety and those fit enough to do so dropped down to join the assembling forces under Bamford.

Then Adams arrived at the gangways with the request from Harrison that Weller send reinforcements east along the parapet wall. He sent Lieutenant Underhill with men of numbers 11 and 12 platoons, but time was passing too quickly and the blockships were drawing closer and closer to the still all-powerful Mole batteries. The din, the smoke, the confusion rose to a crescendo and gradually the initiative passed to the defenders as the element of surprise dissipated and the German gunners brought more and more of their emplaced guns into action. Ashore, military commanders had by now made up their minds as to the pattern of the attack, and were issuing their orders. Grey-clad figures raced through the narrow Zeebrugge streets buckling on their equipment.

In addition to the inferno actually raging on the Mole and around the assault craft, the 15-inch shells of the monitors *Erebus* and *Terror* were landing with thunderous regularity only a mile or so away, and shore batteries were replying. To this uproar *Vindictive's* 11-inch howitzer was adding its not inconsiderable quota, and her 6-inch guns were reaching a stage of near-incandescence. It is thus somewhat doubtful if the urgent requests for reinforcements yelled down the lighthouse telephone by the frantic German guard commander, or his sudden, startled announcement of the appearance of the blockships, were either heard or understood by his superior inshore barracks.

However, the Mole gunners had also seen the blockships, and the Extension guns were swinging around to command the inner approaches and blow these new arrivals out of the water. As further reinforcement, a half-battalion of German infantry were converging on the shore end of the Mole, and its leading company—on bicycles —were already pedalling furiously along the causeway.

On the Mole, the Marines and Bluejackets of the assault force were now hemmed in on three sides: they could not burrow for protection into the solid concrete and it was becoming increasingly dangerous to raise one's head sufficiently to peer along the weapon sights. They clung to the wet shadows and fought bitterly.

The sides of the trap closed in.

◆ ◆ ◆

According to the prepared timetable, the three vessels of Unit K— the two submarines and their attendant picket-boat—should have slipped their tows 56 minutes after passing 'G' buoy and after a brief pause for taking up station, shaped their own course for the viaduct.

When the time came, however, *C 3*—having followed the instructions thus far to the letter—found that her two consorts were no longer in company. Once her own towing hawser had been cleared from the destroyer *Trident* and that vessel had disappeared into the night, *C 3* found herself vastly alone on a gently heaving sea. This condition would be no matter for concern for submariners in normal circumstances but with the particular task which now lay ahead of *C 3* the absence of her sister-ship was disturbing and that of the picket-boat critical.

At midnight, they were one and a half miles from the viaduct, and with a silent tribute to his brother's planning and accuracy Dick Sandford ordered a change of course to approach the steel bridge at right angle to its length. There was the devil's own thunder going on two miles to port, and he could picture the gunners firing like shelling peas. No one had spotted *C 3* as yet—but how long would that last?

With a crack of astonishing violence a star-shell burst immediately overhead, then shore batteries opened fire. Fifty yards to port grey geysers mushroomed from the sea. *C 3* rolled, but kept course. Two more geysers erupted and the shell-scream followed overhead—then surprisingly, the firing ceased. Leading Seaman Cleaver turned on the smoke canisters, but the wind drifted the clouds offshore and slightly ahead, so it failed to hide them, screening the viaduct instead. Cleaver turned the smoke off again and came back aft to the bridge.

On they ran, knowing they were watched, waiting for the shellfire mysteriously withheld. Then a flare burst somewhere just above the water inside the sweep of the Mole, and the whole viaduct was blackly silhouetted against its yellow glow. The piers rose slim but solid, the braces were a web between them, the palisade a wide black margin above. There was movement in the gaps in the bottom quarter of the margin, and an unrecognizable fuzziness among the piers just below it. Then the flare died.

C 3 ran on towards a viaduct which was beginning to loom up.

Two searchlights stabbed down upon them, one from each end of the viaduct, then a third joined in from somewhere ashore near the root of the causeway. On the conning tower, the hard, white light baked the remaining moisture from tongues and mouths gone dry, and salt crystallized on lips and in the furrows above the eyes.

And still the enemy held their fire.

Sandford made the last alteration of course exactly 100 yards from the viaduct. The piers could be seen clearly and the caverns between, with the waiting foe above. As the submarine swung slightly to port, aiming precisely between two of the piers, a thought flickered for a second at the back of Sandford's mind—but was gone before he could catch it.

The sands were running out now and the men must not be trapped below. Sandford ordered them up and they stood crowded together on the bridge, staring ahead as the steel trap loomed higher before them. The gap narrowed. Fascinated, they watched and forgot to breathe.

The *C 3* swept on into black shadow beneath the steel platform, rocked up for'ard like a bucking horse, and with the rasping clangor of ten million files on sheet steel flung herself over and on to the bridgework of girders at nine and a half knots. She only stopped when her conning-tower smashed against solid steel above. All around her cross-braces snapped and molten globules from the scarified hull hissed in the water below. She had ridden up two feet: the floor of the viaduct was less than twelve feet above the steel casing of her bows, which jutted just beyond the far side of the viaduct into the Mole harbor.

Five tons of Amatol rested centrally under the floor of the viaduct.

And still—for the moment—the only signs of life from the enemy close around were the sounds of shouting, of boots on steel plates and of laughter. The Germans were under the impression that the *C 3*—apparently ignorant of the narrow spaces between the viaduct piers—had been attempting to run under the viaduct and into the Mole harbor. Now, they believed, they had caught a British submarine, possibly slightly damaged but basically intact.

And having caught the submarine, they had no intention of allowing the crew to escape.

While Sandford remained on the conning tower to fire the fuse, the others scrambled fore and aft to release the motor-skiff hanging from spars lashed horizontally across the tower. There had been two of these, one each side, but the port one had gone—where and how? The lashings were slipped, the skiff dropped away and as the ropes ran out it bumped down on the *C 3*'s bulges and slid outwards into the water. As the crew piled aboard, there was a sharp and ominous clank, but in the flurry no one noticed.

Then Sandford ripped clean the end of the cordtex, struck it— setting off the long, twelve-minute time fuse—came down off the conning tower like a sack of coals into the skiff. With a lurch the tiny craft yawed clear of the *C 3* and wallowed deep-loaded out from the shadows into the open. Immediately there were screams of anger and barked orders, drowned by the hard stammer of machine guns and the louder, vicious crack of rifles. Flame stabbed down upon the skiff from less than twenty feet above and splinters whipped up from the flimsy hull. The searchlights burst alight again, their beams pinning the skiff down on the sea for the defenders to riddle with fire; lead shrilled close between tight-packed men and smacked through wood, and the sea jetted inboard through a dozen holes.

Stoker Henry Cullis Bindall bit back a grunt and grabbed at the gunwale, and as Sandford's hand went out to help him it seemed to explode in blood. The water slopping in the bottom of the skiff stained bright red, but it lessened in volume as the specially installed pump sprang to life and vomited it over the side again.

The skiff-motor, although operating, whirred uselessly: as the skiff had hit the water, the propeller had smacked hard against the C 3's exhaust and the shaft had snapped. Allan Roxburgh and Petty Officer Harner each manned one of the skiff's diminutive oars but Harner was hit, gasped and rolled sideways off the thwart. The skiff was still only a few yards from the C 3, with a westward set of tide trying to sweep her back under the viaduct, three men out of six were already wounded, and the fire concentrated on them was as thick as raindrops in a summer shower.

As Leading Seaman Cleaver flung himself down in Harner's place, Dick Sandford was hit again and more seriously. He just controlled a convulsive leap which might have capsized the rolling skiff, then gripped his thigh in order to staunch the spurting blood. His face was already white from the tearing agony of a hand wound and the faces of the others blanched at the red torrent which first drenched and then matted his trouser-leg. He rolled away from the tiller and John Howell-Price took command.

Gradually Cleaver and Roxburgh pulled the wallowing, stricken craft out into the waters clear of the Mole; the tide pressed inexorably against them, the oars were trifling, pom-poms from the shore added heavier metal to the leaden hail and inboard the prospect was heartbreaking.

Shortly thereafter C 3 blew up.

The skiff was abreast of the end of the viaduct now, having been pulled northwestwards by the tide: C 3 lay not more than two hundred yards from her—probably much less—and yet such was the enveloping thunder of the battle that the explosion was more seen than heard. . . . a sudden yellow-white light flooded and consolidated the stark details of the scene. From the viaduct a pillar of flame mounted higher and higher into the air and as it rose, the dark outlines of flying girders, railway sleepers, guns and twisted bodies were silhouetted against its brilliance.

Leading Seaman Potter, from his vantage point in the conning tower of *Iphigenia* as she swung in past the lighthouse and shaped course for the canal entrance, noticed other, vaguely unbelievable shapes. Narrow-rimmed wheels spun out across the water, familiarly-bent metal tubes and frames showed momentarily against the white screen: then, perfect and unmistakable, a complete bicycle, its rider still gripping the handlebars in a catalepsy of fright and astonishment, rode high into the air, somersaulted completely, and crashed down into the sea.

The rear files of the bicycle company, unable to stop in time, shot over the edge of the hole which had so unexpectedly opened in front of them and met their deaths in the sea or among the tangled web of steel girders; but theirs were the only bodies ever found, for the majority of the company was blown to pieces. The reinforcements would not now arrive: the pressure on the Marine and Bluejacket assault parties—if not relieved—could not be increased. Communication with the shore was cut.

In the tiny motor-skiff, relief and joy drained the remaining strength from nerves and muscles already over-burdened. Not that it mattered—the searchlights had gone out and the fire bearing on them was lighter: the gunners behind the shore pom-poms were too much shaken by what they had just witnessed to maintain their fire on a target which was anyway no longer illuminated for them.

◆ ◆ ◆

With the viaduct blown and the blockships well on their way in, Carpenter proceeded to tour *Vindictive*. Although he was as yet completely unscathed, bearing apparently a charmed life, his uniform and accouterments bore curious marks. The peak of his cap looked rather as though the mice had been at it and a large hole gaped at the lower left hand corner of his cap badge. It was balanced by another similar hole at the back of the cap, through which some of the lining protruded and there was also an unseamanlike ridge across the crown. His binocular case slung behind him was not likely to be used again either, for shrapnel had passed through its length and his searchlight and smoke goggles hung with shattered lenses from the straps.

As he descended from the bridge, one of the first sights to meet his eyes was that of Lieutenant E. Hilton Young, R. N. V. R. , in his trousers and shirtsleeves, hatless, his right arm bandaged and a large cigar jutting imperturbably from a widely grinning face. He was supervising the work of the 6-inch port battery and had little time to waste on social pleasantries, even with his captain.

"Got one in the arm!" he announced shortly, in reply to inquiries, and before solicitude could suggest his removal to safer spheres, added importantly, "Ah, well. Got to get on, y'know!"

Later Hilton Young decided he'd better check on the Mole position. He was seen standing at the head of one of the gangways, still in his shirtsleeves, still hatless, still blandly puffing at his cigar as he gently rose and fell with the sea-sawing of the plank, gazing appreciatively at the scenes of bitter fighting around him.

Carpenter's progress bore similarities to Dante's experiences in the Inferno. An angry and continual clangor rang from the funnels as shot reduced them to ribbons and ricocheted viciously between the upper works; white-hot shrapnel rained down on the decks, occasionally supplemented by a grey, vicious hail as low-fired shells smashed off pieces of the concrete parapet before howling flatly away into the darkness. *Vindictive* replied. Her mortars threw their screaming bombs over the Mole with regular explosions, the deck Lewis-guns drummed and chattered unceasingly, the howitzers boomed and cracked, huge rockets still whistled alarmingly from the stern ports.

Below decks, if the noise was slightly less the sights and smells were stupefying. Over all, the sickly reek of ether pervaded with its sinister connotations, penetrating even the thick heaviness of exploding cordite and that basic naval odor of tar and corticene. Men lay everywhere—in dark corners if they were dying and could reach them, propped against bulkheads, packing the mess-decks; the walking-wounded helped and consoled the bad cases, the stretcher bearers hurried to and fro, the excess crew who had come for the trip paid their passage a thousand times over in willing service. The surgeons sweated and snipped, the sick-bay attendants swabbed and bandaged.

And everyone wanted news of the battle.

"Have we won, sir? What's happening? Where are the block-ships?"—the questions came to Carpenter from all sides as he made his way along, cheerful, encouraging, assured.

"That'll fix 'em, sir, won't it?" whispered one youngster propped in a corner, a smile of contentment spreading over his face as Carpenter told of probable success. The boy's head fell back against the steel bulkhead but the smile remained. "Blast 'em . . ." he whispered as he died.

In the engine room harsh yellow light glinted through the blue and black jungle and the air was thick with grease and sweat and heat, and the faint sourness of men controlling fear with their minds while denied the blessed release of action. Engine-room and stoke-hold men know too much of death; they have time to think and everywhere they look they see the pipes of scalding steam, the boilers, the fires, the jetting oil; around them steel flails sob as they plunge and rise again.

To add to the closed, trapped atmosphere, ammonia fumes had leaked into the engine room and stokeholds shortly before the arrival at the Mole. During those last few minutes of the approach, while all hell raged outside and the crew expected to see gaping holes torn in the hull, they were forced to endure the extra heat and confinement of goggles and respirators. A few shell-splinters had fallen through but that was all; torpedo-netting piled on the gratings kept out the steel rain from the funnels. But the din had penetrated and told its own story; now they all crowded around Carpenter and found release for tense nerves in bursting cheers and hammerblows on shipmates' shoulders.

Carpenter returned to the bridge. There was little change in conditions—if anything, enemy fire on the upper works had increased. Pom-poms on one of the destroyers opposite were still proving a nuisance, although Lamplough and his Marines of 9 and 10 platoons had attacked the other with hand grenade and rifle, killing several of the crew and silencing the automatic fire.

Further eastward on the Mole, the main assault was going forward but the barbed-wire entanglements precluded a fast sweeping rush against emplaced automatic fire, and the foremost destroyer could still enfilade the flank of an attack. Small parties of Marines worked their way forward under the cover of rail trucks, and bitter, isolated fighting took place across the width of the concrete arena. Exploding shell filled the air with cordite fumes, and metal fragments pockmarked the stone, too often splattering crimson on the grey-white surface.

From the *Vindictive*, Carpenter watched the progress of the action. The blockships had gone past the lighthouse nearly half an hour before—at 0020—and by now they were undoubtedly resting on the sea-bed somewhere—it was to be hoped in the right place. Whether they had been successful or not, their crews by now must, with sheer passage of time, be either lost or rescued; *Vindictive*'s job was surely done, for at no time had there been anything but the heaviest possible concentration of fire upon her, and the diversion she had caused could not have been greater.

The assault parties had been promised twenty minutes' notice of *Vindictive*'s withdrawal and as the last permitted time for leaving the Mole was 0120, the retirement signal must be given in ten minutes anyway. Was there anything to be gained by staying until the last possible moment? Without definite information regarding the blockships he could not be absolutely certain, but one fact was evident; *Vindictive* was held in position solely by *Daffodil*'s efforts and if anything happened to the ferryboat, then *Vindictive* would swing away and the storming parties on the Mole, unable to return aboard, would be lost. *Daffodil*'s position was far more vulnerable than *Vindictive*'s for she was further out, and her vitals were not screened by the mass of the Mole. Moreover Carpenter was beginning to think that some of the damage his ship was suffering came from the heavy shore batteries around Blankenberge—to which *Vindictive* was tangentially unscreened and *Daffodil* thus completely exposed.

The responsibility was Carpenter's and he had no wish to share it: after a brief talk with Rosoman to ensure he had overlooked no vital point, he ordered the retirement signal sounded. As all horns and sirens aboard *Vindictive* had long since been shot away, orders were passed to *Daffodil* to use her horn. There was a half-anxious, half-comic interval while the ferry-boat's pipe spluttered and gurgled, drenching the neighbourhood with rusty foam, black-clotted sludge and luke-warm bathwater, then a low moan became audible, gradually increasing in volume as it rose up the scale until it was emitting a workmanlike, earsplitting yowl. This was repeated several times and retirement began.

It was fraught with difficulty and danger. There seems to be a deep atavistic streak in the British nature which will not allow its warriors to leave their dead on the field: no matter what the price demanded in life and limb, they bring their dead home.

Zeebrugge provided several almost unbelievable examples of this. Of the entire convoy strength, numbering nearly seventeen hundred men, only 49 failed to return to Dover and of these the sea had claimed some and others were prisoners for the very reason that they had refused to leave dangerously and often fatally wounded comrades. This is possibly absurd and probably wasteful: but it has grandeur.

Covered by Lewis-guns on the parapet and the Marines of number 9 platoon holding a tiny perimeter, the sound men on the Mole crossed in spasmodic rushes to the scaling-ladders and ropes, and pulled themselves the 16 feet up to the top—with their backs to an angry enemy and the weight of a wounded or dead comrade across their shoulders: man's spirit is his strength, and in exaltation or compassion his strength is limitless.

In a steady stream the men came down the gangways, often to lay down their burdens and return again to the raging battle to bring in another of the wounded. Padre Peshall's score will never be known —like Harrison he had played football and combined immense physical strength with his devotion.

With the signs of retreat obvious to the enemy. German fire and fury redoubled—it is always easier to be brave against a retreating foe, and indeed, then he is most vulnerable: Carpenter knew that the most dangerous time lay ahead. Since his return to the bridge he had already twice avoided death himself by only millimeters—once when a shell set fire to a stack of boxes containing fused Stokes bombs, and once by direct shellfire. In the first instance, the chief quartermaster, Petty Officer Youlton, dealt with the danger by stentorian orders to everyone in the vicinity (regardless of rank) to remove themselves, while he himself smashed open the burning boxes on the deck and stamped on the contents until they were extinguished. When the fire broke out again later, the position resolved itself into simple factors—which would last longer, the fire or Youlton's boots? It was a near thing, but Youlton received his Conspicuous Gallantry Medal in hospital for reasons other than burnt feet—he was too closely connected with Carpenter's second narrow escape.

Nearly fifteen minutes had passed since the retirement signal, and the stream of survivors from the Mole was thinning. Lieutenant-Commander Rosoman, Carpenter and Youlton were standing outside the conning tower on the alert for the first possible moment of safe withdrawal, when a shell exploded just behind them. Rosoman fell with shrapnel through both legs, Youlton's arm was shattered and Carpenter received a deep flesh-wound in the left shoulder: he was remarkably lucky.

A few minutes later, he received assurances that the last of the attack force had come aboard, but to make doubly certain he went to look for himself. How he avoided death at that moment can never be known; he stood on the foremost gangway, solitary and unmoving, and surveyed the deserted scene. No man moved on the wide expanse of the Mole, but from its edges destruction came at him from every angle—and missed. Satisfied, he returned to the bridge and issued his orders.

Daffodil reversed engines and allowed *Vindictive* to swing away from the Mole, and a tow was passed to her from the bigger ship's bows. As *Daffodil* tugged the tow came taut—and snapped almost immediately. But *Vindictive's* head had started to swing. It was enough: the anchor cable was slipped and Carpenter rang his engines full ahead. Gathering way, the big ship moved along the Mole and as her helm was put over, the last trick in the bag was pulled. Even denser clouds of Brock smoke than had been used in the approach belched from stacks and canisters aboard *Vindictive* and the two ferryboats. As the Germans prepared for a last gigantic onslaught which would wipe out the force which had inflicted this humiliation upon them their quarry disappeared completely from view in a screen as impenetrable and as extensive as the Mole itself —and this time the wind remained constant, gently blowing the screen after the retreating ships and warmly protecting them.

The Brock smoke had given them just sufficient cover to get in: now it was undoubtedly saving them all on the way out—but its resourceful and accomplished creator was missing. For some months afterwards there were persistent stories that Brock had been seen leading a party of Marines in the attack on German gun-positions, that he had attacked the enemy with his bare fists when his revolver was empty, that he removed breeches from the guns himself and flung them into the sea, that he had been wounded and that two Marines had refused to leave him and had last been seen locked in fierce hand-to-hand combat with enemy soldiers above his recumbent form.

The truth has never been established—the last certainty was his disappearance into the observation post, intent on solving the mysteries of German sound-ranging methods. Possessed of a brilliant, questing brain, a charming and affectionate personality, Brock was lost at the height of his powers. The more one reads his notes, his letters, and the opinions of those who knew him best, the greater certainty arises on one point: had he known of his fate beforehand, he would still have gone gaily forward to meet it.

So *Vindictive* left the Mole where she had won more glory in an hour than most ships do in their lifetimes. The gangways crashed over the side as they slid from the parapet, for a moment the wreckage fouled the port propeller but it soon cleared, the mainmast-bumpkin hammered the concrete as it carried out its destined duty protecting the screws and, with clear visibility in front and the densest fog behind, the gallant old ship pelted away into the night. Flames streamed from her gaping stacks until she appeared to be on fire, but her boilers pushed her along at a spanking 15 knots: despite her wounds she had every reason to be satisfied with her night's work.

The same, unfortunately, could not be said for all the assault craft. *Daffodil*, of course, had rendered sterling service. Had it not been for the enormous head of pressure which her engineers kept in her boilers, undoubtedly the storming of the Mole could not have taken place—the blockships would have been sunk before they reached the lighthouse. This achievement was even more remarkable in view of the fact that the engine room was holed and two compartments flooded, but Acting Artificer-Engineer Sutton dealt with the situation with cool and deliberate efficiency—and then returned to the hour-long task of keeping the hands of the pressure gauges at a point considerably past the danger line.

Some of the demolition party aboard *Daffodil* managed to climb up over her bows on to *Vindictive* and eventually reach the Mole (some of the explosive charges had been placed in position but were not blown because of the proximity of our own men)—but in the main her value had been as pin to her parent craft. Campbell had shown superb seamanship and was later most deservedly decorated for his bravery—wounded and half-blind, he had refused to leave the bridge until there was no likelihood whatever of accident or misfortune.

But for poor *Iris* it had been a bitter and frustrating night which ended in dire tragedy.

Despite the self-sacrifice of both Hawkins and Bradford, she had been unable to secure herself to the Mole. For a few minutes after

Bradford's death, the anchor he had placed remained in position—but *Iris* was being flung about to a much greater extent even than *Vindictive*, and eventually the cable was either torn or shot away. Suddenly Commander Gibbs found his vessel surging far out from the Mole and swinging like a pendulum at the end of her starboard main anchor-cable which, unlike her parent ship, she had successfully let go upon first arrival.

Gibbs decided that with his scaling ladders broken and enemy personnel directly overhead, there was little chance of landing his Marines over the parapet. With the object, therefore, of landing them across *Vindictive* Gibbs slipped his anchor cable and steamed in a wide circle around the stern of *Daffodil* to come in on *Vindictive*'s quarter. There was unavoidable delay in securing alongside, for the attention of all on board the larger ships was concentrated on the fighting on the Mole, but eventually help was forthcoming.

Hardly was the task completed, however, when on Carpenter's orders *Daffodil* sounded the retirement signal and *Iris* was instructed to cast off and make her way home. Bitter disappointment and frustration was felt by all on board, but a detached observer could with justice have pointed out that at least her casualty list—in numbers—was not excessive: the quality of the gallantry displayed by Bradford, Hawkins and Hallihan was, of course, unmeasurable.

This cold comfort did not last long.

As she turned away northwards she steamed directly under a salvo of falling shot from shore batteries. There was a violent explosion and *Iris* disappeared behind a vast sheet of flame: when next seen she was lurching away to starboard with the port end of the bridge a smashed ruin, and flames shooting up around the conning positions. Aboard, shock from the stunning violence of the disaster held momentary sway, then men rushed up from below to deal with the fire. They were led by Lieutenant Oscar Henderson who brought up hoses to deal with the flames, but after one look at the bridge he decided that his position was up there.

In the shambles of the control stations he found senior officers Gibbs and Eagles mortally wounded, the navigating officer practically unconscious from loss of blood and the quartermaster desperately trying to bring the ship under control while still fighting off the numbing effects of an 11-inch shell's exploding within ten feet of him.

By now the *Iris* was well off course and circling to starboard—straight into the field of fire of the Mole Extension batteries. The German gunners, denied a target larger than a motor launch for the last fifteen minutes, had witnessed the explosion and had had ample time to prepare their reception. As Henderson rallied the quartermaster, and the navigating officer—Lieutenant George Spencer—willed himself back into a state where he could whisper out a course, *Iris* crossed into the zone of the Mole guns' fire. Immediately the waters erupted around her as 105-mm. and 88-mm. shell crashed through her sides and swept her decks. In seconds, her casualty list rocketed from three to one hundred and fifty—and she was still under fire. One fact alone saved her—Spencer had managed to correct the course during the split second before the shells hammered home. Petty Officer David Smith flung over the helm, and staggering under the repeated blows though she was, *Iris* answered. Slowly she swung around north again, and as she did so, *M. L. 558* under command of Lieutenant-Commander Lionel Chappell came sweeping through the point-blank fire, regardless of her own danger, to cover her in smoke.

The Mole guns still blasted, the fire under the bridge was rapidly getting out of hand and *M. L. 558* was just as subject to the law of averages as any other craft—she could not expect to live much longer in those waters. But aft of the main hatches a cursing, bloody-minded Australian was exhibiting typical disregard for enemy intentions. Acting Artificer-Engineer William Henry Edgar, R. A. N., had arrived on the upper deck and was carrying out necessary repairs to the damaged smoke canisters. As *M. L. 558* swung back for yet another trip through the flames of hell, black smoke suddenly jetted from *Iris*'s stern and she vanished behind her own screens.

Those aboard straightened up with a sigh of relief and *Iris* herself seemed to ride a little easier. Then three more shells from the heavy shore batteries crashed through her decks. Chaos was come again: it was incredible that she did not plunge to the bottom like stone.

Possibly her double hull saved her—but she was desperately hurt, and in the tight confines of her decks the slaughter had been appalling. She was by no means out of danger, even under smoke and limping out of range, for there was still a fire roaring away under her bridge. Incredibly, Henderson was still unhurt, Spencer still conscious and David Smith still at the wheel, steering with one hand while he shone a torch on the compass-needle with the other, blinded by the smoke from the flaming ammunition, which was almost as dense as the Brock screen aft.

Smith looked as though he would last some time longer: Spencer must die if the gods willed, but Henderson's duty was now to organize the fire-party. He threw himself down the bridge ladder and ran around to the foredeck. The solitary survivor of his original volunteers from below was already at work—in fact he had hardly stopped since arriving on deck. Able Seaman F. E. M. Lake had been endeavoring to stifle the fire with buckets of sand and he had received a certain amount of aid from an unlikely source—the terrifying explosions of enemy shell around him had shaken apart the ammunition stacks and the blast had partially blown out the flames, enough to give him a fighting chance.

Now, with the aid of Lieutenant Henderson, the remainder of the conflagration was brought under control, and with the type of courage which earned many a George Cross during World War II, Lake set about sorting out live bombs from the debris and hurling them overboard, some of them disappearing into the sea with a puff of steam and an audible hiss. Disregarding the pain from his blistered hands, Lake then joined Henderson who had taken charge on the bridge (Spencer had collapsed at last, and was dying) and relieved Smith at the wheel. Six hours later he was still there, blackened, dead-tired, but unyielding.

He was in good company—six feet away from him was Signalman Tom Bryant, half-sitting, half-lying in the angle of a bulkhead. Bryant had been on the bridge when it was first hit and was one of the wounded who were quickly carried below to the surgeon. Soon after arrival in the makeshift sick bay, however, he learned that he was the only surviving signalman aboard. Ignoring his injuries, he had himself carried up and placed in a position where he could receive and send the vital messages. He lay there in considerable pain—without morphia, and knowing that both his legs were badly shattered—until finally, in the absence of any other form of relief, unconsciousness mercifully overtook him.

In the sick bay below, Captain Frank Pocock, M. D., was faced with a fearful task: over a hundred men needed his urgent attention and he had not one skilled man to help him—his entire staff had been wiped out. It was several hours before any relief arrived—a surgeon from the monitor *Erebus*—and during all that time Pocock worked without a second's break, in appalling conditions, at a task which requires the highest degree of mental and spiritual concentration. He was still at it when *Iris* arrived at Dover at 2:45 P.M. the following afternoon. He had been on his feet at the makeshift operating table for thirteen and a half hours.

◆   ◆   ◆

After zero hour—at 'D' buoy—the blockships had deliberately steamed at a slower speed than the rest of the convoy: they were due to arrive at the end of the Mole twenty minutes after the *Vindictive*, by which time it was thought that the assault diversion would be at its height.

Leading the blockship flotilla was the *Thetis*. At midnight the men on the bridge could hear the opening thunder of the overture but could see little of the fire and fury due to the slowly approaching smoke screen. Not that they were themselves completely out of danger, for the enemy was under the impression that the action on the Mole was merely the forerunner of a large-scale invasion, and heavy guns of the Friedrichsort and Wuerttemberg Batteries were engaged in putting down a wide barrage some three miles out at sea.

The barrage was nearly half a mile deep and through it *Thetis* led her consorts while those on board endeavored to keep in the forefront of their minds the true but unconvincing dictum that for falling shot there is an enormous area of water to hit, and an incredibly small proportionate target deck. When one is standing on that target deck, however, it does not appear so small: they were all glad when eventually they nosed their way into the smoke screen and the world was reduced to five feet square.

On through the smoke the blockships steamed, and as they approached the Mole, the noise of battle grew. Suddenly they were hailed from *M. L. 558* (the same ship which later saved the stricken *Iris*) and the voice of Captain Ralph Collins, commanding the Zeebrugge M. L.s, shouted a distance and bearing. At twenty minutes past midnight, the smoke suddenly thinned and vanished. Directly before Commander Sneyd's eyes appeared the great masonry buttress of the Mole end and the lighthouse above it, all superbly silhouetted against *Vindictive*'s bursting rockets and the startling, yellow glow of the viaduct explosion. Sneyd put his helm hard over and increased speed, signalling to *Intrepid* and *Iphigenia* to do likewise, and swung around into the sweep of the Mole.

Directly ahead of him lay a barge-boom with a gap at the southern end. Shoreward of the gap lay the buoys of the net defense, and some three-quarters of a mile beyond them—through a witches' brew of fire and smoke—lay the canal entrance. On the Mole Extension the German gunners, having failed to sink *Vindictive* at an average distance of a hundred and twenty-five yards, swung around and opened fire on *Thetis* at less than a hundred: they had learned their lesson—gaping holes opened along *Thetis*'s starboard flank and tons of water flooded inboard. Steam, smoke, fire and tumult spread through the riven hull.

The guns on the foredeck answered to the best of their ability, but there were only three of them left aboard, and the targets were legion. One of these was a gun mounted on the outermost barge but suddenly the smoking barrel canted over, water appeared around its base. Before the gun and water-carriage vanished completely, *Thetis* was past and negotiating other difficulties.

Sneyd endeavored to steer his quivering ship into the gap, but *Thetis*, hammered by the impact of shot and caught by a strong east-flowing set of tide, was swept too far to port. She missed the gap and ploughed through the net defense between the two most northerly buoys—tearing the wire mesh to ribbons—and then, carried by her own momentum, plunged on down towards the canal entrance trailing the wreckage behind her. The Germans on the shore could no longer doubt the true nature of the night's attack; abruptly every gun of the shore batteries which would bear, swung around and added its fire to that of the Mole Extension guns. From near at hand two machine guns raked her decks.

Sneyd gradually edged *Thetis* back into the narrow dredged channel which led to the entrance, but the wire nets were wound around the propeller-shafts: the drag of the long length metal trailing behind tugged *Thetis* to port. As her screws checked and threshed, she gradually lost way and sagged back towards the shore. By now steam was jetting blindingly from cut pipes, and smoke and flame erupted solidly from the battered hull. Three hundred yards from the canal entrance, the laboring engines at last brought up solid. Listing with the weight of water in her hold, she grounded on the port side of the main channel.

Still the enemy pumped shell into her, still her guns fired back defiantly. If she would never reach her own intended destination, she had at least attracted sufficient enemy attention upon herself to give her consorts a better chance of reaching theirs. Through the black smoke which engulfed her, a green light shone from her starboard quarter. In obedience to its message *Intrepid* swept by on that side—unhindered by net and undamaged by shellfire.

Intrepid seems almost to have been ignored, so intent were the enemy upon the destruction of Commander Sneyd and his ship—but *Thetis* had now the advantages as well as the disadvantages of being stationary, and her three 6-inch guns were still miraculously intact. The blackened, sweating guncrews fed in ammunition, and pounded away indomitably at enemy positions, and when *Iphigenia* in her turn swept past, they sped her on her way with resounding cheers.

Then, incredibly, *Thetis* rose to even greater heights.

Telephonic communication between bridge and engine room had long since been shot away, but soon after *Iphigenia* passed, engineer Lieutenant-Commander Ronald Boddie succeeded in getting the starboard engine free, and to everybody's delight the battered ship started bumping heavily forward. Sneyd was too much of a realist to imagine that they could ever reach the canal entrance, but his ship was capable of one more gloriously impertinent act: he put her helm over and swung her head out into the dredged channel. Over and over veered the pair of girders which jutted like a sprit from her bows, then finally stopped as *Thetis* grounded forward.

Messengers from the bridge hurled themselves along the gangways and down the steel ladders, clearing the ship, ordering the boat-keepers to station, turning on the remaining smoke canisters. The forecastle was a veritable inferno under the fury of an exasperated enemy, and the petty officer in charge of the foremost firing-keys was killed. Sneyd therefore ordered the charges in the hull to be blown from auxiliary position, there was a solid and sustained thump as the bottom blew out—and with magnificent aplomb *Thetis* settled down precisely athwart the main channel.

Her decks were awash, she was practically invisible under clouds of steam and smoke, both Sneyd and his First Lieutenant, F. J. Lambert, were wounded and now collapsing under partial asphyxiation: in this emergency, Acting Lieutenant G. A. Belben took charge and succeeded in getting away the only boat still seaworthy. This was the cutter—and even she was badly holed. Eventually, waterlogged but still afloat, they were found by *M. L. 526* (manned by volunteers for the duty), and the survivors taken aboard.

The first blockship, if not completely successful, had nevertheless made a magnificent contribution to the operation.

For Bonham Carter and the *Intrepid* up to the moment when they steamed through the canal entrance, it is not too much to say that it had been a case of "roses, roses all the way." Heavy shrapnel had been fired at them before they rounded the Mole, their way had been illuminated by several light flares, but all these—as Bonham Carter was later so nonchalantly to dismiss them—"were quite useless to the enemy on account of the smoke screen."

As has been mentioned, *Intrepid* steamed past *Thetis* practically unnoticed and completely unscathed, swung to port as though taking part in summer maneuvers and swept majestically into the canal entrance. She was undoubtedly in a position to reach and ram the lock-gates, but in obedience to the plan, Bonham Carter checked her when they reached the line of the coast, ordered full speed ahead starboard engine and full astern port, and with helm hard a'starboard, swung his ship across the width of the channel. This channel, however, was even less efficiently dredged than had been anticipated, with the result that a ship of *Intrepid*'s length—she was just over a hundred yards from stem to stern—could swing only about ten degrees before hitting the silt on each side. In so limited an arc, it was obviously impossible to gather sufficient momentum to bury both bows and stern in the silt, especially as they were more or less slapping broadside on.

For a few minutes, Bonham Carter worked his engines to try to get around further, at the same time ordering his crew (remember he had 87 of them) into the boats. The smoke-canisters were now belching forth thick clouds, which if they hid *Intrepid* and her crew from the enemy, also hid the enemy and the canal banks from Bonham Carter: he forced his ship further and further around, backing and filling with a shattering disregard of the growing attention the enemy was concentrating on him. When it was obvious that he could swing no further, he rang the alarm gongs to clear the engine rooms, brought the charge-keys to the "ready" position and waited for his crew to get clear.

As he did so, *Iphigenia* suddenly loomed up out of the blank fog which now filled the canal-entrance, collided with *Intrepid*'s port bow and pushed her back off the silt: Bonham Carter blew the charges just in time to sink his ship before she slid completely back into the main axis of the canal. Below, engineer Sub-Lieutenant Meikle, E. R. A.s Smith and Farrell, and stoker Petty Officer Smith were still in the engine room, but fortunately only their feelings were hurt.

So were Bonham Carter's, for much of his careful maneuvering had been nullified by the accident of the collision. However, he had no need to worry: Billyard-Leake, after an entrance into the canal mouth similar to Orpheus's descent into the Underworld, had no intention of abandoning the scene until all gaps had been closed.

As *Intrepid* settled, some of the smoke cleared momentarily. *Iphigenia* backed away and her stem swung north and east.

In comparison with her sister ship, *Iphigenia* had had a rough passage. Steaming past *Thetis* she had been hit twice, one of the shells cutting a steampipe in the bows. As a result the forepart of the ship was wreathed in thick white clouds. When these cleared, *Iphigenia*'s bows promptly vanished into a drifting smoke screen which effectively cut Billyard-Leake's vision to about three feet, and when the ship emerged from this it was just in time for him to see that they were practically aboard the western pier.

Only by flinging his helm hard over and slamming both engines astern did this extraordinary competent young officer keep his ship afloat. As it was, she veered to port only just enough to enable her to slide into the canal mouth "more or less scraping along the western bank." She cut sharply between a dredger and a barge, severing the hawser which joined them and pushing the barge up the canal ahead of her. Before she could get clear of this bumping, infuriating menace, she was well into the heart of the hornets' nest stirred up by *Intrepid*. Machine guns hosed *Iphigenia*'s decks, shrapnel burst overhead and whistled between her stacks, and she was engulfed in *Intrepid*'s slowly-drifting smoke screens. Once more Billyard-Leake's vision was cut to a matter of inches.

As the smoke cleared, the collision took place. *Iphigenia* brought up all-standing, hung for a second and then slid slowly backwards, but between *Intrepid*'s bows and the eastern bank was now a gap of some forty yards, and Billyard-Leake knew that it was now up to him to retrieve the position.

He rang engines astern, tugged his ship's bows out of the silt into which they had bounced, and then went ahead again on the same handling as Bonham Carter had used. Like *Intrepid*'s commander, he was forced to back and fill, edging his ship across the width of the canal, with each movement like a motorist trying to park between two trucks. Few motorists, however, have to park their vessels under conditions similar to those which reigned in the canal mouth.

It was now 12:45 A.M. In another five minutes' time, *Daffodil* would sound the recall signal for the men on the Mole. But even if Billyard-Leake had the attention to spare, it was unlikely that he could have heard it through the pandemonium raging about him. At last the enemy had realized the full extent of the blow which had been delivered against them, and could visualize the humiliation they would suffer in the cold light of day: they were out for blood, and that of *Iphigenia*'s captain would do as well as any and better than most.

But if Billyard-Leake was aware of this, he was singularly unconcerned: by now his ship was well across the channel, her bows deep into the silt of the eastern bank, her stern well ashore on the opposite side. He rang the alarm gongs, cleared the engine rooms, blew the charges and sank his ship. When the decks were nearly awash and the majority of his crew aboard the remaining cutter (one had been reduced to matchwood) he descended from the bridge, crossed the deck, stepped over the side and joined them. Hours later, he still—to quote Keyes's words—"might have walked straight out of a military tailor's shop, equipped for the trenches, leather coat, shrapnel helmet all complete, very erect and absolutely unperturbed."

He was just twenty-two years old.

Meanwhile, Bonham Carter had been facing the problems arising from what he euphemistically refers to in his report, as his inability "to get rid of my spare watch of stokers at 'D'." During the run in, excellent employment had been found for these extra hands, passing ammunition and manning one of the foredeck guns, but now their presence was undoubtedly an embarrassment. To evacuate ship there were only two cutters, which would normally accommodate 22 men each, and a skiff into which ten men might be uncomfortably packed.

Part of the problem had already been tackled. By the time Bonham Carter blew *Intrepid*'s charges, one cutter-load was already away. With a freeboard which would have caused raised eyebrows on a canoe-lake, this cutter wallowed out of the canal, across the entire width of the Mole harbor and out into the North Sea, where she was eventually found some miles northeast of the Mole by the destroyer *Whirlwind,* and the men taken aboard. Since the blockship crews had been specifically told that the best they could hope for was a German prison-camp, those on board this cutter no doubt preferred to risk a hundred and twenty mile row across to England: certainly they were extraordinarily fortunate to be picked up once they had reached the open sea.

Eventually the other cutter was filled until it was obvious that she could take no more, and with Sub-Lieutenant Meikle in charge, pushed off in the direction of the canal entrance where they immediately ran into rescue launch *M. L. 526,* standing in after they had taken aboard the crew of *Thetis.* This left on *Intrepid* the skiff and some sixteen men—not including Bonham Carter, his officers, and various senior members of the Petty Officers' Mess who showed a stubborn determination not to abandon *Intrepid* without their Captain. The skiff left. It pulled out under the stern of the *Iphigenia* and almost immediately came alongside *M. L. 282,* which with *M. L. 526* now constituted the entire rescue force. *M. L. 128* had already broken down and *M. L. 110* had been almost blown out of the water. This meant two rescue launches instead of four—one complete steaming crew extra, plus numerous stowaways.

As the skiff went alongside the starboard bow of *M. L. 282, Iphigenia's* cutter—now holed and almost awash—reached her port bow. Men scrambled up on the motor launch's foredeck in a never-ending swarm and soon over a hundred men were packed like sardines on a craft which was built to carry fifty at most. The enemy was now well aware of what was happening and machine guns and pom-poms switched their fire from the smoking but now abandoned blockships to the fragile, thin-skinned and virtually unarmed launch. Lieutenant Dean, in command of the launch decided that for the sake of the men now aboard, those still in the *Iphigenia's* cutter had better stay there; the cutter was roped to the launch's stem which then went slowly astern.

As the M. L. gathered speed and drew away, the enemy fire increased in fury and concentration. On the packed decks the casualty rate was high. Suddenly a brilliant white light flared up from the surface of the water just to seaward of the sunken *Iphigenia*. Once more the enemy switched fire. For the moment, *M. L. 282* enjoyed a respite, but it was not to last long: the white light was a flare fitted to a Carter float—and on the float were Bonham Carter, his first lieutenant, his navigating officer, and his coxswain. They had left the *Intrepid* as soon as the ship was clear below decks. The Carley float had been dropped over the side, and they proceeded to paddle in the direction of the canal entrance. As they were passing under *Iphigenia*'s stern someone accidentally trod on the rescue flare, igniting it. The light attracted a rain of small-arms fire, driving them into the water. The float, with its Holmes Flare still blazing brightly, bobbed slowly away.

Bonham Carter and his party swam on down the canal. The night was dark, the air above was thick with smoke and escaping steam. They were swimming in water lashed by machine-gun bullets and heavily coated with oil; if it caught fire they would be burned to death.

Dean on *M. L. 282* saw the figures in the water and, despite the fact that he was already grossly overloaded, took his M. L. back into the canal. Once more she slowed almost to a complete stop under heavy fire while more survivors of the blockships came aboard over her bows. All except Bonham Carter. He had waited until last ("Actually," he protested, "I was the slowest swimmer"), and was left behind. When Dean put his engines astern under the impression that everyone was aboard, he just managed to grab a trailing rope and was dragged through the water.

Smashed and wrenched by the waves, he was nearing exhaustion when a crewman saw him and shouted to him to hang on. But the pull of the water was too strong. Before the crewman could work his way forward to the bridge, Bonham Carter had reached the end of his endurance. The rope tore through his hands and he watched the M. L. shoot out into the wide area of the harbor. When the pain in his arms had subsided enough for him to move them, he started swimming slowly back towards the eastern pier of the canal entrance.

By the time the deckhand had reached the bridge, Bonham Carter had been left far behind. By the light of German star-shells, however, Dean could see the dark shape of his head in the water. Once more *M. L. 282* went forward into the canal mouth. Firing at close range, German machine-gunners and riflemen raked the deck, causing many more casualties. By the time Bonham Carter was at last aboard, the packed ranks of men on deck were thinning ominously.

With his steering gear jammed and his leading deckhand a casualty, Dean coolly worked his ship out under engines, clearing the canal entrance in a long sweep astern which took them across the harbor and almost into the shadow of the Mole. When they reached a point not far from the wrecked viaduct, he rang his engines ahead. *M. L. 282* picked up speed and proceeded along past the seaplane base, the battered sheds, the torn and scarred enemy destroyers, and under the guns at the end of the Mole extension.

The motor launch was still under fire from rifles and machine guns, and the casualty list mounted inexorably, but the greater danger from the Mole batteries was avoided by keeping so close in to the Mole that the guns could not be depressed sufficiently to fire on them. When they reached and passed the lighthouse, Dean held course so that the guns masked each other until they were out of sight, if not out of range. All this time, *Iphigenia*'s cutter was still bumping alongside at the end of the forward tow and there seems to be a genuine note of regret in Dean's report—as though he was reluctantly parting with an old friend—when he comes to his decision to cut her adrift: all the blockship survivors were now aboard the launch. Then he altered course for the retirement—for the steering was free again and Potter was at the wheel. Dean could now afford to relax enough to take stock of his command and the men aboard her. From the standpoint that it had not been expected that *any* of the blockship crews would be rescued, the position was undeniably first-rate—but from the point of view of immediate, actual circumstance, it left much to be desired. *M. L. 282* was grossly overburdened and of the large number of men aboard, many were dead, some were dying fast and too many would soon join that class if medical aid was not quickly forthcoming.

In addition, one of the after smoke-canisters had exploded. In the resultant fire, damage was caused to the sternpost and decking, and several officers and men (Billyard-Leake and Lieutenant Cory-Wright among them) were partially gassed. Dean was also by no means certain that his engines had not been overstrained, in which case he could shortly expect trouble. Of his original crew, only his engine-room staff were still at their posts: his first lieutenant was badly wounded and his deck crew dead.

He was working out the odds against a safe arrival back at Dover when there was a sudden shout from up in the bows. As he made his way for'ard again, the shout was repeated, then taken up by other voices until they all joined into one vast, swelling cheer. Along the deck, men were struggling to their feet, the badly wounded trying to prop themselves up and pulling at the trousers of the fit men to secure their help, the gassed cases were coughing fitfully and fighting for breath to join in: tears streamed down blackened faces, throats raw from smoke and fire still contributed hoarsely to the excitement.

Then Dean reached the bridge and looked ahead.

Steaming towards them was H. M. S. *Warwick*, the huge silken battle flag at her masthead and Keyes's unmistakable figure on the bridge.* By the time they were alongside, Keyes was leaning over the deckrails, and question and answer were shouted across the intervening gap.

The last pieces of the picture fell into place.

"Keyes," related one of the men who had spent the night with him on the bridge of H. M. S. *Warwick*, "really behaved far better than any of us had a right to expect!"

Certainly those like Tomkinson who knew him well, were as-

* Admiral Roger Keyes, under whose command the raid was made.

tonished at the control Keyes had exerted over himself at moments
when it was obvious that he really wanted to be right in the thick of
the action. During the Dardanelles campaign he had frequently
interpreted his duties as Chief of Staff in a far more executive
manner than was usually associated with that post, and Campbell,
who commanded *Warwick* at Zeebrugge, was fully expecting to be
told to take his ship alongside the Mole so that Keyes could join the
assault parties, alongside the viaduct so that he could take a hand
with the submarines—and finally into the canal so that they could all
go ashore and capture a few heavy batteries.

But although it was frequently noticed that Keyes was eyeing the
crucial areas rather wistfully, he never lost sight of the conception as
a whole. Indeed, there seems to have been a strange feeling in all
units that his was the guiding hand which steered not only the
expedition but each separate individual and craft as well. Keyes had
made the spiritually awkward transition from active to Flag command with unexpected success.

Nevertheless, H. M. S. *Warwick* had not been a mere spectator.

At the time when *Vindictive* was first revealed to the Mole
gunners, *Warwick*—with *Phoebe*—was standing off to the west of
the Mole as outer guard, and Keyes first exhibited this sudden
impressive command by keeping her there despite the thunder of the
battle raging only a matter of cables to the east. When sufficient time
had elapsed for *Vindictive* to have secured, Keyes quietly directed
Campbell to proceed to the Mole end to cover the approach of the
blockships. It was while so engaged that they had experienced the
only close, personal action of the type in which Keyes revelled.

When the *Warwick* had reached the vicinity of the lighthouse the
wind had already done its worst, but it was still freshening and the
small craft in the vicinity were constantly exposed as a result. Until
the blockships actually arrived, *Warwick* joined in with what can
only be described as boyish enthusiasm. Smoke pouring from stacks
and canisters, she had wheeled and circled, emerging from her own
screens to take occasional pot-shots at the battery, then returning
into them or dragging them across some suddenly revealed smaller
craft.

While she was so engaged, the blockships swung around the lighthouse and passed in towards the canal. At about the same time the viaduct blew up with a vast sheet of flame. This was sufficient to bring Keyes back to the solid earth of high command—if indeed he had ever left it, for he had remained unusually detached even during the brief moments of exposure to close fire. He told Campbell to return outside the Mole to see how *Vindictive* was faring.

Somehow they missed *Vindictive* in the smoke screens, and eventually ran alongside the Mole well past the position first occupied by *Iris*. It was from this position that Keyes, standing on the compass platform, saw the blockships all grouped together in the canal mouth. Whether they were in and sunk at this moment was not certain, but Keyes realized that *Vindictive* had served her purpose at about the same time that Carpenter was coming to the same conclusion.

Warwick stood off and waited—for Keyes was showing a most praiseworthy disinclination to interfere with the individual responsibilities of his captains—but at about 0110 he did suggest that they approach *Vindictive* in order to signal the desirability of a withdrawal: as *Warwick* approached *Vindictive*'s position, a star-shell suddenly lit up the area and the gallant old cruiser was seen to be already under way—in fact Campbell had to put *Warwick*'s helm hard over to avoid her as she circled out from the Mole.

They followed for a while to make sure that *Vindictive*'s steaming capabilities were sufficient to take her home, then returned towards the Mole to find and help any of the smaller vessels who needed it. Now the strain on Keyes began to mount to a crisis, for he was still unaware of the success or failure of the operation. *Daffodil* and *Iris* were gone now and the small ships of the smoke patrols were all withdrawing.

Gradually the seas around Zeebrugge were emptying.

Then they saw *M. L. 282* and heard the frantic cheering of the men aboard her. The tiny craft listed heavily as she came alongside and over a hundred men were taken from her, including twenty badly wounded and many dead.

By the time they were all aboard, Keyes knew that two of the blockships were in the canal and that, as far as could be judged at the moment, the canal was blocked. For the first time in many months, he felt the warm, vitalizing glow of concrete achievement.

LAST DAYS

While the Americans were attacking in the Meuse Argonne sector, the British launched an even greater offensive in the north; the French moved cautiously against the German lines in the center of the long front. The British had the greater success, hammering into the German defenses, making slow but steady gains. In Flanders, with the help of Belgian divisions, the British smashed into the German Fourth Army, almost achieving a rout; for a while there seemed to be excellent opportunities for a roll-up of the German right wing, but Allied transport and supplies bogged down in the good old Flanders mud.

Allied victory now seemed inescapable, and the Germans began to think of Armistice. Their allies were falling by the wayside: first Bulgaria, on September 30; Turkey, on October 30; and finally Austria-Hungary on November 3.

Just four days before the Austrian-Hungarian armistice, an act of incredible heroism occurred in the Adriatic.

"It was the fall of 1918, and the Austrian army was being crushed in the climax of the battle of Vittorio Veneto. The Austrian fleet had been weakened by heavy losses, and its morale undermined by sedition which finally culminated in open mutiny.

"The reckless efficiency of the Italian MAS boats (motor torpedo boats) had swept the Adriatic clean of enemy craft; the great ships of Austria were immured behind formidable obstructions in Pola and other harbors, and the entrances to these bases were well protected by a strengthened series of complicated nets and chains and floating booms, which it was impossible to pierce and which no MAS boat was now able to jump.

"The work of the Italian motor-torpedo boats and light craft during World War I was both spectacular and effective. The MAS

---

boat of that day—forty feet or so in length, ten or twelve tons in displacement, twenty or thirty knots on gasoline motors; four or five knots on *silent* electric auxiliary motors; a considerable range, and an armament of two 18-inch torpedoes in brackets and several machine guns—was the ancestor of the motor-torpedo boats of today.

"The entry into Pola Harbor had been attempted many times before the gallant and dramatic venture of Rossetti and Paolucci. The Italians made fourteen raids into Austrian harbors during the course of the war.

"But the Italians were still uneasy; those great ships—*Viribus Unitis, Prinz Eugen,* and their consorts—remained a mighty fleet and a menace to the Italian army's flank along the Adriatic. And so Major (later Lieutenant Colonel) Raffaele Rossetti, a naval constructor, and Surgeon Lieutenant (later Captain) Raffaele Paolucci, Royal Italian Navy, achieved their immortality in the dying days of the war."*

"REMEMBER ALWAYS TO DARE"**

by Hanson Baldwin

It was at 1 P.M. on October 31, 1918, that Rossetti and Paolucci boarded an Italian torpedo boat at Venice. The sea was "dead, dark, and dull in autumnal dreariness." The flat sandy coast and the skyline they knew so well dropped astern, and at about eight in the evening they arrived off Brioni Island, peace-time playground for the wealthy, opposite Pola Harbor. Here they transferred to a MAS

* From *Sea Fights and Shipwrecks,* pp. 121, 132.
** From *Sea Fights and Ship Wrecks.*

boat, and, towing a torpedo-like object astern, proceeded to within two-thirds of a mile of the mole of Pola.

In perfect silence they prepared for death: stripped, were injected with camphor against the cold, and dressed in special watertight rubber suits, with air pouches at chest and back. These gloved them snugly, all except their eyes. Rossetti hung a watch in a watertight glass case about his neck; both fitted to their heads weird headgear, shaped to look like wine casks; and they were ready.

The phosphorescence in the water glowed fitfully about the drifting boat. The enemy searchlights wheeled in the distance. It all seemed strangely dreamlike, but to Rossetti, suddenly buoyant with the beginning of adventure, the chances for life appeared greater than before. Some days previously, during the end of their months of preparation, he had estimated the odds at three to two against their return; now his spirits rose with the sight of the harbor lights, and mentally, like all who hold life dear, he grew more confident in the actual face of danger.

The "torpedo" was hauled alongside; with a whispered farewell and final instructions to the crew of the MAS boat Rossetti and Paolucci slipped into the water, and half sitting upon, half clinging to their strange mechanism, disappeared into the dark.

The forward part of their "torpedo" consisted of two detachable metal barrels, each filled with four hundred pounds of T. N. T., and each fitted with clockwork mechanism, time-firing devices, and gear to fix the mines to the side of a battleship. The long slim cylinder aft, reclaimed from a German torpedo which had failed to explode, housed a great flask of air compressed to a pressure of thirty-nine hundred pounds per square inch; this motivated a small engine driving two screws. There was supply enough to keep them moving at slow speed for many hours. Their queer craft was nine yards long, weighed a ton and a half, and made a speed of two miles an hour; it could be lowered or raised in the water, but normally ran fully awash. It was, in fact, a torpedo; but a torpedo controlled by men, an animate thing, a centaur of the sea.

Paolucci and Rossetti steered by using their arms and feet against the water. They had trained faithfully for this night; Paolucci had swum for hours night after night in the waters of Venetian lagoons; Rossetti had perfected the mechanism after more than two years of work; both together had tested it against obstruction after obstruction, had manhandled it through miles of sea. But the water was far colder off this harbor of Pola than in Venice. The men shivered as spray spurted down the necks of their rubber suits.

The dull gleam of a few lights and the dark blur of the mole grew plainer. It had been 10:13 when they started the engine and shoved off. Their comrades believed they were headed for certain death, but Rossetti felt curiously calm and comfortable now; he found himself looking upon the whole adventure with a detached air, like a scientist performing an uncertain experiment. Paolucci, riding the bow of their contrivance, with his rubber-gloved body bent to the waves like some strange sea god, experienced more fully the sensory perceptions of great but subdued excitement. Yes, the Istrian water was certainly colder than that of the lagoons of Venice, but nevertheless he found himself almost sweating with emotion.

Closer and closer as the minutes passed the two men rode toward Pola. The shape of the mole grew and defined itself out of the dark; the soft, blurred edges sharpened. To starboard loomed that headland they so often had studied on the chart. They edged their craft toward the barrage opening. . . . Then suddenly, stunningly, they felt the glare of light. The wheeling searchlights from the harbor fort had picked them out. Was this so soon the end? They felt naked, exposed, in the searchlight's beam; their eyes were dazzled by the glare; but they hung, inert and motionless, to their slowly drifting craft, their heads bobbling on the surface like empty wine casks, floating shoreward with the tide—The searchlight passed them by.

They came soon afterward to the outer barrage, a mass of floating metal cylinders, linked and interlaced with looped wires and chains. The mole was close by now; they could hear the slow slap of the sea against its base. The tiny whir of their propellers, the faint, muffled chug of the engine seemed like roaring in their ears. They stopped the engine and approached the barrier. There was a new worry now: what if the barrier cylinders contained T. N. T.?

They soon had their answer; they approached the chains, touched them, and there was no explosion. They made their torpedo as buoyant as they could, and pushed and hauled it over the first barrier. Metal rasped on metal with a tiny shriek that cut the silence deeply. They paused, startled, but no one heard.

"Guard the propellers."

They nursed the stern into the water, keeping it safe from the looped chains and wires: if the propellers were damaged, then their task was in vain.

For a time now they swam, dragging their torpedo through the water toward the next obstruction (there were seven). But they made too slow progress; even at the risk of discovery from the mole hard by, they must start the engine. It coughed—and started, purring silently. They proceeded, sometimes blundering off the course in the darkness, shivering, half blinded by the salt water, at times swimming beside their torpedo to lighten her; dragging and pushing here; lifting gently there, struggling on the barriers.

All at once Paolucci gasped. Hard by, and moving toward them, they saw a black mass. Rossetti stopped the engine and they slid silently into the water, pressing their torpedo beneath the waves. The mass took shape, sliding softly nearer. A conning tower—a submarine, running without lights. She came so close that Paolucci had his hand on the control valve, ready to fire the mines—but she passed on into the night.

At last they reached the mole; the outer barriers were behind. While Rossetti floated, wading, Paolucci swam forward, exploring cautiously, his hands scarcely rippling the surface. It was past midnight. The concrete wall of the mole went sheer down into deep water. The two brought their machine close into the shadow of it. They swam like frogs, silently and with elaborate care; the gleaming phosphorescence of disturbed water could mean their death and the failure of their great plan.

It was after midnight, and more and more, as they fended their ton and a half of death off the concrete with bruised tired hands, this seemed a fantastic dream. Their heads floated like wine casks in the waves; the tongues of the searchlights licked through the black night overhead.

Paolucci pulled himself ahead, softly, softly, in the water by the mole, a few feet from its top where sentries kept their watch. A noise overhead! He stopped and glued himself tight to the concrete wall like some great sea leech. Then slowly, slowly, he pushed himself out from the wall, the sea to his mouth. There was a shadow on the mole —motionless. Perhaps now a gun was pointing at his head. He put the thought from him, and rolled his head slightly, as a wine cask might move in a seaway. Nothing happened. Still slowly he turned and went back to Rossetti and their machine, heart pounding, arteries throbbing from the rush of blood, but the cold of the Istrian waters creeping up his numbing legs.

They went on, pushing gently, guiding carefully. They came to the inner barriers, and found a gate in the barrage—closed. It was formed by long floating timbers, joined to one another with intersecting beams. From these protruded steel-tipped spikes three feet long, with their points turned outwards. To some were fixed petrol cans for the obvious purpose of giving sound warnings. The barrier looked formidable, and beyond it a trawler lay, about whose deck a red light moved for a time; but soon this went out.

The tide had turned; by the time Paolucci had finished his inspection the strong ebb was carrying Rossetti and the machine back toward the sea. Struggling, they were scarcely able to tow it back beyond the mole's end. Twice they tried to reach the barrier and failed; the thing was beyond their strength. At last Rossetti started the motor again, and the torpedo swung about and headed for the center of the gate.

Now certainly they must be heard; to their alert ears that loud-seeming engine roared the end of hope. But it had commenced to drizzle, and the sentry on the mole must have heard nothing and seen nothing; nothing except, perhaps, two wine casks, dim in the wet mist, and the slap of little waves.

They pushed and hoisted their torpedo over the gate, and

exhausted, panting, rested at last; but briefly. It was 1 A.M. by Rossetti's watch: three hours in the water, three hours of ceaseless struggle—had life been always struggle?

Rossetti's blood froze in sudden terror; Paolucci had coughed, again, and again, and again—and the guard ship only a few meters away! That uncontrollable fit of coughing was the most terrifying moment yet—but the gods were with them: no one heard.

They swam on, now turning over the motor briefly to give them aid, now swimming silently past some ship moored hard by. They came upon more inner obstructions: stout wire submarine nets armed with explosives set to detonate upon impact. A triple set of these lethal nets extended just off the tapering bowsprit of an anchored sailing ship, whose weather-beaten sides Paolucci saw dimly through the mist and night. They had not expected these nets; this was different from the defense plans as airplane photographs and the Italian intelligence service had compiled them. But they persevered. In the cold rain they wove their way through openings in the steel labyrinth, their bodies chilled, their minds numb with exhaustion and the ceaseless labor.

More hardships were to come, and near disasters. Once the strong ebb took the torpedo in charge and nearly washed it beneath the hull of a guard ship; as they struggled in the dark their weary splashings were almost reckless of discovery. At length they came to the last barrage—and pushed past it, past the guard ships into the dim obscurity of the harbor.

But there was no sudden exultation of accomplishment; it was three in the morning, and they were drained of emotion. They licked their salted lips, shifted their cramped limbs on their slowly moving steed, and set their teeth.

They were far behind schedule; by this time the attack should have been long delivered, and they should have been (if lucky) well on their way back to their rendezvous with the MAS boat on the open sea. But that, too, seemed a part of the dream—the MAS boat they had left so long, long ago.

Rossetti signaled to Paolucci that he wished to speak, and the bow man paddled back along the gleaming cylinder. The air was low!

The gauge showed that less than half the supply remained; what was left was hardly enough for the return, even if they should give up the enterprise now. But they did not hesitate. Return was unthinkable.

The engine turned again; the waves slapped against its gleaming sides and broke in dabs of spume over the leaning hooded men astride it. The rain came down harder, mixed with hail.

And then they saw the lights, the lights of ships anchored in a row, the lights of the Austrian fleet, of the *Radetzky, Erzherzog Franz Ferdinand, Zriny, Prinz Eugen, Tegetthoff,* and, farthest shoreward, identified by its bulk, the great *Viribus Unitis,* flagship and pride. Now, with the engine wide, they rode awash—two men in rubber suits and strange headdresses upon a throbbing cylinder—in an enemy harbor, passing down the long line of the ships.

They were nearly at their goal, the great ship *Viribus Unitis* looming up in the foreground, the dawn graying in the east, and the cold rain falling with the hissing spatter of hail, when suddenly the torpedo began to sink. Desperately they fought, arms heavy with the hours of exertion, but its buoyance was going—going—a gasp came from Rossetti: he had found and closed an open intake valve which was admitting water in the cylindrical shell.

Relief came; relief accompanied by fatigue which was almost pain.

Twice they had to make that last painful hundred-yard approach toward the bow of the *Viribus Unitis,* for once the tide swept them away. It was past 4:30, and the east was brightening when they neared the end. They were close enough now; Rossetti detached one of the forward canisters of death and disappeared from Paolucci's gaze within the shadow of the ship.

They were separated—the two who had dared death together so often in that one night. Paolucci felt tired and utterly lonely as he spraddled the drifting torpedo with its single mine, and floated there in the wet dark—waiting.

Rossetti, with four hundred pounds of T. N. T. clutched to his chest, hurried, his heart sick within him as the light grew in the east. But his hands were numb with cold, the fingers bloodless from the long immersion in the sea. He hastened, but he could not see the clockwork mechanism as he floated there in the dark, clinging to the ship's side with his icy hands. The lever—ah, he had the lever. But careful; he must set it just so; pushed too far that mine, rocking so gently on the little waves, would explode in his arms. His fingers twitched, his tired face showed the agony of his restraint. He felt the dial—and gently, so gently, he pushed the lever to the left. At 6:30 the end would come. He turned a valve; the mine sank hard by the steel ship's side, and it was almost done. But not quite; the mechanism that attached the explosive canister to the ship's side jammed; a cord, wet and stubborn with the water, became tangled at this last moment.

Desperately he struggled as the light waxed and the dark grew gray with day. He (and Paolucci, drifting out there out of sight in the dark) stiffened with dismay as a bugle sang on the decks of the *Viribus Unitis* and lights were switched on and the voices of men rang across the waters. Discovery—But no; they were still safe. And suddenly, as the dawn strengthened, the cord became disentangled, and the thing was done.

At last . . . the thing . . . was done.

Rossetti swam back slowly out of the shadow of the ship to Paolucci, this man he would always love; for had they not lived many lives, died many deaths this night together?

And Paolucci, struggling against the stream with the balky thing that had been their ship and their salvation, saw the broadening band of dawn, noted that it was 5:15, and then with a heart that had never experienced greater joy discovered the floating cask that was Rossetti's head moving toward him out of the shadow.

They turned toward the enemy shore to find rest, perhaps escape —but it was not to be. The phosphorescence in the water at last betrayed them as the dawn stretched its accusing fingers over the sea. A searchlight in the top of the *Viribus Unitis* flashed bright across the bay and pinioned them with its broad swathe of light. Men shouted; a boat shoved off from the ship's side; they braced themselves for the shock of bullets crashing into brain. But no bullets came; the boat flew with strong oars over the sea, and as it came they did their final duty. Paolucci detached the second canister of explosives and set it free in the swirling tideway. Rossetti opened the immersion valve and the "torpedo," gleaming bubbles marking its passing, sank deep into the waters of Pola harbor.

The men turned on their backs, the bright glare of the searchlight in their eyes, a great relief of mind and utter weariness of body their only sensation. They had done their jobs; the rest was in the laps of the gods.

A gutteral hail came from the boat:

"*Wer da?*"

It was a fitting query. In the searchlight glare Paolucci and Rossetti seemed strange creatures risen from primordial ocean— their heads obscured in their strange helmets, their bodies black and glistening in rubber.

"*Italienische Offiziere.*"

They were hauled into the boat, gasping and tired, by men gibbering with excitement. Rest, at last.

But—O God, what was this? *They were being rowed back to the Viribus Unitis!*

It was 5:55 A.M. when they were brought aboard. About them on the upper deck crowded a throng of sailors, and Paolucci noticed with surprise that they were wearing the scrawled characters *Yugoslavia* on their cap ribbons. The crew watched the two men narrowly, like cats. And the clock crawled toward six.

They were taken below and informed that the Austrian admiral had been put ashore just a few hours before and the fleet command turned over to the Yugoslav National Council, by the Emperor of an Austrian Empire that was dying. Rossetti demanded to see the Commanding Officer.

He was taken to the cabin of Captain Ianko Vukovic de Pod-kapelski, a gallant gentleman. With a gesture genuinely dramatic and typically Italian Rossetti extended a dagger, their only arms, and surrendered as prisoners of war.

"Your ship is in serious and imminent danger. I urge you to abandon it and save your men."

The calm captain requested details and asked for an explanation of their presence in the fortified guarded harbor of Pola. Rossetti declined to answer, but urged the necessity of speed. The minutes crawled.

Captain Vukovic passed the word to his men, ordered the boats lowered. Panic spread.

"The Italians have put bombs in the ship!"

Half-clothed men, fresh from the hammocks, dived into the sea; scores worked frantically at the boats; the sailors, mad with mass panic, forgot their two prisoners and tried only to save themselves.

Paolucci and Rossetti, still in their rubber suits, seized the opportunity and dived back into the water, back into the sea in which they had lived the longest eight hours of their lives. But now at last they were surely safe; no longer would their leaping hearts expect each moment the lift of the deck, the crash of sound that meant death. Swim—for their lives.

They swam; but angry shouts followed them. There were those on the *Viribus Unitis* who disbelieved, and calmer minds quelled the panic. They were not a hundred yards away when a boatload of menacing seamen overtook them, and forced them *back to the Viribus Unitis again!*

On deck a threatening mob, some half-naked, some still dripping water, pressed close shouting and gesticulating. Some accused the Italians of deceiving them; others wanted to know where the bombs were. Paolucci edged aft and Rossetti followed him; moved aft again as the crowd surged about them, hemmed them in, aft, always aft, away from the bow. It was 6:27 A.M.

A shout arose from the mob:

"Take them to the hold! Lock them up!"

Angry hands tore off the rubber suits, searched the two prisoners.

"To the hold!"

6:28 A.M.

The two doomed men backed against a bulkhead; Rossetti found a piece of chocolate and munched it. But he could almost hear the minutes tick and the thought of the hold drove terror into his brain. He appealed to the captain: they were prisoners of war and had done nothing not in accord with the rules of war. They had the right to proper treatment, etc., etc. . . . anything for time. The captain, his calm face grave, agreed, and ordered his men away. It was 6:30. . . .

The seconds ticked on, almost the two men counted them, waiting, waiting.

6:31 . . . 6:32. Rossetti looked at Paolucci with half-concealed dread. The minutes wheeled. . . . 6:33 . . . 6:35 . . . 6:40.

The crew, still sullen, milled and muttered; the two Italians slouched weakly against a stanchion. To have died so many deaths for nothing! Their thoughts swam feebly . . . something wrong with the mine . . . two years of work in vain . . . tired, so tired.

They stood in their near-nakedness, and it was suddenly 6:44 . . . and the thing was done.

It was a "dull noise, a deep roaring, not loud or terrible, but rather light." But a great column of foaming water thundered from the wounded bow high toward the brightening sky, roared skyward and splashed down over the stricken decks. The *Viribus Unitis*, pride of the Austrian fleet, trembled. The sullen Slavs ran for the boats, dived into the sea. Some stayed long enough to shake their fists in the lined faces of two Italians who had created death. . . . The thing was done, successful after all . . . the dream.

The Italians shook hands with Captain Vukovic, slid down a rope into the sea, and swam away from the stricken ship. The captain hailed a boat and ordered them taken aboard. The glowering sailors wanted to leave them there to die, but one of Italian descent pulled them in bodily, weak and spent. And there in that small boat floating on the placid waters of Pola Harbor they saw the *Viribus Unitis* go down.

Slowly she settled; her list increased and she heeled more and more, the water racing over her decks, her great turret guns pointing toward the depths. Suddenly she turned over, with a slapping splash, and the green slime of her keel rose above the white water. Then Paolucci saw a man crawling on the slippery bottom; suddenly the black figure rose and stretched to his full height. It was Captain Vukovic, with his ship to the last.

The *Viribus Unitis* took a sudden plunge; screams died in the sea;

there was a cascading whirlpool and a cloud of smoke and steam and jumbled wreckage where Captain Vukovic and the pride of the Austrian Navy had been. A sailor in the boat sobbed:

"My ship! My beautiful ship!"

The two Italians were taken to the hospital ship *Habsburg*, half-frozen and so exhausted that Paolucci almost fainted when a sailor struck him. But they staggered aboard, heads held high, like those Romans who once saluted Caesar only to die. It was then that they learned that their second mine had drifted in the fairway down the line of anchored ships, to explode against the thin steel sides of the auxiliary cruiser *Wien* and sink her. Their great adventure was doubly successful.

AFTERWORD*

by William Manchester

Pershing was lining his sights on Sedan and Metz. Yet they didn't much matter now. The war maps had changed vastly since the first wave of the Seventy-seventh had disappeared into the hazy boscages. On the fourth day of their lonely struggle Von Hindenburg, brooding over his shrinking front, had notified Berlin that an armistice must be sought at once, and three days later he had reported in despair that there was no hope of stopping the Allied tide. The Imperial Chancellor was frantically trying to reach Woodrow Wilson through Switzerland, suggesting a truce based on Wilsonian proposals made nine months before. At the time they had been scornfully branded "The Fourteen Points" by Germany's *Norddeutsche Allgemeine Zeitung*. Now they were all the Germans could hope for—more, in fact, for Wilson coldly referred the note to Foch. The President could read maps, too. The war was rapidly approaching a solution in the field. There wasn't much left to bargain over. In the North Sea the anti-sub barrage was nearly tight. Albert was re-entering his channel towns in triumph, the French were ringing their own church bells in the long lost villages around Lille, and the British were approaching Mons. Everything was slipping away from the Kaiser, including the other Central Powers.

In the West Pershing's advance was renewed November 1. The enemy's last scribbly ditches caved in that afternoon, and four days later he hadn't any front at all. Apart from the stolid machine

* Adapted from "The Great War," published in *Holiday*.

gunners, who kept their murderous barrels hot to the end, German soldiers had become a disorderly mob of refugees. They had lost heart. Reports from the fatherland were appalling. Ludendorff had been sacked, there was revolution in the streets, and the fleet had mutinied when ordered off on a death-or-glory ride against the British. In this final agony the rearguard in France, Sergeant Woollcott wrote, resembled an escaping man who "twitches a chair down behind him for his pursuer to stumble over." Each chill dawn doughboys went roaring over the top in fighting kit, driving the fleeing wraiths in field gray away from their railroad and up against the hills of Belgium and Luxemburg. It was a chase, not a battle. The galloping horses and bouncing caissons could scarcely keep up with the racing troops. Pershing told his generals to forget about flanks, light up the trucks, and see how far they could go—an order which touched off a frantic race for Sedan. Nobody won it, because the French were being sticky, but in the excitement the First Division forgot itself and broke all the rules of military courtesy. Vaulting out of its own sector, it recklessly crossed the boundaries of the Seventy-seventh and the Rainbow, taking Father Duffy prisoner in a hollow square and actually challenging the commander of the Rainbow on his own front line. It was an indignity no general officer could take lightly, but this one was young, proud, and named Douglas MacArthur, and he was mad as hops.

His protests were lost in the news of another border crossing. Kaiser Wilhelm, the Supreme War Lord, had abdicated and entered Holland as a political refugee. Even as the First and the glowering Rainbow jointly occupied the heights opposite Sedan, the Eiffel Tower in Paris was beaming directions to German envoys, telling them which trenches to approach and where to pick up their guides. In Foch's railroad car the first of them signed his dictated terms at 5 A.M. on the morning of November 11. All firing was to cease six hours later, and the moment the hills were tinged with the first faint promise of morning motorcycles spluttered up and down the American front, passing the word that the guerre would be *finis* at eleven sharp. After ten o'clock the front grew noisy—everybody wanted to get in that last shot—but eyes glued to a million watches finally saw minute hands creep upright, and then there was a tremendous silence. It lasted but a moment and was followed by a deafening cheer on both sides. Generals might haggle over words, but soldiers knew this was more than an Armistice. It was a surrender. It was the end of the war, of all wars, and it had come, as editorial writers everywhere noted profoundly, at the eleventh hour of the eleventh day of the eleventh month.

Yet for once the generals were right. It was to be a long truce, but it wouldn't be peace, because more than the guerre was *finis*. There were omens, for those who could read them. The belfries Edith Wharton heard calling joyously to one another across Paris that morning might also have been tolling for a French army broken in spirit and left to politicians like André Maginot. Something had died in France, just as something had been born in Russia; that very morning, as rockets of victory streaked innocently over Mézières, Bolshevik troops mounted an offensive against five thousand American soldiers who had been unwisely diverted to Archangel in the hope of restoring the fallen government there. The administration that had sent them was no blinder than its people. American voters had just defied the Spanish Flu to crowd polling places and discredit Woodrow Wilson, torpedoing his League of Nations and confirming the fears of Winston Churchill, who wondered, as he stood in a London window and heard Big Ben strike eleven, whether the world would return to international anarchy.

It would. But it would not be the same anarchy. An age had reached Journey's End. The door of history had shut on the princes and potentates and plumed marshals and glittering little regular armies—on all the elegance and *fanfaronade* that had marked that disciplined, secure world. The grinning doughboys stacking their arms and swapping cigarettes for Fritz's souvenirs might not know it; the new Congress back home certainly didn't, and the hysterical crowds in Times Square, the Champs Élysées, and the Buckingham Palace grounds knew it least of all, though the English had a kind of sign. As they romped over the mall with firecrackers and confetti the sky suddenly darkened. It began to rain, hard. Some of the celebrators climbed into the arms of Queen Victoria's statue, but after huddling a few minutes in its arms they crept down. They had found little shelter there, and less comfort. The arms had been stone cold.

Here is the story of the "war to end all wars" as it has never before been told—unforgettably recorded through first-hand accounts of men who were a part of it.

A unique history, drama as no fiction could capture it, these pages bring to life the horror, the courage, the tragedy and ironic humor of World War I. Here are eye-witness reports of the great battles fought on land, at sea, and for the first time in the air; deeply personal accounts of the men in the trenches; and combat correspondents' descriptions of the bizarre and bloody events they witnessed daily on the battle fields. (continued on back flap)

From the over-all grand strategy to the perspective of individual soldiers, these writings capture the authors' own immediate emotions as perceptively as they encompass the entire sweep and depth of the war. Here is Robert Grave's description of the Cambrin and Cuinchy trenches; Winston Churchill on the first Battle of the Marne; Alan Moorehead describing the Anzac beachhead; T. E. Lawrence's account of desert warfare; Hanson Baldwin on the Battle of Jutland; Alistair Horne writing of the fall of Fort Douaumont; Alan Clark re-creating the early days of Loos; and reports from such other writers as William Manchester, Richard M. Watt, L. W. Griffith, Leon Wolff, Frederick Oughton and Barrie Pitt. Don Congdon, the editor, provides the reader with a running commentary which establishes the background and chronology of each combat account.

NORTH SEA

London

GREAT BRITAIN

Zeebrugge

FLANDERS

Passchendaele

Ypres

Messines

ENGLISH CHANNEL

Loos

Arras

Somme

Oise

Aisne

Soissons

Marne

Seine

Château-Thierry

Paris

FRANCE

0   25   50   75